Student Learning in Physical Education

Applying Research to Enhance Instruction

Stephen J. Silverman, EdD
University of Illinois

Catherine D. Ennis, PhD
University of Maryland

Editors

Human Kinetics

Library of Congress Cataloging-in-Publication Data

Student learning in physical education: applying research to enhance instruction /
Stephen J. Silverman, Catherine D. Ennis [editors].

    p.   cm.

    Includes bibliographical references and index.

    ISBN 0-87322-714-X

    1. Physical education and training--Study and teaching.
2. Learning.   I. Silverman, Stephen, J. 1954- . II. Ennis,
Catherine D.

    GV361.E65   1996

    796'.07--dc20   95-42629
                                                               CIP

ISBN: 0-87322-714-X

Acquisitions Editor: Rick Frey, PhD; **Developmental Editor**: Elaine Mustain; **Assistant Editors**: Erin Cler, Susan Moore, Sandra Merz Bott, Dawn Cassady, Henry Woolsey, and Jim Burns; **Editorial Assistant**: Amy Carnes; **Copyeditor**: Michael Ryder; **Proofreader**: Jim Burns; **Indexer**: Craig Brown; **Typesetting and Text Layout**: Angela K. Snyder; **Text Designer**: Robert Reuther; **Cover Designer:** Judy Henderson; **Illustrator**: Jennifer Delmotte; **Printer**: Edwards Brothers

Printed in the United States of America

10 9 8 7 6 5 4 3 2 1

Human Kinetics

Web site: http://www.humankinetics.com

United States: Human Kinetics, P.O. Box 5076, Champaign, IL 61825-5076
1-800-747-4457
e-mail: humank@hkusa.com

Canada: Human Kinetics, Box 24040, Windsor, ON N8Y 4Y9
1-800-465-7301 (in Canada only)
e-mail: humank@hkcanada.com

Europe: Human Kinetics, P.O. Box IW14, Leeds LS16 6TR, United Kingdom
(44) 1132 781708
e-mail: humank@hkeurope.com

Australia: Human Kinetics, 57A Price Avenue, Lower Mitcham,
South Australia 5062
(08) 277 1555
e-mail: humank@hkaustralia.com

New Zealand: Human Kinetics, P.O. Box 105-231, Auckland 1
(09) 523 3462
e-mail: humank@hknewz.com

CONTENTS

CONTRIBUTORS

STEPHEN J. SILVERMAN has established a strong reputation as a physical educator in both teaching and research. He is a professor of kinesiology and curriculum/instruction at the University of Illinois at Urbana-Champaign. Steve has developed and tested a model of learning and instruction that provides in-depth insights into the teaching of physical education. A former coeditor of the *Journal of Teaching in Physical Education,* Steve is a fellow in the Research Consortium of the American Alliance for Health, Physical Education, Recreation and Dance (AAHPERD) and a member of the American Educational Research Association (AERA). In addition, he serves as chair-elect of the Curriculum and Instruction Academy of AAHPERD's National Association of Sport and Physical Education. He presented the 1992 AAHPERD Research Consortium Scholar Lecture and the 1993 Physical Education Scholar Lecture at the annual meeting of the AERA. Steve has received an AERA Exemplary Research Paper Award. Steve received his doctorate in education from the University of Massachusetts at Amherst. He and his wife, Patricia Moran, reside in Champaign, IL, where Steve also enjoys running, aquatic sports, and following politics.

CATHERINE D. ENNIS is an associate professor in the Department of Kinesiology at the University of Maryland in College Park. A specialist in curriculum theory and development, Cathy has served as both a graduate and an undergraduate instructor and advisor and has worked extensively on enhancing the physical education curriculum in urban public school districts throughout the U.S. Cathy has published more than 40 research articles in scholarly journals and served as editor of the Pedagogy Section of *Research Quarterly for Exercise and Sport* from 1993 to 1995. She is coauthor of the book *The Curriculum Process in Physical Education* (Brown & Benchmark, 1995). In 1995, she presented the Physical Education Scholar Lecture at the annual AERA meeting. In 1984 Cathy completed her PhD in curriculum theory and development at the University of Georgia. She is a member of the American Education Research Association. She is also active in AAHPERD as a fellow in the Research Consortium and past chair of the curriculum and instruction academy. She serves on the editorial review boards for *Quest* and the *Journal of Teaching in Physical Education.* In 1994 she received the Celebration of Teaching Award from the University of Maryland's Center for Teaching Excellence. A resident of Silver Spring, MD, Cathy enjoys gardening, hiking, and walking.

KAREN P. DEPAUW is professor of kinesiology and leisure studies and associate dean of the graduate school at Washington State University. She is well known for her work in the area of adapted physical activity and sport for individuals with disabilities. Karen has coauthored textbooks and many other publications related to adapted physical education. Prior to becoming a university faculty member, she taught adapted physical education in Los Angeles. She has been president of the National Association of Physical Education in Higher Education and is currently president of the International Federation of Adapted Physical Activity. A member of numerous task forces related to adapted physical education, Karen also serves on the editorial board of the *Adapted Physical Activity Quarterly*.

DON HELLISON is professor in the School of Kinesiology at the University of Illinois at Chicago. He is most well known for his work with at-risk youth and the development of affective approaches to teaching physical education. He received the 1994 AAHPERD C.D. Henry Award for service to minorities, the 1995 University of Illinois at Chicago Excellence in Teaching Award, and the 1995 International Olympic Committee President's Prize for his contributions to sport pedagogy. The author of many books, his most recent is *Teaching Responsibility Through Physical Activity* (Human Kinetics, 1995). He currently serves as editor of *Quest*.

LYNN DALE HOUSNER is currently professor of teacher education and assistant dean in the School of Physical Education at West Virginia University. Prior to assuming the position at West Virginia, Lynn was on the faculties of New Mexico State University and The University of Texas at Austin. Lynn has served as chair of the AAHPERD Curriculum and Instruction Academy, president of the New Mexico Association of Health, Physical Education, Recreation, and Dance, as Professional Preparation chair of the Southwest District AAHPERD, and as an editorial board member for the *Journal of Teaching in Physical Education*. He was the 1994-95 Southwest District (AAHPERD) Scholar.

LESLIE LAMBERT is associate professor and chair of the Department of Education and Physical Education at Roanoke College in Salem, Virginia. In addition to her roles in higher education, she has been a public school teacher, a central-level instructional coordinator for a large, metropolitan school district, and has served as a consultant to numerous school systems across the nation. She is a frequent contributor at national conferences and to the professional literature. Her areas of specialization include curriculum development, school reform, and staff development.

AMELIA M. LEE is professor of kinesiology at Louisiana State University. Her research focuses primarily on teacher and pupil thinking about physical education instruction and learning. She has written widely on these topics and has coauthored two books on physical education for children. For seven years, she was an elementary physical education teacher. She was recipient (with Karen Greenockle and Richard Lomax) of the Exemplary Research Paper Award presented by the AERA Special Interest Group on Research on Learning and Instruction in Physical Education. Two of her doctoral students have received the AERA SIG Group's Award for Outstanding Dissertations. Amelia is a fellow in the American Academy of Kinesiology and Physical Education. She recently completed a term as editor of *Quest* and serves as member of the editorial boards of the *Journal of Teaching in Physical Education* and the *Research Quarterly for Exercise and Sport*.

THOMAS L. McKENZIE is professor of exercise and nutritional sciences at San Diego State University and adjunct associate professor, Department of Community Pediatrics, University of California, San Diego. He is a former public school physical education teacher, administrator, coach, and athletic director and has been a performance-enhancement consultant with the United States National Volleyball Team since 1981. He has authored over 60 refereed papers on physical education, sport, psychology, and pedagogy. He is the physical education director for two large research projects funded by the National Institutes of Health, SPARK (Sports, Play, and Active Recreation for Kids), and CATCH (Child and Adolescent Trial for Cardiovascular Health).

MARY O'SULLIVAN is associate professor and interim director of the School of Health, Physical Education, and Recreation at Ohio State University. She currently serves as the coeditor of the *Journal of Teaching in Physical Education*. She teaches courses on secondary physical education at the undergraduate level and supervises student teachers. She is working on an innovative secondary physical education curriculum unit with two high school teachers and is researching the impact of the curriculum on students' critical awareness of sport and physical activity in their lives, schools, and community cultures. She enjoys Irish and classical music, reading, tennis, hiking, and cycling.

JUDITH H. PLACEK is a faculty member in the Physical Education Teacher Education Program in the School of Education at the University of Massachusetts at Amherst. Judy's interest in integrated curricula began when she developed and taught an integrated curriculum for four years at a Seattle high school. The book based on this experience, *Physical Education in the Secondary Schools: Curricular Alternatives,* coauthored with Hal Lawson, is considered a seminal work on integrating conceptual material into physical education. She has continued her work in this area through presentations and workshops. Her other scholarly interests include qualitative research, teacher education, and teacher socialization. Judy has been a longtime member of the *Journal of Teaching in Physical Education* editorial board.

JUDITH E. RINK is the department chair and a professor in the Department of Physical Education, University of South Carolina, Columbia. Judy is the author of several textbooks dealing with curriculum and instruction in physical education and has been the coeditor of the *Journal of Teaching in Physical Education.* Her research interests are primarily in investigating relationships between what teachers do and what students learn. She has chaired the National Association for Sport and Physical Education (NASPE) Committee to Develop National Standards for School Physical Education Programs and has taught in the public schools of New York and North Carolina. Judy's hobbies are sailing, woodworking, and gardening.

JAMES F. SALLIS received his doctorate in clinical psychology in 1981 from Memphis State University. He was a post-doctoral fellow in cardiovascular disease prevention and epidemiology at the Stanford Center for Research in Disease Prevention. Jim currently is professor of psychology at San Diego State University. His primary research interests are promoting physical activity throughout the life span, with an emphasis on youth. He is the author of over 140 scientific publications and is on the editorial board of 5 journals. He is the coauthor of a health psychology textbook, *Health and Human Behavior.*

DARYL SIEDENTOP is professor in the Sport and Exercise Sciences program and senior associate dean in the College of Education at Ohio State University. His interests are in teacher effectiveness research, curriculum development, sport education, and behavior analysis. Daryl is a fellow of the American Academy of Kinesiology and Physical Education, a recipient of the Honor Award of the Curriculum and Instruction Academy of NASPE, and 1994-95 Alliance Scholar for AAHPERD. He currently serves on the Advisory Board for United States Physical Education. In 1982, he received the Juan Antonio Samaranch Award at the Olympic Scientific Congress. His wife, Bobbie, is an elementary PE specialist. His leisure interests revolve around reading, golf, tennis, running, and dying annual deaths with the Chicago Cubs.

SANDRA A. STROOT is an associate professor in the Sport and Exercise Sciences program in the College of Education at The Ohio State University. Sandy has been working for the past eight years in a collaborative project where faculty from The Ohio State University and teachers and administrators from the Columbus Public Schools have worked to provide assistance to beginning teachers. Her research interests center on the socialization of physical education teachers during their first years of teaching, and the impact of workplace conditions on their ability to be successful in their school context. A second area of interest focuses on the effects of teacher interactions on motor performance of children.

LEAANN TYSON is an associate professor of physical education at Western Washington University in Bellingham, Washington, where she teaches courses in elementary physical education and physical education pedagogy. Her scholarly interests focus on teacher effectiveness and teacher assessment. She was recipient (with Stephen Silverman and Linda Marrs Morford) of the Exemplary Research Paper Award presented by AERA Special Interest Group on Learning and Instruction in Physical Education. She has taught elementary physical education and was physical education and health coordinator for the Round Rock, Texas, Independent School District. She writes a monthly column for the Bellingham paper on physical education and youth sport. LeaAnn is a nationally ranked handball player and has been both singles and doubles national champion.

KAY M. WILLIAMSON has taught in various places, including England, Nigeria, Canada, and the United States. After obtaining her doctorate in physical education at the University of Massachusetts, Kay assumed a position as assistant professor at the University of Illinois at Chicago. Her scholarly work has focused on qualitative research methods, working with inner-city children, and facilitating discussion on equity issues at all educational levels. Kay recently took a new position with a large, multinational corporation.

TERRY M. WOOD is an associate professor in the Department of Exercise and Sport Science at Oregon State University. Specializing in measurement and evaluation, computer applications, and research methods, he earned his PhD from the University of Wisconsin–Madison. Terry currently serves as president of the International Society for Measurement and Evaluation, president-elect of the American Association for Active Lifestyles and Fitness, and is a former chair of the AAHPERD Measurement and Evaluation Council. He has published manuscripts and presented scholarly papers at the state, national, and international levels, has served as measurement and evaluation section editor for the *Research Quarterly for Exercise and Sport,* and has coauthored two measurement and evaluation textbooks.

PREFACE

This book is not a teaching methods text, a curriculum text, or a book on research methodology. It brings a research perspective to inform the areas of teaching, teacher education, and curriculum in physical education and related areas within the physical activity field. We intend it to be a strong step in bridging the gap between research and practice in physical education. Our purpose is to present and help others understand the knowledge base for making educational decisions. By being fully informed of what we know about teaching, curriculum, and teacher training and development, the professional decision-making process can be brought to a new level—where teaching is no longer treated as something one can only learn by experience. Research can be used to inform practice at many levels, and our hope is that those using this book will take the information and apply it in their day-to-day work.

This book is directed to graduate students needing a comprehensive introduction to the area, physical education teachers, physical education supervisors, and teacher educators. We and the authors of the individual chapters have synthesized information to help the reader understand the framework of research and what we know about our field. We believe that research can be understood by interested practitioners when it is written with practical purposes in mind. Some may regard our attempts to make the information in this book as "user friendly" as possible as a lack of rigorous scholarship. We believe, however, that the true sign of the scholar is to be able to explain clearly to a broad audience what he or she does. To that end, we have tried to avoid educational jargon and use an easily readable style.

The book is organized into five parts. The first section provides an overview of the field. In chapter 1, the editors provide definitions and frame the discussion that occurs in the rest of the book. Chapter 2, by Amelia Lee, and chapter 3, by Steve Silverman, focus on the history of the subdiscipline and on how and why we do research in the area. These chapters provide a foundation for reading the remainder of the book.

The second part deals with issues related to diversity in school settings. We believe that every school is different and that diversity, while sometimes a challenge, is manageable. Diversity clearly is an important consideration in educational decision making. Chapter 4, by LeaAnn Tyson, addresses the context of schools in our society. Chapter 5, by Kay Williamson, and Chapter 6, by Karen DePauw, address the specific issues of gender and special needs in physical education. These chapters seek to enhance instructional sensitivity and improve teachers' abilities to individualize content and instruction as necessary for each student.

The third section deals with promoting student learning. In chapter 7, by Cathy Ennis, the influence of teachers' values and context on student learning are discussed. Chapter 8, by Leslie Lambert, addresses curricular issues in physical education, and in chapter 9 Judy Rink summarizes what we know about effective teaching. In the final chapter, Terry Wood discusses the use of assessment in promoting learning. We have found that the assessment process often is divorced from the learning process and believe that need not be the case. The chapters in this section provide a great deal of information about what promotes student learning in physical education.

The fourth section presents approaches to physical education outcomes that have proven track records. The authors of these chapters are scholars with a great deal of practical experience in teaching various aspects of physical education. Fitness and physical activity have received much attention in recent years. Thom McKenzie and Jim Sallis focus on these areas in chapter 11. Daryl Siedentop presents the sport education model as a form of educational reform for physical education in chapter 12. In chapter 13, Don Hellison discusses teaching of self- and social responsibility. Don's tremendous experience in inner-city areas brings a special sense of what can be accomplished through physical activity. Judy Placek, in the last chapter in this section, looks at ways to integrate physical education with other curricular areas.

The fifth section deals with teacher training and development. As the part title ("Learning to Teach: An On-Going Process") suggests, we view this as a continuing and fluid process. Mary O'Sullivan, in the first chapter in the section, discusses preservice teacher education. In chapter 16, Sandy Stroot discusses the literature on socialization into teaching. We hope this research can help beginning teachers understand the induction experience. The last chapter in this section, by Lynn Housner, discusses teacher innovation and change—the process of growing as a teacher. The final section contains a short epilogue.

The contributors to this volume are the leading scholars in their fields. We very much appreciate their willingness to contribute to this book. They bring a variety of perspectives to this volume, which is unique in being directed to practitioners from a research base. The value lies in what each author contributes and in how you use the information.

Stephen Silverman
Catherine D. Ennis

PART 1

Overview of the Field

CHAPTER 1

Enhancing Learning:
An Introduction

Stephen J. Silverman
Catherine D. Ennis

Physical education is an integral part of the curriculum in most schools. Although state-mandated requirements differ (National Association for Sport and Physical Education [NASPE], 1993), many resources are devoted to physical education. In an age of accountability and educational reform, it is our hope that all students enrolled in physical education courses will receive quality instruction throughout a well designed curriculum taught by professional physical educators.

While this goal may seem unattainable to some, we believe that communication between professionals in physical education can influence the quality of physical education programs. This book is an attempt to integrate and synthesize the research on teaching, curriculum, and teacher education in physical education. The volume of research has grown considerably in recent years and provides information that can help teachers and teacher educators make informed decisions.

The field of research in physical education pedagogy, sometimes called *sport pedagogy* in the international community, has made great strides over the past few decades. Twenty years ago, there were few specialists trained to do research on physical education pedagogy. The field was characterized by a lack of research that could be used by teachers, teacher educators, or curriculum developers. At that time, Locke (1977, p. 2) concluded "the profession has no cumulative body of knowledge about teaching motor skills or any of the cognitive and affective learnings which are adjunct to skill acquisition." Although Locke was bemoaning the progress the field had made, he saw a future: The title of his paper was "Research on Teaching Physical Education: New Hope for a Dismal Science."

We have realized some of that hope. As evidenced by the contributors to this book, there are now many well trained researchers in the field of physical education pedagogy. While there once were few focused research efforts, there now are a number of scholars who specialize in a specific subarea within the field. As this book makes clear, the amount and quality of research has grown substantially. Over a decade ago, Piéron and Graham (1984) said that the area was in its adolescence. The growth of physical education pedagogy suggests that the field has now reached young adulthood. A great deal of maturing is yet to come, but we've made substantial progress. There is cause for celebration of the combined efforts of our field.

While we celebrate this growth we must be mindful that there still is much to learn. The database is not complete, and the research synthesized here tells us what we know now. In some instances we know a great deal; in others the available information is sketchy. In a few years we will know more. As with all research in the social sciences, the field continues to evolve—we never will know all that we want to know. That, however, does not mean we should not use the research now available to make informed decisions.

In order to help readers get the most out of this book, we introduce some concepts and definitions in this chapter. In the first section, we provide an overview of the areas within physical education pedagogy. In the second section, we briefly discuss some issues in using research to inform the educational process and enhance learning.

THE FIELD OF
PHYSICAL EDUCATION PEDAGOGY

As the number of research specialists in physical education pedagogy has grown, we have seen an increased specialization within the field. No longer can we think of the field as just one area. In fact, you will note when you look at the chapters that follow that there are many research subareas within each specialization.

We can think of the field of physical education pedagogy as having three subareas: (a) teacher education; (b) curriculum; and (c) teaching. Although these areas are distinct, there is some overlap. As Figure 1.1 suggests, it is even possible for the research in all three subareas to come together as one. Some research easily falls into one of these categories, but other research is not so easily categorized. Nevertheless, the three areas provide a general framework for understanding the subareas within our field.

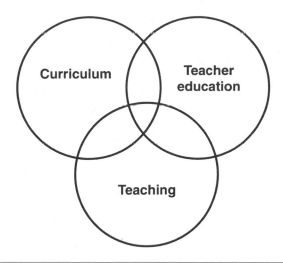

Figure 1.1.   Subareas in physical education pedagogy

Before discussing each of the subareas of pedagogy, it is important to note that each area has both a research side and an applied side. Some people conduct research on teaching physical education, and others teach physical education. The same can be said of teacher education and curriculum. Often, those doing research also may be involved in teacher education and curriculum development; they may teach physical education activity courses as part of their assignment at a college or university. Likewise, teachers enrolled in graduate school may conduct research in one of the subareas while simultaneously teaching physical education. In addition, collaborative research, where teachers and researchers work together, can be designed to merge theoretical and practical information. Both the researcher and practitioner are strong players in the field.

Research on teacher education focuses on teacher training and development. It may ask teacher candidates why they entered the field, how they developed and learned to be teachers, and what factors promoted or inhibited subsequent growth while they were employed as teachers. Research may also address how teachers are trained and which methods seem to be the most beneficial in reaching the goals of a teacher education program. The chapters in section five by Mary O'Sullivan, Sandy Stroot, and Lynn Housner concentrate on these issues.

Although once focusing exclusively on what is taught in physical education, research in curriculum now explores other issues as well. Curriculum researchers study what is taught, why teachers select content for their classes, how teachers' values influence curriculum selection and implementation, and the process by which curriculum is designed. This area deals with the subject matter of physical education and how we determine what should be taught. The chapters by Cathy Ennis and Leslie Lambert in section three review research on curriculum issues.

Research on teaching physical education concentrates on teaching effectiveness from the perspectives of teachers and students. It addresses such issues as the relationships between student and teacher behaviors and student learning, how students mediate the intended instruction from the teacher, and how teaching methods influence learning. Research on teaching physical education mostly has focused on motor skill learning, but also can address other goals related to knowledge, affect, or social development. The chapter by Judy Rink in section three provides a comprehensive overview of this research.

As we noted earlier, the three subareas may overlap. For instance, issues in teaching and curriculum may combine in research on student learning. Curriculum and teacher training issues overlap in studies that focus on teacher training curriculum and its development. Likewise, the areas of teaching and teacher education intersect when we consider the best ways to train prospective physical education teachers, or when teaching appraisal is the research focus. Although the three-way combination complicates things even further, it is less likely that all areas will overlap in one research paper.

Often, such overlap occurs when curriculum is developed and teaching methods are suggested for reaching the curricular goals. In application, teaching and curriculum go hand-in-hand. The chapters in section four by Thom McKenzie and Jim Sallis, Daryl Siedentop, Don Hellison, and Judy Placek show how research and scholarship on teaching and curriculum interact to influence what and how subject matter is taught in physical education.

USING RESEARCH TO ENHANCE LEARNING

Research is the basis for much of the decision making in Western society. Although research is often presented in the news, reporters usually present only the conclusions and implications, ignoring the researchers' caveats. Yet these caveats are important. For instance, when considering whether the results of a medical study have implications for us, we need to know if the subjects were much older or younger than ourselves; had preexisting medical problems; lived in an environment different from our own; or exhibited certain behaviors. It is also possible that the information can change our lives if we are afflicted with a disease, or have no effect if we are not. The details influence the utility of the research.

The situation in physical education is similar. Some research will be helpful, while other research will not. The authors of the chapters that follow have tried to make distinctions and address the topics most important for physical educators. Each author has put a great deal of work into his or her chapter; thoughtful contemplation is necessary to make the information useful to you. All research is situation specific. It occurs at a certain time and place that likely is different, in some ways, from most other situations. It tells us a lot about the situation being studied, but might not be applicable to other situations—or then again, it might. A single study gives us some insight into the problem, but we may not understand how the phenomenon being studied functions in other situations. This is one difficulty in applying research directly to other classes, grade levels, or situations.

How do you know if the research can be helpful in providing solutions to questions about professional practice? There are two important things to consider when examining research. First is the quality of the research. A good research question that is followed by a poorly designed or executed study will tell us little. No matter how good the question and how much we want to know the answer, poor research cannot answer the question. Fortunately, the dramatic rise in the number of physical education researchers over the last few decades has helped improve the overall quality of investigation. Publication outlets have become more rigorous and many manuscripts undergo review by multiple reviewers and an editor. Most research published in "referred" journals has undergone a review that warrants some confidence in the results.

The second thing to consider is whether the situation is similar to yours. If you are teaching physical education and want to apply certain research, you should ask yourself the following: Is the grade level similar to those I teach? Are the students similar? Are my resources (particularly facilities, supplies, and personnel) similar? Do I think I can do what I need to do to implement what I have learned? Do I want to use what I have learned? All of these questions are important. The chapters that follow provide much information about physical education; your answers to the above questions will help you decide whether it can be used in your situation.

No single study, of course, will provide all the answers. Selecting a specific situation (e.g., schools in a certain area) and sample (e.g., middle-school students) for a study is one of the trade-offs that must be made to assure good research. Personnel and financial resources dictate that large, universal studies are rarely possible. Researchers make decisions that influence these trade-offs, and without them, no research would be conducted. A small, well designed study provides valuable information to both researchers and practitioners. The results of these studies can be used for future research. Replication in a variety of environments is good and allows better interpretation of results. As Judy Rink discusses later, in the case of student practice, multiple studies with similar results permit stronger conclusions than can be drawn from a single study.

We believe there is a database available for making educated decisions about physical education teaching, teacher education, and curriculum development. The research is robust. As Gage (1978, 1985) noted in discussing classroom research, no one result can be implemented in isolation from other teaching variables or from the personality and capabilities of the teacher. Helping students to learn is an interactive process, and each new situation and student requires using the available information to the best of our ability. Researchers and teachers make educated decisions and must combine their knowledge and experience to produce sound results.

SUMMARY AND PRELUDE

We assume you, as a reader of this book, are interested in studying the results of research so you can enhance student learning in physical education. It would be easy to dismiss the utility of research without thoroughly examining it. We urge you to be creative as you read and think about the chapters that follow. Trying to implement a new idea and finding it doesn't work is okay and, in our opinion, preferable to not trying.

Both of us have taught canoeing and know that the canoeist who never gets wet never gets better. Such an individual does not try new and challenging things, and his or her repertoire of canoeing skills remains static. Likewise, the teacher or teacher educator who is not adventurous and innovative will stay safe and dry, but will not grow. The tremendous gains in physical education research can only influence teaching if we *use* the information.

The chapters that follow provide an overview of the field. The authors summarize our knowledge and the state of the art. They provide a marvelous resource that can help you explore the field and, we hope, persuade you to think about how you can contribute to it. We encourage you to read and explore and get a little "wet" as you think about applying the knowledge base in our field.

REFERENCES

Gage, N.L. (1978). *The scientific basis of the art of teaching.* New York: Teachers College Press.

Gage, N.L. (1985). *Hard gains in the soft sciences: The case of pedagogy.* Bloomington, IN: Phi Delta Kappa.

Locke, L.F. (1977). Research on teaching physical education: New hope for a dismal science. *Quest, 28,* 2–16.

National Association for Sport and Physical Education (NASPE). (1993). *Shape of the nation 1993: A survey of state physical education requirements.* Reston, VA: Author.

Piéron, M., & Graham, G. (Eds.). (1984). *Sport pedagogy* (The Olympic Scientific Congress proceedings, volume 6). Champaign, IL: Human Kinetics.

CHAPTER 2

How the Field Evolved

Amelia M. Lee

The history of research in physical education pedagogy reflects a gradual change in the way effective teaching and teacher education has been conceptualized. This evolution has determined to a great extent the nature of the research conducted and the extent to which the findings have been deemed useful for informing practice.

The goal of this chapter is to describe the varieties of ways researchers have gone about studying teaching, teacher education, and curriculum in physical education. The alternative forms of research will be described from a historical perspective, with a description of the relationships between practitioners and researchers along the way. In general, researchers have taken two perspectives, which can be illustrated by a comparison to an observer with a pair of binoculars. The earlier researchers "focused their binoculars" on a particular component of the teaching-learning setting and tried to analyze every part in great detail. We looked at capacities and actions of teachers and learners, seeking to discover relationships and differences, meticulously analyzing the teaching/learning process.

Because of a dissatisfaction with the narrow lens for studying teaching and learning, a broader conceptualization is evolving, with researchers focusing more on the perspectives of the participants. Careful consideration is now given to the interaction of participants, their backgrounds, and the context. The goals, thoughts, feelings, expectations, and attitudes of teachers, teacher educators, and students are accepted by researchers as important data. These researchers use a wider angle to view the learning environment and study the significance of social, cultural, and political influences.

For years, research has been used to gain a theoretical and practical understanding of teaching, teacher education, and curriculum in physical education. Questions are formulated to help us better understand what constitutes good teaching and how to prepare teachers who can implement quality instructional programs in schools and gymnasiums. This chapter seeks to introduce the various approaches that have been used to formulate answers to pedagogical questions in our field.

THE EVOLVING CURRICULUM
AND EARLY RESEARCH EFFORTS

To understand the contributions of groups of scholars and the types of influences guiding their research efforts, let's look briefly at how the curriculum in physical education has evolved over the years. The history of physical education reflects the cultural, economic, social, and political forces of the times, and an understanding of the curriculum from a historical perspective can assist in the interpretation of research findings.

THE FIRST PROGRAMS

Physical education programs in the United States appeared in the early 1800s and were primarily therapeutic exercises. At the turn of the 20th century there was a shift in focus, and the concern for individual development brought about new aims and objectives for physical education programs (Jewett, Bain, & Ennis, 1995). *The Cardinal Principles of Education,* published by the Commission on the Reorganization of Secondary Education in 1918, had a role in making physical education an established offering in the schools, with an emphasis on worthy use of leisure time. The influence of John Dewey created a philosophy stressing total development through natural problem solving, and this approach for education was directly applied to physical education programs in the form of sports and games.

The programs of the early 1900s replaced rigid exercises with natural play and recreational activities and became known as the "education through the physical" approach. While physical education struggled to survive the educational crisis during the Depression of the 1930s, the new program continued to gain support, and the concept of total development through physical activities shaped the program of activities until the 1960s. During the 1940s and 1950s the concerns brought about by World War II and the perceived need to promote physical well-being resulted in an increased attention to fitness programs in our schools. Even with the emphasis on physical fitness, sport was the dominant curricular offering.

RESEARCH EFFORTS

Pedagogical research began in the 1940s with attempts to find teacher characteristics or presage variables (e.g., social class of parents, number of siblings) that would correlate highly with teacher effectiveness or product variables. The criteria of teacher effectiveness in this early model were typically teacher ratings by administrative personnel or by students. These researchers tried to identify personal traits of teachers, such as appearance or enthusiasm, that were thought to be linked to good teaching. Another form of early classroom research compared the measured achievement of classes taught by one method with that of classes taught by another (Brophy & Good, 1986). These approaches failed to produce relevant and consistent findings about what constitutes effective teaching. According to Medley (1979), the early research using the teacher rating scales produced no evidence to show that teachers possessing certain characteristics were actually more effective in promoting student achievement or any of the goals of education. The methods studies were inconclusive because the differences in the methods were not sufficient to show differences in student achievement (Medley, 1979).

Over the years pedagogical researchers in physical education have used findings from generic classroom research to formulate the questions and issues for study. In an early review of research on teaching physical education, Nixon and Locke (1973) report only one study designed to relate personal characteristics of preservice teachers to teacher success (Dawson, 1969). In a later review, Locke (1984) describes a study which used numerous presage variables to predict the success of student teachers as measured by the ratings of cooperating teachers. The author accounted for 80 percent of the variance in the ratings given to the teachers. Locke concludes that the findings of this study were astonishing, but "as such ratings have no known relationship to teaching success, or to anything else, it is difficult to convert the results into either interesting theory or useful rules for practice" (p. 24). Despite these warnings, many teacher educators adapted these rating scales for judging the performance of student teachers, and many are still in use today.

RESEARCH ON MOTOR SKILL ACQUISITION

At the time that classroom pedagogical researchers were interested in defining the desirable traits of effective teachers and how they used effective methods (Medley, 1979), researchers in physical education were concerned with identifying ways that teachers could facilitate the acquisition of motor skills. Most of the research activity during this time was produced by physical educators specializing in motor learning. Before 1960, physical education was defined only as a teaching field, so the student population was limited to those preparing to be teachers. Thus, researchers in motor learning, as well as in other specializations within the field of physical education, were concerned with directing their findings to practicing or prospective teachers. Nixon and Locke (1973) described studies of schedule patterns (e.g., three days a week versus two days a week for skill practice), class size, the usefulness of mechanical learning aids, the effects of different ways to present, and analyses of the practice task. A typical methods study in physical education, for example, compared two methods of teaching beginning basketball (Whilden, 1956).

Although Nixon and Locke's 1973 review focused on the research in physical education that was most concerned with teaching as a means of facilitating the acquisition of motor skills, they warned that knowing how students learn and knowing how to help them learn are two different kinds of knowledge. These authors concluded that because of a host of methodological difficulties, including the general absence of theory as a tool in designing the research, the findings did not provide any information that would improve teaching practice in physical education. While Nixon and Locke concluded with some suggestions for teachers (e.g., the use of augmented knowledge of performance for closed skills), they complained about voids in which the teacher's actions must depend on tradition, chance, or intuition (e.g., how to guide a learner's response after feedback). They also called for more descriptive analytic research in motor skill learning, where methods for the systematic recording of events and behaviors could be devised and tested.

During the next decade, interest in systematic observation of teachers and events in the gymnasium led to the development of a number of instruments to collect and describe quantitative data on teaching. These efforts, along with the influence of those who continued to criticize low-inference measurement of teaching events (Dunkin & Biddle, 1974), helped to define the process-product research programs of the 1970s, which yielded more consistent results.

MAJOR CHANGES IN PROGRAMS

Several events in the 1960s changed how the field of physical education was conceptualized. An article by Franklin Henry described physical education as an academic discipline (Henry, 1964). We became interested in defining a body of knowledge for our field and offering undergraduate majors for students seeking careers outside of teaching (Bain, 1990). There was concern for establishing a scientific knowledge base for the discipline, and many groups began to rename their programs to reflect an academic major rather than a teaching field. These changes led to some confusion about the nature of the subject matter of our field as well as the range of goals researchers, curriculum designers, and teachers were expected to accomplish.

Proponents of a movement approach to teaching physical education challenged the traditional sports and fitness emphasis in the 1960s, recommending that a Laban-based movement education framework be used to structure content in games, dance, and gymnastics (Barrett, 1985). Movement education, borrowed from British curricular models based on Rudolph Laban's movement theory, emphasized an understanding of movement concepts through problem solving and discovery and offered legitimate competition for the dominant sport curriculum. Critics were concerned that research efforts had not provided support for the approach. Nixon and Locke (1973) pointed out that the pattern of results from experimental studies of movement education at the elementary school, high school, and college levels had been nonsignificant, and indicated a concern about a host of methodological weaknesses. While the movement approach had an impact on some elementary school programs in the country, the subject matter of physical education, for the most part, continued to be sport and fitness.

Subsequent growth of the subdisciplinary areas and the various definitions of goals resulted in a lack of agreement about the nature of the physical education curriculum. Jewett et al. (1995) explain that curriculum planning is based to a large extent on professional judgment and public policy. The focus of the curriculum has changed throughout history according to national and personal priorities related to social, economic, and political concerns. From the 1960s to the present time there have been many different views and resulting curricular models described (e.g., fitness model, conceptual model). While these changes made the researcher's job more complex, the resulting growth in both the number of specialists in the field and in the quality of their pedagogical research was positive. Even though some viewed the research role of the subdiscipline specialist as more prestigious than that of the pedagogical specialist, the development of more sophisticated research methodology has resulted in increased research productivity. Efforts after the major changes of the 60s have produced a well founded knowledge base related to teaching and teacher education in physical education.

RESEARCH PROGRESS

While the early research in physical education generated little knowledge concerning teaching, researchers became aware of the difficulties involved in providing useful information. Efforts of succeeding years focused on overcoming these shortcomings and research on teaching made great strides.

DESCRIPTIONS OF TEACHERS AND CLASSES

By the 1970s pedagogical researchers were ready to give up on the methods focus of the 50s and 60s and eager to consider the use of observational instruments that classroom researchers had collected. Another event helping to redirect the field of research on teaching was the publication of Dunkin and Biddle's *The Study of Teaching* (1974). Dunkin and Biddle developed a model that organizes the variables in teaching into presage, context, process, and product categories. Presage variables (characteristics of the teachers) and product variables (teaching outcomes) had been used in earlier research, but high inference scales had been used to measure outcomes.

Dunkin and Biddle's framework was helpful in designing and discussing research and served to guide research efforts for many years. Context variables were defined as the conditions to which the teacher must adjust, and process variables referred to the activities in the class, or what teachers and students do. They discussed the merits of conducting studies using valid and reliable instruments for systematic observation and coding of behaviors and events occurring in teaching-learning environments. Physical educators followed the lead of classroom researchers and began to focus on the development and standardization of systematic observation instruments for recording and analyzing teacher and student behaviors in the gymnasium. Locke (1977) says that the development and use of instruments for systematic observation was significant because this methodology allowed researchers to gather data through direct observation of teachers teaching.

Anderson and Barrette (1978) took the lead when they described the behaviors of teachers and students in physical education classes. Other work by Cheffers (1973) adapted the Flanders Interaction Analysis System (CAFIAS) for use in physical education. At The Ohio State University, Siedentop and his colleagues (Siedentop & Hughley, 1975) developed the O.S.U. Teacher Behavior Instrument, which was used originally with student teachers, but later with cooperating teachers as well as inservice teachers. These initial efforts led to the development of other instruments, which were eventually compiled and published (Darst, Zakrajsek, & Mancini, 1989).

While many different types of observation systems have been used in pedagogical research, the Academic Learning Time-Physical Education (ALT-PE) instruments (Siedentop, Tousignant, & Parker, 1982) have probably been used most often. Siedentop and his colleagues (Siedentop, Birdwell, & Metzler, 1979) adapted the Academic Learning Time model from the Beginning Teacher Evaluation Study (BTES) (for an overview, see Fisher et al., 1978) and presented a series of papers examining how the ALT-PE concept could be used as a process measure in physical education. After a series of studies which extended through the 1980s (Aufderheide, 1983; Godbout, Burnelle, & Tousignant, 1983; Metzler, 1980; Piéron & Haan, 1979; Placek, Silverman, Shute, Dodds, & Rife, 1982; Silverman, Dodds, Placek, Shute, & Rife, 1984), Metzler (1989) concluded that students spend a small proportion of time engaged in motor activities related to motor skill achievement. Other descriptive work in physical education has shown that the environment in physical education is predominantly teacher centered (Anderson & Barrette, 1978; Cheffers & Mancini, 1978; Lombardo & Cheffers, 1979).

TEACHER BEHAVIOR RESEARCH

Following the development of instruments for systematic observation, researchers became involved in a whole line of teacher effectiveness studies in which low-inference measures of teaching behaviors were used as process variables. This approach was an improvement over earlier attempts that relied on high-inference scales of teacher effectiveness, but the results were mixed and thus disappointing to both researchers and teacher educators. One popular technique used was a correlational design in which various teacher behaviors (process) were correlated with student achievement (product). Using teacher explanations as the process variable, Oliver (1980) and Taylor (1976) reported relationships between teacher behavior and student achievement. Other researchers (Yerg, 1981a; 1981b; Yerg & Twardy, 1982) found that none of the teacher behaviors measured were associated with student achievement.

Because of a strong belief in the value of teacher feedback, many pedagogical researchers have studied the relationship of feedback to achievement. A recent review of the feedback studies in physical education (Lee, Keh, & Magill, 1993) indicated that the results from this line of research were inconsistent. Most of the studies concluded that teacher feedback, measured objectively in a variety of different ways, was not related to increased achievement (Godbout, Burnelle, & Tousignant, 1987; Salter & Graham, 1985; Silverman, Tyson, & Krampitz, 1992).

While the early process-product studies helped to define physical education pedagogy as an important focus for research, several researchers in the field, some of them involved in the early research, began to call attention to important methodological issues. Problems cited to explain the inconsistent results included short periods of instructional time and the competence level of the teachers (Graham, Soares, & Harrington, 1983; Yerg, 1981a). In the early 80s, for example, Graham and his colleagues (Graham & Heimerer, 1981; Graham et al., 1983) argued that successful teaching requires an orchestration of teaching behaviors and a single behavior such as feedback will rarely be powerful enough to discriminate more and less effective teachers. Other researchers (Rink & Werner, 1987) emphasized the need to focus on important variables other than teacher behaviors, which had thus far yielded limited results. In a much earlier report, Dunkin and Biddle (1974) had warned researchers of the risks involved in reporting patterns of teacher behaviors without considering context factors such as grade level, teacher objectives, and subject matter, noting that more complex designs are needed before findings could be meaningful.

CHANGING TEACHER BEHAVIOR

Based on the picture of the typical physical education class presented by the observational research evidence, many physical educators set out to determine the behaviors of good teachers, define precisely what those behaviors are, and teach them to novices. Believing that higher frequencies of certain teacher behaviors would result in greater student learning, researchers trained teachers to change the type and quality of information delivered to students.

One study, for example, defined and trained enthusiastic teaching behavior in a group of student teachers (Rolider, Siedentop, & Van Houten, 1984). Using applied behavior analysis, these researchers and others (e.g., Carlisle & Phillips, 1984) concluded that teachers can be trained to increase their level of enthusiastic behavior. Another teacher behavior used in several intervention studies over a period of several years was teacher feedback. Researchers (Hawkins, Wiegand, & Landin, 1985; Landin, Hawkins, & Wiegand, 1986) trained student teachers to modify their feedback behavior and increase the rate of appropriate levels of positive feedback to students. Cusimano (1987) and van der Mars (1987) also used planned intervention to increase the amount of specific, positive feedback inservice teachers gave to students regarding skill performance.

These studies showed that teacher behavior can be changed through behavioral analytic techniques and systematic feedback, and this finding had great appeal to researchers studying teacher effectiveness. In an earlier review, Locke (1984) had been somewhat pessimistic about using research findings (from physical education or classroom research) to prescribe rules for teachers, discussing the problem of transfer from training to actual teaching. In a rather recent review of research on teaching, Locke (1987) explained that "it has been established beyond question that physical education teachers at preservice or inservice levels can acquire new behaviors, alter old patterns of instruction, adapt methods to the unique demands of local context, and do so without the assistance of elaborate and expensive training interventions" (p. 84).

Others began to question whether focusing on a single "best way to teach" was productive for teacher education, and in the research programs that followed scholars and teacher educators took a different approach. It became more and more important for researchers to explain their findings, and while the research describing relationships between what teachers do in physical education classes and what their students learn did not produce consistent results, the methodology was promising. It was a step forward from the earlier focus on comparison of teaching methods and led the way to a mature, respectable area of inquiry for those interested in the study of teaching and teacher education.

A FOCUS ON TIME

Just as the process-product research program got underway, critics began to direct attention to its weaknesses. First, while some teacher behaviors might be associated with student achievement, the correlations were usually low and not always significant. A more serious concern seemed to be the difficulty in explaining the reasons for the relationships (Brophy & Good, 1986). Thus, at the same time teacher behavior research was gaining momentum in the late 70s and early 80s, a student mediating paradigm was offered as an alternative. Based on a belief that attention to the immediate responses of students would provide better estimates of the effects of teaching (Shulman, 1986), the observable activities of the learners during class became viewed as mediators of instruction. Using concepts from the work of Carroll and Bloom (Carroll, 1963; Bloom, 1974), student engaged time became the variable of interest. Initial research efforts using time as a student mediating variable in pedagogical research were found in the BTES (Fisher et al., 1978). These researchers theorized that the amount of time a student was engaged with the subject at an appropriate difficulty level was the crucial variable underlying successful teaching. Thus, within this modified process-product framework, the variable identified as Academic Learning Time (ALT) was accepted as the process variable linking measures of teacher behavior to student learning. Even though Doyle (1977) advocated the study of a broader range of student mediating processes that govern learning, ALT emerged as the quantitative measure used in research for the next several years.

CONTRIBUTIONS OF ALT-PE RESEARCH

With the availability of the revised ALT-PE Instrument (Siedentop et al., 1982), research relating student engaged time to achievement was a logical step. After the series of studies describing how time is spent in physical education classes, researchers shifted the emphasis toward process-product designs using student engaged time as the process variable. The first attempts by physical educators to demonstrate a relationship between ALT-PE and student achievement were not successful (Godbout et al., 1987; Silverman, 1983; Yerg, 1983; Yerg & Twardy, 1982), probably because task difficulty and the quality of student practice were difficult to determine. More recent research, considering the context in which instruction occurs and the nature of the task being taught, has shown that engaged time is related to achievement. For example, in a study using the class as the unit of analysis, Silverman, Tyson, and Morford (1988) found that time spent in practice with feedback was positively related to achievement and that the type of practice was important. Studies using the number of practice trials in which correct technique was used as a measure of successful practice have found the expected relationships between engagement and achievement (Ashy, Lee, & Landin, 1988; Buck, Harrison, & Bryce, 1991; Dugas, 1984; Silverman, 1985, 1990). It appears that the quality rather than the total amount of practice is more important to student learning (Ashy et al., 1988; Silverman, 1990).

UNDERSTANDING MORE ABOUT TEACHER DEVELOPMENT

At the same time some researchers were interested in quantifying desirable teacher actions, others were interested in determining why teachers behave as they do in the gymnasium. This approach recommended taking a broader view, and emphasized the need to move beyond the detailed analysis of one or two aspects of teacher behavior. In one viewpoint, first set forth by Lortie (1975), an individual's biography, rather than a teacher education program, is viewed as the primary determinant in how effective a teacher will be. In this perspective, personal dispositions, educational experiences as a student, early role models, and the school environment serve as socializing agents for teachers and are difficult to offset in teacher education.

Another perspective found in the literature of the 1970s was that prospective teachers enter the educational system without any opinions or impressions and are passive recipients in the social structure of the system. There was some early evidence to support the notion that effects of teacher education programs are washed out by the educational social structure (Templin, 1979).

In the 1980s it became apparent that both of the early approaches overlooked the interaction between the teacher's personal perspectives and the social structure. Another early study by Templin (1981) indicated that students serve as socializing agents. Thus, from an interactive viewpoint, socializing agents can include numerous forces that influence the development of teachers. Teachers react to both student and classroom influences, and the reciprocal nature of this process shapes teacher behavior in significant ways.

According to Locke (1984), physical educators were slow to recognize the value of the socialization model in formulating research questions. With the exception of Templin's (1979, 1981) work, there were few early efforts to understand the extent to which teacher education influences the practice of teaching. In an extensive review of research on teacher education from 1960 through 1981, Locke (1984) concluded that: "Teachers can be caused to acquire particular teaching behaviors. What is less clear from the research is what impact particular teacher behaviors have on student achievement in the natural setting, how well skills acquired in training programs transfer to the natural setting, and under what conditions teachers will persist in using the pedagogy they have acquired through formal teacher education" (p. 36).

While there was no early program of research comparable to the teacher effectiveness efforts (Bain, 1990), there was much written about the salient influences in the process of teacher socialization. Physical education scholars in this tradition have played a critical role in alerting other professionals to question the value of available research for guiding the practice of teachers. The most recognized spokesperson for this research focus is Lawson (1983a, 1983b, 1986, 1988, 1990), whose work emphasized the importance of understanding the roles that various socializing agents play in the development of effective physical education teachers.

In an early article, Lawson (1983a) synthesized information concerning the socialization process for physical education, setting forth five basic assumptions. The socialization process, according to Lawson, is a lifelong process, not beginning with a teacher education program, but instead beginning early in life and continuing throughout the educational career. He suggested that operations in the physical education world are institutionalized and therefore are resistant to change. Lawson viewed socialization as problematic rather than automatic, in that socialization occurs when incompatibilities or inconsistencies occur. He stated that differences in school programs and teacher education programs exist which contribute to the complex nature of socialization of physical education teachers, and that judgments regarding what is effective or functional socialization reflect the orientation of those who are making the evaluation.

In 1989, Templin and Schempp (1989) delineated an interactive view of teacher socialization that sees the prospective teacher as an active agent in his or her own socialization, controlling the direction of both biography and social structure. These authors put together a volume of essays which summarized the major influences in the process of teacher socialization in physical education. In a more recent monograph edited by Stroot (1993), various authors summarized the research completed thus far using the occupational socialization model defined by Lawson (1986). Stroot's chapter in this book also reviews some of this material. The research reported examined recruitment into physical education (e.g., Dodds, Placek, Doolittle, Pinkham, Ratliffe, & Portman, 1992), the socialization process during teacher preparation (e.g., Graber, 1991), and experiences of teachers as they enter the school setting (e.g., O'Sullivan, 1989).

Research (Schempp, 1989) has identified the individual's biography as the fundamental base for teacher socialization, advancing the notion that primary influences on the socialization process occur before teacher education. Other researchers (Graber, 1989; Solmon, Worthy, & Carter, 1993; Solmon, Worthy, Lee, & Carter, 1991) have studied the interaction between the teacher's personal perspective and the social structure of the educational system. Findings from these studies support the view of the teacher as an active agent controlling the direction of biography and social structure in the socialization process. In other recent work, the life history approach has been used (Templin, Sparkes, & Schempp, 1991) to gather in-depth information about the lives of teachers and influences of the socialization process.

Taken together, the findings from this line of research support the view that teaching is a complex endeavor and socialization into teaching involves several dimensions. Based on the research available, Lawson and Stroot (1993) conclude that socialization is interactive, problematic, and has variable impacts upon individuals. A more complete analysis of socialization research is provided in chapter 16.

THE INFLUENCE OF INFORMATION PROCESSING AND COGNITIVE SCIENCE

As the research literature increased during the 1980s, the focus broadened to include the study of teacher and student thinking as well as behavior. Scholars in this tradition (Clark & Peterson, 1986; Wittrock, 1986) brought attention to the need for researchers to go beyond describing what teachers and students do in classes, relating what teachers do to student behavior, and planning intervention programs to change the behavior of teachers. The study of thought processes represents an approach to research based on the assumption that what teachers and students do is affected by what they think.

Basing their work on research in cognitive psychology, which describes the thinking and actions of experts and novices in a variety of fields (Chi, Glaser, & Rees, 1982), many researchers have investigated the cognitive components of teaching expertise. A recent review by Dodds (1994) summarized research conducted on how knowledge of a particular topic is organized by expert and novice physical education teachers. According to Dodds (1994), several researchers have examined expertise in observational skill, finding that experts differ from novices in diagnosing movement skills. Expert teachers have developed complex cognitive schemata which enable them to notice correct and incorrect aspects of motor skill performance, easily selecting and prioritizing salient cues for the task (Pinheiro & Simon, 1992). On the other hand, while novice teachers have difficulty extracting the salient clues from the teaching environment, they can be taught observational skills during field experiences (Barrett, Allison, & Bell, 1987; Bell, Barrett, & Allison, 1985). Other studies have also demonstrated that the movement analysis capabilities of novices can be improved through training (Beveridge & Gangstead, 1988).

Using different forms of cognitive mapping techniques, researchers have studied the knowledge bases of expert and novice teachers (Ennis, Mueller, & Zhu, 1991; Housner, Gomez, & Griffey, 1993; Rink, French, Lee, Solmon, & Lynn, 1994). Findings from this research indicate that experts have more complex knowledge structures about teaching and the curriculum, but until the work is extended beyond a description of broad generic categories of schemata, these findings have limited value. With the exception of Ennis et al. (1991), these studies have not looked at content-specific levels of knowledge structures. Moreover, none of the studies have traced the teachers' knowledge about teaching to actual teaching processes. Dodds (1994) concludes that the expert-novice research completed thus far has defined expertise in a narrow way and argues for a broader conception. The available data tell us little about that part of teaching expertise related to creating equity for students by addressing motor elitism, racism, sexism, homophobia, and other social justice issues (Dodds, 1994).

TEACHER THINKING AND DECISION MAKING

The chapter on "Teachers' Thought Processes" (Clark & Peterson, 1986) in the *Third Handbook of Research on Teaching,* was helpful in conceptualizing the domain of teachers' thought processes into the categories of preactive planning, interactive decision making, and teacher theories and beliefs. The first two categories represent a temporal distinction between teacher thought processes occurring prior to teaching (pre-active) or during teaching (interactive). The third category examines the influence of teachers' theories and beliefs on planning and decision making.

Teacher planning has been an area of research interest in physical education since 1979, when Sherman (1979) compared the planning of expert and novice gymnastics teachers. Since that time, several other researchers have focused on various aspects of teacher planning (Byra & Sherman, 1993; Griffey & Housner, 1991; Housner & Griffey, 1985; Placek, 1984; Solmon & Lee, 1991; Stroot & Morton, 1989; Twardy & Yerg, 1987). With the exception of Placek (1984), who gathered data through observation in a naturalistic setting, and Stroot and Morton (1989), who analyzed actual plans and interviews, researchers have used a think-aloud technique in which teachers are asked to verbalize their thoughts during the planning session. Their responses are recorded and analyzed to determine the frequency and type of planning decisions made. Findings from the planning studies, for the most part, indicate that planning decisions, regardless of level of expertise, are related to the activities and content of the lesson rather than the goals and objectives.

The traditional planning model (Tyler, 1950) accepted by most teacher education programs emphasizes the consideration of objectives as a first step, but because of these research findings this basic model is being questioned. The finding by Placek (1983) that teachers plan to keep students "busy, happy, and good" has caused many disgruntled teacher educators to reevaluate the effectiveness of current training programs. Teachers in the study by Stroot and Morton (1989) provided a different and more optimistic view of teacher planning. These teachers, who were identified as being effective, based on objective data and reputation, were concerned with student learning and planned extensively following the basic Tyler model. The expert-novice studies suggest that more and less experienced teachers differ in their thinking and decision making during pre-active planning. When compared to inexperienced teachers, more experienced teachers request more information about the teaching situation, plan in more detail, and make more decisions concerning strategies for implementing instructional tasks.

Many of the researchers interested in the thought processes of teachers have used a stimulated recall interview to study teachers during actual instruction (Byra & Sherman, 1993; Housner & Griffey, 1985; Walkwitz & Lee, 1992). Though there is some variation in the data-collection techniques used, teachers generally view a videotape of a lesson recently completed and answer a series of questions regarding their thoughts and decisions during the lesson. Findings from the studies comparing experienced and inexperienced teachers (Byra & Sherman, 1993; Housner & Griffey, 1985) indicate that experienced teachers are more likely to implement alternative teaching routines when lessons are perceived as not progressing as intended. Inexperienced teachers, on the other hand, tend to continue according to their plan, even when they perceive that the lesson is not progressing as planned. The study by Walkwitz and Lee (1992) indicated that experienced teachers could translate knowledge of their subject matter into classroom events.

The studies of teachers' pre-active and interactive thoughts have produced little information that can guide research or inform teaching. The findings from the planning studies have alerted teacher educators to the possibility that planning principles introduced during preservice education were never transferred into teaching practice. The interactive studies have been criticized for using frequency counts of thoughts and feelings which were believed to precede behavior (Shulman, 1986). This approach to analysis is very similar to the early process-product work and probably lacks the complexity needed to answer important questions about teaching.

The research in physical education that has focused on the influence of beliefs and values on teachers has been conducted, for the most part, by Ennis and her colleagues (Ennis, Mueller, & Hooper, 1990; Ennis, Ross, & Chen, 1992; Ennis & Zhu, 1991). In a recent review of the influence of beliefs on the knowledge acquisition and utilization of teachers, Ennis (1994) points out that teachers develop educational belief systems that influence their decisions about selection of content, teaching strategies, and tasks in physical education (also see chapter 7). She provides evidence that individuals may choose to resist knowledge that conflicts with their belief systems (e.g., Faucette, 1987). Consistent with these findings is Veal's (1988, 1992) research on teachers' beliefs about assessment. This work indicates that teachers and teacher educators differ in their beliefs about assessment and that what teachers actually do is not always consistent with their self reports.

STUDENT THINKING

Cognitive studies of how students learn from teaching are beginning to appear in the literature. This work is an extension of the time mediating research which focused on student behavior and ignored the covert responses students have during instruction. Grounded in a belief that teachers do not directly influence achievement but rather cause students to think and behave in certain ways, these studies emphasize the role that student perceptions, motivations, affective processes, and attention play in achievement (Lee & Solmon, 1992). This line of research has identified background variables that influence the extent to which students choose to participate in tasks defined by the teacher (Greenockle, Lee, & Lomax, 1990) and has analyzed how the thoughts and feelings of students as they practice a motor skill mediate the instruction provided by the teacher (Lee, Landin, & Carter, 1992). Other research has studied student perception of teacher behavior and supports the notion that student thoughts mediate learning. Martinek's (1988) recent research focusing on how teacher expectancy effects are mediated by student perceptions found that learners in high- and low-expectation groups perceive specific teacher behaviors in different ways. Other work (Hanke, 1987) focusing on student cognition has described how students perceive and give meaning to teachers' instructional behaviors in different ways.

Some researchers interested in defining how students mediate learning have found social cognitive models of student motivation useful. Research (Solmon & Lee, in press) has demonstrated that students' entry characteristics, such as skill level, as well as their motivational beliefs and use of learning strategies, play an important role in their actual participation patterns during instruction. An extension of this work includes the construct of student goal orientation to understand achievement motivation in motor skill settings (Solmon & Boone, 1993). While this line of research seems promising, it requires the use of self-report data, which some traditional researchers find limited because subjects may not always be truthful.

However, because the integration of social and cognitive mediational constructs can help explain some complex dimensions of student achievement motivation and learning, the subjective measures of student cognition are valuable. Collected and analyzed with care, self reports can be a reliable source of data. This work suffers, however, from the same weaknesses of some of the earlier process-product designs. The researchers, thus far, have paid little attention to the variations among teachers and how subject matter and context interact with motivational and cognitive beliefs of students (Shulman, 1986). We do not know yet how different teaching strategies or different types of movement tasks influence the ways that students mediate instruction.

ECOLOGY IN THE GYM

Rather than focusing on one or two aspects of a teaching-learning environment and analyzing thoughts and actions in great detail, some researchers are interested in viewing the interactive processes occurring in the classroom. Although the thoughts and feelings of the participants are important in this research, it places more emphasis on teacher and student interaction in the context of the learning environment. The setting in which the research is conducted is believed to be a key in determining reasons for teacher and student behavior in physical education. From this perspective, researchers tend to focus on unwritten rules which might define activities and behaviors that are appropriate and expected for the various subgroups in the class. These expected patterns of behavior, or the roles defined for different students in the class, are believed to be constructed by the interactions in the specific context.

Such research is interested in equality of opportunity based on gender, ethnicity, or social class. Physical education studies by Griffin (e.g., 1985) and Bain (1985) have described the limits placed on groups defined by gender and levels of obesity. These researchers used ethnographic methodology to reconstruct the social realities of the classroom. They were not interested in studying the effectiveness of the teacher in terms of student movement outcomes. Rather, the purpose was to describe how the structure of a typical physical education class failed to serve the needs of some student subgroups.

More recently, researchers have explored how students in physical education perceive or assign meaning to instructional events (Pissanos & Allison, 1993; Solmon & Carter, 1995) and how teachers come to understand and accept a teaching approach (Rovegno, 1993). These studies are framed using a constructivist educational viewpoint which assumes that individuals actively construct knowledge based on their interpretations of their experiences in the situation and these interpretations are influenced by existing knowledge and expectations. One interesting finding emerging from the research by Pissanos and Allison (1993) and Solmon and Carter (1995) is that gender influenced the construction of meaning in physical education. This group of researchers is concerned with the importance of events to the participants, especially those that are interpreted differently because of gender, social class, or skill level. They seek to reconstruct the meanings students assign to the events in the class and to uncover the basis for the constructed meanings.

A CONCERN FOR BROADER ISSUES

The researchers interested in ecological research look for interactive processes from a broad perspective and reject the notion of identifying some isolated factors for description or correlational analysis. They seek detailed information about the interactions in the classroom but argue that these processes are influenced by conditions outside the school, including family and cultural characteristics. These researchers might define an effective teacher as one who provides equal opportunity for males and females or skilled and unskilled students. They would look within the structure of the class for effectiveness rather than use student achievement measures.

The limited amount of ecological research conducted in physical education has uncovered and explained some features of the hidden curriculum. Based on this research and the initial conceptualization of the hidden curriculum in physical education by Bain (1975), a rather large group of researchers has attempted to describe more accurately the knowledge and skills students learn as an unintentional consequence of the formal teaching and learning processes (e.g., Kirk, 1992; Fernandez-Balboa, 1993). The research recommended by these scholars is more interpretative and critical in nature. They argue that the focus must be on communication and meaning-making in the classroom and the research tools must shift more toward the use of participant observation, case studies, and other qualitative methodology (Kirk, 1992).

During the brief history of pedagogical research in physical education, there have been different and sometimes conflicting concepts of "good research" and how it can improve practice. In recent years, many of the controversies have centered on the value of a technological orientation to teaching and learning. Many teacher educators, through the years, have taken results of descriptive and process-product work and simplified them into a set of desirable behaviors that all teachers must acquire. The critics of the process-product research argue that this model has little chance of improving educational practice (e.g., Tinning, 1991). Lawson (1993) has recently concluded that the extent to which pedagogical research, disseminated during teacher education, can be used by teachers to improve practice is limited. He believes that knowledge for practice must be derived from practice, and research that is relevant to one set of practices is not necessarily useful in others. Action research has been proposed as a way for teachers to research their own practice.

SUMMARY

The history of research on teaching and teacher education has been characterized by a gradual shift from a narrow to a broader focus. Much of the early research could be compared to an observer with a pair of binoculars searching for particular behaviors and techniques that might lead to a better understanding of what constitutes good teaching. Research describing the minute details of teacher and student behavior and defining relationships between teaching processes and desirable student outcomes dominated the efforts of many researchers during the 1970s and 1980s.

Researchers who advocated a broader study of teaching and teacher education argued that the process-product research did not provide theoretical explanations for why certain behaviors and processes were related to student outcomes. Using a wider angle lens, they directed attention away from counting events and behaviors toward a study of teaching learning processes from the perspective of students and teachers. These approaches are concerned with explanations of thoughts as well as actions and consider prior knowledge, attitudes, goals, and feelings as mediating variables. Those using the wide-angle approach are more concerned with the interactions between teachers and contexts and fear that a narrow focus will result in a list of rules imposed on teachers. This makes them quite uneasy because of their strong belief that a specific set of competencies reflects a technological rather than a reflective orientation.

The past two decades have been productive for pedagogical researchers in physical education, with findings leading to a greater understanding of how learning occurs from teaching in the gymnasium. The research has been conducted from a range of perspectives, and efforts to refine earlier models which used a more narrow lens provided opportunities for professional dialogue and debate. Discussion of theoretical and conceptual research issues is a healthy sign, and the future for the field looks promising. During the next decade new methods for conducting research will be identified and additional problems will be uncovered.

REFERENCES

Anderson, W.G., & Barrette, G.T. (Eds.). (1978). What's going on in gym: Descriptive studies of physical education classes. *Motor Skills: Theory Into Practice, Monograph 1*.

Ashy, M.H., Lee, A.M., & Landin, D.K. (1988). Relationship of practice using correct technique to achievement in a motor skill. *Journal of Teaching in Physical Education, 7*, 115–120.

Aufderheide, S. (1983). ALT-PE in mainstreamed physical education classes. *Journal of Teaching in Physical Education Monograph 1*, 22–26.

Bain, L.L. (1975). The hidden curriculum in physical education. *Quest, 24*, 92–101.

Bain, L.L. (1985). A naturalistic study of students' responses to an exercise class. *Journal of Teaching in Physical Education, 5*, 2–12.

Bain, L.L. (1990). Physical education teacher education. In W.R. Houston (Ed.), *Handbook of research on teacher education* (pp. 758–781). New York: Macmillan.

Barrett, K.R. (1985). The content of an elementary school physical education program and its impact on teacher preparation. In H.A. Hoffman & J.E. Rink (Eds.), *Physical education preparation: Insight and foresight* (pp. 9–25). Reston, VA: American Alliance for Health, Physical Education, Recreation and Dance.

Barrett, K., Allison, P., & Bell, R. (1987). What preservice physical education teachers see in an unguided field experience: A follow-up study. *Journal of Teaching in Physical Education, 7,* 12–21.

Bell, R., Barrett, K., & Allison, P. (1985). What preservice physical education teachers see in an unguided, early field experience. *Journal of Teaching in Physical Education, 4,* 1–90.

Beveridge, S., & Gangstead, S. (1988). Teaching experience and training in sport skill analysis. *Journal of Teaching in Physical Education, 7,* 103–114.

Bloom, B.S. (1974, September). Time and learning. *American Psychologist, 29,* 682–688.

Brophy, J., & Good, T.L. (1986). Teacher behavior and student achievement. In M.C. Wittrock (Ed.), *Handbook of research on teaching* (3rd ed., pp. 328–375). New York: Macmillan.

Buck, M., Harrison, J.M., & Bryce, G.R. (1991). An analysis of learning trials and their relationship to achievement in volleyball. *Journal of Teaching in Physical Education, 10,* 134–152.

Byra, M., & Sherman, M.A. (1993). Preactive and interactive decision-making tendencies of less and more experienced preservice teachers. *Research Quarterly for Exercise and Sport, 64,* 46–55.

Carlisle, C., & Phillips, D.A. (1984). The effects of enthusiasm training on selected teacher and student behaviors in preservice physical education teachers. *Journal of Teaching in Physical Education, 4,* 64–75.

Carroll, J.B. (1963). A model of school learning. *Teachers College Record, 64,* 723–733.

Cheffers, J. (1973). *The validation of an instrument designed to expand the Flanders System of Interaction Analysis to describe nonverbal interaction, different varieties of teacher behavior and pupil responses.* Unpublished doctoral dissertation, Temple University, Philadelphia.

Cheffers, J., & Mancini, V. (1978). Teacher-student interaction. In W. G. Anderson & G.T. Barrette (Eds.), What's going on in gym: Descriptive studies of physical education classes. *Motor Skills: Theory Into Practice, Monograph 1,* 39–50.

Chi, M., Glaser, R., & Rees, E. (1982). Expertise in problem solving. In R.J. Sternberg (Ed.), *Advances in the psychology of human intelligence* (pp. 7–75). Hillsdale, NJ: Erlbaum.

Clark, C., & Peterson, P.L. (1986). Teachers' thought processes. In M.C. Wittrock (Ed.), *Handbook of research on teaching* (3rd ed., pp. 255–296). New York: Macmillan.

Cusimano, B.E. (1987). Effects of self-assessment and goal setting on verbal behavior of elementary physical education teachers. *Journal of Teaching in Physical Education, 6,* 166–173.

Darst, P., Zakrajsek, D., & Mancini, V. (1989). *Analyzing physical education and sport instruction* (2nd ed.). Champaign, IL: Human Kinetics.

Dawson, W. (1969). *The relation of personal data to teaching competence of male physical education majors.* Unpublished doctoral dissertation, University of Utah, Provo.

Dodds, P. (1985). Are hunters of the function curriculum seeking quarks or snarks? *Journal of Teaching in Physical Education, 4,* 91–99.

Dodds, P. (1994). Cognitive and behavioral components of expertise in teaching in physical education. *Quest, 46,* 153–163.

Dodds, P., Placek, J.H., Doolittle, S., Pinkham, K.M, Ratliffe, T.A., & Portman, P.A. (1992). Teacher/coach recruits: Background profiles, occupational decisional factors, and comparisons with recruits into other physical education occupations. *Journal of Teaching in Physical Education, 11,* 161–176.

Doyle, W. (1977). Paradigms for research on teacher effectiveness. In L.S. Shulman (Ed.), *Review of research in education* (Vol. 5, pp. 163–198). Itasca, IL: Peacock.

Dugas, D.M. (1984). Relationships among process and product variables in an experimental teaching unit. *Dissertation Abstracts International, 44,* 2709A. (University Microfilms No. 84-00, 193)

Dunkin, M.J., & Biddle, B.J. (1974). *The study of teaching.* New York: Holt Rinehart & Winston.

Ennis, C.D. (1994). Knowledge and beliefs underlying curricular expertise. *Quest, 46,* 164–175.

Ennis, C.D., Mueller, L.K., & Hooper, L.M. (1990). The influence of teacher value orientations on curriculum planning within the parameters of a theoretical framework. *Research Quarterly for Exercise and Sport, 61,* 360–368.

Ennis, C., Mueller, L., & Zhu, W. (1991). Description of knowledge structures within a concept-based curriculum framework. *Research Quarterly for Exercise and Sport, 62,* 309–318.

Ennis, C.D., Ross, J., & Chen, A. (1992). The role of value orientation in curricular decision making: A rationale for teachers' goals and expectations. *Research Quarterly for Exercise and Sport, 63,* 38–47.

Ennis, C.D., & Zhu, W. (1991). Value orientations: A description of teachers' goals for student learning. *Research Quarterly for Exercise and Sport, 62,* 33–40.

Faucette, N. (1987). Teachers' concerns and participation styles during in-service education. *Journal of Teaching in Physical Education, 6,* 425–440.

Fernandez-Balboa, J.M. (1993). Sociocultural characteristics of the hidden curriculum in physical education. *Quest, 45,* 230–254.

Fisher, C.W., Filby, N.N., Marliave, R., Cahen, L.S., Dishaw, M.M., Moore, J.E., & Berliner, D.C. (1978). *Teaching behaviors, academic learning time and student achievement: Final report of Phase IIIB, Beginning Teacher Evaluation Study* (Technical Report V-1). San Francisco: Far West Laboratory.

Godbout, P., Burnelle, J., & Tousignant, M. (1983). Academic learning time in elementary and secondary physical education classes. *Research Quarterly for Exercise and Sport, 57,* 11–19.

Godbout, P., Burnelle, J., & Tousignant, M. (1987). Who benefits from passing through the program? In G. Barrette, R.S. Feingold, C.R. Rees, & M. Piéron (Eds.), *Myths, models and methods in sport pedagogy* (pp. 183–197). Champaign, IL: Human Kinetics.

Graber, K.C. (1989). Teaching tomorrow's teachers: Professional preparation as an agent of socialization. In T. Templin & P. Schempp (Eds.), *Socialization into physical education: Learning to teach* (pp. 59–80). Indianapolis, IN: Benchmark Press.

Graber, K.C. (1991). Studentship in preservice teacher education: A qualitative study of undergraduates in physical education. *Research Quarterly for Exercise and Sport, 62,* 41–51.

Graham, G., & Heimerer, E. (1981). Research on teacher effectiveness: A summary with implications for teaching. *Quest, 33,* 14–25.

Graham, G., Soares, P., & Harrington, W. (1983). Experienced teachers' effectiveness with intact classes: An ETU study. *Journal of Teaching in Physical Education, 2,* 3–14.

Greenockle, K., Lee, A., & Lomax, R. (1990). The relationship between selected student characteristics and activity patterns in a required high school physical education class. *Research Quarterly for Exercise and Sport, 61,* 59–69.

Griffey, D., & Housner, L.D. (1991). Planning, behavior and organization climate differences of experienced and inexperienced teachers. *Research Quarterly for Exercise and Sport, 62,* 196–204.

Griffin, P.S. (1985). Boys' participation styles in a middle school physical education sports unit. *Journal of Teaching in Physical Education, 4,* 100–110.

Hanke, U. (1987). Cognitive aspects of interaction in physical education. In G.T. Barrette, R.S. Feingold, C.R. Rees, & M. Piéron (Eds.), *Myths, models, and methods in sport pedagogy* (pp. 135–141). Champaign, IL: Human Kinetics.

Hawkins, A., Wiegand, R., & Landin, D.K. (1985). Cataloguing the collective wisdom of teacher educators. *Journal of Teaching in Physical Education, 4,* 241–255.

Henry, F.M. (1964). Physical education: An academic discipline. *Journal of Health, Physical Education, and Recreation, 35,* 32–39, 69.

Housner, L., & Griffey, D. (1985). Teacher cognition: Differences in planning and interactive decision-making between experienced and inexperienced teachers. *Research Quarterly for Exercise and Sport, 56,* 45–53.

Housner, L.D., Gomez, R.L., & Griffey, D.C. (1993). Pedagogical knowledge structures in prospective teachers: Relationships to performance in a teaching methodology class. *Research Quarterly for Exercise and Sport, 64,* 167–177.

Jewett, A.E., Bain, L.L., & Ennis, C D. (1995). *The curriculum process in physical education* (2nd ed.). Dubuque, IA: William C. Brown.

Kirk, D. (1992). Physical education, discourse, and ideology: Bringing the hidden curriculum into view. *Quest, 44,* 35–56.

Landin, D.K., Hawkins, A., & Wiegand, R. (1986). Validating the collective wisdom of teacher educators. *Journal of Teaching in Physical Education, 5,* 252–271.

Lawson, H. (1983a). Toward a model of teacher socialization in physical education: The subjective warrant, recruitment, and teacher education (Part I). *Journal of Teaching in Physical Education, 2,* 3–16.

Lawson, H. (1983b). Toward a model of teacher socialization in physical education: Entry into schools, teachers' role orientations, and longevity in teaching (Part 2). *Journal of Teaching in Physical Education, 3,* 3–15.

Lawson, H. (1986). Occupational socialization and the design of teacher education programs. *Journal of Teaching in Physical Education, 5,* 107–116.

Lawson, H. (1988). Occupational socialization, cultural studies, and the physical education curriculum. *Journal of Teaching in Physical Education, 7,* 265–288.

Lawson, H. (1990). Sport pedagogy research: From information-gathering to useful knowledge. *Journal of Teaching in Physical Education, 10,* 1–20.

Lawson, H. (1993). Teachers' uses of research in practice: A literature review. *Journal of Teaching in Physical Education, 12,* 366–374.

Lawson, H., & Stroot, S. (1993). Footprints and signposts: Perspectives on socialization research. In S. Stroot (Ed.), Socialization into physical education. *Journal of Teaching in Physical Education, [Monograph], 12*(4), 437–446.

Lee, A., Keh, N., & Magill, R. (1993). Instructional effects of teacher feedback in physical education. *Journal of Teaching in Physical Education, 12,* 228–243.

Lee, A., Landin, D., & Carter, J. (1992). Student thoughts during tennis instruction. *Journal of Teaching in Physical Education, 11,* 256–267.

Lee, A., & Solmon, M. (1992). Cognitive conceptions of teaching and learning motor skills. *Quest, 42,* 57–71.

Locke, L. (1977). Research on teaching physical education: New hope for a dismal science. *Quest, 28,* 2–16.

Locke, L. (1984). Research on teaching teachers: Where are we now? *Journal of Teaching in Physical Education, Monograph 2.*

Locke, L. (1987). The future of research on pedagogy: Balancing on the cutting edge. *American Academy of Physical Education Papers, 20,* 83–95. Champaign, IL: Human Kinetics.

Lombardo, B., & Cheffers, J. (1979). The observation and description of teaching behaviors of selected physical education teachers. In R.H. Cox (Ed.), *Symposium papers: Teaching behavior and women in sport* (pp. 32–36). Washington, DC: AAHPERD.

Lortie, D. (1975). *Schoolteacher: A sociological study.* Chicago: University of Chicago Press.

Martinek, T.J. (1988). Confirmation of a teacher expectancy model: Student perceptions and causal attributions of teaching behaviors. *Research Quarterly for Exercise and Sport, 59,* 118–126.

Medley, D. (1979). The effectiveness of teachers. In P. Peterson & H. Walberg (Eds.), *Research on teaching: Concepts, findings, and implications* (pp. 11–27). Berkeley, CA: McCutchan.

Metzler, M.W. (1980). The measurement of academic learning time in physical education. *Dissertation Abstracts International, 40,* 5365A. (University Microfilms No. 80-90, 314)

Metzler, M.W. (1989). A review of research on time in sport pedagogy. *Journal of Teaching in Physical Education, 8,* 87–103.

Nixon, J.E., & Locke, L. (1973). Research on teaching in physical education. In M.W. Travers (Ed.), *Second handbook of research on teaching* (pp. 1210–1242). Chicago: Rand McNally.

Oliver, B. (1980, April). *Process-outcome relationships and motor skills learning.* Paper presented at the annual meeting of the American Educational Research Association, Boston.

O'Sullivan, M. (1989). Failing gym is like failing lunch or recess: Two beginning teachers' struggle for legitimacy. *Journal of Teaching in Physical Education, 8,* 227–242.

Piéron, M., & Haan, J. (1979, July). Interactions between teacher and students in a physical education setting: Observation of student behaviors. Paper presented at the International Council of Health, Physical Education, and Recreation Congress, Kiel, FRG.

Pinheiro, V., & Simon, H. (1992). An operational model of motor skill diagnosis. *Journal of Teaching in Physical Education, 11,* 288–302.

Pissanos, B.W., & Allison, P.C. (1993). Students' constructs of elementary school physical education. *Research Quarterly for Exercise and Sport, 63,* 425–435.

Placek, J. (1983). Conceptions of success in teaching: Busy, happy, and good? In T.J. Templin & J.K. Olson (Eds.), *Teaching in physical education* (pp. 46–56). Champaign, IL: Human Kinetics.

Placek, J. (1984). A multi-case study of teacher planning in physical education. *Journal of Teaching in Physical Education, 4,* 39-49.

Placek, J., Silverman, S., Shute, S., Dodds, P., & Rife, F. (1982). Active learning time (ALT-PE) in a traditional elementary physical education setting: A descriptive analysis. *Journal of Classroom Interaction, 17*(2), 41–47.

Rink, J., French, K., Lee, A., Solmon, M., & Lynn, S. (1994). A comparison of pedagogical knowledge structures of preservice students and teacher educators in two institutions. *Journal of Teaching in Physical Education, 13,* 140–162.

Rink, J., & Werner, P. (1987). Student responses as a measure of teacher effectiveness. In G.T. Barrette, R.S. Feingold, C.R. Rees, & M. Pieron (Eds.), *Myths, models, and methods in sport pedagogy* (pp. 199–206). Champaign, IL: Human Kinetics.

Rolider, A., Siedentop, D., & Van Houten, R. (1984). Effects of enthusiasm training on subsequent teacher enthusiastic behavior. *Journal of Teaching in Physical Education, 3,* 47–59.

Rovegno, I. (1993). Content knowledge acquisition during undergraduate teacher education: Overcoming cultural templates and learning through practice. *American Educational Research Journal, 30,* 611–642.

Salter, W.B., & Graham, G. (1985). The effects of three disparate instructional approaches on skill attempts and student learning in an experimental teaching unit. *Journal of Teaching in Physical Education, 4,* 212–218.

Schempp. P. (1989, April). *A case study of one physical education teacher's knowledge for work.* Paper presented at the annual meeting of the AERA, San Francisco.

Sherman, M. (1979, December). *Teacher planning: A study of expert and novice gymnastics teachers.* Paper presented at the Pennsylvania State Association of HPER Annual Convention, Philadelphia.

Shulman, L. (1986). Paradigms and research programs in the study of teaching: A contemporary perspective. In M.C. Wittrock (Ed.), *Handbook of research on teaching* (pp. 3–36). New York: Macmillan.

Siedentop, D., Birdwell, D., & Metzler, M. (1979, March). *A process approach to measuring teacher effectiveness in physical education.* Paper presented at the AAHPERD Annual Conference, New Orleans.

Siedentop, D., & Hughley, C. (1975). O.S.U. teacher behavior rating scale. *Journal of Physical Education and Recreation, 46,* 45.

Siedentop, D., Tousignant, M., & Parker, M. (1982). *Academic learning time-physical education coding manual.* Columbus, OH: The Ohio State University.

Silverman, S. (1983). The student as the unit of analysis: Effect on descriptive data and process-outcome relationships in physical education. In T. Templin & J. Olson (Eds.), *Teaching in physical education* (pp. 277–285). Champaign, IL: Human Kinetics.

Silverman, S. (1985). Relationship of engagement and practice trials to student achievement. *Journal of Teaching in Physical Education, 5,* 13–21.

Silverman, S. (1990). Linear and curvilinear relationships between student practice and achievement in physical education. *Teaching and Teacher Education, 6,* 305–314.

Silverman, S., Dodds, P., Placek, J., Shute, S., & Rife, F. (1984). Academic learning time in elementary physical education (ALT-PE) for student subgroups and instructional activity units. *Research Quarterly for Exercise and Sport, 55,* 365–370.

Silverman, S., Tyson, L.A., & Krampitz, J. (1992). Teacher feedback and achievement in physical education: Interaction with student practice. *Teaching and Teacher Education, 8,* 333–344.

Silverman, S., Tyson, L.A., & Morford, L.M. (1988). Relationships of organization, time, and student achievement in physical education. *Teaching and Teacher Education, 4,* 247–257.

Solmon, M.A., & Boone, J. (1993). The impact of student goal orientation in physical education classes. *Research Quarterly for Exercise and Sport, 64,* 418–424.

Solmon, M.A., & Carter, J.A. (1995). Kindergarten and first grade students' perceptions of physical education in one teacher's classes. *Elementary School Journal, 95,* 355–365.

Solmon, M.A., & Lee, A.M. (1991). A contrast of planning behaviors between expert and novice adapted physical education teachers. *Adapted Physical Activity Quarterly, 8,* 115–127.

Solmon, M.A., & Lee, A.M. (in press). Entry characteristics, practice variables, and cognition: Student mediation of instruction. *Journal of Teaching in Physical Education.*

Solmon, M.A., Worthy, T., & Carter, J.A. (1993). Interaction of school context and role identity of first year teachers. *Journal of Teaching in Physical Education, 12,* 313–328.

Solmon, M., Worthy, T., Lee, A., & Carter, J. (1991). Teacher role identity of student teachers in physical education: An interactive analysis. *Journal of Teaching in Physical Education, 10,* 188–209.

Stroot, S. (1993). Socialization into physical education. *Journal of Teaching in Physical Education* [Summer Monograph].

Stroot, S., & Morton, P. (1989). Blueprints for learning. *Journal of Teaching in Physical Education, 8,* 213–222.

Taylor, J.L. (1976). Development and use of the physical education observation instrument for rating patterns of teacher behaviors in relationship to student achievement. *Dissertation Abstracts International, 37,* 2615A. (University Microfilms No. 76-26, 009)

Templin, T. (1979). Occupational socialization and the physical education student teacher. *Research Quarterly, 50,* 482–493.

Templin, T. (1981). Student as socializing agent. *Journal of Teaching in Physical Education, Introductory Issue,* 71–79.

Templin, T., & Schempp, P. (Eds.). (1989). *Socialization into physical education: Learning to teach.* Indianapolis: Benchmark Press.

Templin, T., Sparks, A., & Schempp, P. (1991). The professional life cycle of a retired physical education teacher: A tale of bitter disengagement. *Physical Education Review, 14,* 143–156.

Tinning, R. (1991). Teacher education pedagogy: Dominant discourses and the process of problem setting. *Journal of Teaching in Physical Education, 11,* 1–20.

Twardy, B.M., & Yerg, B.J. (1987). The impact of planning on inclass interactive behaviors of preservice teachers. *Journal of Teaching in Physical Education, 6,* 136–148.

Tyler, R.W. (1950). *Basic principles of curriculum and instruction.* Chicago: University of Chicago Press.

U.S. Office of Education. (1918). *Cardinal principles of secondary education.* Washington, D.C.: Author.

van der Mars, H. (1987). Effects of audiocueing on teacher verbal praise of students' managerial and transitional task performance. *Journal of Teaching in Physical Education, 6,* 157–165.

Veal, M.L. (1988). Pupil assessment practices and perceptions of secondary teachers. *Journal of Teaching in Physical Education, 7,* 327–342.

Veal, M.L (1992). Pupil-based theories of pupil assessment: A case study. *Research Quarterly for Exercise and Sport, 63,* 48–59.

Walkwitz, E., & Lee, A. (1992). The role of knowledge in elementary physical education: An exploratory study. *Research Quarterly for Exercise and Sport, 63,* 179–185.

Whilden, P. (1956). Comparison of two methods of teaching beginning basketball. *Research Quarterly, 27,* 235–242.

Wittrock, M.C. (1986). Students' thought processes. In M.C. Wittrock (Ed.), *Handbook of research on teaching* (3rd ed., pp. 297–314). New York: Macmillan.

Yerg, B.J. (1981a). Reflections on the use of the RTE model in physical education. *Research Quarterly for Exercise and Sport, 52,* 38–47.

Yerg, B.J. (1981b). The impact of selected presage and process behaviors on the refinement of a motor skill. *Journal of Teaching in Physical Education, 1,* 38–46.

Yerg, B.J. (1983). Re-examining the process-product paradigm for research on teaching effectiveness in physical education. In T. Templin & J. Olson (Eds.), *Teaching in physical education* (pp. 310–317). Champaign, IL: Human Kinetics.

Yerg B.J., & Twardy, B.M. (1982). Relationship of specified instructional teacher behaviors to pupil gain on a motor skill task. In M. Piéron & J. Cheffers (Eds.), *Studying the teaching in physical education* (pp. 61–68). Liege, Belgium: Association Internationale des Superieures d'Education Physique.

CHAPTER 3

How and Why We Do Research

Stephen J. Silverman

The research process sometimes seems mystical. An individual or a group collects data, writes a report, and finally publishes it. Often these research papers are difficult for nonresearchers to read—even if they are practitioners in the same field. As with any skill, understanding and applying research requires learning and practice.

Because researchers often provide conclusions that can improve the educational process, it will benefit practitioners to understand the investigative process better and, perhaps, read some of the original research. In order to evaluate its applicability, they need to know a little about the mechanics of research. Practitioners must be able to decide if researchers' suggestions are appropriate for the situation in which they are working or whether the results warrant the conclusions presented.

This chapter will not duplicate the work of those references (e.g., Borg & Gall, 1989; Denzin & Lincoln, 1994; Locke, 1989; Locke, Spirduso, & Silverman, 1993; Thomas, 1993; Thomas & Nelson, 1990) that can help you get a more complete view of research. Rather, it will provide a foundation for reading the chapters that follow. I will first discuss why we do research in physical education and present a way of thinking about the research process. Next, I will discuss how we can use the results of research in physical education. In the final section, I will present an overview of the methods used for research on teaching, teacher education, and curriculum in physical education. This discussion will focus on the concepts needed to understand later chapters in this book and, perhaps, provide a framework for reading research reports.

WHY WE DO RESEARCH AND
WHY DOES IT MATTER?

As noted earlier, the research process is often seen as mystical and difficult. I can remember reading the preface of a statistics textbook a few
years ago in which the author noted that the best way to have people
avoid you at a cocktail party is to tell them you teach statistics and
research methods. This suggests that many people either don't understand
research or view researchers and what they do in a less than positive
light. Kerlinger (1973) notes that we often think of the researcher as a
nerd in a lab jacket desperately seeking facts in an attempt to expand
some arcane theory or find a cure for cancer that is many years away.

In actuality, the research process is more dynamic. Researchers develop
ideas based on their experiences and on previous research. They have
many false starts and some satisfying conclusions to their efforts. They try
out their ideas and the interpretation of results with others—colleagues,
graduate students, teachers—who may provide different and valuable
insight. They worry as they progress, hoping all goes well until the data
are ready for a research report. Once a researcher submits a paper for
publication there may be additional worries every time he or she checks
the mail, wondering if the paper will be accepted and published. The
research process, particularly in an area like physical education where
research often is conducted in schools, is a human enterprise. Sometimes
it's fun and goes well, sometimes it doesn't.

When research doesn't go well or the initial experience of doing research
is not satisfying, why do researchers persist? People conduct research for
many reasons. Sometimes a research project is required for a graduate
degree or, it may be that a faculty member is conducting research and
publishing to keep his or her job and earn tenure. Those of us who have
made a career in which research and scholarship play a major role originally may have conducted research for those reasons. I believe, however,
the motivation for continuing research is different. Most of the reasons
for conducting research in physical education fall into two categories: (a)
providing information to improve physical education and (b) contributing
to the theoretical bases of physical education.

As the distinguished researcher Nathanial Gage (1966) noted a number of
years ago, many people study educational issues because they want to improve
teaching. They see issues in instructional settings and design research they
believe will lead to informed improvement of their field. Much research is
done with the aim of improving the way professionals conduct business. Most
researchers hope their work will be valuable sometime to someone practicing
in their field, even if this is a distant prospect or never happens.

Extending theory, or as Doyle (1978) suggested, understanding educational processes, is another reason for conducting research. Understanding why things happen and why in certain situations they do not happen

provides a theoretical base for a field. Knowing something works is one thing; knowing *why* provides different information and can result in a deeper understanding of the field. Some would claim that only research that immediately extends theory is valuable (see Gage, 1994 and Garrison & Macmillan, 1994 for a discussion of this issue in teaching research), but in reality it takes a focused research program conducted over a number of years to provide greater understanding of the phenomenon being studied.

Some people believe that research that cannot be readily used is merely an academic exercise; others insist that research with ambiguous theoretical implications is fluff. These positions, however, polarize the issue. In the best situation, the researcher has both practical and theoretical reasons for conducting physical education research. Sometimes one motivation or the other dominates. The knowledge obtained from research often occurs progressively, in small increments, until eventually everything comes together and the whole makes more sense.

Whether the goal of research is improvement or understanding—or both—we can think of the research process as problem solving. We all do research in our everyday lives. We encounter problems and try to find the answers. Sometimes we use trial and error and other times we know a little more and have strategies for finding a solution. Research is just a sophisticated and formalized version of problem solving.

We all are familiar with the ways in which teachers solve problems, even if we don't think of it as research. For example, a teacher may note that many students are misbehaving. She asks herself why, and notices that the misbehavior mostly occurs near the end of a practice session. She decides to switch activities so students don't become bored and notices that misbehavior is reduced drastically. In effect, the teacher has asked a question, proposed a solution, and observed the results.

A similar situation occurs in more formal research. The researcher may ask "what if" questions (Locke et al., 1993) that have theoretical or practical implications. The question being asked is refined, a method that answers the question is devised, and then the researcher collects data to answer the question. He or she has posed a question and then provided an answer. This answer may not be of immediate value for others who are in different situations or who believe that more evidence is needed through replication, but it provides one insight into the question.

USING THE RESULTS OF RESEARCH

If we view research as problem solving, then when reading research we need to determine whether it applies to problems that occur in our situation. Alternatively, if you identify a problem or want to examine other ideas, you may want to go to the literature and see if someone has investigated the topic. You will often find helpful research reviews. Certainly, the other chapters in this book provide a review and summary of a rich literature on physical education.

If you decide to read an original research paper, to follow up on ideas learned here, or for any other reason, there are a variety of ways to ease your task and make the most of the information. My first recommendation is to read the abstract and see if the information still looks interesting or helpful to you. Next, skim the article and see if it again seems applicable. Ask yourself, does this situation seem similar to mine? Is it close enough that I might get something useful out of the paper? If, at this point, you think the paper is worth pursuing, read it to figure out what the researcher did and what implications the information may have for you.

Normally, research papers have four sections: (a) introduction; (b) method; (c) results; and (d) discussion. The introduction sets the stage and explains the importance of the research. The question or purpose of the research usually is presented near the end of this section. Often this section is placed in the context of previous research and may or may not discuss practical issues. The method section explains what the researcher did to answer the question. The subjects and setting are especially important in determining whether the paper is applicable to your situation. For instance, if you work in an urban public school and the research was conducted in a private preparatory school, you may decide the situations are so different that no comparison is possible. Or if the research occurred in a setting with a very small group of students, the suggestions may not work for the 30 students you teach in each class. (I would note, however, that it is possible for research papers to provide valuable information even in contexts that are quite different.) The results section presents the author's findings based on the questions that were asked. This section may have tables, statistical symbols, narratives, or other ways of presenting information. Finally, the discussion section interprets the results for theory or application, or both. The section may include conclusions for practice or future research.

Many people, as noted earlier, find research reports difficult to read. Some papers are easier to read than others. Some will be of greater interest and, therefore, will sustain greater effort. The use of system language (terms that have specific meaning to researchers), jargon, statistical terms, and other peculiarities of the research report contribute to the difficulty. Researchers and journal editors strive to make their work clear, but even the best written research paper may be difficult for those without a background in research.

When reading research papers you should concentrate on what *you* need from the paper, not everything the author wrote. A friend of mine, a long-time public school teacher, reads the introduction to find the purpose of the study. She next reads the method to determine if the setting, students, and intervention, if any, are relevant to her situation. When reading the results, she looks for summary statements and ignores the technical discussion. For example, she may read the topic sentence describing the result and then forego the statistical discussion that follows.

Finally, she reads the discussion to see if the conclusions or suggestions can be helpful and provide her with greater insight. Her strategy allows her to read information of interest without getting bogged down in the parts that have little impact on the problems she faces. My friend doesn't get everything out of the paper, but she does get a lot of help.

There are two other things that might be of value in reading and understanding research. First, don't give up too easily. Ask for help; from faculty members at universities, curriculum directors with research training, and others. A discussion with someone else also may help. Second, if you have had a graduate research methods course or have experience reading research, you can learn by helping others. We all benefit when we discuss with or help others. I have found that some of the most interesting discussions I've had with colleagues occurred when the topic was their research. You may find the same.

When seeking information from research, the bottom line is, "Will this paper help me?" Researchers read many papers they will never cite. This reading helps provide a base for understanding the broad field (Locke et al., 1993). The same goes for practitioners. You should not expect every paper to be helpful. Some will help you understand what won't work or may not be applicable to your situation. Others will apply directly to it. The more you explore the literature, the easier it will be to select among papers.

One concern often expressed about educational research is that the results are obvious and that any reasonably intelligent person would come to a similar conclusion. Gage (1991, 1994) strongly states that this isn't the case. Among his reasons are:

- This only occurs in hindsight and not before research is conducted.
- Research provides specificity for a more complete understanding by answering questions like "how much?" and "how often?"
- By examining different contexts, research shows where results are not applicable.

Research provides information that can be obtained in no other way.

METHODS OF RESEARCH IN PHYSICAL EDUCATION

Research is conducted using a variety of methods guided by different types of questions. Research in physical education may focus on teaching, teacher education, or curriculum. In order to understand research and follow the discussion in this book, it is important to have a basic understanding of the different research paradigms, or models, used in physical education, and their characteristic methods. In this section, I will discuss the importance of defining questions as a preliminary step in research; why different approaches are used; and the major ways research is conducted in physical education.

THE IMPORTANCE OF DEFINING QUESTIONS

If we take the view that research is a form of problem solving, then the problem is the key to research. If the researcher doesn't have at least a general idea of the problem, it's difficult to conduct good research. A good problem, stated as a question or hypothesis, guides research and makes a research paper easier to comprehend.

We can ask different types of questions about physical education. For instance, we may want to know how teachers develop and implement curriculum, how student teachers mature and gain pedagogical content knowledge, or about the relationship between feedback and learning in physical education. Each question has a different focus and also may require a different paradigm, or approach, to answer the question being posed. As Lee noted in the previous chapter, many different questions have been addressed in physical education and the questions have evolved over the years. Research paradigms and methods have expanded, and there are many tools available to do research.

THE MERITS OF DIFFERENT PARADIGMS

There has been much debate over whether one research paradigm is superior to another (e.g., O'Sullivan, Siedentop, & Locke, 1992; Schempp, 1987, 1988; Siedentop, 1987). At times this debate has been acrimonious. My position is similar to that of Guba (1985, p. 87) that "no single paradigm provides more than a partial picture." We must have research in a variety of subareas and by a variety of approaches to attain a fuller understanding of our field. As you will surely note as you read the chapters that follow, many methods are used and each provides information necessary for a broad picture of physical education.

The different paradigms often present research in different ways and require different criteria for writing the research report and communicating information (Bruce & Greendorfer, 1994). This diversity, in my mind, is good. You will see some of this diversity reflected throughout this book, as the contributors refer to individual research papers. While there is diversity in the methods used, it is important to note that much of the research conducted across paradigms occurs in natural settings with real teachers, students, student teachers, and teacher educators. This common factor has been important to the advancement of knowledge in physical education.

METHODS OF RESEARCH

Many discussions of research paradigms begin with a presentation of the philosophical underpinnings of each paradigm. That discussion is beyond this chapter, as we can read research and get an idea of its value without a detailed discussion of these issues. If you are interested in pursuing the philosophical issues, a basic introduction can be found in the first chapter of Creswell (1994). Here I will discuss the research paradigms that have been widely used in physical education research or are emerging in the field, along with their characteristic methods. I will provide an overview of each method and a few references as places to start to get more information. In addition, I will cite literature using the method so, if you wish, you can read an example of the research method in an actual physical education study. Although research can be categorized in different ways, research paradigms can be broadly classified as qualitative or quantitative. These two classifications can be further broken down. Figure 3.1 provides a diagram of the major paradigms and subparadigms that are used in physical education and will be discussed in this chapter.

Each of the paradigms and subparadigms has different names in different literature and uses research methods that may or may not also be

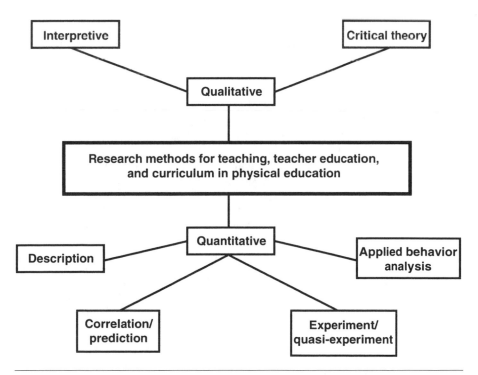

Figure 3.1.   Common research methods in teaching, teacher education, and curriculum in physical education

used in a closely related subparadigm. Devotees of one method may think alternative methods are very different, while others may think they are very similar. In this chapter, I will discuss four quantitative methods: (a) description; (b) correlation/prediction; (c) experimental and quasi-experimental; and (d) applied behavior analysis or single subject research. Qualitative paradigms can be classified into two broad categories, interpretive and critical theory. Table 3.1 presents an overview of the general aim, common names, and the primary research techniques for quantitative research and for both qualitative categories. I have presented interpretive and critical methods separately in the table to illustrate the differences between these approaches.

QUANTITATIVE RESEARCH

The general aim of quantitative research is the description, prediction, and explanation of the situation being studied. Most research methods

Table 3.1 Aims, Common Names, and Primary Research Techniques of the Research Paradigms

	Quantitative	Interpretive	Critical theory
General aim	The description, prediction, and explanation to understand specific aspects of the environment.	Understanding a situation from the perspective of the participant.	The critique and understanding of power within society.
Commonly used other names	• Positivism • Post-positivism • Descriptive • Correlational • Experimental • Behavior analysis	• Ethnography • Constructivism • Phenomenology • Participant observation • Interpretive-interactionism • Hermeneutics	• Feminist • Marxist • Critical ethnography • Deconstruction • Post-modernism • Post-structuralism
Primary research techniques	• Observation instruments • Paper and pencil inventories • Surveys • Implementing treatments • Reliable measurement of variables • Statistical analysis	• Observation and use of field notes • Examination of materials (lesson plans, curricula, etc.) • Interviews • Narratives and case studies	• Analysis of print materials, popular culture, and society • Documentation of empowerment activities

books (e.g., Borg & Gall, 1989; Thomas & Nelson, 1990) provide a good overview of these methods. As the name implies, quantitative research reports data using numbers and statistics. As Lee discussed in her chapter, there is a long history of various types of quantitative research in physical education. Each of the groupings presented below can be conducted in isolation. Or, as Rosenshine and Furst (1973) suggested, the various methods can be combined in programmatic research.

A common aspect of much of the quantitative research in physical education over the past two decades, particularly teaching research, is the use of observation of teacher and student behavior (Silverman, 1991). As Locke (1977) discussed in an early paper on physical education research, the use of observation was a requirement for improving the research at that time. Early research did not collect direct data on physical education (Nixon & Locke, 1973), and the results were not very helpful to practitioners or researchers. A description of some of the common observation instruments used in physical education can be found in Darst, Mancini, and Zakrajsek (1989).

Description

The general goal of descriptive studies is to find out what is occurring in a situation. "How do students spend time in physical education classes?," "What kind and how much feedback do teachers give students in physical education?," or "What goals do teachers have for their classes?" are typical of the questions used to guide descriptive research. There is no attempt to describe relationships or measure the effectiveness of an intervention. Providing a description of what occurred in the group being studied and in various subgroups is the focus. Means and standard deviations, bar charts, and tables often represent the data.

The best example of a large-scale descriptive project in physical education is the work of Bill Anderson and his students at Teachers College, Columbia University (Anderson & Barrette, 1978). The research group videotaped many physical education classes, designed instruments to analyze and describe what was on the tapes, and presented a multidimensional view of physical education. This research program influenced many who subsequently engaged in physical education research.

Correlation/Prediction

Correlation and prediction studies use similar techniques to understand the relationships between two variables or among a number of variables. Questions such as, "Is there a positive relationship between student time-on-task and student achievement?" and "Is there a relationship between teachers' control ideology and their goals for physical education?" examine the relationship between two variables. A more complex study might ask, "What are the interrelationships of student and teacher variables in predicting student achievement in physical education?" In such a case many variables are measured and used in combination. Papers using this methodology report simple and multiple correlation coefficients, percent variation of the criterion variable (student achievement in the last question above) accounted for by the other variables (usually reported as an R^2), or may report complex models of the interrelations among variables.

The work that I have done with valuable assistance from students and colleagues represents this type of research (e.g., Silverman, 1990, 1993; Silverman, Kulinna, & Crull, 1995; Silverman & Tyson, 1994; Silverman, Tyson, & Krampitz, 1992; Silverman, Tyson, & Morford, 1988). A large group of students were pretested and posttested and received instruction between the tests. The instruction was videotaped and process data (e.g., amount of time spent in various categories, the amount and type of student practice, and teacher feedback to students) were collected from the videotapes. The process data obtained by observation were correlated with student achievement in the individual studies cited above. Finally, the data from all the studies were combined to examine the interrelationships of the variables in predicting student achievement.

Experimental and Quasi-Experimental Research

Experimental and quasi-experimental research involves the analysis of differences between groups. Some research in this category may compare students randomly assigned to treatments versus those in a control group (experiments). Other research may use already existing, intact groups and compare differences in a dependent variable (quasi-experiments). The difference between randomly assigned groups and intact groups determines, to a degree, what kind of conclusions can be made about a treatment. Although many would suggest that experiments yield the best knowledge (see Campbell & Stanley, 1963, for the classic discussion), it is very difficult to do good experiments in natural settings (Cook & Campbell, 1979; Silverman, 1985). Randomization just is not possible in many school settings. A study using an experimental or quasi-experimental design might ask questions such as, "Do high-skilled students receive more teacher feedback than low-skilled students?," "Does the reciprocal style result in greater motor skill learning than the command style?," or "What is the difference in the amount of physical activity between fitness and skill-based curricula?" Again, the purpose is to determine group differences in means on one or more variables. This is established by various statistical techniques, and papers using this paradigm report means and standard deviations and the results of t-tests, analysis of variance, or multiple analysis of variance.

The work of Mike Goldberger and his students (Goldberger, 1983; Goldberger & Gerney, 1986, 1990) is a good example of experimental research in physical education. They have conducted a systematic examination of Mosston's spectrum of teaching styles (Mosston & Ashworth, 1994), comparing the effect of various teaching styles on student achievement in motor skills and other common goals of physical education. Students in these studies were pretested on the dependent variables, randomly assigned to treatments (teaching style) where they received instruction, and then posttested. In addition, the researchers observed and collected data during instruction to verify that the teaching style was being implemented as intended.

Applied Behavior Analysis

Applied behavior analysis or single subject research uses a small number of subjects to determine if an intervention can change the behavior of a subject. Borg and Gall (1989) discuss this category of research design in the context of behavior modification. Questions that might be posed by researchers using this paradigm are, "Will the use of students' names reduce off-task behavior?," "Will student teachers viewing videotapes with a focused observation use gym space more efficiently?," or "Will a reward system increase student physical activity outside of physical education classes?" In single subject research, at the basic level, baseline data on the behavior of interest are collected, the intervention is implemented, and then the intervention is stopped. Data collection continues through the intervention and for a period afterwards. The researcher plots the data to see if the desired effect occurs during the intervention and if removing the intervention reduces the behavior back to the baseline. Visual inspection of the data is used for making conclusions about the intervention's effectiveness.

A good example of single subject research is a study by Hans van der Mars (1987) in which he was interested in increasing teachers' use of verbal praise. The research was conducted with a student teacher. Observational data were collected to establish a baseline, and data collection continued throughout the study. The intervention was by way of an audio cue—the student teacher wore a tape recorder with an earphone providing prompts to provide praise. In this study, the intervention was removed and then reimplemented to chart the effect.

QUALITATIVE RESEARCH

The use of qualitative research has grown greatly in the past decade. In particular, interpretive research methods have flourished and are being represented frequently in the literature. Many good references now exist for all forms of qualitative research. Denzin and Lincoln (1994) provide a very comprehensive discussion of qualitative research. You may find, however, that the paper by Locke (1989) and the commentaries which follow (Bain, 1989; Sage, 1989; Schutz, 1989; Siedentop, 1989) are a good place to start for interpretive research and that Thomas (1993) is a readable text on critical methods.

Interpretive Research

Interpretive researchers work to provide a rich description and understanding of a situation from the perspective of those being studied. The interpretive researcher wants to get beyond mere description and provide an in-depth understanding of what is occurring and how the participants view the situation. Questions that might be asked in an interpretive research study are, "What is the relationship between student teachers and their supervisors during student teaching?," "How do teachers adapt and adjust during the first three years of teaching?," and "How do teacher educators work to revise their curriculum when restrictions are imposed by state mandate?" Among the methods interpretive researchers use are interviews, analysis of materials such as lesson plans and curriculum guides, and intense observation. This type of observation is different from that used in quantitative research, discussed earlier. Interpretive researchers observe a wide range of activities and use field notes to record information.

Published papers of interpretive research report themes that were found during data collection. These themes are supported by quotes, vignettes, and detailed descriptions. The data presentation is in prose, and a results section may read like a newspaper story (i.e., here's what I found and why).

As Williamson notes in her chapter, the work of Pat Griffin (1984, 1985a, 1985b) examining equity issues in junior high school is an excellent example of interpretive research. She used observation, informal and formal interviews, and material collection to examine the roles boys and girls play in physical education and how teachers view and influence students. Her description is must reading for physical education teachers interested in equity in their classes.

Critical Theory

Critical theory researchers approach their task from a different perspective. The critical theorist views research as a way to analyze power inequities in a situation or in society. An alternative form of critical research seeks to document the empowerment of individuals through interventions, counseling, or group activities. There is no pretense of objectivity in critical research. In fact, many critical researchers approach their work as a political enterprise with the goal of influencing change. Critical researchers may ask questions such as, "Does participation in physical activity utilizing tools for self-responsibility empower the participants to take control of their lives?," or "How does the use of traditional teaching strategies affect the teacher-student relationship in physical education?" The first question relates to documenting empowerment activities and the second to examining power in a relationship.

The critical theorist researcher may use observation, field notes, and interviews. In addition, the researcher examining power may analyze textual material, television programs, movies, or any other cultural phenomena. Reports examining power relationships present the question and the viewpoint of the author, then provide detailed support for the contention. As noted above, the paper may take a position from the start. Empowerment documentation papers may read like a combination of the other critical papers and interpretive research reports.

The work of Don Hellison (see chapter 13) is among the few focusing on empowerment in physical education. He has implemented a program, outside of school hours, in inner-city Chicago that focuses on social and self responsibility of students using physical activity as the instructional medium. The goal is not acquisition of motor skills or fitness, but becoming responsible adults. The use of notes and interviews documents the progress of children in this program.

David Kirk's (1989) examination of the research-practice gap in physical education is a good example of a critical paper that examines power. He argues that the dominant approaches to research on teaching physical education have not resulted in curriculum changes. He discusses strategy, power, and politicization as he critiques what he calls the "orthodox view" (p. 124) and concludes by providing an alternative view.

USING QUALITATIVE AND QUANTITATIVE METHODS IN THE SAME STUDY

Much debate has centered on combining quantitative and qualitative research methods in a single study (Howe, 1988; Phelan, 1987; Smith & Heshusius, 1986). Some believe that the methods are so different that researchers cannot use multiple paradigms without sacrificing the tenets of one or the other method. The debate among proponents of each method has become so divisive at times that Gage (1989, p. 4) termed the discussion "the paradigm wars." As Locke et al. (1993) have noted, while the discussion continues multiple paradigmatic research is underway, providing valuable information.

Cathy Ennis (1994) provides an excellent example in physical education of combining qualitative and quantitative methods in one study. She measured teachers on their goal orientations using a quantitative instrument (see chapter 7). From this information she selected a subgroup of teachers with a specific orientation. Interpretive research methods then were used to gain greater insight into the curriculum and instructional choices of these teachers. The overall report and the information it provides would not be possible if the methods were not combined.

SUMMARY

Research in physical education has made great advances over the past two decades. The quality and quantity of research has improved and, as will be noted throughout the rest of this book, the information available is impressive. A significant, positive development in physical education research is that trained researchers are now using a variety of research methods. Physical educators—researchers and practitioners alike—should appreciate the progress and encourage this diversity in the future.

REFERENCES

Anderson, W.G., & Barrette, G.T. (Eds.). (1978). What's going on in gym: Descriptive studies of physical education classes. *Motor Skills: Theory Into Practice, Monograph 1.*

Bain, L.L. (1989). Interpretive and critical research in sport and physical education. *Research Quarterly for Exercise and Sport, 60,* 21–24.

Borg, W.R., & Gall, M.D. (1989). *Educational research: An introduction* (5th ed.). New York: Longman.

Bruce, T., & Greendorfer, S.L. (1994). Post modern challenges: Recognizing multiple standards for social science research. *Journal of Sport and Social Issues, 18,* 258–268.

Campbell, D.T., & Stanley, J.C. (1963). *Experimental and quasi experimental designs for research.* New York: Rand-McNally.

Cook, T.H., & Campbell, D.T. (1979). *Quasi-experimentation: Design and analysis issues from field settings.* Chicago: Rand-McNally.

Creswell, J.W. (1994). *Research design: Qualitative and quantitative approaches.* Thousand Oaks, CA: Sage.

Darst, P., Mancini, V., & Zakrajsek, D. (1989). *Analyzing physical education and sport instruction* (2nd ed.). Champaign, IL: Human Kinetics.

Denzin, N., & Lincoln, Y.S. (Eds.). (1994). *Handbook of qualitative research.* Thousand Oaks, CA: Sage.

Doyle, W. (1978, April). *Research on the realities of the classroom: Who needs it?* Paper presented at the annual meeting of the American Educational Research Association, Toronto, Canada.

Ennis, C.D. (1994). Urban secondary teachers' value orientations: Social goals for teaching. *Teaching and Teacher Education, 10,* 109–120.

Gage, N.L. (1966). Research on cognitive aspects of teaching. In Association for Supervision and Curriculum Development and National Education Association, *The way teaching is* (pp. 29–44). Washington, DC: Author.

Gage, N.L. (1989). The paradigm wars and their aftermath. *Educational Researcher, 18*(7), 4–10.

Gage, N.L. (1991). The obviousness of social and educational research results. *Educational Researcher, 20*(1), 10–16.

Gage, N.L. (1994). The scientific status of research on teaching. *Educational Theory, 44,* 371–383.

Garrison, J.W., & Macmillan, C.J.B. (1994). Process-product research on teaching: Ten years later. *Educational Theory, 44,* 385–397.

Goldberger, M. (1983). Direct styles of teaching and psychomotor performance. In T. Templin & J. Olson (Eds.), *Teaching in Physical Education: Big Ten Body of Knowledge Symposium Series, volume 14,* (pp. 211–223). Champaign, IL: Human Kinetics.

Goldberger, M., & Gerney, P. (1986). The effects of direct teaching styles on motor skill acquisition of fifth grade children. *Research Quarterly for Exercise and Sport, 57,* 215–219.

Goldberger, M., & Gerney, P. (1990). Effects of learner use of practice time on skill acquisition of fifth grade children. *Journal of Teaching in Physical Education, 10,* 84–95.

Griffin, P.S. (1984). Girls' participation patterns in a middle school team sports unit. *Journal of Teaching in Physical Education, 4,* 30–38.

Griffin, P.S. (1985a). Boys' participation styles in a middle school physical education team sports unit. *Journal of Teaching in Physical Education, 4,* 100–110.

Griffin, P.S. (1985b). Teachers' perceptions of and responses to sex equity problems in a middle school physical education program. *Research Quarterly for Exercise and Sport, 56,* 103–110.

Guba, E.G. (1985). The context of emergent paradigm research. In Y.S. Lincoln (Ed.), *Organizational theory and inquiry: The paradigm revolution* (pp. 79–104). Beverly Hills, CA: Sage.

Howe, K.R. (1988). Against the quantitative-qualitative incompatibility thesis: Or dogmas die hard. *Educational Researcher, 17*(8), 10–18.

Kerlinger, F.N. (1973). *Foundations of behavioral research* (2nd ed.). New York: Holt, Rinehart and Winston.

Kirk, D. (1989). The orthodoxy in RT-PE and the research/practice gap: A critique and an alternative view. *Journal of Teaching in Physical Education, 8,* 123–130.

Locke, L.F. (1977). Research on teaching physical education: New hope for a dismal science. *Quest, 28,* 2–16.

Locke, L.F. (1989). Qualitative research as a form of scientific inquiry in sport and physical education. *Research Quarterly for Exercise and Sport, 60,* 1–20.

Locke, L.F., Spirduso, W.W., & Silverman, S.J. (1993). *Proposals that work: A guide for planning dissertations and grant proposals* (3rd ed.). Newbury Park, CA: Sage.

Mosston, M., & Ashworth, S. (1994). *Teaching physical education* (4th ed.). New York: Macmillan.

Nixon, J.E., & Locke, L.F. (1973). Research on teaching in physical education. In M.W. Travers (Ed.), *Second handbook of research on teaching* (pp. 1210–1242). Chicago: Rand-McNally.

O'Sullivan, M., Siedentop, D., & Locke, L. (1992). Toward collegiality: Competing viewpoints among teacher educators. *Quest, 44,* 266–280.

Phelan, P. (1987). Compatibility of qualitative and quantitative methods: Studying child sexual abuse in America. *Education and Urban Society, 20,* 35–41.

Rosenshine, B., & Furst, N. (1973). The use of direct observation to study teaching. In M.W. Travers (Ed.), *Second handbook of research on teaching* (pp. 122–183). Chicago: Rand McNally.

Sage, G.H. (1989). A commentary on qualitative research as a form of scientific inquiry in sport and physical education. *Research Quarterly for Exercise and Sport, 60,* 25–29.

Schempp, P.G. (1987). Research on teaching in physical education: Beyond the limits of natural science. *Journal of Teaching in Physical Education, 6,* 109–110.

Schempp, P.G. (1988). Exorcist II: Reply to Siedentop. *Journal of Teaching in Physical Education, 7,* 79–81.

Schutz, R.W. (1989). Qualitative research: Comments and controversies. *Research Quarterly for Exercise and Sport, 60,* 30–35.

Siedentop, D. (1987). Dialogue or exorcism? A rejoinder to Schempp. *Journal of Teaching in Physical Education, 6,* 373–376.

Siedentop, D. (1989). Do the lockers really smell? *Research Quarterly for Exercise and Sport, 60,* 36–41.

Silverman, S. (1985). Critical considerations in the design and analysis of teacher effectiveness research in physical education. *International Journal of Physical Education, 22*(4), 17–24.

Silverman, S. (1990). Linear and curvilinear relationships between student practice and achievement in physical education. *Teaching and Teacher Education, 6,* 305–314.

Silverman, S. (1991). Research on teaching in physical education. *Research Quarterly for Exercise and Sport, 62,* 352–364.

Silverman, S. (1993). Student characteristics, practice and achievement in physical education. *Journal of Educational Research, 87,* 54–61.

Silverman, S., Kulinna, P., & Crull, G. (1995). Skill-related task structures, explicitness, and accountability: Relationships with student achievement. *Research Quarterly for Exercise and Sport, 66,* 32-40.

Silverman, S., & Tyson, L. (1994, April). *Modeling the teaching-learning process in physical education.* Paper presented at the annual meeting of the American Educational Research Association, New Orleans, LA.

Silverman, S., Tyson, L., & Krampitz, J. (1992). Teacher feedback and achievement in physical education: Interaction with student practice. *Teaching and Teacher Education, 8,* 333–344.

Silverman, S., Tyson, L., & Morford, L.M. (1988). Relationships of organization, time, and student achievement in physical education. *Teaching and Teacher Education, 4,* 247–257.

Smith, J.K., & Heshusius, L. (1986). Closing down the conversation: The end of the quantitative-qualitative debate among educational inquirers. *Educational Researcher, 15*(1), 4–12.

Thomas, J. (1993). *Doing critical ethnography.* Newbury Park, CA: Sage.

Thomas, J.R., & Nelson, J.K. (1990). *Research methods in physical activity* (2nd ed.). Champaign, IL: Human Kinetics.

van der Mars, H. (1987). The effects of audiocueing on teacher verbal praise and students' managerial and transition task performance. *Journal of Teaching in Physical Education, 6,* 157–165.

PART 2

Addressing the Needs of Diverse Students

CHAPTER 4

Context of Schools

LeaAnn Tyson

A "school" is generally considered to be an institution for teaching, a place of learning, or even a group of individuals who share common influences, beliefs, or opinions. Rarely, if ever, is it defined as a workplace for teachers. How teachers perceive and interpret conditions of their workplace influence how they teach, how they interact, and in some cases, how they survive. However, a school does not operate and teachers do not function in isolation. The context of schools is created by conditions which impact the nation, education, and students. Examining these conditions, or *contextual factors*, helps us understand the teacher's work environment and how teachers interpret their roles, which in turn affects students and what they learn.

The many contextual factors include characteristics of the community, the school's physical setting, its organization and culture, and the students within (Griffin, 1985; Grossman & Stodolsky, 1994; Pinkham, 1994; Smyth, 1992). Although these factors are interrelated and intertwined, they each contribute separately to the teaching and the learning environment. These factors can facilitate teachers' abilities to perform their work effectively by creating positive conditions, or they can hinder and constrain teachers, creating dissatisfaction (Templin, 1989). In some cases, teachers have the power to influence and change their workplace, making it a more satisfying and rewarding place to teach (Smyth, 1992). These factors also can influence how students feel about learning and how well they do learn.

Much research in education and physical education, particularly process-product research, has examined teaching and learning without considering context (Lawson, 1993; Talbert & McLaughlin, 1992). In addition, previous research in education has taken a *top-down* approach; that is, looking at how school contexts (such as tracking or student grouping) affect student learning, or looking at school characteristics and their impact on educational outcomes (such as effective schools research) (Edmonds, 1979; Talbert & McLaughlin, 1992). Considering the diversity of school districts, schools, and individuals within schools, it is logical to explore the variety of settings where and conditions under which physical educators work (Lawson, 1993). Just as important is to examine how teachers respond to these settings and conditions. This *bottom-up* approach can provide greater insight as to why teachers and students do what they do, feel how they feel, and how they make sense of their work.

This chapter presents an overview of what is known about the school environment and how it might impact a teacher's work and a student's learning. A global examination of changes that have occurred and current conditions in the nation, in education, in schools, and in students is presented first, followed by a discussion of contextual factors which specifically impact the physical education learning environment. Lastly, suggestions for the physical education context are offered.

THE CHANGING NATION

Changes that occur throughout the nation (and world) ultimately affect schools. Today's society is influenced by a multitude of cultures. Early immigration into the United States was primarily from Europe (Graham, 1993). As more immigrants arrived from other parts of the world, awareness of ethnic diversity, especially in terms of inequality, emerged (Woods, 1992). No longer did the "melting pot" theory, which attempted to assimilate all cultures into one, prevail. In the 1960s and 1970s, many ethnic groups rightly demanded and received attention and inclusion, at times resulting in racial conflict (Woods, 1992). Despite this tension, interracial understanding increased and the nation began to view itself as culturally diverse. Asia and South America became the leading source of immigration in the 1980s (Amstutz, Beglau, Whitson, Naumann & Sherritt, 1992; Hodgkinson, 1988). Ethnic minority populations are now the fastest growing groups. It is estimated that by the year 2010, the state of California will have an adult majority minority population (Hodgkinson, 1988). Today, a pluralistic view is dominant and individuals work to maintain separate, yet contributing, identities. Collectively, the numerous cultures create today's "salad bowl," replacing yesterday's "melting pot."

Today's society is also technology dependent. Tinning and Fitzclarence (1992) describe an "information society," with strong influences from cinema, television, computers, telephone, and radio. Not only does the American population already have tremendous access to information via home computers, but advanced information networks now allow Americans to participate in a global economy based upon global interdependence (Hodgkinson, 1988; Wilson, 1991). This increasing technology, however, has not occurred without associated problems such as computer viruses, "hackers," technotheft, and ethical issues which surround such things as genetic engineering and freezing of embryos (Wilson, 1991). In addition, technical advances in medicine have increased survival rates of very premature babies, contributing to the number of children with disabilities (Hodgkinson, 1988).

Longevity is increasing for many as a result of improved living conditions and greater control of some diseases. The "Graying of America" suggests that there are and will be more older people in the workforce. Members of this population will require more health services, possibly competing for the same resources as their younger counterparts. Because dependent elderly will have greater medical costs and youngsters need educational services, especially as infant and preschool programs multiply, it is suggested that intergenerational conflict will result (Hodgkinson, 1988; Wilson, 1991).

Health care concerns have risen, partially attributable to Americans living longer and the growing number of newborns who have been exposed to alcohol and illegal drugs before birth. Furthermore, despite the medically supported recognition that physical activity is a means to prevent disease, 24 percent of the country's adults are totally sedentary and 54 percent are inadequately active (Van Camp, 1993). This seems to run contrary to the evidence that fewer American high school students report watching five or more hours of television daily in 1990 as compared to 1980 (9.1 as opposed to 27.3 percent) (National Center for Education Statistics, 1993). However, with so many alternatives to television viewing—many of which are also sedentary—afforded to youth, these findings may not be surprising. The fact remains, however, that only about 22 percent of American adults are adequately active, or active enough to receive health benefits from physical activity (Van Camp, 1993).

Poverty continues to be a concern. From 1971 to 1991, the percent of Americans living below the poverty level has increased from 12.5 to 14.2 percent (National Center for Education Statistics, 1993), and it is predicted that the trend will continue (Wilson, 1991). Housing is already far from adequate, and the fastest growing homeless group is families with children (Amstutz et al., 1992). In 1987, 21 percent of all children were considered poor (Amstutz et al., 1992). Currently, 50 percent of African American children are raised in lower income households by a single, female parent (Smith, 1991). In addition, there will be a widening gap between the poor that are technologically illiterate and those that are literate (Wilson, 1991). The country is becoming increasingly diverse in socioeconomic status.

Although these are certainly not all the issues which exist in a changing nation (and additional information will be presented in discussions to follow), they *do* have a great impact on education, schools, teachers, and students. Schools are a reflection of and respond to developments in the nation and the world. Conversely, schools work to influence and reshape the state of the nation and the world. School reform, which will be discussed in the next section, can only happen with social reform brought on by combined efforts of communities, businesses, higher education, and families (Graham, 1993).

CHANGING EDUCATION

Some would argue that education and schools have been slow to respond to a changing world. Others would suggest that the role of education and the school has changed significantly during the last century (Graham, 1993). When families immigrated to this country, primarily from Europe, schools worked to assimilate the children in attempts to form a more homogeneous society. As the country developed and prospered, schools assisted children in adjusting to modern life and preparing them for adult life, assuming roles of male breadwinner and female homemaker or teacher. Attempts to assimilate increasingly diverse students and prepare students for a nation and world that was changing too rapidly were not adequate. The school's role then became that of accommodation and accessibility. Schools became concerned with expanded and equitable opportunities for education (Graham, 1993). Desegregation efforts, Title IX, dropout prevention programs, Public Law 94–142, college education assistance, and "reentry" tools such as Veterans' Educational Assistance Amendments, General Equivalence Degree (GED) credentials, and programs for "nontraditional" learners have provided accommodation and access to education for diverse students (Kett, 1993; National Center for Education Statistics, 1993; Woods, 1992). According to Graham (1993), Americans had been more concerned with creating the system than seeing if the system actually worked.

More recently, however, the role of education has been to insure learning, and this has placed American education under close scrutiny by policy makers, parents, and students. This is evidenced by reform efforts that focus on the quality of teaching through teacher assessment (Kirst, 1993; Tyson & Silverman, 1994a, 1994b). In physical education, authors have focused on accountability and outcomes for learning (Lawson, 1993; Siedentop, 1993). Concerns about the competitiveness of America in a global economy, assimilation and accessibility efforts that did not meet the needs of a dynamic student population, and the belief that all children should achieve and perform have led to numerous changes and movements in education (Bedell, 1992; Education Commission of the States, 1992; Sedlak, 1993).

Recent educational themes such as teaching "the whole child," cooperative learning, integrated instruction (see chapter 14 by Placek),

multicultural/diversity education, critical thinking, and parent involvement have been met by many teachers with enthusiasm and by some
with frustration and a "This too shall pass" attitude. Some of these movements, such as multicultural education, have not been proven adequate
or successful (Woods, 1992). Many of these themes have found their way
into the physical education curriculum (Barta & Anderson, 1982; Daley,
1991; Hellison, 1991; King, 1994; McBride, 1991; Rees, Feingold & Barrette, 1991; Swisher & Swisher, 1986; Werner, 1994; Wessinger, 1994;
Woods, 1992), although the movement has been somewhat slower than
into other content areas.

Reforms have included identification of characteristics of "effective
schools" for other schools to model (Edmonds, 1979) and establishing
specific, national, educational goals for the year 2000. These particular
goals address graduation rates, school readiness, student achievement,
adult literacy, safe and disciplined learning environments, parental
involvement, citizenship, mathematics and science, and professional development for teachers (United States Department of Education, 1991).
Although not specifically mentioned in any of the goals, access to physical
education is identified as one of the objectives necessary to meet the goal
of student achievement and citizenship. When polled in 1992, parents
indicated their perceptions of progress toward specific goals (National
Center for Education Statistics, 1993). When given choices of "A great
deal," "Quite a lot," "Not too much," "None at all," and "Don't know," the
answer receiving the highest percentage of responses for each identified
goal was "Not too much." In every instance, "A great deal" received the
lowest percentage of responses (ranging from 2 to 5 percent) (National
Center for Education Statistics, 1993). The educational goals and concern
for outcomes have come under criticism because they are viewed as unrealistic without parallel social reform. They do not provide specific strategies
(and funding) to help students attain the outcomes (Delattre, 1992; Graham, 1993; Hodgkinson, 1988). For this reason, they have become the
focus of education reform.

The challenge for reform has not been limited to education in general.
Recently, there has been a call to think differently about physical education—its role and the way in which it is delivered, particularly at the
secondary level (Locke, 1992; O'Sullivan, Siedentop & Tannehill, 1994;
Rink, 1993; Siedentop, 1993; Stroot, 1994; Tinning & Fitzclarence, 1992).
Siedentop (1993) suggests that the education goals for the year 2000
should be viewed as a "window of opportunity" for physical educators.
The increased attention to health care, the recognition of the role that
activity plays in disease prevention, and the examination of current, often
inadequate, programs have no doubt contributed to this attention.

In most cases, physical education continues to maintain a lower status
than most other content areas for several reasons: (a) it is not considered
an "academic" subject such as math or science; (b) it is not a subject which
typically offers a hierarchy of classes (such as math sequence); (c) it is

not recognized as core to the mission of the school; and (d) weak physical education programs help maintain its low status (Grossman & Stodolsky, 1994; Rink, 1993; Sparkes, Templin & Schempp, 1993). Because budget constraints are forcing priorities in education, some quality elementary physical education programs have been eliminated and secondary physical education has been curtailed in the curriculum (Rink, 1993). Unfortunately, this comes at a time when physical inactivity contributes to more than 250,000 deaths per year and the American College of Sports Medicine and others recommend developing and implementing effective health promotion strategies in the schools (Lawson, 1993; Van Camp, 1993). Although this is important in all schools, it has particular significance in urban and minority schools, as the lack of physical activity is greater in groups of lower socioeconomic status and ethnic minorities (Van Camp, 1993).

Preparing students to function in tomorrow's world is a very challenging task in a dynamic society combined with a reactive educational system. As is discussed in the next section, schools have been given tasks that are more than academic. As Ravitch (1993) states, "The challenge before us is to develop a thoughtful process to decide what knowledge is of the most worth, and what knowledge is most valuable to children who will live and work in the 21st century" (p. 334). Skills and competencies which were adequate years ago are no longer so: The "new literacy" for all students includes critical and creative thinking skills for problem solving, conflict resolution skills, team process skills such as cooperation and collaboration, foreign language, word processing skills, understanding and appreciation of other cultures, and an understanding of economics and finance (Amstutz et al., 1992; Education Commission of the States, 1992; Graham, 1993; Wilson, 1991). Lifelong learning must be emphasized and educational opportunities for older adults must be expanded (Wilson, 1991). Even in physical education, attention to life-span activity is recommended (Siedentop, 1993).

Computer literacy and the ability to access information have already received a great deal of attention in the educational system. From the fall of 1981 to the fall of 1990, the proportion of public schools with computers grew from 18 to 97 percent (National Center for Education Statistics, 1993). In 1989, 39 percent of students in high school and college and 52 percent of elementary students used computers in school (National Center for Education Statistics, 1993). Because of the increasing number of adults using computers in the workplace, technology and computer literacy must be integrated into instruction, not taught as a separate subject area (Wilson, 1991). Hopefully, education will continue to endeavor to provide all students access to and training in technology.

The role of education has changed throughout the decades. Currently, the focus of education revolves around accountability—accountability of teachers to produce learning and accountability of students to demonstrate outcomes. Actual and anticipated changes in the world and nation create change in education. Today's teachers must prepare all students to function, and to succeed, in tomorrow's world.

CHANGING SCHOOLS

The school is a reflection of the community—economically, socially, and ethnically (Amstutz et al., 1992). Hence, community issues and problems become school issues and problems. As a result of a changing world and changing communities, schools have been given a tremendous amount of responsibility in the last couple of decades, and they may not be equipped (with personnel, curriculum, or facilities) to meet all the needs of all the students. Sedlak (1993) suggests that some children attending schools are faced with emotional, social, and physical problems because their parents are incapable of creating nurturing, supportive families or leading healthy, productive lives. Graham (1993) states, "While families and communities are much more powerful influences upon children than their schools, nonetheless, it is the schools that remain the institutions that the public attempts to manipulate to form the children" (p. 3). In addition to being responsible for educating children—all children—schools have had to expand their curricula, health, and social services to provide essentials that many parents and families cannot (Graham, 1993). In schools and classrooms, there are times and circumstances when achieving academic goals becomes secondary to improving a child's nurturing and life conditions. Over 20 percent of public school teachers polled in the 1990-91 school year identified "promoting personal growth" as the most important goal for education (National Center for Education Statistics, 1993). Only "building basic literacy skills" was identified by a greater percentage of teachers as the most important goal.

Although goals for education and reform in general have been established, many school districts and individual campuses have distinct and dramatically different goals for students. School context is an important consideration in examining the work of teachers and the learning environment of students. In describing high schools, McLaughlin (1992) suggests that depending on the type of school context, different goals for students may exist. For example, in what is categorized as an "academic elite" school, the goal for teachers is to prepare highly motivated and high-achieving students for prestigious universities. In an "alternative high school," which typically includes students who have not been successful in "traditional" schools, the most important goal for students might be personal growth. In "typical" high schools, the goals are less consistent and the context of the department may have a greater influence on the teachers' instruction of students (Grossman & Stodolsky, 1994; McLaughlin, 1992; Siskin, 1990).

As communities change, schools continue to become more culturally, academically, and economically diverse. Many urban schools are already faced with critical levels of violence, absenteeism, drug abuse, racism, poverty, student turnover, and youngsters with illegal status (Griffin, 1985; McLaughlin, 1992). One national education goal aims at making every school in the United States free of drugs and violence by the year 2000 (United States Department of Education, 1991). Although few would argue its worthiness, many would claim it is not realistic. For 16 of the first 20 years of the Gallup poll on education, "discipline" was identified as the most pressing problem in America's schools (Reese, 1993). Beginning in 1986, however, "drug use" became the number one problem, although it was tied with "lack of financial support" in 1992 (National Center for Education Statistics, 1993). Interestingly, while the general public saw drug use as a major concern, only 7.2 percent of elementary and secondary public school teachers identified student drug use as a serious problem. Lack of parental involvement, student apathy, poverty, parent alcoholism and drug abuse, student use of alcohol, student disrespect for teachers, student absenteeism, student tardiness, verbal abuse of teachers, lack of academic challenge, students dropping out, student pregnancy, and physical conflicts among students were all identified as more serious problems (National Center for Education Statistics, 1993).

It should be understood that the vast majority of students have never tried inhalants, marijuana, crack, cocaine, or psychedelic drugs, although 37.8 percent of eighth graders and 58.9 percent of tenth graders reported drinking alcohol six or more times (National Center for Education Statistics, 1993). Although alcohol appears to be the most often used drug, the percent of high school seniors who reported using alcohol within the last 30 days dropped from 72 percent in 1980 to 51 percent in 1992 (National Center for Education Statistics, 1993).

Attention to school violence and crime has increased. School vandalism and personal violence increased in the 1960s and 1970s, prompting the use of newly developed alarm systems and cameras (Reese, 1993). Although approximately 3 million school crimes were reported in 1988, at least 82 percent of eighth graders and 89 percent of tenth graders claimed they were never robbed or attacked (National Center for Education Statistics, 1993; Reese, 1993). More students reported being threatened or involved in physical fights. Current efforts to reduce school violence include the use of metal detectors, police or school guards, conflict resolution training, student identification cards, cameras, alarm systems, restricted access, and more visible identification of visitors. Student behaviors are being addressed by banning beepers, gang clothing or insignia, and expensive clothing and shoes which might attract crimes of theft (Reese, 1993). An additional trend has been to limit the use of school facilities after hours, despite recommendations that schools should become more available to the community (Amstutz et al., 1992; Reese, 1993; Wilson, 1991). Many of these efforts are proving successful, and schools in some neighborhoods are much safer than the students' homes and communities (Reese, 1993).

Schools are faced with more issues and have more responsibility, the most critical of which is meeting the needs (academic and otherwise) of all children. In the future, schools will be educating more children. Although elementary and secondary enrollments declined in the 1970s and early 1980s, since 1985 the number of students has continued to grow, particularly at the elementary level (National Center for Education Statistics, 1993). It is estimated that from the 1992–93 school year to the 2003–04 school year, there will be a 13 percent increase in the number of children in kindergarten through grade 8 and an increase of 22 percent in the number of students in grades 9 through 12, or an overall increase of 15 percent in schools (Hussar, 1993). During that same time, it is predicted that there will be a 12 percent increase in the number of elementary teachers and a 23 percent increase in secondary teachers (National Center for Education Statistics, 1993). Resources will continue to be a concern, and competition for resources is bound to increase.

Already, resource availability in many schools and districts is problematic. Currently, most school districts are supported by local property taxes, leading to inequities in funding. As many states struggle to revise funding formulas and equal educational opportunities for students, districts demonstrate incredible diversity. Districts vary tremendously in size (from 84 to 950,000 students), in the amount of state and federal revenues received, and in administrative expenditures (Hannaway, 1992). An issue which continues to receive much attention is per pupil expenditure (Kozol, 1991). Graham (1993) reports that one school district spends $4,322 per student per year (at the high school level) and another district less than 40 miles away spends $10,510 per student. It is not surprising that, although the gap is decreasing, the number of students from families with income levels of more than $74,999 report far more computer usage at school than students with family incomes of less than $5,000 per year (National Center for Education Statistics, 1993). For the most part, these students are not attending the same schools.

Many school districts and schools have altered their organization and administrative structure. The *effective schools correlates* identified in the late 1970s and 1980s (Edmonds, 1979) suggested that strong schools had strong administrative leadership. Principals became "instructional leaders." As it was recognized that schools knew more about the needs of the students and parents they served than did a centralized office or administration, site-based management and restructuring became the keys to effective leadership in diverse schools. Districts vary dramatically in the amount of school autonomy they permit. The degree of autonomy may be affected by state and federal revenues, the strength of parent and teachers' union influence, and other conditions of the political environment (Hannaway, 1992). However, site-based management continues to be a recommendation and movement in many districts (Education Commission of the States, 1992). As principals are empowered to make more decisions, including budget decisions, content areas seen as marginal by some—such as physical education—may be greatly affected.

Considering the current state of schools and predictions for the future, numerous recommendations have been made; some in light of the national education goals. In addition to previously discussed new forms of management and organization, new policies, politics, instruction, and assessment are suggested (Education Commission of the States, 1992). Recommended changes to the school curricula include additional science, math, technology, diversity/multicultural instruction, and prevention strategies for substance abuse (Wilson, 1991). School schedules, too, should be rethought (Education Commission of the States, 1992). Already, many schools have altered traditional school schedules with year-round schooling, extended blocks of time for content areas (instead of 55-minute periods), rotating schedules, and opportunities for instruction outside (before and after) the normal school day. Parallel recommendations have been made for physical education—restructuring schedules, rethinking content to match student needs, reorganization of the class structure, and so on (Siedentop, 1993).

A call has gone out for businesses, universities, and schools to work as partners in educating children and communities (Amstutz et al., 1992). Along those lines, it is recommended that schools expand their use of facilities for community instruction, recreation, and older adult programs (Amstutz et al., 1992; Wilson, 1991). Strong community education programs do exist which include summer programs for youth, school libraries for public use, enrichment classes for the community, rooms set aside in schools to make parents feel welcome, and family literacy programs (Amstutz et al., 1992). Also, as families become more diverse (to be discussed later), more schools will need to provide child care and family services, and become more flexible in the timing of activities that involve parents, especially single parents who work during the day (Wilson, 1991). Schools also need to expand their instructional facilities beyond the classroom more often: Museums, businesses, community service centers, health care facilities, and such can all be used for learning (Amstutz et al., 1992). In physical education, the "classroom" can expand to include health and fitness facilities, which many programs already use.

There are indications that conditions in schools are improving. Even though it appears that students are consuming less alcohol and school violence and vandalism peaked in the 1970s, the question remains, "Is it good enough?" Possibly the strongest (and most logical) recommendation is to encourage and reward schools for innovation and thoughtful risk-taking (Education Commission of the States, 1992; Siedentop, 1993). Exciting, innovative programs and changes are being tried, although measures of success may not be available at this point. The key, however, is in the attempt.

THE CHANGING STUDENT BODY

Few would argue with the idea that students of today are different than students of generations past. Examining and understanding characteristics of the changing student body helps school districts and teachers address the needs of youngsters in today's schools, and teacher education programs prepare teachers to educate tomorrow's students.

DIVERSITY AND DEMOGRAPHICS

As indicated in Table 4.1, on any given day children face many challenges. The numbers are quite disturbing, and the majority of these children will be or have been part of the educational system. In addition to these issues, children and teenagers currently in school are "distracted" by after-school jobs (not all out of necessity, but desire) and responsibilities left unfulfilled by parents (Talbert & McLaughlin, 1992). Because so many of these children have and see such limited opportunities for success, it is not surpris-

Table 4.1   Every Day in America

---

3 children die from child abuse.

15 children die from guns.

27 children—a classroomful—die from poverty.

95 babies die before their first birthday.

564 babies are born to women who had late or no prenatal care.

788 babies are born at low birthweight (less than 5 pounds, 8 ounces).

1,340 teenagers give birth.

2,217 teenagers drop out of school each day.

2,350 children are in adult jails.

2,699 infants are born into poverty.

3,356 babies are born to unmarried women.

8,189 children are reported abused or neglected.

100,000 children are homeless.

135,000 children bring guns to school.

1,200,000 latchkey children come home to a house in which there is a gun.

From *The State of America's Children Yearbook* by Children's Defense Fund, 1995, Washington, DC: Children's Defense Fund. Copyright 1995 by Children's Defense Fund. Reprinted with permission.

ing that attaining the national educational goals for the year 2000 appear unrealistic (Delattre, 1992).

Diversity in family structure has contributed to the changing student body. Single-parent and blended families are growing more numerous; families considered "traditional," less so (Amstutz et al., 1992; Hodgkinson, 1988; National Center for Education Statistics, 1993). Many believe there are more dysfunctional families and that this may contribute to problems seen in the schools. Risk factors for teenagers include

- family history of high-risk behaviors, such as alcoholism and drug abuse;
- family management problems, which might include lack of clear expectations for children's behavior, failure of the parent(s) to monitor children, and inconsistent or excessively severe punishment; and
- parents who model inappropriate behaviors, such as committing crimes, using or tolerating drugs, and drinking (Logg, 1994).

As family structure changes, family roles may be changing as well, as evidenced by increasing mothers in the workforce (Amstutz et al., 1992). This may be problematic because girls and women have not received equitable quality of educational experiences in the past, as Williamson indicates in chapter 5. As recommended, schools must accommodate diverse family structures by offering additional services and having more flexibility in scheduling parent programs or conferences.

As previously mentioned, students are becoming increasingly culturally diverse. The largest school districts in the country already have majority minorities (Amstutz et al., 1992). Many teachers and programs appear ill-equipped to handle diverse students (Bedell, 1992; Griffin, 1985). In addition to different languages, different cultures might also have different child-rearing practices and sex-role socialization norms which would affect the students' educational experiences (Smith, 1991). As will be discussed later, students of various ethnic groups also perceive physical education differently. Ethnic minority students also appear to have different educational opportunities at home, as well. In 1989, the percent of students using computers at home for school work was 10.7 percent for children classified as "White, non-Hispanic," 3.4 percent for children in the category of "Black, non-Hispanic," and 3.6 percent for Hispanic children (National Center for Education Statistics, 1993).

Schools are seeing an increase in prognosis and diagnosis of children with disabilities (Hodgkinson, 1988). In the 1976–77 school year, 8.33 percent of public school students were served in federally supported programs for the disabled (National Center for Education Statistics, 1993). By the 1990–91 school year, it was 11.57 percent. Children with specific learning disabilities increased from 1.8 to 5.17 percent during that same time period. Some of these children were exposed to and/or inherited dependency to alcohol and illegal drugs *in utero*, were malnourished, had acquired drug and alcohol dependency, and/or were exposed to sexually transmitted diseases (Amstutz et al., 1992; Delattre, 1992). Such children pose special challenges to teachers (specific implications in physical education for children with disabilities will be presented in chapter 6). Some children, however, have been labeled "unsuccessful" simply because they do not fit into the norm or because their needs have not been met in the traditional educational system (Amstutz et al., 1992). Consequently, there is a disproportionate number of minority students placed in special education, and they tend to remain in the programs longer (Bedell, 1992). Students and parents report that there may be low expectations and inappropriate learning goals and objectives for students with disabilities, contributing to a 36 percent dropout rate (National Council on Disability, 1989).

The American population is becoming more educated. In 1980, 69 percent of the population 25 years old and older had completed high school. In 1991, that percent had risen to 78 percent (National Center for Education Statistics, 1993). Despite these measures, dropout rates remain of national importance. One of the educational goals for the year 2000 states that there will be a 90 percent graduation rate of high school students (United States Department of Education, 1991). Research measuring the dropout rate is difficult to compare because of inconsistencies in defining a "dropout" (Kett, 1993). By some definitions, students who simply quit attending are dropouts, while other definitions specify the number of days missed without enrolling in another public or private school. It is suggested that there are increased dropout rates with Hispanic students (Kett, 1993); but overall, graduation rates have increased (Hodgkinson, 1988; National Center for Education Statistics, 1993). African American students do appear to be dropping out less, but the rate is still higher than their Anglo American counterparts (Kett, 1993; National Center for Education Statistics, 1993). States which have high ethnic diversity and high poverty have higher dropout rates (Hodgkinson, 1988). Differences in dropout rates among ethnic groups are problematic if minority student populations are growing, which they are.

Student achievement measures are showing mixed results (National Center for Education Statistics, 1993). For children who were 9 and 13 years old, achievement in science increased from the late 1970s to the late 1980s, but the same age group showed no improvement in reading from 1971 to 1990. Scholastic Aptitude Test (SAT) scores showed increases in the mathematics component between 1982 and 1992, while scores declined slightly in the verbal section. When both scores were combined, African American and Asian American students' scores increased much more than those of Anglo American students (National Center for Education Statistics, 1993).

STUDENT ATTITUDES

What do students think about school? In 1988, when 8th graders were administered a Likert-type scale which included statements about school climate (National Center for Education Statistics, 1993), the statement that received the highest percentage (80.2 percent) of "strongly agree" or "agree" responses was "Teaching is good." When 10th graders were polled in 1990, the percentage increased slightly. More than 60 percent of 8th grade and 10th grade students (both years) gave the "strongly agree" or "agree" response to the following additional statements: "Students get along well with the teacher"; "There is real school spirit"; "Rules for behavior are strict"; "Discipline is fair"; "Other students often disrupt class"; "Teachers are interested in students"; and "Teachers listen to what I have to say." The statements which received the lowest percentages (less than 22 percent) of the same responses in each year were "I often feel 'put down' by my teachers" and "I don't feel safe in school." In addition, when given choices of "Understood the material," "Try very hard," and "Feel challenged," the majority of 10th graders in 1990 selected "Try very hard" in regard to the four subject areas identified—mathematics, English, history, and science (National Center for Education Statistics, 1993). The combined results indicate that, overall, the students were positive about school climate and perceived that they try hard in their classes.

To physical educators, student attitudes and perceptions in physical education class are deemed important because they may be related to participation in activity outside of class, either during free time or later in life. Questions about these attitudes and perceptions have been raised in various studies. Rice (1988) reported that 85 percent of high school students enjoyed physical education, whereas Tannehill, Romar, O'Sullivan, England and Rosenberg (1994) found that more than 40 percent of the students indicated they liked physical education less than math, science, English, history, and foreign language. Students appreciated teachers who were friendly (Rice, 1988), who had high expectations and were focused on learning (Luke & Sinclair, 1991), and who were sensitive and cared about students (Luke & Sinclair, 1991; Stinson, 1992). In a high school dance class, Stinson (1992) found that if students liked the teacher, they tended to like the class/subject. Rice (1988) also reported that 73 percent of the high school students considered their physical education teachers to be good role models.

In various studies, secondary students indicated they liked or enjoyed physical education because of the variety of activities offered (Rice, 1988); specific outcomes, such as serving a ball over the net and winning (Tannehill et al., 1994); the atmosphere of fun and freedom (Luke & Sinclair, 1991); and the fact that they could be with friends (Tannehill & Zakrajsek, 1993). Negative aspects of physical education that have been reported include class periods that are too brief (Rice, 1988); clothing or changing clothes for physical education (Luke & Sinclair, 1991; Rice, 1988); methods of evaluation (Luke & Sinclair, 1991); and feeling uncomfortable or at risk in performing skills (Tannehill et al., 1994). In addition, it has been reported that some students do not exert themselves in physical education class (Templin, Sparkes, Grant & Schempp, 1994). Carlson (1993) reported on middle school students for whom physical education also had little meaning. Similarly, Tinning and Fitzclarence (1992) found Australian high school students saw physical education as "irrelevant and boring," and Browne (1992) found the main reason Australian students did not elect to take physical education was that it was not relevant to their career plans. Low-skilled sixth graders (Portman, 1993) and middle school students (Carlson, 1993) who had negative experiences in physical education class generated strategies to cope, partly by withdrawing.

When asked about the importance of physical education, 57 percent of the students in the Tannehill and Zakrajsek (1993) study reported that it was important, although the responses differed according to ethnic group. Only 31 percent of the high school students in the Tannehill et al. (1994) study indicated that physical education was important or very important. There are mixed responses regarding the value of coeducational physical education (Luke & Sinclair, 1991; Tannehill et al., 1994).

For the most part, aspects of team sports have been identified as important to students in physical education. Rice (1988) found that high school boys and girls preferred team sports over individual sports. Tannehill and Zakrajsek (1993) found that more than 80 percent of the middle and high school African American students surveyed preferred learning team sports. Similarly, Tannehill et al. (1994) found that approximately 70 percent of high school boys and girls reported that team sport skills and learning to play team sports should receive the most emphasis in physical education courses. Fitness or fitness improvement was also identified as being an important learning goal by the majority of high school boys and girls (Tannehill et al., 1994) and by Asian, Hispanic American, Anglo American, and African American middle and high school boys and girls (Tannehill & Zakrajsek, 1993). Running was the most frequently cited activity disliked by middle and high school boys and girls (Luke & Sinclair, 1991; Tannehill & Zakrajsek, 1993). In one instance, more than 70 percent of Asian American students and middle and high school boys opposed learning dance (Tannehill & Zakrajsek, 1993), while another study (Tannehill et al., 1994) reported that high school boys indicated that dance should not be taught and the girls were ambiguous on the question. Curriculum content, or what is taught, was found by Luke and Sinclair (1991) to be the most influential factor in determining positive and negative attitudes of high school boys and girls in the physical education class.

As communities change, schools and students change. Students are becoming more diverse and they have different needs. Because physical educators work in a complex environment with many variables, meeting the learning needs and interests of all students is quite challenging.

ISSUES AND CONDITIONS THAT AFFECT PHYSICAL EDUCATION

As early as 1975, Locke described the physical educator's work. He identified positive aspects, such as long vacations and close association with sports, that serve to attract and (it is to be hoped) retain physical education teachers. He also described the realities of the job—lack of collegial interactions with other adults, large class sizes, lack of rewards—with which physical educators deal daily. Since then, much has been written to assist in understanding the context in which physical educators perform and physical education students learn.

Many conditions and issues have an impact on physical education as a learning and teaching environment. Socialization research (see Stroot's chapter 16) examines the process of how teachers are socialized into their workplace and work culture. Workplace conditions—such as support of the subject matter (versus marginalization), autonomy (versus neglect), collegial interactions (versus isolation), opportunities (versus lack of) for professional growth, and job responsibilities other than teaching—can facilitate or hinder the teaching of physical education (Gay, 1993; Griffin, 1985; Lambdin, 1993; O'Sullivan, 1989; O'Sullivan & Dyson, 1994; O'Sullivan, Stroot & Tannehill, 1989; Siedentop, Doutis, Tsangaridou, Ward & Rauschenbach, 1994; Smyth, 1992; Smyth, 1993; Solmon, Worthy & Carter, 1993; Sparkes, Templin & Schempp, 1993; Stroot, Collier, O'Sullivan & England, 1994; Templin, 1988; Templin, 1989; Templin et al., 1994). Rather than attempt to make distinctions between whether these conditions result from or contribute to the effect of context, the reader should seek to understand the complexity of the gymnasium and study the contributions of these intertwined factors.

SCHEDULING AND CLASS SIZE

Overall, teachers report that scheduling and class time are job inhibitors (Lambdin, 1993; O'Sullivan, 1989; Smyth, 1992; Smyth, 1993; Stroot et al., 1994). At the elementary level, classroom teachers often deliver classes that are scheduled back to back. Even though elementary physical education specialists may teach up to 10 to 12 classes a day, the number of classes is not the only problem. When classroom teachers deliver classes late, and the classes are scheduled one after another with no consideration to logical sequence or time to rearrange equipment, it makes the educator's job all the more challenging. Smyth (1992) points out that it is especially difficult for a first-year teacher. In addition, secondary students are usually scheduled into physical education without regard to abilities or activity preferences (Siedentop et al., 1994).

Teachers often feel frustrated at the lack of time allotted for physical education. Despite recommendations to lengthen physical education classes to help meet health goals (Nelson, 1991), elementary specialists in some districts are being eliminated and secondary physical education programs are losing curricular time. Granted, the allotted time is often wasted, resulting in decreased academic learning time. Many teachers, however, would like to be part of the decision-making process regarding scheduling and class time. Unfortunately, the amount of time—not the level of student learning—drives teaching (Stroot et al., 1994; Templin, 1989).

For the most part, teachers express concern or say class size creates a hindrance to quality instruction (O'Sullivan, 1989; O'Sullivan & Dyson, 1994; Solmon et al., 1993; Templin, 1989). Especially at the secondary level, the number of students in the physical education class exceeds that of other classes. With large classes, the physical educator's role becomes that of monitor rather than teacher.

Many quality programs exist wherein physical educators take part in the scheduling and class sizes are consistent with those of other academic content areas. These are, more than likely, programs that are not marginalized.

RESOURCES, FACILITIES/SPACE, AND EQUIPMENT

For the teachers in Stroot et al.'s (1994) study, equipment and facilities were some of the most commonly mentioned job enhancers. It could be assumed that teachers with adequate to superior facilities and equipment feel they can do a better job teaching. However, many teachers express the need for more equipment, better facilities, and better (priority) use of facilities (Griffin, 1985; Lambdin, 1993; Smyth, 1993). At the elementary level, the gymnasium is often a multipurpose room, which can double as a cafeteria, place for assemblies, community voting center, meeting place, and so on. Given current educational reforms and recommendations for the future, physical educators may be sharing facilities and equipment with community programs and extended programs (those involving recreation for the community and older adults). This arrangement may be less palatable to teachers if access is already limited during the day.

As a result of inadequate resources, teachers make adjustments. In some cases, curricular choices are affected. In one example, canoeing was eliminated from the program when resources which supported canoeing were reduced (Siedentop et al., 1994). Inadequate facilities and space in an urban middle school prompted a change of schedule to one longer class period per week to accommodate travel time to a community facility (Griffin, 1985).

STUDENT LEARNING AND ASSESSMENT

Teacher education programs promote the goal of student learning and assessment. However, teachers are often socialized into a system where there is no accountability for student learning; thus, the need to assess does not exist. This may be because teachers sense that the expectations for student learning are low, or because assessment is difficult considering the number of students and the time required to keep track of them (Templin, 1989). Teachers may also believe that students might not enjoy the class as much if there were more focus on learning skills (Siedentop et al., 1994). As a result, grading in physical education is based on attending, dressing out, and participating. In other words, if students comply with procedures and routines, they are relatively safe from receiving a poor grade, regardless of quality of performance. This is not always the case, however.

O'Sullivan et al. (1989) describe elementary teachers with different degrees of experience continuing to focus on student learning. Despite the sometimes overwhelming pressures on first-year teachers, Solmon et al. (1993) and O'Sullivan (1989) describe novice physical educators who felt successful because they taught routines and rules, changed student attitudes toward physical education, and observed progress in their students.

Education reform efforts are now focused on accountability. Teachers must get away from the "busy, happy and good" syndrome (Placek, 1983) and the "participation means an A" mentality. The profession will continue to be marginalized if physical educators are not accountable for learning (Lawson, 1989). If a student does not receive any learning from physical education, there is little justification for the requirement. If it is not required, it becomes a peripheral luxury. These are the aspects of schools and education that are eliminated.

OTHER FACTORS—POLICIES, PERSONAL EVENTS, PLACES, AND PARENTS

Many other factors have an impact on physical education. Central office policies (which might mandate grading procedures or student assignment to classes) can influence a teacher's work (Griffin, 1985). A critical event in a teacher's personal life may affect the way he or she teaches (Templin et al., 1994). In some cases, the location of the school changes the conditions of work. Griffin's (1985) study identified qualities which are unique to urban, multiracial schools. Teachers were affected by not only language differences, but differences in dress and attitude of students. In addition, teachers must address personal prejudices that might influence their teaching. Some teachers teach in a context where the socioeconomic level is very low and very high at the same time. These teachers teach students who do not have the benefit of outside movement experiences, as well as students who have had a significant amount (Smyth, 1993).

Most teachers value parental support, and many teachers make strong efforts to garner it. The research demonstrates that some teachers perceive little support from parents, perhaps because of the parents' own bad experiences or because their child received a low grade in physical education (Smyth, 1993; Stroot et al., 1994; Templin, 1989). Even when teachers do sense support from parents, the parents may not believe physical education is important and are not happy when their child is given a low grade (O'Sullivan, 1989).

REWARDS

The teaching profession is not plentiful in extrinsic rewards such as status, salary, and power. Intrinsic, or psychic, rewards can include (primarily) student learning and growth or collegial stimulation and support (Sandholtz, 1990). Because of some of the previously discussed contextual factors and workplace factors which will be discussed in chapter 16, these psychic rewards can be very limited. For example, teachers who feel strong support from administrators or other teachers feel more valued. Significant collegial interactions with colleagues prevent teachers' feelings of isolation and professional separation. In Stroot et al.'s (1994) study, teachers reported supportive administrations and "teamwork and cooperation among colleagues" as job enhancers.

Reward for physical educators is also derived from visible student learning. If a teacher monitors instead of teaches, student learning is less likely to occur. Keeping students "busy, happy and good" (Placek, 1983) provides little opportunity to view learning. If assessment on student learning does not occur, student progress is less likely to be seen.

Although they get limited praise from administrators (Templin, 1989), physical educators do report a sense of reward in their teaching. Teachers said students and interactions with the students were most important or the sources from which they received the greatest reward (O'Sullivan et al., 1994; Stroot et al., 1994). Solmon et al. (1993) and O'Sullivan (1989) found that first-year teachers felt successful in their accomplishments which focused on student progress.

CONCLUSIONS

The contextual factors of schools and physical education are worth examining. This research sheds light on the complexity of teaching, learning, and the school, but it also exposes that which must be improved. In some cases, the context of the teacher's and student's world is the result of external factors, such as national trends; in other cases, the factors are locally determined and manipulated. In some instances, aspects of the learning environment may need improvement or change. Some of these changes can be implemented through joint efforts by districts, policy makers, administrators, and others. In other instances, only teachers can create change. In these situations, teachers should initiate and take responsibility for attempting change (Smyth, 1992; Stroot et al., 1994). (Teacher innovation and change is discussed in detail in chapter 17 by Housner.) Other suggestions to make positive impacts on school context, which parallel what is happening in the nation and education in general, include, but are not limited to

- making physical education more relevant to students (Tinning & Fitzclarence, 1992);
- having programs which meet the needs of all students (Tannehill & Zakrajsek, 1993);
- implementing technology to help students maintain interest (O'Sullivan et al., 1994); and
- attempting to learn about various cultures, from learning how to pronounce each student's name correctly to understanding the unique characteristics of specific cultures (religious holidays, interactions with members of opposite sex, etc.) (Daley, 1991; Smith, 1991; Swisher & Swisher, 1986).

Lawson (1989), however, cautions that efforts need to consider the diversity of backgrounds of teachers, the diversity of the programs that prepared them, and the diversity of the contexts in which they work. The purpose of these changes, of course, is to create a better learning environment—one that prepares today's students for tomorrow's world.

REFERENCES

Amstutz, D., Beglau, M., Whitson, D., Naumann, D., & Sherritt, C. (1992). *Community involvement in school improvement.* Laramie, WY: Wyoming Center for Educational Research. (ERIC Document Reproduction Service No. ED 352 732)

Barta, S., & Anderson, T. (1982). *Multicultural nonsexist education: Physical education in Iowa schools.* Des Moines, IA: Iowa State Department of Public Instruction, Educational Equity Section. (ERIC Document Reproduction Service No. ED 219 358)

Bedell, F.D. (1992). Educational needs of minorities with disabilities. In T. J. Wright & P. Leung (Eds.), *Proceedings of The Unique Needs of Minorities With Disabilities: Setting an Agenda for the Future* (pp. 193–202). Jackson, MS. (ERIC Document Reproduction Service No. ED 358 593)

Browne, J. (1992). Reasons for the selection or nonselection of physical education studies by year 12 girls. *Journal of Teaching in Physical Education, 11,* 402–410.

Carlson, T.B. (1993). Alienation in the gymnasium [Summary]. *Proceedings of the Special Interest Group Research on Learning and Instruction in Physical Education of the American Educational Research Association,* 44–46.

Children's Defense Fund. (1995). *The state of America's children: Yearbook 1995.* Washington, DC: Author.

Daley, D. (1991). Multicultural issues in physical education. *The British Journal of Physical Education, 22* (1), 31–32.

Delattre, E.J. (1992, April). *Our children's lives.* Paper presented at the Annual International Study Conference of the Association of Childhood Education International, Chicago. (ERIC Document Reproduction Service No. ED 352 114)

Edmonds, R. (1979). Effective schools for the urban poor. *Educational Leadership, 37* (1), 15–27.

Education Commission of the States. (1992). *Renewing public dialogue. 1992 education agenda.* Denver: Author. (ERIC Document Reproduction Service No. ED 351 760)

Gay, D.A. (1993). Data Bank II: Case studies of outstanding physical education programs, case 3. (Doctoral dissertation, Columbia University Teachers College, 1993). *Dissertation Abstracts International, 54,* 3698A.

Graham, P. (1993). Antiquarianism and American education: Assimilation, adjustment, access. In D. Ravitch & M. Vinovskis (Eds.), *Historical perspectives on the current educational reforms* (pp. 16–55). Washington, DC: Office of Educational Research and Improvement. (ERIC Document Reproduction Service No. ED 359 623)

Griffin, P.S. (1985). Teaching in an urban, multiracial physical education program: The power of context. *Quest, 37,* 154–165.

Grossman, P.L., & Stodolsky, S.S. (1994). Considerations in the content and circumstances of secondary school teaching. In L. Darling-Hammond (Ed.), *Review of research in education* (pp. 179–221). Washington, DC: American Educational Research Association.

Hannaway, J. (1992, October). *School districts: The missing link in education reform.* Paper presented at the annual meeting of the Public Policy and Management Association, Denver. (ERIC Document Reproduction Service No. ED 359 644)

Hellison, D. (1991). The whole person in physical education scholarship: Toward integration. *Quest, 43,* 307–318.

Hodgkinson, H. (1988, October). *The context of 21st-century civics and citizenship.* Paper presented at the National Conference on the Future of Civic Education, Washington, DC. (ERIC Document Reproduction Service No. ED 310 984)

Hussar, W.J. (1993). *Pocket projections of education statistics to 2004.* Washington, DC: National Center for Education Statistics.

Kett, J. (1993). Dead end or detour? School leaving in historical perspective. In D. Ravitch & M. Vinovskis (Eds.), *Historical perspectives on the current educational reforms* (pp. 503–559). Washington, DC: Office of Educational Research and Improvement. (ERIC Document Reproduction Service No. ED 359 623)

King, S.E. (1994). Winning the race against racism. *The Journal of Physical Education, Recreation and Dance, 65* (9), 69–74.

Kirst, M. (1993). Recent history of U.S. governance. In D. Ravitch & M. Vinovskis (Eds.), *Historical perspectives on the current educational reforms* (pp. 56–110).

Washington, DC: Office of Educational Research and Improvement. (ERIC Document Reproduction Service No. ED 359 623)

Kozol, J. (1991). *Savage inequalities.* New York: Crown Publishers.

Lambdin, D.D. (1993). Elementary school teachers' lives and careers: An interview study of physical education specialists, other subject specialists, and classroom teachers. (Doctoral dissertation, University of Massachusetts, 1992). *Dissertation Abstracts International, 53,* 3441A.

Lawson, H.A. (1989). From rookie to veteran: Workplace conditions in physical education and induction into the profession. In T.J. Templin & P.G. Schempp (Eds.), *Socialization into physical education: Learning to teach* (pp. 145–164). Indianapolis: Benchmark Press.

Lawson, H.A. (1993). Teachers' uses of research in practice: A literature review. *Journal of Teaching in Physical Education, 12,* 366–374.

Locke, L.F. (1975). The ecology of the gymnasium: What the tourists never see. *Proceedings of SAPECW* (pp. 38–50). (ERIC Document Reproduction Service No. ED 104 823)

Locke, L.F. (1992). Changing secondary school physical education. *Quest, 44,* 361–372.

Logg, C. (1994, March 5). Researchers identify teen risk factors. *The Bellingham Herald,* p. A2.

Luke, M.D., & Sinclair, G.D. (1991). Gender differences in adolescents' attitudes toward school physical education. *Journal of Teaching in Physical Education, 11,* 31–46.

McBride, R.E. (1991). Critical thinking—An overview with implications for physical education. *Journal of Teaching Physical Education, 11,* 112–125.

McLaughlin, M.W. (1992). *What matters most in teachers' workplace context?* Stanford, CA: Center for Research on the Context of Secondary Teaching, Stanford University, School of Education. (ERIC Document Reproduction Service No. ED 342 755)

National Center for Education Statistics. (1993). *Digest of education statistics 1993.* Washington, DC: Author.

National Council on Disability. (1989). The education of students with disabilities: Where do we stand? Washington, DC: Author.

Nelson, M.A. (1991). The role of physical education and children's activity in the public health. *Research Quarterly for Exercise and Sport, 62,* 148–150.

O'Sullivan, M. (1989). Failing gym is like failing lunch or recess: Two beginning teachers' struggle for legitimacy. *Journal of Teaching in Physical Education, 8,* 227–242.

O'Sullivan, M., & Dyson, B. (1994). Rules, routines, and expectations of 11 high school physical education teachers. *Journal of Teaching in Physical Education, 13,* 361–374.

O'Sullivan, M., Siedentop, D., & Tannehill, D. (1994). Breaking out: Codependency of high school physical education. *Journal of Teaching in Physical Education, 13,* 421–428.

O'Sullivan, M., Stroot, S.A., & Tannehill, D. (1989). Elementary physical education specialists: A commitment to student learning. *Journal of Teaching in Physical Education, 8,* 261–265.

Pinkham, K.M. (1994). Perspectives of secondary school physical educators on the school as a workplace. *Proceedings of the Special Interest Group Research on Learning and Instruction in Physical Education of the American Educational Research Association,* 17–19.

Placek, J.H. (1983). Conceptions of success in teaching: Busy, happy and good? In T.J. Templin & J.K. Olson, (Eds.), *Teaching in physical education* (pp. 46–56). Champaign, IL: Human Kinetics.

Portman, P.A. (1993). Experiences and behaviors of low-skilled sixth grade students in physical education classes: The significance of being chosen last [Summary]. *Proceedings of the Special Interest Group Research on Learning and Instruction in Physical Education of the American Educational Research Association,* 31.

Ravitch, D. (1993). Standards in American educational history. In D. Ravitch & M. Vinovskis (Eds.), *Historical perspectives on the current educational reforms* (pp. 288–335). Washington, DC: Office of Educational Research and Improvement. (ERIC Document Reproduction Service No. ED 359 623)

Rees, C.R., Feingold, R.S., & Barrette, G.T. (1991). Overcoming obstacles to collaboration and integration in physical education. *Quest, 43,* 319–332.

Reese, W. (1993). From "Reefer Madness" to "A Clockwork Orange"? In D. Ravitch & M. Vinovskis (Eds.), *Historical perspectives on the current educational reforms* (pp. 657–722). Washington, DC: Office of Educational Research and Improvement. (ERIC Document Reproduction Service No. ED 359 623)

Rice, P.L. (1988). Attitudes of high school students toward physical education activities, teachers, and personal health. *Physical Educator, 45* (2), 94–99.

Rink, J.E. (1993). What's so critical? In J.E. Rink (Ed.), *Critical crossroads: Middle and secondary school physical education* (pp. 1–16). Reston, VA: National Association for Sport and Physical Education.

Sandholtz, J.H. (1990). *Demands, rewards, and effort: A balancing act for teachers.* Stanford, CA: Center for Research on the Context of Secondary School Teaching, Stanford University, School of Education. (ERIC Document Reproduction Service No. ED 338 591)

Sedlak, M. (1993). Historical perspectives on school-based social services in the United States. In D. Ravitch & M. Vinovskis (Eds.), *Historical perspectives on the current educational reforms* (pp. 111–158). Washington, DC: Office of Educational Research and Improvement. (ERIC Document Reproduction Service No. ED 359 623)

Siedentop, D. (1993). Thinking differently about secondary physical education. In J.E. Rink (Ed.), *Critical crossroads: Middle and secondary school physical education* (pp. 7–10). Reston, VA: National Association for Sport and Physical Education.

Siedentop, D., Doutis, P., Tsangaridou, N., Ward, P., & Rauschenbach, J. (1994). Don't sweat gym! An analysis of curriculum and instruction. *Journal of Teaching in Physical Education, 13,* 375–394.

Siskin, L.S. (1990). *Different worlds: The department as context for high school teachers.* Stanford, CA: Center for Research on the Context of Secondary School Teaching, Stanford University, School of Education. (ERIC Document Reproduction Service No. ED 338 592)

Smith, Y.R. (1991). Issues and strategies for working with multicultural athletes. *Journal of Physical Education, Recreation and Dance, 62* (3), 39–44.

Smyth, D.M. (1992, April). *The kids just love him: A first year teacher's perceptions of how the workplace has affected his teaching.* Paper presented at the annual meeting of the American Educational Research Association, San Francisco. (ERIC Document Reproduction Service No. ED 355 177)

Smyth, D.M. (1993, April). *First year physical education teachers' perceptions of their workplace.* Paper presented at the annual meeting of the American Educational Research Association, Atlanta. (ERIC Document Reproduction Service No. 361 308)

Solmon, M.A., Worthy, T., & Carter, J.A. (1993). The interaction of school context and role identity of first-year teachers. *Journal of Teaching in Physical Education, 12,* 313–328.

Sparkes, A.C., Templin, T.J., & Schempp, P.G. (1993). Exploring dimensions of marginality: Reflecting on the life histories of physical education teachers. *Journal of Teaching in Physical Education, 12,* 386–398.

Stinson, S.W. (1992). Meaning and value: Reflections about what students say about school. *Journal of Curriculum and Supervision, 8,* 216–238.

Stroot, S.A. (1994). Contemporary crisis or emerging reform? A review of secondary school physical education. *Journal of Teaching in Physical Education, 13,* 333–341.

Stroot, S.A., Collier, C., O'Sullivan, M., & England, K. (1994). Contextual hoops and hurdles: Workplace conditions in secondary physical education. *Journal of Teaching in Physical Education, 13,* 342–360.

Swisher, K., & Swisher, C. (1986). A multicultural physical education approach: An attitude. *Journal of Physical Education, Recreation and Dance, 57* (7), 35–39.

Talbert, J.E., & McLaughlin, M.W. (1992). Understanding teaching in context. Stanford, CA: Center for Research on the Context of Secondary School Teaching, Stanford University, School of Education. (ERIC Document Reproduction Service No. ED 342 756)

Tannehill, D., Romar, J.E., O'Sullivan, M., England, K., & Rosenberg, D. (1994). Attitudes toward physical education: Their impact on how physical education teachers make sense of their work. *Journal of Teaching in Physical Education, 13,* 406–420.

Tannehill, D., & Zakrajsek, D. (1993). Student attitudes toward physical education: A multicultural study. *Journal of Teaching in Physical Education, 13,* 78–84.

Templin, T.J. (1988). Teacher isolation: A concern for the collegial development of physical educators. *Journal of Teaching in Physical Education, 7,* 197–205.

Templin, T.J. (1989). Running on ice: A case study of the influence of workplace conditions on a secondary school physical educator. In T.J. Templin & P.G.

Schempp (Eds.), *Socialization into physical education: Learning to teach* (pp. 165–197). Indianapolis: Benchmark Press.

Templin, T.J., Sparkes, A., Grant, B., & Schempp, P. (1994). Matching the self: The paradoxical case and life history of a late career teacher/coach. *Journal of Teaching in Physical Education, 13,* 274–294.

Tinning, R., & Fitzclarence, L. (1992). Postmodern youth culture and the crisis in Australian secondary school physical education. *Quest, 44,* 287–303.

Tyson, L.A., & Silverman, S. (1994a). An analysis of physical education and non-physical education teachers at the elementary and secondary levels on statewide teacher assessment. *Journal of Teaching in Physical Education, 14,* 85–98.

Tyson, L.A., & Silverman, S. (1994b, April). *An analysis of statewide teacher appraisal scores across four years.* Paper presented at the annual meeting of the American Educational Research Association, New Orleans.

United States Department of Education. (1991). America 2000: An education strategy. Washington, DC: Author.

Van Camp, S. (1993, October). *The role of physical activity and prevention in health care reform in the United States.* Paper presented at the meeting of the Members of the House Ways and Means Subcommittee on Health, Washington, DC.

Werner, P. (1994). Whole physical education. *The Journal of Physical Education, Recreation and Dance, 65* (6), 40–44.

Wessinger, N.P. (1994). Celebrating our differences—Fostering ethnicity in homogeneous settings. *The Journal of Physical Education, Recreation and Dance, 65* (9), 62–68.

Wilson, C. (Ed.). (1991). *A vision of a preferred curriculum for the 21st century.* Rochester, MI: Oakland University, School of Education and Human Services. (ERIC Document Reproduction Service No. ED 344 275)

Woods, L.A. (1992). Development of an inventory to assess multicultural education attitudes, competencies, and knowledge of physical education professionals (Doctoral dissertation, University of Georgia, 1992). *Dissertation Abstracts International, 53,* 2295A.

CHAPTER 5

Gender Issues

Kay M. Williamson

I have a dream that people will not kill whales or animals and the world will be a better place to live in. And that girls will be respected in this [fourth grade] class and other classes as well, and boys will be more thoughtful.

> Kenyanna Dos Santos, 4th Grade, *The Tribal Tribune*,
> (January 28, 1994, p. 2).

Kenyanna was in fourth grade when she wrote her thoughts about the world and fairness. By the age of nine, she was aware of gender differences in the way girls were treated in class and perceived boys as less thoughtful. When the world is defined by gendered behaviors, then both boys and girls suffer from the pressure of imposed expectations. The purposes of this chapter are to describe how gender can affect a student's ability to learn and to suggest ways that teachers can look at each student as unique. It is important that teachers respond to individual actions and efforts of students rather than hold different expectations for boys or girls. This chapter is divided into five sections: (a) gender roles and society; (b) gender research in education; (c) gender research in sport, exercise, and physical activity; (d) gender research in physical education; and (e) challenging gender role stereotypes.

GENDER ROLES AND SOCIETY

It is important to define the term gender, as nomenclature with different meanings have been used synonymously in the literature. The terms gender and sex are often used interchangeably; however, there are distinctions in the meaning and use of these terms. The term sex refers to the biological differences between men and women, whereas gender represents the social, cultural, and psychological processes through which femininity and masculinity are constructed and reproduced in society (Oakley, 1972).[1] As Scraton (1992) emphasized, the definition of gender can vary across cultures and time. The importance of making this distinction is that myths have been constructed about the abilities of the sexes based on their biological differences. Scraton's statement, "...it is the social construction of gender that is important, not biological differences" is a pivotal premise for an understanding of gender inequalities (p. 8).

SOCIALIZATION AND GENDER ROLE STEREOTYPING

There are several societal influences that affect children's perceptions of their gender roles. For example, when I was looking at clothes to buy for my newborn niece the gender color code of blue for boys and pink for girls was clear; I once heard a friend's four-year-old daughter refuse a sheet of blue paper because, she said, "That's for boys!" Given the messages children receive at such an early age, it is not surprising that they identify specific colors related to gender. Children's birthday cards and toys also have gender ramifications: Girls are associated with homely duties such as vacuuming, cooking, looking after dolls, and caring for "cute" creatures; while boys are identified with action-packed or often violent activities with guns, trucks, and sports. (Haywood, 1986; Streitmatter, 1994). Many people are socialized into "gender appropriate" behavior, which leads them to believe these stereotypes. For example, how many times have we heard or said, "Boys will be boys"? The labels we associate with gender roles often become self-fulfilling prophecies for the individuals being stereotyped as well as those who do the stereotyping (King, Miles, & Kniska, 1991; Snyder, 1982).

Gould (1978) wrote about society's obsession with gender role stereotypes in an article entitled "X." The article recounted a fictitious experiment with a child, whose sex remained a secret to everyone except the scientists and parents. The child loved to play with dolls and computerized robots, shoot baskets, and weave baskets. The adults became angry and frustrated because they did not know what kinds of "gender appropriate" clothes or toys to buy for the child, or whether the child was interacting with children of the opposite sex in a "proper" manner. The frustration and situations that are depicted in this article, while humorous, emphasize the extent to which we try to categorize and label children as soon as they are born. I have found this a useful reading for helping university students to understand the explicit and subtle ways boys and girls are stereotyped.

It often prompts teachers to consider that societal norms and expectations may be different from the child's subjective reality.

GENDER RESEARCH IN GENERAL EDUCATION

Notions of "gender appropriate" behavior in society can also be reinforced in schools. A study with elementary school students (Adler, Kless, & Adler, 1992) illustrated how children constructed idealized images of masculinity and femininity from which they modeled their behavior in peer groups. A boy's popularity was based on his athletic ability, coolness, toughness, social skills, and success in cross-gender relationships. A girl's popularity was based upon her parents' socioeconomic status, physical appearance, social skills, and academic success.

CURRICULUM AND SUBJECT AREAS

Title IX of the 1972 Education Amendments was an attempt to provide access for girls and boys to all aspects of the school curriculum. It stated that educational opportunities may not be offered separately based on the sex of students (Stromquist, 1993). Despite this legislation, bias is still evident more than two decades later. Unfortunately, due to historic association and teachers' and career counselors' stereotypic views of subjects as masculine or feminine (AAUW, 1992; Grossman & Grossman, 1994), students often identify "gender appropriate" content areas in the curriculum by the end of elementary school. Research has shown that girls, boys, and teachers considered reading to be a feminine activity, while math, science, and computers were considered masculine pursuits (Streitmatter, 1994; Sutton, 1991). Boys and girls do achieve different levels of success in some subjects (American Association of University Women [AAUW], 1992). For example, the AAUW stated that "differences between boys and girls in math achievement is declining. Yet in high school, girls are still less likely than boys to take the most advanced courses and be in the top scoring math groups" (p. 4). These differences are further perpetuated as gender-based assumptions become apparent in career choices. Although changes are taking place with students crossing gender stereotypic lines, Streitmatter (1994) emphasized, "Many career areas continue to reflect considerable gender overrepresentation" (p. 91). Grossman and Grossman (1994) noted that "women comprise 90% of vocational classes in cosmetology, clerical, home economics, and health courses, and less than 10% of students in agriculture, technology, electronics, appliance repair, auto mechanics, carpentry, welding, and small engine repair" (p. 26). Such disparity in career choices reflects the power of gender socialization. The pressure and opportunity for either sex to challenge career stereotypes can be difficult if teachers are unaware how they perpetuate traditional expectations for boys and girls in the classroom (Streitmatter, 1994).

INSTRUCTIONAL MATERIALS
AND PEDAGOGICAL PRACTICE

Textbooks, bulletin boards, school plays, and other means of presenting and displaying information can reinforce gender stereotypes of "appropriate roles" for boys and girls (AAUW, 1992; Streitmatter, 1994). Instructional materials also can marginalize or ignore women and minorities. Although the days of "Dick and Jane" readers are supposedly passed, gender and race biased textbooks are still prevalent in schools (AAUW, 1992).

A teacher's use of various instructional materials and pedagogical practices, however, either inhibits or promotes gender stereotyping. Teachers can create and maintain gender stereotypes in how they provide feedback and attention to students. Gender differences can be communicated in how teachers model sexist behavior—and reinforce students for behaving in different gender stereotypic ways (Grossman & Grossman, 1994). Some teachers continue to use instructional materials and pedagogical strategies to interact differently with girls and boys. In one study, the AAUW (1992) reported that teachers favored and encouraged boys by giving them more praise, opportunities to respond to questions, and constructive feedback on work. Again, such instructional bias places pressure on both boys and girls; boys can develop domineering and aggressive behaviors in seeking teacher attention, while girls can become silent and submissive because their voices go unheard.

Race and socioeconomic status are also factors that add another layer of discrimination in how boys and girls are treated, which also can bias a teacher's perceptions and interactions with children (Parish, Eubanks, Aquila, & Walker, 1989; Sutton, 1991). In a study by Grossman and Grossman (1994), European American teachers treated African American and European American girls differently. African American girls were dealt with more harshly when they misbehaved and praised for their social skills rather than academic and intellectual performance (Grossman & Grossman, 1994). Grant (1984) suggested such teacher interactions can lead African American girls to perceive themselves as being more suited to such stereotypic roles as housekeepers, maids, and nannies.

From these examples, it is apparent that teachers are in powerful positions to influence children (Ayers, 1989; Sloan, 1995). Yet, one of the dilemmas of gender biased actions is that, for the most part, they are unintentional and unconscious (Streitmatter, 1994). Gender bias is difficult to confront because it tends to be insidious and pervasive. Later in this chapter, I will focus on recognizing and confronting teacher bias.

GENDER RESEARCH IN SPORT, EXERCISE, AND PHYSICAL ACTIVITY

Research in sport, exercise, and physical activity mirrors concerns related to findings in education in general. Gender expectations in these areas are historically specific, rigid, and extreme. Over the centuries, the biological functions of a woman were given as reasons for her not participating in activity. In Victorian society, it was feared that a woman's reproductive system would be damaged if she exercised. During the 1920s and 1930s such myths were questioned and proven inaccurate. A new set of fears emerged for women; if they participated in vigorous activity they could begin to look masculine and lose social approval (Griffin, 1992). For men, participation in sports, exercise, and physical activity was consistent with Western society's definition of masculinity: aggressive, competitive, and tough (Streitmatter, 1994). Again, societal expectations exerted pressure for both men and women to behave "gender appropriately."

Various authors offer insight into female sport participation. Weiss and Glenn (1992) described socialization practices, psychological development, and biological maturation as they relate to female sport participation, and their findings are described in the following two sections. As Greendorfer and Brundage (1987) emphasized, when differences occur between boys and girls in learning motor skills, "we not only accept them but tend to expect them" (p. 125).

SOCIAL AND PSYCHOLOGICAL PERSPECTIVES OF MOVEMENT PARTICIPATION

Societal expectations delineate specific roles for men and women. I experienced this as a child at the Conservative Club, an exclusive association for supporters of the Conservative political party in Britain. When I was 12 years old, John Spencer, a British snooker champion, played an exhibition game at the local Conservative Club. (Snooker is a game similar to pool.) My 10-year-old brother, Paul, was able to attend, but I had to stay home because only males were allowed to observe this event. I recall feeling this was unfair, but it was not until 1989, when I was 34 and a similar situation arose, that I questioned the apparent injustice. Margaret Thatcher was the Conservative prime minister of England and my father had become manager of a Conservative Club. When my brothers and I visited him, we decided to have a game of snooker. I was poised with my cue ready to take a shot, when I was hastily informed by a flustered Chairman of the Club that women could not play snooker because it was "unladylike and inelegant." I was furious and, with Mrs. Thatcher's portrait beaming at me from the wall, I expressed my anger to the Chairman and my dad at the different rules that existed for men and women—

especially when a woman was head of the government! This situation is mirrored in the United States, where some private golf clubs still do not allow women and minorities access to facilities (Coakley, 1994).

Women, faced with situations like those described above, have had to overcome various societal hurdles to participate in physical activity. Three factors are important in how both women and men are socialized into physical activity:

1. Reinforcement from significant others, such as parents, coaches, teachers, and peers.
2. Opportunities available in the school and neighborhood.
3. Personal attributes, such as self perception, physical ability, maturation, motivation, and the value one places on activity (Weiss & Glenn, 1992).

Because sport and activity are associated with masculine tendencies, women can experience role conflict when participating in sports (Blinde & Greendorfer, 1992; Coakley, 1994). Role conflict for female students can be reduced if members of their social support network, such as parents and peers, recognize and value sport activities (Goldberg & Chandler, 1991).

Role conflict can also result from media images of how men and women are portrayed in sports (Theberge, 1991; Weiss & Glenn, 1992). Generally, women's activities are underrepresented and trivialized (Talbot, 1986; Weiss & Glenn, 1992). Examples are evident when watching sports on television or reading sport related magazines or newspapers. For this reason, it is important that teachers present positive images of both male and female athletes in their physical education classes. Such role models help motivate all students to participate.

Other factors associated with motivation to participate in activities include self-confidence, achievement goal orientation, and locus of control (Weiss, & Glenn, 1992; Lirgg, 1992). Parents, teachers, and coaches provide feedback, an influential aspect in formulating self-perceptions and self-confidence (Weiss & Glenn, 1992). Because girls tend to be stereotyped as less athletically competent than boys (Eccles & Harold, 1991), they may not respond positively when receiving reinforcement from others for fear of appearing "boyish." Boys are inclined to be more confident in their physical abilities than girls because it is expected of them (Greendorfer & Brundage, 1987; Lirgg, 1992).

BIOLOGICAL FACTORS

Differences between students are not as important as how we perceive these differences and allow them to determine expectations and behaviors. For example, the relative impact of biological differences on human performance may be the most controversial issue to confront in overcoming gender bias. As mentioned earlier, everyone receives messages about the roles of men and women from various sources: society, the media, parents, teachers, and coaches. Thus, it can be difficult to challenge our ingrained values and beliefs. A major question is to what extent "biological differences" are a result of heredity, the environment, or the social setting in which we live.

Research has indicated that, prior to puberty, there is no statistically significant difference in the physical capabilities of boys and girls (Thomas & Thomas, 1988). Various studies have shown that muscle tissue of men and women will improve equally with exercise (Rich, 1994; Wells, 1992). Thomas and Thomas emphasized, however, that it was difficult to ascertain to what extent societal expectations affect female participation in activity after adolescence. Other studies have shown that gender differences are more a consequence of cultural and societal expectations than "natural or biological" differences for students (Carlson, 1994; Eccles & Harold, 1991; Greendorfer & Brundage, 1987).

LIMITATIONS OF RESEARCH AND GENDER BIAS

Research on gender differences in sport and physical activity tends to be biased and limited (Bredemeier, 1992). One important issue that researchers have overlooked is the variability within groups (Bredemeier, 1992). As Bredemeier stated, "Averaging the mean scores of biological sex groupings doesn't tell us much about the development of individual females and males . . . Usually even the most reliable differences are found to be relatively trivial" (pp. 197-198). This alternative approach to data analysis emphasizes both the variability within a group of boys and girls and the degree of overlap between the sexes (Bredemeier, 1992). If the variability within and across groups was reported more carefully, parents, teachers, and students might draw different conclusions about the capabilities of boys and girls.

IMPLICATIONS FOR GIRLS' AND BOYS' PARTICIPATION IN ACTIVITY

Even though there are many opportunities for men and women to participate in various sports today, many physical activities remain associated with masculinity or femininity. Gender role definition for participating in different forms of movement is still apparent, despite the passage of Title IX (Hutchinson, 1995). For example, Isaac's (1992) report reflected the gender stereotypic patterns of participation in a local parks and recreation program. Girls' participation accounted for 18% of the team sports, 48% of the recreation sports (e.g., tennis, bowling), and 92% of the dance and movement participants. A primary factor to consider in accounting for these differences was the amount of encouragement girls and boys received to participate in the various movement activities. If certain activities are perceived to be either masculine or feminine, then either sex could be discouraged from participating in cross-gender activities.

Homophobia (fear of lesbians and gay men) can reinforce gender stereotypes and influence participants to stay within the bounds of "gender appropriate" activities (Coakley, 1994). Homophobic name calling can be directed at students who cross gender-specific activities. For example, boys who take part in figure skating and girls who play rugby could be labeled "sissies, or fags" and "tomboys, lezzies, or dykes" (Coakley, 1994; Griffin, 1989a; Grossman & Grossman, 1994). Ironically, for girls, the term "tomboy" in some contexts is highly regarded and a form of praise if this term reflects male qualities (Coakley, 1994; Talbot, 1986). The pressure of homophobia can be extreme. For example, girls participating in what is perceived as a male activity may shave their legs and put ribbons in their hair to ensure that their femininity is preserved (Lenskyj, 1994).

Homophobia can enforce gender stereotypes and impede boys and girls from participating in various movement activities (Coakley, 1994; Griffin, 1992; Williamson, 1993). As Coakley emphasized, "Gender equity is not just a women's issue; equity involves opening up spaces for men to participate in forms of sport that are not based on dominant forms of masculinity" (p. 225). Physical education in its purest sense must provide a variety of movement experiences for boys and girls which are contrary to gender stereotypes (Leaman, 1986).

GENDER RESEARCH IN PHYSICAL EDUCATION

Given the socialization of children into gender roles at home, school, and in sport settings, achieving gender equity in physical education classes can be challenging (Griffin, 1989b; Grossman & Grossman, 1994). Physical education is another area where the social construction of gender can be maintained and perpetuated (Dewar, 1987) unless teachers are willing to examine their values, beliefs, and teaching practices to provide a more equitable learning environment. This section reviews gender research in physical education and includes: (a) Title IX and curricular choices, (b) student participation patterns, and (c) teacher and student interactions.

TITLE IX AND CURRICULAR CHOICES

As mentioned earlier, Title IX emphasized that students should not be separated for curricular choices on the basis of sex. In physical activity, however, there are exceptions for boys and girls to be segregated when participating in contact sports such as wrestling, boxing, rugby, and ice hockey (Bruce, 1993; Lay, 1990). Despite Title IX, sex segregation still is widely practiced in physical education, even in activities that are not contact sports (Griffin, 1989b; Knoppers, 1988; Lay, 1990).

A pre-Title IX legacy that has been difficult to overcome is that physical education classes were segregated at all levels of education, except perhaps in the elementary school. Since 1972, implementing coeducational classes has proved a struggle for many teachers. Also, private schools are exempt from Title IX, and it is still common practice to have gender segregated physical education in these schools (Madrigal & Williamson, 1994; Williams & Williamson, 1995).

One of the problems that occurred with the implementation of Title IX was that teachers were not consulted, involved, or prepared to incorporate gender equity into their classes (Griffin, 1985a). Over 20 years later, many still struggle to achieve gender equity in physical education. Teachers need to be aware of how they label activities in their curriculum, and how certain curricular offerings have become gender stereotyped. For example, gender stereotypes are perpetuated if jumping rope and skipping are reinforced as girls' activities while baseball and football are classified as boys' activities (Ignico, 1989). The following two examples, relating to dance and fitness testing, emphasize problems that have occurred in trying to implement coeducational physical education.

Dance

Dance usually is associated with feminine qualities in North America (Crawford, 1994). As Ferdun (1994) stated, "Labeling dance as female prevents dance from functioning as an educational medium. It limits participation by anyone who does not want to be associated with stereotyped gender images and practices" (p. 46). Effective suggestions are provided for how to confront and overcome gender stereotypes associated with dance by Ferdun (1994) and Kerr-Berry (1994). Besides having positive male role models, other instructional strategies include:

- Discussing gender as a conscious variable in dance.
- Teaching dance as a "wholeness" in relation to the body, culture, and a way of communication.
- Teaching a broad range of dance genres.
- Promoting empathy in dance experiences by practicing and imagining what it is like to move as someone else.
- Providing dance experiences that promote gender equality.
- Using percussion instruments to reduce movement barriers (Ferdun, 1994; Kerr-Berry, 1994).

To achieve these ends in a subject such as dance, teachers also have to monitor their gender bias relative to how they approach students and present images (Kerr-Berry, 1994).

Fitness Testing

Fitness testing is another example of how gender inequities can be perpetuated in physical education (Williamson, 1993). Various fitness tests such as: Chrysler-AAU (1987); FITNESSGRAM (Cooper Institute for Aerobics Research, 1992); Physical Best (American Alliance for Health, Physical Education, Recreation and Dance, 1988); and the Presidential Fitness Awards Program (U.S. Department of Health and Human Services, 1987) use different standards for boys and girls from ages 5 or 6 through 18. This results in the perpetuation of gender stereotypes and expectations. As stated earlier, differences between boys' and girls' performance are not significant before puberty, and even after puberty the effects of socialization make generalizations difficult to assert (Oldenhove, 1989; Thomas & Thomas, 1988). One troubling factor is how some fitness organizations have admitted to arbitrarily setting standards (Safrit & Looney, 1992). Only recently (Cooper Institute for Aerobics Research, 1992) have fitness organizations begun to address this issue. The main factor, however, is how teachers use fitness tests and to what extent they discuss gender stereotypes in their classes.

Discrepant standards for boys and girls place pressure on both sexes; boys are expected to outperform girls or be subject to humiliation, while girls are not expected to perform as well as boys. To ascertain to what extent interpreting fitness scores was subject to gender bias, the data from 215 children aged 10 to 13 who took part in the Physical Best fitness program were analyzed (Rozdilsky, Williamson, & Wilkinson, 1992). The performance of each child was compared to the boys' standards, and the results showed no significant differences between the performance of boys and girls between 10 and 12 years of age. The analysis reflected that discrepant standards were inappropriate for children of this age. Although the girls' performance declined after age 12, debate continues over whether this was the result of nature or nurture.

STUDENT PARTICIPATION PATTERNS

Even in schools where coeducational physical education supposedly is taking place, there are concerns about how classes are organized and taught (Griffin, 1985a; Lay, 1990; Lock, 1993). Even though boys and girls may be in the same gymnasium, gender segregation can take place in the way that subjects are scheduled. For example, if Flag football and aerobics are activity choices offered at the same time, and students perceive Flag Football to be a "boy's activity" and aerobics to be a "girl's activity," then gender segregation is encouraged if students choose to participate in an activity because it is "gender appropriate" (Griffin, 1989a; Chepyator-Thomson, 1990).

Socialization of students into specific gender roles and a teacher's lack of understanding about gender equity can make coeducational physical education classes intimidating places for girls (Griffin, 1983, 1989b; Hutchinson, 1995; Talbot, 1986; Turvey & Laws, 1988). Intimidation for girls is reflected in boys' harassment, little opportunity to participate, and reinforcement of stereotypic gender roles (Evans, 1986; Felshin & Oglesby, 1986; Griffin, 1983, 1989b; Turvey & Laws, 1988). Coeducational classes also can be humiliating for less athletic boys, as Griffin (1985b) showed in her research on boys' participation styles in physical education. Less able boys were labeled as wimps and were subject to physical and verbal abuse during class. Other students stuffed grass down their shirts and called them homophobic names. Griffin's studies (1984, 1985b) emphasized vividly how gender stereotyping played out among the students. Another interesting outcome of Griffin's work was that there were more differences in physical ability within the group of boys and within the group of girls than between the two groups. Again, this supports Bredemeier's (1992) notion that research should focus on differences within a group of boys or girls rather than drawing dichotomous conclusions about the sexes.

The choice of curricular offerings is the main determinant of students' positive or negative attitudes toward physical education (Luke & Sinclair, 1991). Researchers have suggested that curricular offerings be thoroughly scrutinized. As students progress through school they become less physically active (Freedson & Rowland, 1992). To keep students actively engaged, it has been suggested that traditionally sex stereotyped sports such as football and softball be removed from the curricula (Vertinsky, 1992). Another alternative is to redesign team sports to emphasize developing personal skill, and "offering a broader range of optional and learner centered activities (including self-defense) with the potential of becoming long-term leisure pursuits" (Vertinsky, 1992, p. 385).

Other skills that move away from the traditionally competitive emphasis can be developed through physical activity. For example, teaching cooperation, social skills, and self- and social responsibility are alternative foci to that of learning physical skills (Hellison & Georgiadis, 1992; Mercier, 1992; Williamson & Georgiadis, 1992). Again, teachers will need help in implementing appropriate strategies to achieve these educational ends (Vertinsky, 1992).

TEACHER AND STUDENT INTERACTIONS

Teachers are a potent force in students' positive or negative attitudes toward participation in physical education (Luke & Sinclair, 1991). Research on teacher interactions with students in physical education, however, tends to reflect educational research in general: Teachers display gender-biased perceptions and explanations for student behavior (Arrighi, Young, & O'Neil, 1985; Brawley, Landers, Miller, & Kearns, 1979; Griffin, 1985a; Macdonald, 1990), and interact with boys more than girls (Dunbar & O'Sullivan, 1986). If students perceive that teachers have stereotypic expectations for boys and girls, they are likely to respond to these expectations, resulting in the self-fulfilling prophecy (Martinek, 1989; Martinek, Crowe, & Rejeski, 1982). McBride (1990) suggested that gender stereotyping by physical education teachers may not be as extreme as assumed, though he cautioned that his results should not be generalized due to the small sample size of six teachers.

Some researchers have suggested that if negative emotional climates exist in the gymnasium against which students cannot be protected, the short-term solution might be single-sexed classes (Scraton, 1993). This controversial suggestion reflects a failure to bring about fairness in the gymnasium. Griffin (1985a) described, however, how a teacher who had taken courses in equity awareness provided a more equitable learning environment in his coeducational physical educational classes than veteran teachers who had no such preparation.

Teacher awareness of how inequities can occur is important when reviewing how race, religion, social class, and physical ability add various layers of discrimination that can affect girls' and boys' participation in physical education (Carroll & Hollinshead, 1993; Chepyator-Thomson, 1990; Smith, 1992; Sparks, Templin, & Schempp, 1993). In a study of high school students, Chepyator-Thomson (1990) reported that students formed their own cliques based on gender and racial groups, which interfered with class participation. For example, in frisbee class, students threw to friends in their gender and racial groups and excluded others not in their clique. With regards to activity opportunities, African-American women have been described as the most oppressed group in America. They are disproportionately placed at the bottom of the socioeconomic ladder and have fewer opportunities than others to participate in sports such as swimming, tennis, gymnastics, and golf (Smith, 1992).

Teacher sensitivity toward the implications of student diversity is important so as to enhance participation in physical education for all students. Carroll and Hollinshead (1993) provided a vivid example of how physical education teachers' lack of cultural understanding of girls from Bangladesh and Pakistan inhibited their participation. The students recounted that they were made to dress and perform activities that contradicted the way their families and communities expected them to live their lives. In contrast, Sloan (1995) emphasized how teachers in her school tried to develop culturally sensitive approaches to include girls in activity. Girls from India were allowed to wear long-sleeved shirts and pants in order to take part in swimming.

A teacher's use of language when interacting with students is another indication of social awareness and can contain implicit messages (Knoppers, 1988; Wright & King, 1990). For example, "girls' pushups" is inappropriate because of the gender connotation associated with girls seeming less competent than boys (Rich, 1994). Descriptions such as "level 1, 2, or 3" can be substituted for "girls' pushups," with each level reflecting a progressively more difficult developmental phase for doing a pushup. This allows students to select a level based on ability rather than gender. It is important for a teacher to reflect on the inclusiveness of language; for example, terminology such as *sportsmanship, first baseman, and man-to-man defense* can be replaced with *fair play, first base, and player-to-player defense* (Williamson, 1993).

Strategies teachers use to address situations in class also reflect their implicit beliefs about gender. As mentioned earlier, homophobic name calling reinforces gender stereotypes. A teacher's decision to interrupt or ignore such an occurrence indicates to students a teacher's approval or disapproval of such behavior. Messages relative to social values are communicated either intentionally or unintentionally. This phenomenon is referred to as the hidden curriculum (Bain, 1990; Dodds, 1985; Fernandez-Balboa, 1993): Students may come to understand sexist and discriminatory messages insidiously relayed tacitly by the teacher through language use, interaction with students, and labeling of activities as gender-specific. The results of the aforementioned studies emphasize the need for teachers to examine their own beliefs and practices when reflecting on their teaching methods.

CHALLENGING GENDER ROLE STEREOTYPING

With appropriate awareness preparation, teachers can create more equitable learning environments for students (Griffin, 1985a; Griffin & Placek, 1983; Hutchinson, 1995; Williamson & Williams, 1990). Lock (1993), however, cautions against attaining technical skills for overcoming gender bias in isolation from a discussion of the political nature of this struggle in schools. It is imperative that gender inequity is addressed with students and teachers in schools, as well as undergraduates in teacher preparation programs (Dodds, 1993; Scraton, 1993; Tinning, 1991).

Teachers can create a more equitable learning environment in physical education by

- understanding how social issues such as gender stereotyping can be perpetuated in physical education;
- acknowledging that such issues need to be confronted and dealt with in teaching;
- examining and perhaps changing current teaching practices; and
- advocating for support on issues of social justice in the school and community.

TEACHERS' VALUES, BELIEFS, AND PRACTICE

Teachers' beliefs can be transmitted to children and also can affect their participation in physical education. Examining personal beliefs and practices, however, can be difficult (Evans, 1989; Griffin, 1989c). If teachers are open to change, creating a more equitable environment is possible. A first step is understanding the process of bringing about change in teaching. Bressan and Weiss (1982) developed a theory of instruction to help teachers change current practice and enhance student learning.

Research on teacher values indicates that the majority of female and male professionals are supportive of such issues as women's rights and concerned about equality and social justice (Duquin, Bredemeier, Oglesby, & Greendorfer, 1984). It seems that although the majority of teachers know that gender differences can exist, it is less clear to what extent such issues are addressed in practice.

There are various articles to help teachers reflect on their biases and improve teaching practices (Dodds, 1993; Evans, 1989; Griffin, 1989c; Griffin & Placek, 1983; Hutchinson, 1995; Macdonald & Jobling, 1992; Williamson, 1993). These articles deal with issues such as teachers' assumptions about girls' and boys' skill levels and their use of inclusive language, implementing a variety of teaching strategies to enhance learning for all students, group formation, curricula offerings, methods of assessment and evaluation, student interactions, and discussion of equity issues with students.

In a recent qualitative study of four physical education teachers (Tsangaridou, 1993), teacher sensitivity to gender issues was very apparent. The teachers explained how reflective they had become about social issues in their teaching and how important it was to address such issues in class. Pedagogical strategies included taking time to discuss gender issues with students; encouraging students to work with a partner focusing on skill development, as opposed to being overly concerned about the sex of the partner; and bringing in female graduates of the school who had gone on to become successful high school athletes to talk to and act as role models for grade 4, 5, and 6 students. Two problems that teachers confronted, however, were the embedded gender socialization that students brought into the classroom and sexist language used by other teachers in the school building. It is difficult to promote equity in the gymnasium unless education colleagues are also committed to the task (Griffin, 1989c; Williamson, 1993). This also extends to the support of other teachers in the school and school policy itself.

PARENTAL AND COMMUNITY SUPPORT

Society places pressure on boys and girls to behave in certain ways. These behaviors begin at home. Griffin (1989c) emphasized that parental and community support were ". . . crucial to successfully implementing co-ed classes" (p. 21). Griffin raised an important issue about parents giving appropriate support if they perceive physical education to be an important part of their child's curriculum. Parental and community advocacy, however, is an area in which physical educators need to improve (Sloan, 1995).

A recent study revealed that few parents of high school students were physically active (Tannehill, Romar, O'Sullivan, England, & Rosenberg, 1994). The researchers suggested that as so many parents were inactive, there was probably a lack of meaningfulness in the parents' own physical education experiences. This lack of parental activity may have also contributed to their less than supportive role for their children's physical education experiences.

SUMMARY

Confronting gender inequity within ourselves can be a difficult challenge. This task is compounded when the media invariably bombard us with attempts to dichotomize the "differences" between boys and girls. Titles of articles such as "Boys *Will* Be Boys" (Fiely, 1995) and "Sizing Up the Sexes" (Gorman, 1992) reiterate the way the media can accentuate differences rather than similarities between boys and girls. As teachers, however, it is our task to reflect within ourselves and examine the extent to which we can help promote a more equitable learning environment for all children. This may involve "unlearning" assumptions that we have held in the past. By looking more critically at our own beliefs and teaching practices, we may expand the educational opportunities of our students.

Change starts with the individual, but it also needs the support of colleagues, administrators, and the community. Perhaps with better public relations—and teachers' willingness to challenge and change current teaching practices—physical education classes can be places in which all students experience success, feel emotionally safe, and learn skills for participating in lifelong activity.

---

[1]The American Psychological Association ([APA], 1994) does not recognize that this distinction is quite so clear. It is stated that "gender is cultural and is the term to use when referring to men and women as social groups. Sex is biological; use it when biological distinction is predominant." APA stated that as the term sex can be confused with sexual behavior the term gender is preferable in writing as it "helps keep meaning unambiguous" (p. 47).

REFERENCES

Adler, P.A., Kless, S.J., Adler, P. (1992). Socialization to gender roles: Popularity among elementary school boys and girls. *Sociology of Education, 65,* 169–187.

American Alliance for Health, Physical Education, Recreation and Dance. (1988). *Physical Best: The American Alliance physical fitness education & assessment program.* Reston, VA: Author.

American Association of University Women. (1992). *How schools shortchange girls.* Wellesley, MA: The Wellesley College Center for Research on Women.

American Psychological Association. (1994). *Publication manual of the American Psychological Association* (4th ed.). Washington, DC: Author.

Arrighi, M., Young, J., & O'Neil, L. (1985). Equity in the gymnasium: Curricular and instructional implications. *Proceedings of the Fourth Conference on Curriculum Theory in Physical Education* (pp. 168–183). Athens, GA: University of Georgia.

Ayers, W. (1989). Childhood at risk. *Educational Leadership, 46*(2), 70–72.

Bain, L.L. (1990). A critical analysis of the hidden curriculum in physical education. In D. Kirk & R. Tinning (Eds.), *Physical education, curriculum and culture: Critical issues in the contemporary crisis* (pp. 23–42). London: The Falmer Press.

Blinde, E.M., & Greendorfer, S.L. (1992). Conflict and college sport experience of women athletes. *Women in Sport and Physical Activity Journal, 1*(1), 97–113.

Brawley, L.R., Landers, D.M., Miller, L., & Kearns, K.F. (1979). Sex bias in evaluating motor performance. *Journal of Sports Psychology, 1*(1), 15–24.

Bredemeier, B.J.O. (1992). "And ain't I a woman?" Toward a multicultural approach to gender and morality. *Quest, 44,* 179–209.

Bressan, E.S., & Weiss, M.R. (1982). A theory of instruction for developing competence, self-confidence, and persistence in physical education. *Journal of Teaching in Physical Education, 1,* 38–47.

Bruce, T. (1993). Title IX: 21 years of progress? *Women in Sport and Activity Journal, 2*(1), 73–79.

Carlson, T.B. (1994). *Why students hate, tolerate, or love gym: A study of attitude formation and associated behaviors in physical education.* Unpublished doctoral dissertation, University of Massachusetts, Amherst.

Carroll, B., & Hollinshead, G. (1993). Equal opportunities: Race and gender in physical education. In J. Evans, (Ed.), *Equality, education, & physical education* (pp. 154–169). London: The Falmer Press.

Chepyator-Thomson, J.R. (1990). *Stratification in an American secondary school: Issues of race, gender, and physical ability in physical education.* Unpublished doctoral dissertation, University of Wisconsin, Madison.

Chrysler Fund-Amateur Athletic Union (AAU). (1987). *Physical fitness program.* Bloomington, IN: Author

Coakley, J.J. (1994). *Sports in society: Issues and controversies* (5th ed.). St. Louis: Mosby.

Cooper Institute for Aerobics Research. (1992). *The Prudential FITNESSGRAM technical reference manual.* Dallas: Author.

Crawford, J.R. (1994). Encouraging male participation in dance. *Journal of Physical Education, Recreation and Dance, 65*(2), 40–43.

Dewar, A.M. (1987). The social construction of gender in physical education. *Women's Studies International Forum, 10,* 453–465.

Dodds, P. (1985). Are hunters of the functional curriculum seeking quarks or snarks? *Journal of Teaching in Physical Education, 4,* 91–99.

Dodds, P. (1993). Removing the ugly 'isms' in your gym: Thoughts for teachers on equity. In J. Evans (Ed.), *Equality, education, & physical education* (pp. 28–29). London: The Falmer Press.

Dos Santos, K. (January 28, 1994). The sound of great voices. *The Tribal Tribune, 20* (1), p. 2.

Dunbar, R.R., & O'Sullivan, M.M. (1986). Effects of intervention on differential treatment of boys and girls in elementary physical education lessons. *Journal of Teaching in Physical Education, 5,* 166–175.

Duquin, M.E., Bredemeier, B.J., Oglesby, C., & Greendorfer, S.L. (1984). Teacher values: Political and social justice orientations of physical educators. *Journal of Teaching in Physical Education, 3,* 9–19.

Eccles, J.L., & Harold, R.D. (1991). Gender differences in sport involvement: Applying the Eccles' expectancy-value model. *Journal of Applied Sports Psychology, 3*(1), 7–35.

Evans, J. (1986). A look at the team selection process. *Canadian Association of Health, Physical Education, and Recreation Journal, 52*(5), 4–9.

Evans, J. (1989). Equality and opportunity in the physical education curriculum. *The Australian Council for Health, Physical Education, and Recreation National Journal,* (123), 8–11.

Felshin, J., & Oglesby, C.A. (1986). Transcending tradition: Females and males in open competition. *Journal of Physical Education, Recreation and Dance, 57*(3), 44–47, 64.

Ferdun, E. (1994). Facing gender issues across the curriculum. *Journal of Physical Education, Recreation and Dance, 65*(2), 46–47.

Fernandez-Balboa, J.M. (1993). Sociocultural characteristics of the hidden curriculum in physical education. *Quest, 45,* 230–254.

Fiely, D. (September 1, 1995). Boys *will* be boys. *The Columbus Dispatch,* Section F, 1–2.

Freedson, P.S., & Rowland, T.W. (1992). Youth activity versus youth fitness: Let's redirect our efforts. *Research Quarterly for Exercise and Sport, 63,* 133–136.

Goldberg, A.D., & Chandler, T.J.L. (1991). Sport participation among adolescent girls: Role conflict or multiple roles? *Sex Roles, 25,* 213–225.

Gorman, C. (1992). Sizing up the sexes. *Time, 139*(3), 42–51.

Gould, L. (1978). *X: A fabulous child's story.* New York: Daughters Publishing.

Grant, L. (1984). Black females' "place" in desegregated classrooms. *Sociology of Education, 57,* 98–110.

Greendorfer, S.L., & Brundage, C.L. (1987). Gender differences in children's motor skills. In M.J. Adrian (Ed.), *Sports women* (pp. 125–137). New York: Karger.

Griffin, P. (1983). Gymnastics is a girls' thing: Student participation and interaction patterns in a middle school physical education unit. In T. Templin & J. Olsen (Eds.), *Teaching in physical education* (pp. 71–85). Champaign, IL: Human Kinetics.

Griffin, P. (1984). Girls' participation styles in a middle school physical education team sports unit. *Journal of Teaching in Physical Education, 4,* 30–38.

Griffin, P. (1985a). Teachers' perceptions of and responses to sex equity problems in a middle school physical education program. *Research Quarterly for Exercise and Sport, 56,* 103–110.

Griffin, P. (1985b). Boys' participation styles in a middle school physical education team sports unit. *Journal of Teaching in Physical Education, 4,* 30–38.

Griffin, P. (1989a). Homophobia in physical education. *Canadian Association of Health, Physical Education, Recreation Journal, 55*(2), 27–31.

Griffin, P. (1989b). Equity in the gym: What are the hurdles? *Canadian Association of Health, Physical Education, Recreation Journal, 55*(2), 23–26.

Griffin, P. (1989c). Assessment of equitable instructional practices in the gym. Canadian Association of Health, Physical Education, Recreation Journal, 55(2), 19–22.

Griffin, P. (1992). Changing the game: Homophobia, sexism, and lesbians in sport. *Quest, 44,* 251–265.

Griffin, P., & Placek, J. (1983). *Fair play in the gym.* Amherst, MA: University of Massachusetts.

Grossman H., & Grossman, S.H. (1994). *Gender issues in education.* Boston, MA: Allyn & Bacon.

Haywood, K. (1986). *Life span and motor development.* Champaign, IL: Human Kinetics.

Hellison, D., & Georgiadis, N. (1992). Teaching values through basketball. *Strategies, 5*(4), 5–8.

Hutchinson, G. E. (1995). Gender-fair teaching in physical education. *Journal of Physical Education, Recreation and Dance, 66*(1), 42–47.

Ignico, A.A. (1989). Elementary physical education: Color it androgynous. *Journal of Physical Education, Recreation and Dance, 60*(2), 23–24.

Isaac, T. (1992). Lexington Division of Parks and Recreation studies gender equity programming. *The Full Court Press: Citizens for Sports Equity, 6*(1), 9.

Kerr-Berry, J.A. (1994). Using the power of West African dance to combat gender issues. *Journal of Physical Education, Recreation and Dance, 65*(2), 44–45, 48.

King, W.C., Miles, E.W., & Kniska, J. (1991). Boys will be boys (and girls will be girls): The attribution of gender role stereotypes in a gaming situation. *Sex Roles, 25,* 607–623.

Knoppers, A. (1988). Equity for excellence in physical education. *Journal of Physical Education, Recreation and Dance, 59*(6), 54–58.

Lay, N.E. (1990). A Title IX dialogue. *Journal of Physical Education, Recreation and Dance, 61*(5), 83–84.

Leaman, O. (1986). Physical education and sex differentiation. *British Journal of Physical Education, 17,* 123–124.

Lenskyj, H.J. (1994). Girl-friendly sport and female values. *Women in Sport and Physical Activity Journal, 3*(1), 35–45.

Lirgg, C.D. (1992). Girls and women, sport, and self-confidence. *Quest, 44,* 158–178.

Lock, R. (1993). Women in sport and physical education: A review of the literature in selected journals. *Women in Sport and Physical Activity Journal, 2*(2), 21–49.

Luke, M.D., & Sinclair, G.D. (1991). Gender differences in adolescents' attitudes toward physical education. *Journal of Teaching in Physical Education, 11,* 31–46.

Macdonald, D. (1990). The relationship between sex composition of physical education classes and teacher/pupil verbal interaction. *Journal of Teaching in Physical Education, 9,* 152–163.

Macdonald, D., & Jobling, I. (1992). A checklist for gender equity in school sport. *The Australian Council for Health, Physical Education and Recreation National Journal,* (135), 23–25.

Madrigal, K., & Williamson, K M. (1994). Sports, fitness, and fun: A male teacher's and female students' perceptions and practice of physical education. *Illinois Journal for Health, Physical Education, Recreation, and Dance, 34* (Spring), 37–46.

Martinek, T.J. (1989). Children's perceptions of teaching behaviors: An attributional model for explaining teacher expectancy effects. *Journal of Teaching in Physical Education, 8,* 318–328.

Martinek, T., Crowe, P., & Rejeski, W. (1982). *Pygmalion in the gym: Causes and effects of expectations in teaching and coaching.* Champaign, IL: Leisure Press.

McBride, R.E. (1990). Sex-role stereotyping behaviors among elementary, junior, and senior high school physical education specialists. *Journal of Teaching in Physical Education, 9,* 249–261.

Mercier, R. (1992). Beyond class management—Teaching social skills through physical education. *Journal of Physical Education, Recreation and Dance, 63*(6), 83–87.

Oakley, A. (1972). *Sex, gender, and society.* London: Temple-Smith.

Oldenhove, H. (1989). The Commonwealth Sex Discrimination Act (1984) and children's sport: Policy and implications. In K. Dyer (Ed.), *Sportswomen towards 2000* (pp. 188–192). Richmond, South Australia: Hyde Park Press.

Parish, R., Eubanks, E., Aquila, F.D., & Walker, S. (1989). Knock at any school. *Phi Delta Kappan, 70,* 386–394.

Rich, N.C. (1994). Female strength and neuromuscular response time: A review. *Women in Sport and Physical Activity Journal, 3*(1), 47–72.

Rozdilsky, R., Williamson, K.M., & Wilkinson, S. (1992, April). *The perpetuation of sexism through physical fitness testing.* Paper presented at the Annual Conference of the American Alliance for Health, Physical Education, Recreation and Dance, Indianapolis.

Safrit, M.J., & Looney, M.A. (1992). Should the punishment fit the crime? A measurement dilemma. *Research Quarterly for Exercise and Sport, 61,* 124–127.

Scraton, S. (1992). Shaping up to womanhood: Gender and girls' physical *education.* Philadelphia: Open University Press.

Scraton, S. (1993). Equality, coeducation and physical education in secondary schooling. In J. Evans (Ed.), *Equality, education, & physical education* (pp. 139–153). London: The Falmer Press.

Sloan, J. (1995). Keeping the dreams alive. In J.A. Williams & K.M. Williamson (Eds.), *Beginning to teach physical education: The inside stories* (pp. 75-81). Dubuque, IA: Kendall/Hunt.

Smith, Y.R. (1992). Women of color in society and sport. *Quest, 44,* 228–250.

Snyder, M. (1982, July). Self-fulfilling stereotypes. *Psychology Today,* pp. 60–68.

Sparkes, A.C., Templin, T.J., & Schempp, P.G. (1993). Exploring dimensions of marginality: Reflecting on life histories of physical education teachers. In S. Stroot (Ed.), Socialization into physical education [Monograph]. *Journal of Teaching in Physical Education, 12*(4), 386–398.

Streitmatter, J. (1994). *Toward gender equity in the classroom: Everyday teachers' beliefs and practices.* Albany, NY: State University Press.

Stromquist, N.P. (1993). Sex-equity legislation in education: The state as promoter of women's rights. *Review of Educational Research, 63,* 379–409.

Sutton, R.E. (1991). Equity and computers in the schools: A decade of research. *Review of Educational Research, 61,* 475–503.

Talbot, M. (1986). Gender and physical education. *British Journal of Physical Education, 17,* 120–122.

Tannehill, D., Romar, J.E., O'Sullivan, M., England, K., & Rosenberg, D. (1994). Attitudes towards physical education: Their impact on how physical education teachers make sense of their work. *Journal of Teaching in Physical Education, 13,* 406–420.

Theberge, N. (1991). A content analysis of media coverage of gender, women and physical activity. *Journal of Applied Sport Psychology, 3*(1), 36–48.

Thomas, J.R., & Thomas, K.T. (1988). Development of gender differences in physical activity. *Quest, 40,* 219–229.

Tinning, R. (1991). Teacher education pedagogy: Dominant discourses and the process of problem setting. *Journal of Teaching in Physical Education, 11,* 1–20.

Tsangaridou, N. (1993). *Teachers' reflection and its role in shaping their educational values and practices: A naturalistic study of experienced physical education teachers.* Unpublished doctoral dissertation, The Ohio State University, Columbus.

Turvey, J., & Laws, C. (1988). Are girls losing out? The effects of mixed-sex grouping on girls' performance in physical education. *The British Journal of Physical Education, 19,* 253–255.

U.S. Department of Health and Human Services. (1987). *The Presidential Physical Fitness Award Program: Instructor's guide.* Washington, DC: Author.

Vertinsky, P.A. (1992). Reclaiming space, revisioning the body: The quest for gender-sensitive physical education. *Quest, 44,* 373–396.

Weiss, M.R., & Glenn, S.D. (1992). Psychological development and females' sport participation: An interactional perspective. *Quest, 44,* 138–157.

Wells, C.L. (1992). Issues and future directions for lifelong physical activity. The physiological perspective for women. *Women in Sport and Physical Activity Journal, 1*(1), 1–17.

Williams, J.A. & Williamson, K.M. (Eds.). (1995). *Beginning to teach physical education: The inside stories.* Dubuque, IA: Kendall/Hunt.

Williamson, K.M. (1993). Is your inequity showing? Ideas and strategies for creating a more equitable learning environment. *Journal of Physical Education, Recreation and Dance, 64*(8), 15–23.

Williamson, K.M., & Georgiadis, N. (1992). Teaching an inner-city after-school program. *Journal of Physical Education, Recreation and Dance, 63*(8), 14–18.

Williamson, K.M., & Williams, J.A. (1990). Promoting equity awareness in the preparation of undergraduate physical education students. *Teaching Education, 3*(1), 117–123.

Wright, J., & King, R.O.C. (1990). "I say what I mean," said Alice: An analysis of gender discourse in physical education. *Journal of Teaching in Physical Education, 10,* 210–225.

CHAPTER 6

Students With Disabilities in Physical Education

Karen P. DePauw

Although individuals with disabilities have existed in society throughout history, their widespread inclusion and acceptance in public life is a modern phenomenon (DePauw, 1986; Hewett & Forness, 1974). The inclusion of students with disabilities in public schools is a rather recent development, a process characterized by varying educational systems and approaches. With strong advocacy for individuals with disabilities (starting in the 1970s and receiving its greatest emphasis to date with the passage of the Americans with Disabilities Act of 1990), disability rights (civil rights) have come to the forefront. This has been demonstrated by the push toward integration of individuals with disabilities in society and our public schools, including physical education classes. Recent statistics indicate that 93% of individuals with disabilities are being educated in regular education settings (including physical education) (United States Department of Education, 1991). Thus, it is important that physical educators not only be aware of but also be trained to teach students with disabilities. Our task is to provide physical education courses which enable students of all capabilities to develop and learn. For many physical educators, this represents a challenge not previously confronted; but it is one we are most capable of accomplishing. It begins with an understanding of disability and adapted physical activity which can be translated into practice (Block, 1994a, 1994b; Craft, 1994a; DePauw & Goc Karp, 1994a).

DEFINITIONS

The terms which follow are used throughout this chapter. Other terms which may be unfamiliar to the reader will be defined in the context of discussion.

Impairment, disability, and handicap are three terms which have been applied somewhat interchangeably to the performance or appearance of individuals who are perceived to deviate from that defined as "normal." In this context, impairment is defined as an identifiable organic or functional condition which an individual exhibits. Disability is defined as ". . . a loss or reduction of functional ability and/or activity" (World Health Organization, 1980). Although used previously in legislation, handicap is now thought to imply devaluation as a result of the impairment or disability and a socially constructed view of "typical" performance (Seaman & DePauw, 1989).

The most acceptable of these terms is disability. Using "people first" language—placing emphasis on the person instead of the disability—translates into terminology such as "individuals with disabilities." Disabilities vary not only in degree but in kind. The legally defined categories and prevalence of disabilities among the school-age population are presented in Table 6.1. As shown, approximately 10% of the school-age population are identified as students with disabilities.

Physical education is among the services mandated by federal law to be provided to school-age individuals with disabilities. In 1952, adapted physical education was defined as a "diversified program of developmental activities, games, sport, and rhythms suited to the interests, capacities,

Table 6.1 Prevalence of Disability Found Among the School-Age Population

Category	Prevalence (%) 1984-1985	Estimated
Learning impairments	4.1	2.0–4.0
Speech/language impairments	2.5	3.4–5.0
Mental retardation	1.6	2.5–3.0
Serious emotional disturbance	0.8	2.0–3.0
Multiple impairments	<0.2	
Hearing impairments	<0.2	0.6–0.8
Health impairments	<0.2	
Orthopedic impairment	<0.1	0.5
Visual impairments	<0.1	0.1

From *Eighth Annual Report to Congress on Implementation of the Education of the Handicapped Act*, 1986.

and limitations of students with disabilities who may not safely or success-fully engage in unrestricted participation in the vigorous activities of the general physical education programs" (AAHPERD, 1952). Although adapted physical education still refers to school-based programs of physical education provided to students with disabilities, current programs assume different forms ranging from regular physical education to highly specialized programs in segregated settings.

It is important that physical educators be familiar with two other terms: *adapted physical activity* and *disability sport*. Adapted physical activity has become an umbrella term used worldwide to encompass such areas as physical education, recreation, dance, sport, fitness, and rehabilitation for individuals with impairments across the life span (DePauw & Doll-Tepper, 1989; Poretta, Nesbitt, & Labanowich, 1993). Adapted physical activity refers to a cross-disciplinary study which attempts to: identify and solve motor problems throughout the life span of affected individuals; develop and implement theories which support access to sport and active lifestyle; and develop cooperative home-school-community service delivery and empowerment systems (DePauw & Sherrill, 1994).

Obviously, adapted physical activity needs to be dealt with in programs beyond those which are typical in the schools. Disability sport is one of these additional programs. It refers to sport that has been designed for, modified to include, or practiced in its unrestricted form by individuals with disabilities (DePauw & Gavron, 1995). Given the increasing emphasis on connections among school, family, and community, it is important that physical educators be aware of activity-based opportunities for individuals with disabilities that exist beyond the schoolyard.

HISTORICAL PERSPECTIVES ON DISABILITY

There have been individuals with perceived or real differences throughout history, but the ways in which these persons were treated varied depending on the individual, the perceived nature of the impairment, and the societal or cultural values and norms of the time. At one time or another, these individuals were destroyed, tortured, exorcised, sterilized, ignored, exiled, exploited, pitied, cared for, categorized, educated, and even considered divine (Hewett & Forness, 1974; for more detailed discussion, see also DePauw, 1990a).

Survival and superstition were key elements of ancient society (3000 BC to 500 BC); individuals considered to be obviously physically deformed or physically incapable of hunting for food or defending themselves were left to face the consequences of the harsh environment—the ultimate consequence being death (Davies, 1975). Sometimes superstition resulted in the belief that individuals with mental impairments were possessed:

Those possessed with "good spirits" were revered, those with "bad spirits" were indulged to prevent their seeking revenge (Hewett & Forness, 1974). Persons born with impairments continued to face a harsh physical environment and the possibility of infanticide through Greek and Roman history from 500 BC to 400 AD, except for a "brief period of humanitarian reform" initiated by Plato and Hippocrates (Hewett & Forness, 1974). They advocated care, not exile, or exorcism, for those with mental impairment. Additionally, physical activity or exercise, hydrotherapy, massage, and exposure to sunshine were provided to individuals with disabilities.

The Middle Ages (AD 400–1500) brought the religious influence to bear on the evolving perspective of disability. During the same historical period, the Laws of Moses forbade the Hebrews from putting to death those who were deformed, but individuals with disabilities were not allowed to pray in the Temple (Davies, 1975). The rise of Christianity resulted in distinct differences in the treatment of people with various mental impairments. For example, those with mental retardation were thought to be "children of God," while those with mental illness were viewed as "possessed by the devil." Mentally retarded individuals were protected and tolerated, but their quality of life was quite limited. Those thought to be possessed were subject to exorcism and torture, and witch burning persisted (Hewett & Forness, 1974).

During the 16th and 17th centuries, science and medicine influenced the treatment of individuals with disabilities. Although severe persecution of individuals with noticeable differences continued, and the belief in demonology persisted, those with hearing impairments and mental retardation received more humanitarian treatment. For example, deaf children were provided with education afforded only to a privileged few, and mental retardation was studied from psychological and educational perspectives.

Initial acceptance of individuals with disabilities occurred during the 18th century. This period was characterized by the transition from fear, superstition, and hostility toward individuals with disabilities to caring, understanding, and education of these same individuals. The French Revolution awakened the sense of individual responsibility and led to humane treatment of individuals considered to be mentally ill. Treatment during this period involved the use of asylums, hospitals, or schools as residential institutions, and a tradition of humanitarian teaching was begun. In addition to institutions for individuals with mental illness, schools for children who were blind and deaf appeared by the end of the 18th century.

The development of such institutions led to the beginnings of educational treatment during the 19th century. Due to the efforts of such individuals as Jean Marc Itard, Eduoard Sequin, and Maria Montessori, an individualized, clinical (medical) methodology and an educational system evolved that stressed physical, intellectual, and moral development. Residential institutions, such as those in Europe for persons who were deaf, blind, or considered mentally retarded (or feeble-minded), appeared in the United States.

The 20th century is viewed as a period of social reform; a period influenced by the return home of many injured veterans of war, increased governmental intervention on behalf of individuals with disabilities, and the emergence of concern about disability, especially in the fields of education, psychology, and medicine. Identification and proliferation of handicapping conditions resulted. Society continued to label those who were different, resulting in the proliferation of terminology applying to handicapping conditions. Special education flourished; adapted physical education evolved. During the 1990s, the disability rights movement dramatically altered the social reforms of the earlier 20th century. For a critique and analysis of events during this period, see DePauw (1986) and Shapiro (1993).

CURRENT PERSPECTIVES ON DISABILITY

Our current notions about disability have historical roots in the medical profession (Chappell, 1992), which tended to view disability as a problem of the individual (Barnes, 1990). This approach to disability emanated from a theory of deviance (e.g., Freidson, 1965) and stigma (e.g., Brown & Smith, 1989; Goffman, 1963) and has resulted in a proliferation of labels for individuals with handicapping conditions, or impairments. The emphasis on conditions or characteristics (impairments) has perpetuated a categorical approach to treatment and intervention, leading to the development of segregated adapted physical education programs and specialized physical education programs for individuals with specific disabilities (e.g., for persons with mental retardation, or for persons who are blind).

The current disability rights movement challenges us to consider disability not as an individual problem but rather as a societal one (Chappell, 1992; Hanks & Poplin, 1981)—as a social role that has become legitimized over time (e.g., Haber & Smith, 1971; Lemert, 1951; Shapiro, 1993). At the core of this movement is the belief that disability is neither tragic nor pitiable (Shapiro, 1993, p. 20), and that those with disabilities take pride in defining themselves as being disabled and reject the stigma or shame traditionally associated with their condition. When disability is seen as a personal problem, the individual is "blamed" and thus the individual alone must change. Only when disability is seen in the context of social relationships is serious societal change possible.

Although full participation by individuals with disabilities in many societies is still far from a reality, the general trend has been one of progressive inclusion and acceptance (DePauw, 1986). Individuals with disabilities who were excluded from society and schools are now being included. Physical education and sport programs have been forced to change as a result of progressive inclusion (DePauw, 1986), but complete inclusion must await a fully accessible society in which all persons have and are able to exercise freedom of choice. There must be increased access to regular physical education programs, a decrease in special schools and segregated settings, and inclusion of athletes with disabilities in Paralympic and Olympic-level competition.

HISTORICAL PERSPECTIVES ON ADAPTED PHYSICAL EDUCATION

The history of adapted physical education dates back to ancient China, where various forms of exercise were used to alleviate physical disorders and illness (Seaman & DePauw, 1989). The early Greek and Roman cultures also recognized the relationship between physical activity and well being. Over the centuries, the name and nature of physical activity programs for individuals with disabilities would change: medical, therapeutic, rehabilitative, healing, remedial, corrective, curative, special, developmental, and adapted (Sherrill, 1988). The populations served changed along with the role and scope of various service delivery systems (McKenzie, 1909; Rathbone, 1934; Sherrill, 1993). For a detailed discussion of the changing nature of adapted physical education, see Sherrill and DePauw (1996) and DePauw and Sherrill (1994).

Adapted physical education today is strongly influenced by a perspective that combines medical and educational theories drawn from 19th century Europe (Sherrill & DePauw, 1996). Per Henrik Ling (1776–1839) of Sweden advanced medical gymnastics. Sensory motor training evolved from the work of Jean Marc Itard (1775-1839) of France. The medical gymnastics approach was used in American public schools to prevent illness and to promote health, so early physical education in the United States took on a medical orientation—the first physical educators were physicians. Later physical education adopted a developmental emphasis, and this emphasis was incorporated early in adapted physical education, in which sensory motor training was used by special educators and perceptual motor theorists.

It wasn't until the 1950s that these two approaches became connected. Special education became a public school responsibility and the American Alliance for Health, Physical Education, Recreation and Dance (AAHPERD) took the first step toward acknowledging that physical education instruction, facilities, and equipment should be adapted to meet individual needs of both regular and special education students (Sherrill & DePauw, 1996). Adapted physical education programs were few and far between until the enactment of federal legislation in 1975.

CURRENT PERSPECTIVES ON ADAPTED PHYSICAL EDUCATION

Legislation mandating civil rights of individuals with disabilities was first passed in 1958 and continues to be proposed to the present day. The rights of persons to access programs, facilities, education (including physical education), and sport have been secured through a number of laws:

- PL 90-170, Elimination of Architectural Barriers Act (1968);
- PL 93-112, the Rehabilitation Act (1973), which prohibits discrimination on the basis of disability;
- PL 94-142, Education of All Handicapped Children's Act (1975), which mandates education, including physical education, for children with disabilities;
- PL 95-606, Amateur Sports Act (1978), which recognizes athletes with disabilities as part of the United States Olympic Movement; and
- the Americans with Disabilities Act of 1990 (ADA), a comprehensive law which extends the broad protections offered by the Civil Rights Act of 1964 to individuals with disabilities.

In addition to federal legislation, laws are in place that secure these same rights on a state and local level. Although some particulars might vary across the states, the basic rights remain the same. Among the key concepts of federal legislation for individuals with disabilities are free, appropriate public education (including physical education) in the least restrictive environment and the individualized education plan (IEP). Appropriate placement of students with disabilities is determined by a multidisciplinary team based upon the goals and objectives specified in the IEP.

The legal mandates of the 1970s helped transform adapted physical education from a medical model approach to an educational approach. Henceforth, programs were to be based on the assessment and selection of the least restrictive placement and services. Today, the traditional physical education class is viewed as the appropriate, least restrictive environment for students with disabilities. In addition, the emphasis is now on a cross-disciplinary, ecological, life-span model which empowers persons with disabilities to adopt healthy lifestyles and to use recreation and sport resources beyond the classroom (Seaman & DePauw, 1989; Sherrill, 1993; Sherrill & DePauw, 1996).

Adapted physical education must no longer be viewed as a place (regular versus adapted physical education), but rather as a service that allows individuals with disabilities to be fully integrated with nondisabled peers while accommodating special needs through consultation visits, team teaching, peer tutoring, and specially trained paraprofessionals (Sherrill & DePauw, 1996). In order to meet the needs of students with disabilities in physical education, the adapted physical education delivery system has evolved to one that is generally administered by an adapted physical education specialist employed by a school district to organize and implement the following services (Sherrill, 1993):

- Planning for the total community
- Assessment of individuals referred as having special needs
- Prescription/placement
- Teaching/consulting
- Evaluation of service delivery
- Coordination of resources
- Advocacy

Recently, adapted physical education has broadened in scope by offering programs that address the needs of diverse populations (e.g., at-risk youth, those affected with HIV/AIDS, and persons with severe and multiple impairments) and challenge individuals with disabilities (e.g., competitive sports and high-risk sports, such as mountain climbing and sky diving). Today's physical education programs provide more individualized activities and offer more choices; less emphasis is placed upon the activity and more on the individual's interests and needs. The categorical approach (e.g., restrictive activities based on specific disabilities and segregation of students with disabilities), which characterized much early adapted physical education, is finally giving way to programs that promote integration and inclusion.

To keep up with the changing nature of public school adapted physical education programs, professional preparation programs in colleges and universities must change. A current goal of many professional preparation programs is to infuse regular education courses with content about disability and individual differences, as well as to structure separate courses for awareness for all and specialization for some (DePauw & Goc Karp, 1994a, 1994b). This infusion philosophy is also evident in public school workshops and state and national conferences which serve as inservice training vehicles for experienced teachers.

HISTORICAL PERSPECTIVES ON RESEARCH

Research on adapted physical activity (adapted physical education and disability sport) has been conducted since the early 1900s (Broadhead, 1986; DePauw, 1988, 1992; Pyfer, 1986; Stein, 1983) (see note at end of chapter). Throughout, research questions have continued to evolve, research designs and methodology have improved, and numbers and groupings of individuals have increased. For an overview of research related to fitness and physical activity, see Shephard (1990).

Prior to the 1960s, adapted physical activity research described the growth and development of individuals with specific types of impairments, identified postural disorders, and determined impairment-specific motor characteristics. The populations studied included those with mental retardation, mental illness, and sensory impairment (auditory and visual), primarily from institutional settings.

Research conducted in the 1960s and 1970s examined the initial effects of fitness and exercise as well as perceptual motor programs for individuals with disabilities. Early intervention programs, program effectiveness, mainstreaming, behavior management approaches, and assessment/evaluation were studied during this time. In addition, the motor characteristics of selected disability groupings were identified; these groupings included autism, asthma, cerebral palsy, deafness, emotional disturbance, learning disability, mental retardation, obesity, and visual impairment.

During the 1970s, research on sport for individuals with disabilities was studied for the first time. Physiological (fitness, response to exercise) and biomechanical aspects (wheelchair propulsion) of sport performance were the two primary topics studied in the early days of disability sport research. These initial sports investigations were conducted in rehabilitation settings with males who had spinal cord injuries or polio. Disability sport research has progressed rapidly from investigations of sports for rehabilitation to research about, on, and for athletes with disabilities.

Research of the 1980s and 1990s increased the depth and breadth of our knowledge and understanding of adapted physical education. Specifically studied were

- scientific bases for motor performance,
- effects of physical activity,
- teaching and learning physical activity, and
- influences upon physical activity (DePauw, 1992).

Although research activity increased, the selected general findings presented below must only be viewed as preliminary, and the number of studies on any given topic remains limited.

1. In general, individuals with disabilities exhibit physiological responses to exercise similar to those found among able-bodied athletes. Differences in functional muscle mass due to paralysis, amputation, or osteoporosis in paralyzed limbs contribute to different responses to exercise. Differences in difficulty of comprehension, motivation, or mechanical inefficiency related to a specific condition (e.g., mental retardation, cerebral palsy) due to the severity of a physical impairment were also noted (Shephard, 1990). Based on the results of these studies, it is unclear whether differences in physiological responses are due to differences in physiological functioning or assessment techniques.

2. Despite the effect that a specific disability may have on the degree of intensity, duration, and frequency of exercise, evidence suggests that individuals with disabilities can benefit from training and improve performance.

3. Efficiency of wheelchair propulsion has been examined through studies of rim diameter, stroke frequency, seat height, technique, speed, level of impairment, and sporting event (sprint vs. distance). In particular, investigators have reported improved athletic performance (movement efficiency) due to a decrease in the mass of the chair as well as individual adaptations of seat height and inclination, camber of the wheels, and variations in handrim sizes.

4. Training and instructional physical activity programs have been reported as being beneficial to individuals with disabilities. The effectiveness of these programs depends on the specific type of program provided (e.g., fitness, balance, flexibility, motor skills).

It is important to highlight here the studies that have been undertaken in the area of sport pedagogy and individuals with disabilities. Findings are summarized in Table 6.2, and the following sections focus on these topics: (a) effective teaching and learning (time on task, management strategies, information processing, teacher behaviors); (b) attitudes toward individuals with disabilities; and (c) integration. For additional reading, see Block and Vogler (1994); DePauw and Goc Karp (1992); Vogler, DePaepe, and Martinek (1990); and Webster (1993).

EFFECTIVE TEACHING AND LEARNING

Although a body of knowledge exists about effective teaching and effective teachers, relatively little research has been conducted utilizing students with disabilities (Vogler, DePaepe, & Martinek, 1990; Webster, 1993). However, the available research does include studies which examined regular physical education, integrated or mainstreamed, and adapted physical education settings. Two early studies concluded that teaching strategies effective with able-bodied children were also effective with students with disabilities (Mawdsley, 1977; Taylor & Loovis, 1978). This initial research speaks to the commonality among students in physical education rather than to assumed differences based on disabilities.

TIME ON TASK

Effective teaching is said to be linked to student learning. A key issue related to student learning is Academic Learning Time-Physical Education (ALT-PE). This issue has been studied as it relates to individuals

Table 6.2 Summary of Selected Research Findings and Implications for Physical Education Instruction

Findings	Implications
Effective Teaching and Learning	
– Teaching strategies effective for able-bodied students effective for students with disabilities	– Select teaching strategies and modify as necessary
– Students with disabilities spent little time engaged in appropriate motor activity	– Increase time engaged in motor activity
– Primary and secondary reinforcers increased learning among students with severe/profound impairments	– Use meaningful, tangible reinforcers dependent upon type and level of impairment
– Individualized contingency and token economy effective with mild and behaviorally disordered students	
– Feedback improved performance	– Provide quality feedback
– Individualized instruction increased time on task	– Use peer tutors and individualized instruction
– Peer tutoring effective in increasing performance	
– Reverse chaining or random order more effective than blocked practice or drill for students with mental retardation	– Modify practice and learning strategies for students with mental retardation
– Teachers had lower expectations for students with disabilities	– Educate teachers about appropriate expectations
– Experienced teachers had greater repertoire of strategies for effective teaching	– Provide preservice teachers with more experience
Attitudes About Students With Disabilities	
– Perceived teacher competence best predictor of positive attitude toward students with disabilities	– Enhance competence of teachers
– Previous experience with individuals with disabilities resulted in more favorable attitudes	– Increase experiences with disabled persons
– Physical educators preferred students with learning impairments than physical impairments	– Help teachers modify activities for physically impaired
Integration	
– Integrated physical education did not cause differential learning	– Teach students with disabilities in integrated physical education settings
– For students with mild and moderate impairments, social and motor performance enhanced by inclusion	

with disabilities (Aufderheide, McKenzie, & Knowles, 1982; DePaepe, 1985; Gagnon, Tousignant & Martel, 1989; Miller, 1985; Webster, 1987). These studies indicated that students with disabilities spent relatively little time engaged in appropriate motor activity (e.g., 16%); nearly half their class period was spent waiting. As suggested by Webster (1993), strategies to facilitate individual attention, minimize disruptive behaviors, and enhance on-task performance are needed to increase student learning.

MANAGEMENT STRATEGIES

Effective classroom management strategies, appropriate placement, individualized instruction, and peer tutoring can enhance the meaningful participation of students with disabilities in physical education. Aufderheide et al. (1982) found that students with disabilities in an integrated setting with individualized instruction were engaged in motor activity at an appropriate level of difficulty more frequently than students who did not receive individualized instruction. Individualized instruction involves strategies such as individual tasks and practice, specific attention by the teacher, and peer tutoring.

Peer tutoring has been found to be effective not only in increasing ALT-PE, but also in actual, measured performance; increased static and dynamic balance (DePaepe, 1985); and increased gross motor proficiency among students with mental retardation (Bechtold, 1977). Webster (1987) found increases in activity levels of students with mental retardation with peer tutors regardless of the degree of training received by tutors. A study by DePaepe (1985) found that peer tutoring could be implemented effectively in either a segregated, or adapted, physical education as well as an integrated setting, but that effectiveness was dependent upon the ability of the student with a disability.

To increase time on task, adapted physical education teachers use a variety of behavior management techniques. Bishop and French (1982) studied the use of reinforcers with students with severe mental retardation and found that primary and sensory reinforcers were more effective than social praise in classes with students with severe mental retardation. Music was also determined to be a successful reinforcer which facilitated enhanced performance and increased time on task of students with profound mental retardation (Silliman & French, 1988). Thus, teachers are encouraged to identify specific reinforcers that are meaningful to the individual student and that facilitate attention to task (Bishop & French, 1982).

Jeltma and Vogler (1985) examined the effects of an individual contingency on students with behavioral disorders in physical education. They found that an individual contingency can be an effective behavioral strategy in modifying disruptive behavior and increasing on-task behavior.

These results were similar to those found by Vogler and French (1983), who studied group contingencies (i.e., Good Behavior Game) in activity-based programs. Further, the usual forms of behavior management (such as establishment of rules, simple social reinforcement, and warnings and admonitions) were ineffective with students with behavioral disorders.

For students with mild impairments, the use of a token economy was found to be effective. Bennett, Eisenman, French, Henderson, and Shultz (1989) used a single-subject, multiple baseline design to investigate the effect of a token economy on the exercise behavior and cardiovascular fitness of females with Down's Syndrome. The authors found that a token economy was effective in increasing exercise behavior. Token economy plus knowledge of results (KR) and token economy with KR and response cost were found to be more effective in increasing time on task than just knowledge of results (KR) or no reinforcement (Croce & Rock, 1988). Although students with disabilities demonstrated improved performance with feedback, Gauthier (1981) found that disabled students in a mainstreamed physical education class were less likely than their able-bodied counterparts to receive feedback following a movement response. Just as they do with all students, physical educators are encouraged to provide feedback to students with disabilities and to expect improvement in their performance.

An inverse relationship between the amount of teacher talk and the quality of teacher-student relationship was found. With more talk by the teacher, the students tended to tune out; students with disabilities were not able to process all the verbal information provided to them. In addition, Mawdsley (1977) found an inverse relationship between the amount of teacher criticism and the quality of teacher-student relationship; criticism contributed to negative classroom climate. On the other hand, an increase in teacher questioning correlated significantly with an increase in quality of student-teacher relationship. Thus, it appears that questioning promotes positive relationships and a positive climate.

Information Processing

A few studies have attempted to understand information processing and the effect of practice among students with mental retardation. Students with mild mental retardation performed significantly more accurately after they learned a task in random or sequenced format than in blocked order (Del Rey & Steward, 1989). Related, forward, and reverse chaining (sequencing) was studied by Hsu and Dunn (1984) using subjects with mental retardation. They found that those students in the reverse chaining group required significantly fewer trials and physical assists to learn motor tasks.

It is important to understand the variations inherent in an activity and to define them for students with disabilities prior to initiating practice (Poretta, 1988). Support for the utility of random practice schedules was found by Edwards, Elliott, and Lee (1986). The performance of subjects in their study who received random practice was more consistent than that of those who received blocked practice. This suggests that a drill type approach to motor skill acquisition may not be the best procedure, and that teachers should stress variability and variety when planning instructional sessions (Edwards, et al., 1986).

Teacher Behaviors

The success of any physical education program depends in part upon the teacher. Karper and Martinek (1982) found that teachers held lower expectations for motor performance of children with disabilities than those of able-bodied children, even though there was no significant variability in their performance in class. In addition, teachers expected more positive social relations with able-bodied students than with students with disabilities (Martinek & Karper, 1981). Inasmuch as expectations influence teacher behavior, teachers must not only provide feedback, but also distinguish between its types; in particular, the feedback needs to be specific and congruent with focus of task (Karper & Martinek, 1982). Vogler, van der Mars, Cusimano, and Darst (1992) studied experience, expertise, and teaching effectiveness with mainstreamed and able-bodied children in physical education. They found that (a) teacher behavior differed little as a function of either experience or expertise and (b) although mainstreamed students spent less time on task, and less time on tasks at a motor-appropriate level, than able-bodied students, neither teacher experience nor expertise altered those differences.

Solmon and Lee (1991) found that experienced teachers had superior knowledge and a better repertoire of teaching strategies for teaching students with disabilities. They were prepared with contingency plans based on the actions and abilities of students with disabilities, while novice teachers generated plans that were unidirectional and failed to accommodate the range of ability levels in the class (Solmon & Lee, 1991). The authors suggest that novice teachers should receive supervised training in teaching students with disabilities, develop effective management skills, and plan lessons to incorporate both variety and individualized instruction by involving all students at an appropriate level of difficulty with minimal waiting time. Further, Webster (1993) suggested that teachers (a) adapt and adjust to match the contextual environment, (b) maximize actual time on task for all students, (c) provide congruent, specific skill and behavior feedback, and (d) organize practice that promotes learning and retention.

ATTITUDES ABOUT DISABILITY

Research has been done on how attitudes about disability held by preservice students, physical education teachers, and physical education students influence meaningful physical activity programs. Much of the current body of knowledge has come from research by Terry Rizzo and his colleagues.

Physical education teachers' attitudes toward individuals with disabilities vary according to the students' type of impairment (Aloia, Knutson, Minner, & von Seggern, 1980; Rizzo, 1984; Rizzo & Wright, 1988). Specifically, physical educators prefer teaching students with learning impairments rather than students with physical impairments. Students with learning impairments were viewed more favorably than students with mild mental retardation or behavioral disorders (Rizzo & Vispoel, 1991). Perceived teacher competence was found not only to be significantly correlated with positive teacher attitudes (Rizzo & Wright, 1988) but as the best predictor of positive attitudes (Rizzo & Vispoel, 1991).

In another study, the age of the teacher was found to be negatively correlated with attitude; as the age of the teacher increased, positive attitudes decreased (Rizzo, 1985). This is probably because many older teachers received professional preparation which neglected adapted physical education, and failed to address the inclusion of individuals with disabilities in physical education.

Physical education and preservice students were found to hold varying attitudes about individuals with disabilities. Previous exposure to individuals with disabilities as well as to coursework in adapted physical education and special education was correlated to favorable attitudes among college students (Jansma & Shultz, 1982; Marston & Leslie, 1983; Rizzo, 1985). Rizzo (1984) found that students with disabilities were perceived more favorably by their peers in elementary school than in higher grades.

DePauw and Goc Karp (1990) studied selected college students (physical education, special education, and recreation majors) and found that most held stereotyped attitudes toward individuals with disabilities. In addition, the students expressed concern about the integration of students with learning and physical disabilities into school and community-based settings. These concerns tended to be centered on the logistics of integration (e.g., time limitation, additional burden on teacher, potential discipline problems) rather than its benefits—most agreed that integration could be beneficial to all students. It is interesting to note that special education majors were found to favor segregation or separate classes for individuals with disabilities more strongly than physical education or recreation majors.

INTEGRATION

Initial research on integration was undertaken with both students with mild and those with severe disabilities, but was limited to the classroom setting. Much of this research focused on benefits of inclusion on the academic achievement and social adjustment of students with disabilities;

examination of student-teacher interaction and behaviors; and effective teaching strategies and learning (see Block & Vogler, 1994). Now that the professional debate over the value of inclusion has subsided, research has moved toward ". . . implementation and organizational models of inclusion . . ." (p. 41).

Little research has focused on the integration of students with disabilities into regular physical education (Vogler, DePaepe, & Martinek, 1990) or on implementation and organizational models. As noted previously, much of the relevant research has compared student and teacher behaviors across educational settings (Silverman, Dodds, Placek, Shute, & Rife, 1984; Vogler, van der Mars, Cusiamano, & Darst, 1992) and found that education in integrated settings or "inclusion did not seem to be an obstacle to the learning process" of students with disabilities in physical education (Block & Vogler, 1994, p. 41). Specifically, Vogler et al. (1990) found that, based on time devoted to academic content and emotional climate, the mainstreamed environment was a good context for effective teaching, and that education in an integrated physical education setting did not cause differential learning. Furthermore, inclusion enhanced the social and motor performance of students with mild and moderate impairments (Beuter, 1983; Karper & Martinek, 1983).

RESEARCH DIRECTIONS

Research is needed to help teachers understand and effectively teach students with disabilities in physical education. In this regard, Block and Vogler (1994) suggested three directions for future research:

1. Comparison of integrated and segregated physical education placements upon motor development and performance of students with disabilities.
2. Determination of teacher factors that positively influence integration.
3. Effectiveness of specific curricular and instructional adaptations to integration.

Although such studies might effectively examine inclusion and the specific experience of students with disabilities, they fall short of revising our thinking about the teaching/learning process and incorporating disability as another variable in the process. Inasmuch as learning (or change) can be viewed as the result of the individual-environment interaction, DePauw and Goc Karp (1992) proposed an alternative framework for pedagogical research on teaching physical education to include diverse populations. The framework, shown in Figure 6.1, was adapted from Dunkin and Biddle (1974).

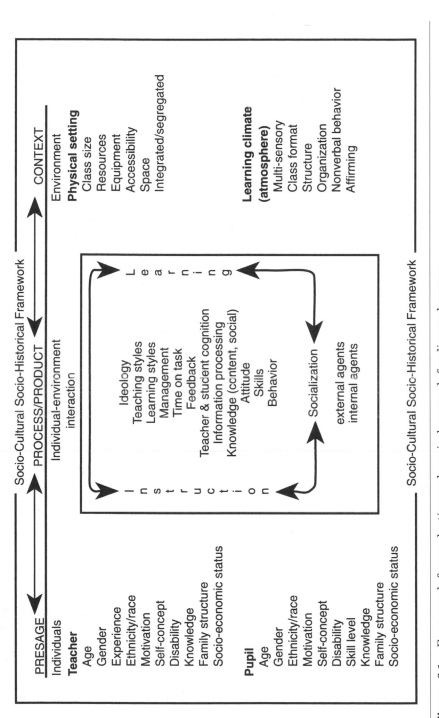

Figure 6.1. Framework for conducting pedagogical research for diverse learners

From "Framework for Conducting Pedagogical Research in Teaching Physical Education to Include Diverse Populations," by K.P. DePauw and G. Goc Karp. In *Sport and Physical Activity: Moving Toward Excellence* by T. William, L. Almond, and A. Sparkes (Eds.), 1992, London: E & FN Spon. Copyright 1992. Reprinted with permission.

This framework emphasizes

(a) interaction among variables which influence the teaching/learning process,
(b) a dynamic, not static, view of pedagogy,
(c) more attention to process than to product, and
(d) the influence of socio-historical and socio-cultural perspectives which are brought into the learning environment (DePauw & Goc Karp, 1992).

The inclusion of a broader societal context helps us realize that "forces such as politics, economics, social mores, cultural values, legal mandates and traditions" (p. 246) do influence the attitudes, beliefs, expectations, and motivations of teachers and pupils and the learning environment, as well as the interaction among variables. Research conducted using this framework must be viewed as dynamic, involving both qualitative and quantitative research designs; action research would be natural. Such a framework promotes the examination of disability as a social construct in the context of social relationships, rather than as an individual's problem.

CONCLUSION: INCLUSION

Although adapted physical education programs for students with disabilities are common, the inclusion of students with disabilities in regular physical education is rapidly becoming the reality (Block & Krebs, 1992). This means that physical education programs need to change in both curriculum and instruction. Innovative implementation and instructional models such as equal-status relationships through reciprocal modeling (Sherrill, Heikinaro-Johansson, & Slininger 1994) and collaboration (Maguire, 1994) need to be developed and evaluated.

For a lengthy discussion and debate about inclusion and least restrictive environment concepts, see the Spring 1994 issue of *Palaestra* (Block, 1994b; Sherrill, 1994). Specific programming tips and strategies for successful inclusion can be found in the feature on "Inclusion: Physical Education for All," edited by Craft (1994b) in the January 1994 issue of *Journal of Physical Education, Recreation and Dance* and in the book by Block, *A Teacher's Guide to Including Students with Disabilities in Regular Physical Education* (1994a).

In keeping with changes underway in the public schools, colleges and universities need to change the ways in which they prepare physical educators. A few have already adopted an infusion approach to the physical education/teacher education curriculum (e.g., DePauw, Lepore, Kowalski, Henderson, & Craft, 1993; Lepore & Kowalski, 1992). For more information and particulars about the role of higher education in preparing physical educators for inclusion and an infusion model for integrating knowledge of disability through the physical education curriculum, see DePauw and Goc Karp (1994a, 1994b).

Increasingly, physical education teachers can no longer rely on highly trained adapted physical education specialists to teach students with disabilities in segregated settings. The segregated settings have given way to integrated physical education settings and, more recently, to inclusion as a base for physical education instruction. Although adapted physical education specialists will be available as teachers and consultants, much of the responsibility for teaching students with disabilities will fall upon the shoulders of the regular physical education teachers.

The provision of physical education to individuals with disabilities does not need to be an overwhelming experience for teachers. Most physical educators already possess much of the basic knowledge and many of the skills necessary to teach individuals with disabilities, but have yet to be challenged to apply such knowledge or provided with a context in which to enhance their skills and abilities. The information contained in this book—and specifically this chapter—should help physical educators prepare for those challenges with reasonable expectations for success.

NOTE

The adapted physical education research literature is found in journals such as the *Adapted Physical Activity Quarterly, Palaestra, Physician and Sports Medicine, Research Quarterly for Exercise and Sport, Rehabilitation Yearbook, Journal of Teaching Physical Education, Medicine and Science in Sport and Exercise, Physical Educator, Physical Education Review, Journal of Biomechanics*, and *Journal of Applied Physiology*, as well as other journals which emphasize special education, rehabilitation, therapy (physical, occupational, corrective), and recreation. In addition, adapted physical activity research has been reported in volumes of compiled research such as *Completed Research in Health, Physical Education, Recreation & Dance* and *Abstracts of Research Presentations at American Alliance for Health, Physical Education, Recreation & Dance Convention*, initially published as separate volumes but now published as a supplement to *Research Quarterly for Exercise and Sport*.

REFERENCES

Aloia, G.F., Knutson, R., Minner, S.H., Von Seggern, M. (1980). Physical education teachers' initial perceptions of handicapped children. *Mental Retardation, 18* (2), 85–87.

American Alliance for Health, Physical Education, Recreation and Dance. (1952). Guiding principles for adapted physical education. *Journal of Health, Physical Education and Recreation, 23,* 15.

Aufderheide, S.K., McKenzie, T.L., & Knowles, C.J. (1982). Effect of individualized instruction on handicapped and nonhandicapped students in elementary physical education classes. *Journal of Teaching in Physical Education, 1,* 51–57.

Barnes, C. (1990). *Cabbage Syndrome: The social construction of dependence.* London: The Falmer Press.

Bechtold, W.W. (1977). The effect of a tutorial relationship between high school student volunteers and peer-aged moderately mentally retarded students participating in individually prescribed programs of physical activity. *Dissertation Abstracts International, 41,* 1472–74A.

Bennett, F., Eisenman, P., French, R., Henderson, H., & Shultz, B. (1989). The effect of a token economy on the exercise behavior of individuals with Down's Syndrome. *Adapted Physical Activity Quarterly, 6,* 230–246.

Beuter, A. (1983). Effects of mainstreaming on motor performance of intellectually normal and trainable mentally retarded students. *American Corrective Therapy Journal, 37,* 48–52.

Bishop, P., & French, R. (1982). Effects of reinforcers on attending behavior of severely handicapped boys in physical education. *Journal for Special Educators, 18,* 48–58.

Block, M.E. (1994a). *A teacher's guide to including students with disabilities in regular physical education.* Baltimore: Paul H. Brookes.

Block, M.E. (1994b). Why all students with disabilities should be included in regular physical education. *Palaestra, 10,* 17–24.

Block, M.E., & Krebs, P.L. (1992). An alternative to least restrictive environments: A continuum of support to regular physical education. *Adapted Physical Activity Quarterly, 9,* 97–113.

Block, M.E., & Vogler, E.W. (1994). Inclusion in regular physical education: The research base. *Journal of Physical Education, Recreation and Dance, 65,* 40–44.

Broadhead, G.D. (1986). Adapted physical education research trends: 1970-1990. *Adapted Physical Activity Quarterly, 3,* 104–111.

Brown, H., & Smith, H. (1989). Whose 'ordinary life' is it anyway? *Disability, Handicap & Society, 4* (2), 105–119.

Chappell, A.L. (1992). Towards a sociological critique of the normalization principle. *Disability, Handicap & Society, 7* (1), 35–50.

Craft, D.H. (1994a). Implications of inclusion for physical education. *Journal of Physical Education, Recreation and Dance, 65,* 54–56.

Craft, D.H. (1994b). Inclusion: Physical education for all. *Journal of Physical Education, Recreation and Dance, 65,* 23–24.

Croce, R., & Rock, S. (1988). The effects of varying types of reinforcement on the fine motor skill acquisition of mentally retarded adults. In D.L. Gill (Ed.), *Abstracts of research papers* (p. 244). Reston, VA: AAHPERD.

Davies, E.A. (1975). *Adapted physical education.* New York: Harper & Row.

Del Rey, P., & Steward, D. (1989). Organizing input for mentally retarded subjects to enhance memory and transfer. *Adapted Physical Activity Quarterly, 6,* 247–254.

DePaepe, J.L. (1985). The influence of three least restrictive environments on the content motor-ALT and performance of moderately mentally retarded students. *Journal of Teaching in Physical Education, 5,* 34–41.

DePauw, K.P. (1986). Toward progressive inclusion and acceptance: Implications for physical education. *Adapted Physical Activity Quarterly, 3,* 1–6.

DePauw, K.P. (1988). Sport for individuals with disabilities: Research opportunities. *Adapted Physical Activity Quarterly, 5,* 80–89.

DePauw, K.P. (1990a). Sport, society, and individuals with disabilities. In G. Reid (Ed.), *Problems in motor control* (pp. 319–337). New York: Elsevier Science.

DePauw, K.P. (1990b). Teaching and coaching individuals with disabilities: Research findings and implications. *Physical Education Review, 13,* 12–16.

DePauw, K.P. (1992). Current international trends in research in adapted physical activity. In T. William, L. Almond, & A. Sparkes (Eds.), *Sport and physical activity: Moving toward excellence* (pp. 221–228). London: E & FN Spon.

DePauw, K.P., & Doll-Tepper, G.M. (1989). European perspectives on adapted physical activity. *Adapted Physical Activity Quarterly, 6,* 95–99.

DePauw, K.P., & Gavron, S.J. (1995). *Sport and disability.* Champaign, IL: Human Kinetics.

DePauw, K.P., & Goc Karp, G. (1990). Attitudes of selected college students toward including disabled individuals in integrated settings. In G. Doll-Tepper, C. Dahms, B. Doll, & H. von Selzam (Eds.), *Adapted physical activity: An interdisciplinary approach* (pp. 149–157). Berlin: Springer-Verlag.

DePauw, K.P., & Goc Karp, G. (1992). Framework for conducting pedagogical research in teaching physical education to include diverse populations. In T. William, L. Almond, & A. Sparkes (Eds.), *Sport and physical activity: Moving toward excellence* (pp. 243–248). London: E & FN Spon.

DePauw, K.P., & Goc Karp, G. (1994a). Integrating knowledge of disability throughout the physical education curriculum: An infusion approach. *Adapted Physical Activity Quarterly, 11,* 3–13.

DePauw, K.P., & Goc Karp, G. (1994b). Preparing teachers for inclusion: The role of higher education. *Journal of Physical Education, Recreation and Dance, 65,* 51–53, 56.

DePauw, K.P., Lepore, M., Kowalski, E., Henderson, H., & Craft, D. (January, 1993). *Infusion of knowledge about individuals with disabilities into the physical education curriculum.* Paper presented at the National Association for Physical Education in Higher Education (NAPEHE) Annual Conference, Fort Lauderdale, FL.

DePauw, K.P. & Sherrill, C. (1994). Adapted physical activity: Present and future. *Physical Education Review, 17,* 6–13.

Doll-Tepper, G., Dahms, C., Doll, B., & von Selzam, H. (Eds.) (1990). *Adapted physical activity: An interdisciplinary approach.* Berlin: Springer-Verlag.

Dunkin, M.J., & Biddle, B.J. (1974). *The study of teaching.* New York: Holt, Rinehart & Winston.

Edwards, J.M., Elliott, D., & Lee, T.D. (1986). Contextual interference effects during skill acquisition and transfer in Down's Syndrome adolescents. *Adapted Physical Activity Quarterly, 3,* 250–258.

Freidson, E. (1965). Disability as social deviance. In M.B. Sussman (Ed.), *Sociology and rehabilitation* (pp. 71-99). New York: Amercian Sociological Association.

Gagnon, J., Tousignant, M., & Martel, D. (1989). Academic learning time in physical education classes for mentally handicapped students. *Adapted Physical Activity Quarterly, 6,* 280–289.

Gauthier, R.A. (1981). A descriptive analytic study of teacher-student interaction in mainstreamed physical education classes. *Dissertation Abstracts International, 41*(8), 3474-A.

Goffman, E. (1963). *Stigma: Notes on the management of spoiled identity.* Englewood Cliffs, NJ: Prentice-Hall.

Haber, L.D., & Smith, R.T. (1971). Disability and deviance: Normative adaptations of role behavior. *American Sociological Review, 36,* 87–97.

Hanks, M., & Poplin, D.E. (1981). The sociology of physical disability: A review of literature and some conceptual perspectives. *Deviant Behavior: An Interdisciplinary Journal, 2,* 309–328.

Hewett, F.M., & Forness, S.R. (1974). *Historical origins.* Boston: Allyn & Bacon.

Hsu, P.Y., & Dunn, J.M. (1984). Comparing reverse and forward chaining instructional methods on a motor task with moderately mentally retarded individuals. *Adapted Physical Activity Quarterly, 1,* 240–246.

Jansma, P., & Shultz, B. (1982). Validation and use of a mainstreaming attitude inventory with physical educators. *American Corrective Therapy Journal, 36,* 150–158.

Jeltma, K., & Vogler, E.W. (1985). Effects of an individual contingency on behaviorally disordered students in physical education. *Adapted Physical Activity Quarterly, 2,* 127–135.

Karper, W.B., & Martinek, T.J. (1982). Differential influence of various instructional factors on self-concepts of handicapped and nonhandicapped children in mainstreamed physical education classes. *Perceptual and Motor Skills, 54,* 831–835.

Karper, W.B., & Martinek, T.J. (1983). Motor performance and self-concepts of handicapped and nonhandicapped children in integrated physical education classes. *American Corrective Therapy Journal, 37,* 91–95.

Lemert, E.M. (1951). *Social pathology.* New York: McGraw-Hill.

Lepore, M., & Kowalski, E. (1992, October). *Infusion: A new look at an old idea.* Paper presented at the North American Federation of Adapted Physical Activity (NAFAPA) Conference, Montreal, Canada.

Maguire, P. (1994). Developing successful collaborative relationships. *Journal of Physical Education, Recreation and Dance, 65,* 32–36.

Marston, R., & Leslie, D. (1983). Teacher perceptions from mainstreamed vs. nonmainstreamed teaching environments. *The Physical Educator, 40,* 8–15.

Martinek, T.J., & Karper, W.B. (1981). Teachers' expectations for handicapped and nonhandicapped children in mainstreamed physical education classes. *Perceptual and Motor Skills, 53,* 327–330.

Mawdsley, R.H. (1977). *Comparison of teacher behaviors in regular and adapted movement classes.* Unpublished doctoral dissertation, Boston University School of Education.

McKenzie, R.T. (1909). *Exercise in education and medicine*. Philadelphia: W.B. Saunders.

Miller, B.E. (1985). *A descriptive analysis of academic learning time and teacher behaviors in regular, mainstreamed and adapted classes*. Unpublished doctoral dissertation, Ohio State University.

Poretta, D. (1988). Contextual interference effects on the transfer and retention of a gross motor skill by mildly mentally handicapped children. *Adapted Physical Activity Quarterly, 5*, 332–339.

Poretta, D.L., Nesbitt, J., & Labanowich, S. (1993). Terminology usage: A case for clarity. *Adapted Physical Activity Quarterly, 10* (2), 87–96.

Pyfer, J. (1986). Early research concerns in adapted physical education. *Adapted Physical Activity Quarterly, 3*, 95–103.

Rathbone, J. (1934). *Corrective physical education*. Philadelphia: W.B. Saunders.

Rizzo, T.L. (1984). Attitudes of physical educators toward teaching handicapped pupils. *Adapted Physical Activity Quarterly, 1*, 263–274.

Rizzo, T.L. (1985). Attributes related to teachers' attitudes. *Perceptual and Motor Skills, 60*, 739–742.

Rizzo, T.L., & Vispoel, W.P. (1991). Physical educators' attributes and attitudes toward teaching students with handicaps. *Adapted Physical Activity Quarterly, 8*, 4–11.

Rizzo, T.L., & Wright, R.G. (1987). Secondary school physical educators' attitudes toward teaching students with handicaps. *American Corrective Therapy Journal, 41*, 52–55.

Rizzo, T.L., & Wright, R.G. (1988). Selected attributes related to physical educators' attitudes toward teaching students with handicaps. *Mental Retardation, 26*, 307–309.

Seaman, J.A., & DePauw, K.P. (1989*). The new adapted physical education: A developmental approach*. Mountain View, CA: Mayfield Publishing Company.

Shapiro, J. (1993). *No pity: People with disabilities forging a new civil rights movement*. New York: Times.

Shephard, R.J. (1990). *Fitness in special populations*. Champaign, IL: Human Kinetics.

Sherrill, C. (Ed.). (1988). *Leadership training in adapted physical education*. Champaign, IL: Human Kinetics.

Sherrill, C. (1993). *Adapted physical activity, recreation, & sport: Crossdisciplinary and lifespan*. Dubuque, IA: Brown.

Sherrill, C. (1994). Least restrictive environments and total inclusion philosophies: Critical analysis. *Palaestra, 10*, 25–28, 31, 34–35, 52–54.

Sherrill, C. & DePauw, K.P. (1996). History of adapted physical activity and education. In J.D. Massengale & R.A. Swanson (Eds.), *History of exercise and sport science*. Champaign, IL: Human Kinetics.

Sherrill, C., Heikinaro-Johansson, P., & Slininger, D. (1994). Equal-status relationships in the gym. *Journal of Physical Education, Recreation and Dance, 65*, 27–31, 56.

Silliman, L.M., & French, R. (1988). The influence of selected reinforcers on the motor performance time-on-task of profoundly mentally retarded children. In D. L. Gill (Ed.), *Abstracts of research papers* (p. 243). Reston, VA: AAHPERD.

Silverman, S., Dodds, P., Placek, J., Shute, S., & Rife, F. (1984). Academic learning time in elementary school physical education (ALT-PE) for student subgroups and instructional activity units. *Research Quarterly for Exercise and Sport, 55,* 365–370.

Solmon, M.A., & Lee, A.M. (1991). A contrast of planning behaviors between expert and novice adapted physical education teachers. *Adapted Physical Activity Quarterly, 8,* 115–127.

Stein, J.U. (1983). Bridge over troubled waters: Research review and recommendations for relevance. In R.L. Eason, T.L. Smith, & F. Caron (Eds.), *Adapted physical activity* (pp. 189–198). Champaign, IL: Human Kinetics.

Taylor, J.L., & Loovis, E.M. (1978). *Measuring effective teacher behavior in adapted physical education.* Paper presented at the Midwest District of the American Alliance for Health, Physical Education, and Recreation. Indianapolis. (ERIC Document Reproduction Service, No. ED 156660).

United States Department of Education. (1991). *Thirteenth annual report to Congress: Implementation of Individuals with Disabilities Act.* Washington, D.C.: U.S. Government Printing Office.

Vogler, E.W., DePaepe, J., & Martinek, T. (1990). Effective teaching in adapted physical education. In G. Doll-Tepper, C. Dahms, B. Doll, & H. von Selzam (Eds.), *Adapted physical activity: An interdisciplinary approach.* (pp. 245–250). Berlin: Springer-Verlag.

Vogler, E.W., & French, R.W. (1983). The effects of a group contingency strategy on behaviorally disordered students in physical education. *Research Quarterly for Exercise and Sport, 54,* 273–277.

Vogler, E.W., van der Mars, H., Cusimano, B.E., & Darst, P. (1992). Experience, expertise, and teaching effectiveness with mainstreamed and nondisabled children in physical education. *Adapted Physical Activity Quarterly, 9,* 316–329.

Vogler, E.W., van der Mars, H., Darst, P., & Cusimano, B.E. (1990). Relationship of presage, context, and process variables to ALT-PE of elementary level mainstreamed students. *Adapted Physical Activity Quarterly, 7,* 298–313.

Webster, G.E. (1987). Influence of peer tutors upon academic learning time—physical education of mentally handicapped students. *Journal of Teaching Physical Education, 6,* 393–403.

Webster, G.E. (1993). Effective teaching in adapted physical education: A review. *Palaestra, 9,* 25–31.

World Health Organization. (1980). *International classification of impairments, disabilities, and handicaps: A manual of classification relating to the consequence of disease.* Geneva, Switzerland: Author.

PART 3

Promoting Student Learning

CHAPTER 7

A Model Describing the Influence of Values and Context on Student Learning

Catherine D. Ennis

Teaching physical education would be so much easier if all physical educators agreed on a single set of goals for their students—that is, if we all agreed that children graduating from our physical education programs should accomplish the same fitness and skill goals at the same level of performance. Of course, we would all need similar class time, equipment, and facilities—and about the same budget each year to replace old equipment with new. It would also be helpful if we had homogeneous groups of students who came to us with similar skills and past experiences with physical activity. They would be motivated and interested in a common set of movement, sport, and fitness activities. It would then be clear what and how we should teach and how well students should learn our content.

If all educators believed that students should graduate with the same skills, what skills would they be? Many physical educators answer this question with a detailed list of movement, sport, and fitness activities similar to those found in a textbook or curriculum guide. Other teachers explain that they have limited time, equipment, or facilities and must narrow the list to a few they can teach students to perform successfully. Still others emphasize the challenges associated with teaching diverse students in their classes. They point out that some students already know how to play most sports on the list or are already engaged in fitness activities, while others in the same class have never participated in some sports and may not want to engage in new activities. These examples represent just a few of the unique challenges in physical education and suggest why it is so difficult to develop a single, concise set of goals for teaching it. They may also explain why physical education programs in the United States vary so widely in content and quality.

Differences in physical education programs also stem from diverse educational values and beliefs that influence curricular and instructional decisions that we as teachers make in the gym. When we believe that our students should be skilled and fit, we structure our classes to teach skill and fitness content. We provide opportunities for practice and test students to be sure they have learned these skills. If we believe students should learn to work with and respect others, we structure our programs to emphasize the social skills needed to play together. We test students by placing them in challenging cooperative or competitive situations (De-Busk & Hellison, 1989). While these two goals are not mutually exclusive, the limited amount of time available in most physical education programs suggests that we must plan carefully. Keeping the focus on a few, important goals will ensure that students receive the practice time needed to reach each goal successfully.

Physical education content is very important to the health and well being of students throughout their lives. Movement, sport, and fitness activities make an important contribution to an individual's education and quality of life. Many students find enjoyment and satisfaction in participating in physical activity. It is important, though, to understand the factors that either help or hinder us as we attempt to teach physical education. We want to take advantage of the positive factors and reduce the negative whenever possible.

In this chapter I will describe the educational values and teaching contexts that characterize different physical education programs. I will then present a values/context model that can contribute both to curricular decision making and to research on teaching and learning.

DESCRIPTIONS OF VALUES AND CONTEXT IN EDUCATIONAL SETTINGS

Each time teachers or coaches decide what content to teach, they are answering the most basic curriculum question: "What knowledge is of most worth to students?" (Broudy, 1982). Answers reflect the teacher's beliefs about physical education content (curriculum), how the content should be conveyed to students (instruction), and the extent to which the content should be mastered or learned by the student (evaluation). Scholars such as Eisner (1992) and Schrag (1992) describe several different orientations to curricular decision making that place the priority for learning on three important aspects of curriculum: teaching the subject matter; considering the needs and interests of the learner; and accommodating the cultural expectations of the society or community in which the education is occurring.

VALUE ORIENTATIONS IN CURRICULAR DECISION MAKING

Jewett, Bain, and Ennis (1995) have proposed five value orientations that appear to influence curricular decision making in physical education.

DISCIPLINARY MASTERY AND LEARNING PROCESS

Advocates of two orientations, disciplinary mastery and learning process, believe that knowledge about the subject matter of physical education should be the major emphasis of the curriculum. Disciplinary mastery educators (e.g., Rink, 1993; Siedentop, 1994) would answer the question, "What knowledge is of most worth?," by pointing out that students should learn human movement patterns and skills that lead to more complex movements, such as those used in dance, swimming, gymnastics, team sports, and fitness activities. They would argue that students should meet specific criteria to demonstrate their knowledge (e.g., Taggert, 1985).

Learning process teachers agree with their disciplinary mastery colleagues that having the ability to perform and knowledge about performance are central to being a "physically educated person." Learning process teachers, though, would offer alternative ways to teach students. They believe that students must not only perform skillfully, but must also know how to solve problems about movement, sport, and exercise. For example, instead of teaching a set play for a throw-in in soccer, coaches and teachers challenge students to create their own plays, using the soccer skills and strategies they have learned. Students in a physical education class or on a soccer team might create five or more different solutions to the problem. They can then teach each other these strategies, taking ownership of the content. They must synthesize knowledge about the throw-in with an understanding of offensive and defensive strategies to create their own solutions. Learning process teachers expect students to work independently. They encourage them to use knowledge to solve problems and to focus on the process of solving the problem as well as the product, or solution, itself (Ennis, 1992).

AFFECTIVE AND SOCIAL ORIENTATIONS

Although the disciplinary mastery and learning process value orientations have strong support in physical education textbooks and programs, there are three other value orientations that teachers discuss when describing physical education: self-actualization, social responsibility, and ecological integration.

The self-actualization approach places the students' needs and interests at the center of the curriculum (Maslow, 1979). Self-actualization teachers attempt to match their curriculum to the interests and motivation levels of their students. A self-actualization curriculum orientation uses movement, sport, and exercise as means to help students develop positive self-esteem. It encourages students to try activities they think are difficult and helps them to move from dependence on external rewards to a more self-fulfilling, intrinsic reward system (Hellison & Templin, 1991). Chapter 13 by Don Hellison in this book provides a detailed explanation of this perspective.

Teachers who advocate social responsibility are most concerned about developing positive, interpersonal relationships among their students. They use movement, sport, and fitness content to provide opportunities for students to work with others. They focus on teaching students how to cooperate and accept personal responsibility for their roles in game play or group problem solving. They encourage students to develop the ability to lead others and to support their captain or group leader in difficult situations (Giebink & McKenzie, 1985).

Teachers who advocate ecological integration (Jewett & Ennis, 1990) emphasize that the knowledge base, the learner, and the social group are equally important. They point out to students the benefits of acquiring knowledge to solve personal or group challenges. Ecological integration teachers help students learn physical fitness, personal, and social skills so they can participate successfully in future group activities (Jewett & Mullan, 1977). Students learn that personal needs must sometimes give way to group concerns; similarly, the group learns that sometimes it must be sensitive to the needs of the individual.

TEACHER VALUES AND CONTEXT

Researchers in general education (Richardson, Anders, Tidwell, & Lloyd, 1991) and in physical education (Lambdin & Steinhardt, 1992) point out that teachers are not always able to design a curriculum consistent with their value orientations. Lambdin and Steinhardt found that, though teachers believed they had the knowledge necessary to be effective in their jobs, there were other barriers in the school context that limited their ability to reach their curricular goals. Such barriers may include student characteristics, administrative nonsupport, large class sizes, or inadequate equipment (Graham, Hopple, Manross, & Sitzman, 1993; Solmon, Worthy, & Carter, 1993; Talbert, McLaughlin, & Rowan, 1993).

Teachers who advocate particular value orientations try to create unique environments to facilitate their educational goals. Each school or class setting contains a blend of contextual factors which enhances the implementation of some goals while limiting others. Context factors affect teachers with different educational value orientations in unique ways.

DISCIPLINARY MASTERY TEACHERS AND CONTEXT

Disciplinary mastery teachers are most effective when they have access to facilities and equipment needed to enhance student performance. Students who are interested in learning about movement, sport, and exercise gain the greatest benefits from disciplinary mastery teachers. While it is difficult for all teachers to work with large class sizes or disruptive or unmotivated students, it is especially difficult for disciplinary mastery teachers. In these instances, even effective class managers report they spend more time keeping children on task than they do providing instruction or giving specific, corrective feedback (Ennis, 1992).

LEARNING PROCESS TEACHERS AND CONTEXT

Learning process teachers create effective environments or contexts for learning by challenging their students to think about how and why certain movement or fitness activities lead to particular results. In other words, they teach students how to analyze a situation and how to alter their own behavior to be most successful. Learning process teachers are very successful when they work in a school or program with goals that focus on critical thinking or problem solving (Ennis, 1990; McBride, 1991). Students come to physical education already expecting to work independently and in groups to solve problems. They are receptive to applying knowledge, such as that associated with biomechanics or physiology, to their motor performance (Lawson & Placek, 1981). It is especially difficult for learning process teachers to create a learning environment in a situation in which students are not motivated to learn. These students may not value the educational experience or may be experiencing other problems, such as attention deficit disorder, that limit their ability to work independently or focus on the problem.

THE SELF-ACTUALIZATION APPROACH AND CONTEXT

Self-actualization teachers focus on helping students to develop a positive self-concept and to set and meet relevant personal goals. They are personally interested in the lives of their students and work to incorporate knowledge that is important to the students into their physical education programs. Their curricula are flexible to respond to the diversity of their students. These teachers have particular difficulty teaching in situations where the school administrators or other teachers require a strict adherence to a rigid set of goals or objectives. These teachers prefer a loosely structured approach that gives students a voice in the selection of goals and learning activities. Teachers need the flexibility to shape a curriculum that entices uninterested, unmotivated, or disruptive students to engage in the program.

SOCIAL RESPONSIBILITY TEACHERS AND CONTEXT

Social responsibility teachers focus on the interpersonal relationships among students in their classes. They design situations in which students must work cooperatively to achieve success. These teachers work especially well with students who may come to school not knowing or wanting to work with others, participate on a team, or follow directions (Wandzilak, Carroll, & Ansorge, 1989). The focus is on developing appropriate personal and social behaviors to respond to a variety of situations. Students learn patience, negotiation, and self-control (Hellison & Templin, 1991). The instructional plan includes a series of small, social progressions leading to increased levels of social responsibility. Like the self-actualization teachers, social responsibility teachers have most difficulty when required to follow rigid, knowledge-based approaches to physical education. For example, the requirement to administer individually oriented fitness tests may be inconsistent with their focus on cooperative goals. Social responsibility teachers argue that until students learn to work cooperatively, they will have difficulty learning knowledge in group situations both in and out of schools (Ennis, 1994b).

ECOLOGICAL INTEGRATION TEACHERS AND CONTEXT

Ecological integration teachers attempt to balance the influence of the knowledge base, the needs and interests of the learner, and the expectations of the community. They help students learn how knowledge connects to meaningful aspects of their lives (Jewett & Mullan, 1977). They see the physical education program as an ecosystem. Events that happen in one part of the program affect every other part of the program. They help students learn to connect knowledge learned in science and mathematics class, for example, with activities they are learning in the gym. Students are successful when they use knowledge to make personal and social decisions that are in the best interest of the school or their classmates.

Ecological integration teachers find it especially difficult to teach when teaching time is limited (either due to scheduling restrictions or large class sizes). They have difficulty finding adequate time to teach students knowledge and social responsibility content while providing activities that contribute to the development of personal goals (Ennis, 1992).

SETTING REALISTIC CURRICULUM GOALS

As you have read these descriptions of value orientations, you may have been attracted to one or more orientations as most consistent with your personal value perspective. Certainly, they each represent valid goals that are important for all students in physical education. So why can't we teach them all? Why not have our curriculum include all of these goals? Unfortunately, it is not that easy. There are a number of barriers that limit our ability to teach these to our students. For example, limited teaching time (some as limited as one semester of physical education at the high school level) severely constrains the efforts of even the most effective teachers. Thus, the curriculum question, "What content is most important to students?," requires the realistic acknowledgment that there are certain factors in the school context that influence our ability to present content to students and the extent to which students can learn that content. Specifically, the context in which teachers work greatly influences their ability to teach effectively within their value orientation. In the next section I will present a model describing the influence of values and context on student learning.

INFLUENCE OF VALUES AND CONTEXT ON STUDENT OUTCOMES

There are many influences that shape values and context within school settings. A model is needed to help us understand how these influences affect student learning. Models provide a visual organization of abstract phenomena and their relationships to each other. The values/context model, shown in Figure 7.1, provides a framework for thinking about curricular decision making that directly affects what, how, and how much students learn in physical education. It treats teacher beliefs as an outcome of working within a particular school context and as a predictor of student learning.

The values/context model incorporates a variety of influences on physical education teachers that shape their beliefs and teaching skills which lead to different student outcomes. The first set of variables described in column one are exogenous context variables. These are variables that are global and pervasive. They affect every aspect of the school experience.

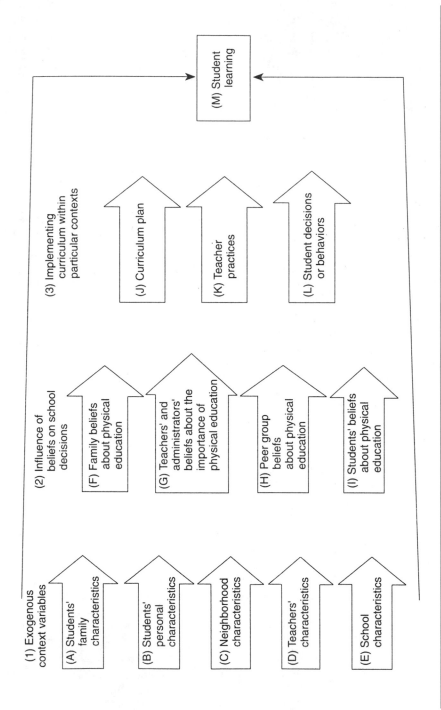

Figure 7.1. Model of the influence of values and context on student learning

They include characteristics of families, students, neighborhoods, teachers, and schools that make up the unique climate of the school and the physical education setting. The variables included in these boxes influence all of the other variables listed in the other boxes. The second column includes more specific beliefs held by families, teachers and administrators, peer groups, and students that more directly influence the teaching-learning process. These in turn affect the curriculum plan, teacher practices, and students' decisions and behaviors. The column at the far right focuses the entire process on the student. It reminds us that the point of teaching is student learning. Decisions made because of context and values directly influence student learning by shaping the teachers' choice of teaching and evaluation strategies. The next sections will describe each box in Figure 7.1 in more detail.

EXOGENOUS CONTEXT VARIABLES (COLUMN 1)

Each box in the Exogenous Context Variables column represents critical characteristics of primary participants in the school setting. The variables are defined broadly in order to encompass the wide variety of circumstances that indirectly influence student learning.

Students' Family Characteristics (Box A)

Historically, we have viewed the student as an isolated individual who comes to school for the primary purpose of learning. Recently, greater consideration has been given to the influence of students' backgrounds and family environments on their interest in and readiness to learn in school settings. Goals, attitudes, and interests held by family members influence students' interests and levels of motivation to participate in certain activities (Collins, 1990).

Family interests often translate into prior experiences with sports and recreational activities that enhance students' openness to new physical education activities. Influential variables include the education level of the parents and siblings and the financial resources available to create opportunities for children. Closely related to this is the employment and marital status of parents and the number of children in the family (Kantor & Brenzel, 1992). While many children with one parent who loves them and cares for them are quite successful in school, other students may not be so fortunate. Even children in two-parent families may experience difficulties, especially when the general mental health and psychological resources of the family are not strong (Eccles & Harold, 1993). Family characteristics appear to be major factors in students' readiness for school and their interest and motivation to be successful in educational settings.

Students' Personal Characteristics (Box B)

Teachers and administrators are often most aware of the individual student's personal characteristics that contribute to or detract from learning. Students' age, maturity (Malina & Bouchard, 1990), gender (Huston & Alvarez, 1990), and ethnicity (Lucas, Henze & Donato, 1990; Peshkin & White, 1990) play a powerful role in their ability to respond positively to school settings and to the teachers and learning environments they experience (Eccles & Midgley, 1990). In addition, students' past performances also influence their future opportunities and the extent to which they appreciate or are prepared to learn new information. Each student takes with them test scores that document their aptitudes, talents, and interests. In physical education, many teachers keep extensive records of student performance in a variety of activities. Students also become well known for their personality or temperament (Boggess, Griffey, & Housner, 1986). These factors influence adult expectations about what and how much students can learn. Oakes (1992) and Martinek (1989) documented positive and negative consequences of adult expectations on student learning.

Neighborhood Characteristics—Social System (Box C)

We can view each of the components in this column as part of a large social system that influences what we value and choose to become involved in (Banks, 1993). Most in-school populations include students from several different neighborhoods. Cohesive groups from a particular neighborhood enhance opportunities for group members to become involved in club activities and provide a ready welcome on athletic teams. Belonging to these groups gives individuals confidence and increases their comfort with school. Social groups function within set norms that are explicitly or tacitly valued by the group (Eisenberg & Mussen, 1989). While neighborhood groups contribute to cohesion, they may also act negatively as social controls to limit group members' individuality. In the extreme, negative codes of social behavior held by gangs require individuals to become involved in illegal activities to maintain or increase their status within the group.

Teachers and administrators are becoming increasingly aware of the negative influences of neighborhood or social group structures on individual students (Wehlage, Rutter, Smith, Lesko, & Fernandez, 1989). Some students look to cliques or gangs for the social support that they may not be receiving at home or school. Sometimes such students are encouraged by peers to be disruptive or verbally or physically aggressive to win approval. Teachers often work with these students in support groups and conflict resolution teams to defuse aggressive behavior. They try to provide opportunities for students to receive rewards for positive, socially appropriate behaviors (National School Boards Association, 1993). Teachers' perceptions of neighborhood or peer influences often affect activities they choose to offer in physical education class (Ennis, 1994a, 1994b). At times they may avoid content that is controversial; or they may include specific content, such as lessons on social responsibility (Ennis, 1995, 1996).

Teachers' Characteristics (Box D)

Teachers' backgrounds, experiences, and levels of teaching skills influence many aspects of their teaching. In addition, teachers control many factors in their classes. They can hold high expectations for students and focus their own energy, motivation, and enthusiasm for teaching. They can also make an effort to understand the interests and concerns of students, neighborhood groups, and families. This is essential to maintaining a positive climate in their classes (Carlisle & Phillips, 1985). A teacher's age, sex, and ethnicity are also important factors in their ability to present and manage physical education programs in particular contexts (Ennis, 1994a). Teachers' mastery of a variety of class management, disciplinary, and teaching strategies contributes to their ability to enhance student learning. Years of experience at different teaching levels (elementary, middle, high school, university) and with different kinds of students (e.g., ethnicity, gender, urban/ rural) also influences their curricular decisions (Figley, 1985; Tannehill, Romar, O'Sullivan, England, & Rosenberg, 1994).

School Characteristics (Box E)

Schools are more than a building or group of athletic fields that serve as work places for teachers and students (Pinkham, 1994). They also encompass the values and beliefs of the educational participants. Communities fund schools to transmit certain basic knowledge and appropriate behaviors to young citizens. Thus, they have a mandate to provide opportunities for learning to take place (Metz, 1978). To carry out this mandate, principals and teachers develop rules, policies, and guidelines that protect students and provide for uniform delivery of diverse programs. In school districts that incorporate school-based management, teachers are involved in the daily operation of the school. They influence decisions involving individual students and funding for each subject area. Schools may differ in the type or age of the students they service (elementary, middle, disabled, gifted) and resources to which they have access.

Schools may also differ in their size and climate (Anderson, 1982). Students enrolled in large high schools comment at times that they become lost in the masses of people who crowd the halls and facilities. While large schools are more economical for the school district, they often require administrators to develop creative organizational structures. For example, administrators can divide students into teams with teachers and facilities assigned specifically to meet their needs. Physical education classes may also be large, forcing teachers to find innovative ways to provide corrective feedback and individualized instruction. Both large and small schools may develop a climate that is warm and inviting to students. School or class climate reflects many tangible and intangible qualities that assist students in bonding with the school and its staff. Students are more likely to become engaged in schools with a warm, welcoming climate. One factor that contributes to a warm climate is the extent to which parents are involved with their children in school activities (Eccles & Midgley, 1990; Fine, 1993). Parents often assist schools to develop special programs that provide enriched educational opportunities for students.

INFLUENCE OF BELIEFS ON SCHOOL DECISIONS (COLUMN 2)

The school social system consists of the interactions among many different people who have a variety of goals and expectations for education (Pajares, 1992). Beliefs about the importance of the physical education experience in the total school curriculum affect resource allocations to the physical education program. They influence decisions about content, teaching strategies, and evaluation (Schubert, 1990). Beliefs may focus on the physical education program or be specific to a particular child or group of children. The boxes in this part of the model represent the beliefs of key individuals and groups—such as families, teachers and administrators, peer groups, and students—that ultimately determine the program's success in enhancing student learning.

Family Beliefs About the Importance of Physical Education (Box F)

Families with school-age children are usually most involved in schools and most concerned with the quality of the educational experience (Eccles & Harold, 1993). It is critical, therefore, for parents to be supportive of the physical education program and understand its benefits for their children, both now and across the life span. Parents' prior experiences often frame their expectations for their children's physical education program. Some parents may have been involved in quality physical education and athletic experiences and need little encouragement to support the program. Others may not remember much about physical education or may have had a negative experience during their school years. These parents may question the value of physical education in the school curriculum. Teachers may need to make an extra effort to convince these parents of the value of the physical education program for children.

Parents may also have beliefs or expectations specific to their own children. They may have preconceived perceptions of their children's abilities and interests that influence their expectations for achievement. They may have differing beliefs about what content is most important for their children to learn. While some parents value physical education as a way to enhance their children's athletic ability, others may value physical education because of its socialization goals. They may see it as an avenue for the development of interpersonal relationships (Wentzel, 1991). Parents whose children are more successful in physical education than they are in other school subjects may value physical education because it enhances their children's self-esteem.

Teachers' and Administrators' Beliefs About Physical Education (Box G)

Teachers must believe in the value of physical education to remain enthusiastic and motivated throughout their careers. They rely on administrator support to create strong programs and maintain class control (Ratliffe, 1986). When administrators value physical education highly, physical education teachers are encouraged to set goals leading to student learning. The five value orientations, described earlier in this chapter, influence teachers' decisions about content in physical education. Teachers also have beliefs about their own abilities to teach. Their sense of self-efficacy may include their ability to teach particular activities, work with certain types of students, or teach using different strategies.

Teachers also have specific beliefs or expectations for students (Martinok, 1989). These may be directed toward particular students or more broadly focused on groups of students, such as neighborhood groups. Teachers may have expectations for student achievement that are helpful in structuring interesting and challenging activities. They may also under or overestimate a student's potential, perhaps because of his or her size (e.g., too short, overweight), limiting students' opportunities to be successful.

Peer Group Beliefs About Physical Education (Box H)

Adolescent students are particularly concerned about being accepted by their peer group. Peer groups can form "subcultures" or cliques that have their own sets of understandings, dress, and language (Eisenberg & Mussen, 1989). Teachers and coaches often address this need for affiliation by organizing teams and clubs. Students are motivated to enhance their performance so they can join the jump rope team or the soccer club. While teams and clubs provide a positive opportunity for students to affiliate with others, there may be other group situations that are not socially positive or productive. The groups' values may be inconsistent with those of the school or the goals and activities stated in the physical education class. In extreme cases, students' disruptive behaviors influence the climate of the classroom, negating the positive aspects of the program (Wehlage et al., 1989).

Peer group pressures affect students in unique ways. Friends or rivals may influence students positively with creative ideas or negatively through verbal or physical intimidation (Berndt & Perry, 1990). Many students find it almost impossible to ignore the demands of their peers. They feel they must comply with the group's wishes or be isolated from peer group support. Teachers may be unwilling or unable to convince students to participate in an activity when the group has decided that the activity is not interesting (Ennis, 1994b).

Students' Beliefs About Physical Education (Box I)

Students also have strong beliefs about and expectations for physical education (Tannehill & Zakrajsek, 1993). They may enter the class with prior experiences that influence their willingness to engage physically and cognitively in the activities (see Stinson, 1993, for examples from high school dance education). They also have their own expectations for performance. Some students believe that they are physically talented and cannot wait to demonstrate their skills. Others feel that they are not very skilled or cannot learn skills, and hesitate or even refuse to participate in physical activity (Martinek & Griffith, 1994). They also value some skills more than others. Valued skills are usually those that they feel successful performing, or those that their peer or ethnic group values. Students have beliefs about the role of the physical educator in structuring recreational or educational experiences. They may simply want to play the game and avoid instructional drills. Others hope that instruction can help them be better performers, enhancing their status in the peer group.

IMPLEMENTING CURRICULUM WITHIN PARTICULAR CONTEXTS (COLUMN 3)

The first two columns in this model apply to the role of context (column 1) and values (column 2) in the curriculum decision-making process. Of course, these two constructs continuously interact, shaping and reshaping each other. The curriculum plan represents a blueprint of teacher beliefs and activities planned to facilitate student learning. Teachers often base their teaching practices on what works successfully in a particular context. The belief that a unit or lesson must "work" (Richardson, 1992) within a context to be considered successful reflects the influence of context on teachers' efforts to plan and implement lessons. A key ingredient in the success of the lesson is the response that students have to the content and the extent to which they are willing to participate.

Curriculum Plan (Box J)

Effective curricular plans are sensitive to family and community values and student characteristics. They reflect the beliefs of teachers and emphasize the skills and abilities that teachers use to enhance student learning. Plans are also consistent with the opportunities and limitations found within the school. They promote a warm climate by reflecting a sensitivity to students' needs and interests. The curriculum may include plans for an entire program, a year in that program, or units and lessons. The goals and activities within the plan build progressively across lessons, units, and years to enhance student achievement systematically. Curricular plans may vary considerably across school districts and individual schools based on the context and the beliefs of the participants in the curricular decision-making process.

Student learning is the result of carefully planned decisions that affect what is taught and how it is taught to students (Goc-Karp & Zakrajsek, 1987). Teachers must understand the variables in the school context and design a program that achieves essential educational goals. Teachers must control, at least to some extent, the diverse factors in the context that let them teach effectively (Arrighi & Young, 1987). They must be able to present content and learning tasks in a way that is interesting and meaningful to students. They try to instill in students a desire to learn and a belief that with effort and practice they can learn.

Teacher Practices (Box K)

Teachers' management, discipline, and teaching strategies may vary based on their value orientation, the content to be taught, and the students in their classes. Some content (e.g., weight training, wrestling, rock climbing, etc.) can be dangerous and must be taught in a direct, teacher-controlled manner to minimize injuries. This method also helps the teacher know immediately which students understand and can perform effectively. Goals such as creative thinking, cooperation, and leadership can be taught using other methods that let students control more of the curricular and instructional decisions. Teaching practices are also influenced by the opportunities and limitations in the context. Large class sizes and limited facilities can make teaching and learning difficult. Teachers must work to develop effective management and control strategies that allow them to teach content. They must present content effectively and then monitor student progress. Teachers work constantly to identify problems and offer specific, corrective feedback to enhance performance. When working with diverse students it is critically important to teach using a variety of methods that have been selected specifically to respond to student interests and needs.

Richardson (1992) points out that a critical factor in teachers' decisions to select a particular curriculum approach or teaching strategy is the extent to which the plan or strategy "works." To work, a curriculum must fit within the context and the teachers' value orientation. It must also be acceptable to students, who may accept or reject a program based on the extent to which it meets their expectations for physical education. It must fulfill their need for knowledge about movement, sport, or exercise. It also must be sensitive to them as individuals and be socially acceptable to their peer group. If students do not believe that they can participate successfully in a curriculum, some will respond by simply choosing not to take part (Ennis, 1994a). In other classes, students may feel that the program is enjoyable and exciting and are quite willing to respond positively.

Student Decisions or Behaviors (Box L)

Student responses to situations or issues are often the catalyst for teacher-initiated change in the curriculum plan and teaching strategies (Erickson & Shultz, 1992). For example, as students become more aware of the importance of healthy lifestyles, they are more interested in content related to fitness and nutrition. They are more willing to engage in vigorous activities and to set and meet personal fitness and nutrition goals.

Students also are constantly responding to the social context in which they live. When other students confront them, they often feel they must defend themselves to avoid future problems. Teachers should monitor the level of student conflict in their classes. When they detect rising feelings of aggressiveness resulting, for example, in verbal harassment of low skilled students, they may choose to make changes in their curriculum that require students to work together positively to be successful. Teachers and students can measure achievement as a group score, focusing on the teams' ability to work cooperatively. Teachers respond daily to changes in the context and students' responses to school situations. It is important that they continue to monitor the changing environment and modify their program to match students' constantly changing needs.

STUDENT LEARNING (Box M)

Student learning is the focus of the curriculum planning and teaching process. All the participants in the school have a direct responsibility to contribute to the learning process. Each box presented in the framework represents a critical component necessary for learning. Administrative and parental support is critical when creating a positive environment for students to learn. Students and peer groups must take responsibility for mentally and physically preparing themselves to learn. They must be open to the learning process and facilitate effective teaching through responsive behavior.

While some students learn because they are interested and excited about the subject matter of physical education, other students need to be helped to value physical activity. Teachers can encourage student learning by selecting content that is interesting and meaningful to them. Teachers are obligated to help students make connections between the content and their lives. For example, some students may not realize how crucial physical activity is for a healthy life. Teachers can help students understand how activity promotes health. They can also promote learning by presenting content using teaching styles that involve students directly in the learning process. This helps students organize the content and use it in their lives. Teachers also promote learning by controlling or managing the instructional setting so that every student has the opportunity to participate. Teachers promote learning by monitoring student progress on important content goals. Students need to understand what they are expected to learn and to be held accountable for learning. When teachers grade students solely on dress and participation, they trivialize the knowledge base of physical education. Students are more likely to value physical education when they are held accountable for learning content that they believe is valuable and meaningful in their lives.

SUMMARY

Values and context are critical factors that influence the decisions teachers make in physical education. Scholars describe values as teacher value orientations and as beliefs held by participants about the importance of physical education. The value orientations of disciplinary mastery, learning process, self-actualization, social responsibility, and ecological integration are useful in understanding the content that teachers feel is most important for students to learn. Value orientations also influence teachers' selection of content and teaching and evaluation strategies.

Factors that shape values and context in particular settings are influential in the curricular decision making process. These range from exogenous variables in the community or the society to parents' and teachers' beliefs about physical education. It is important also to remember that students must function within a peer group-influenced social system. Students often behave quite differently with their classmates than they do when they are talking individually with teachers or other adults. Teacher practices often reflect a synthesis of educational ideas they believe will work in the class setting. They often test several different strategies before finding one that is consistent with their beliefs about teaching and effective within the context in which they teach.

The model proposed in this chapter can be used to clarify and focus one's perspective on the school setting. Because so many different factors appear to impact school teaching, the model may be useful in organizing and emphasizing those that appear most important in shaping student learning. It reminds us not to underestimate the power of the social context and individual beliefs to influence student learning. The model boxes describe broad concepts that may or may not be influential in a particular school setting. It is important for individuals who are studying the teaching-learning process to consider the impact of each variable in classes and schools they are observing. It is hoped that the model will be a flexible tool for examining the influence of context and values in educational decision making.

REFERENCES

Anderson, C.S. (1982). The search for school climate: A review of the research. *Review of Educational Research, 52,* 368–420.

Arrighi, M.A., & Young, J.C. (1987). Teacher perceptions about effective and successful teaching. *Journal of Teaching in Physical Education, 6,* 122–135.

Banks, J.A. (1993). Multicultural education: Characteristics and goals. In J. A. Banks & C.A.M. Banks (Eds.), *Multicultural understanding* (pp. 1–28). Boston: Allyn & Bacon.

Berndt, T.J., & Perry, T.B. (1990). Distinctive features and effects of early adolescent friendships. In R. Montemayor, G.R. Adams, & T.P. Gullotta (Eds.), *From childhood to adolescence: A transitional period?* (pp. 269–290). Newbury Park, CA: Sage.

Boggess, T.E., Griffey, D.C., & Housner, L.D. (1986). The influence of teachers' perceptions of student temperament on managerial decision making. *Journal of Teaching in Physical Education, 5,* 140–148.

Broudy, H.S. (1982). What knowledge is of most worth? *Educational Leadership, 39,* 574–578.

Carlisle, C., & Phillips, D.A. (1985). The effects of enthusiasm training on selected teacher and student behaviors in preservice physical education teachers. *Journal of Teaching in Physical Education, 4,* 64–75.

Collins, W.A. (1990). Parent-child relationships in the transition to adolescence: Continuity and change in interaction, affect, and cognition. In R. Montemayor, G.R. Adams, & T.P. Gullotta (Eds.), *From childhood to adolescence: A transitional period?* (pp. 85–106). Newbury Park, CA: Sage.

DeBusk, M., & Hellison, D. (1989). Implementing a physical education self-responsibility model for delinquency-prone youth. *Journal of Teaching in Physical Education, 8,* 104–112.

Eccles, J.S., & Harold, R.D. (1993). Parent-school involvement during the adolescent years. *Teachers College Record, 94,* 568–587.

Eccles, J.S., & Midgley, C. (1990). Changes in academic motivation and self-perception during early adolescence. In R. Montemayor, G.R. Adams, & T.P. Gullotta (Eds.), *From childhood to adolescence: A transitional period?* (pp. 134–155). Newbury Park, CA: Sage.

Eisenberg, N., & Mussen, P.H. (1989). *The roots of prosocial behavior in children.* Cambridge, UK: Cambridge University Press.

Eisner, E.W. (1992). Curriculum ideologies. In P.W. Jackson (Ed.), *Handbook of research on curriculum* (pp. 302–326). New York: Macmillan.

Ennis, C.D. (1990). Discrete thinking skills in two teachers' physical education classes. *Elementary School Journal, 91,* 473–487.

Ennis, C.D. (1992). Curriculum theory as practiced: Case studies of operationalized value orientations. *Journal of Teaching in Physical Education, 11,* 358–375.

Ennis, C.D. (1994a). Urban secondary teachers' value orientations: Social goals for teaching. *Teaching and Teacher Education, 10,* 109–120.

Ennis, C.D. (1994b). Urban secondary teachers' value orientations: Delineating curricular goals for social responsibility. *Journal of Teaching in Physical Education, 13,* 163–179.

Ennis, C.D. (1995). Teachers' responses to noncompliant students: The realities and consequences of a negotiated curriculum. *Teaching and Teacher Education, 11,* 445-460.

Ennis, C.D. (1996). When avoiding confrontation leads to avoiding content: Disruptive students' impact on curriculum. *Journal of Curriculum and Supervision, 10,* 145–162.

Erickson, F., & Shultz, J. (1992). Students' experience of the curriculum. In P.W. Jackson (Ed.), *Handbook of research on curriculum* (pp. 465–485). New York: Macmillan.

Figley, G.E. (1985). Determinants of attitudes toward physical education. *Journal of Teaching in Physical Education, 4,* 229–240.

Fine, M. (1993). [Ap]parent involvement: Reflections on parents, power, and urban public schools. *Teachers College Record, 94,* 682–710.

Foshay, A.W. (1993). Values as object matter: The reluctant pursuit of heaven. *Journal of Curriculum and Supervision, 9,* 41–52.

Giebink, M.P., & McKenzie, T.L. (1985). Teaching sportsmanship in physical education and recreation: An analysis of interventions and generalization effects. *Journal of Teaching in Physical Education, 4,* 167–177.

Goc-Karp, G., & Zakrajsek, D.B. (1987). Planning for learning—Theory into practice. *Journal of Teaching in Physical Education, 6,* 377–392.

Graham, G., Hopple, C., Manross, M., & Sitzman, T. (1993). Novice and experienced children's physical education teachers: Insights into their situational decision making. *Journal of Teaching in Physical Education, 12,* 197–214.

Hellison D.R., & Templin, T.J. (1991). *A reflective approach to teaching physical education.* Champaign, IL: Human Kinetics.

Huston, A.C., & Alvarez, M. (1990). The socialization context of gender role development. In R. Montemayor, G.R. Adams, & T.P. Gullotta (Eds.), *From childhood to adolescence: A transitional period?* (pp. 156–183). Newbury Park, CA: Sage.

Jewett, A.E., Bain, L.L., & Ennis, C.D. (1995). *The curriculum process in physical education.* Madison, WI: Brown and Benchmark.

Jewett, A.E., & Ennis, C.D. (1990). Ecological integration as a value orientation for curricular decision making. *Journal of Curriculum and Supervision, 5,* 120–131.

Jewett, A.E., & Mullan, M.R. (1977). *Curriculum design: Purposes and processes in physical education teaching and learning.* Reston, VA: American Alliance for Health, Physical Education, and Recreation.

Kantor, H., & Brenzel, B. (1992). Urban education and the "truly disadvantaged": The historical roots of the contemporary crisis, 1945-1990. *Teachers College Record, 94,* 278–314.

Kliebard, H.M. (1987). *The struggle for the American curriculum: 1893-1953.* New York: Routledge & Kegan Paul.

Lambdin, D.D., & Steinhardt, M.A. (1992). Elementary and secondary physical education teachers' perceptions of their goals, expertise, and students' achievements. *Journal of Teaching in Physical Education, 11,* 103–111.

Lawson, H., & Placek, J.H. (1981). *Physical education in secondary schools: Curricular alternatives.* Boston: Allyn & Bacon.

Lucas, T., Henze, R., & Donato, R. (1990). Promoting the success of Latino language-minority students: An exploratory study of six high schools. *Harvard Educational Review, 60,* 315–340.

Malina, R.M., & Bouchard, C. (1990). *Growth and physical activity.* Champaign, IL: Human Kinetics.

Martinek, T.J. (1989). Children's perceptions of teaching behaviors: An attributional model for explaining teacher expectancy effects. *Journal of Teaching in Physical Education, 8,* 318–328.

Martinek, T.J., & Griffith, J.B. (1994). Learned helplessness in physical education: A developmental study of causal attributions and task persistence. *Journal of Teaching in Physical Education, 13,* 108–122.

Maslow, A.H. (1979). Humanistic education. *Journal of Humanistic Psychology, 19,* 13–27.

McBride, R. (1991). Critical thinking—An overview with implications for physical education. *Journal of Teaching in Physical Education, 11,* 112–125.

Metz, M.H. (1978). *Classrooms and corridors: The crisis of authority in desegregated secondary schools.* Berkeley: University of California Press.

National School Boards Association. (1993). *Violence in the schools.* Alexandria, VA: Author.

Oakes, J. (1992). Can tracking research inform practice? Technical, normative, and political considerations. *Educational Researcher, 21*(4), 12–21.

Pajares, M.F. (1992). Teachers' beliefs and educational research: Cleaning up a messy construct. *Review of Educational Research, 62,* 307–332.

Peshkin, A., & White, C.J. (1990). Four Black American students: Coming of age in a multiethnic high school. *Teachers College Record, 92,* 21–38.

Pinkham, K.M. (1994, April). *The school as a workplace: The perspectives of secondary school physical educators.* Paper presented at the annual meeting of the American Educational Research Association, New Orleans.

Ratliffe, T. (1986). The influence of school principals on management time and student activity time for two elementary physical education teachers. *Journal of Teaching in Physical Education, 5,* 117–125.

Richardson, V. (1992). Significant and worthwhile change in teaching practice. *Educational Researcher, 19*(7), 10–18.

Richardson, V., Anders, P., Tidwell, D., & Lloyd, C. (1991). The relationship between teachers' beliefs and practices in reading comprehension instruction. *American Educational Research Journal, 28,* 559–586.

Rink, J.E. (1993). *Teaching physical education for learning.* St. Louis, MO: Times Mirror/Mosby.

Schrag, F. (1992). Conceptions of knowledge. In P.W. Jackson (Ed.), *Handbook of research on curriculum* (pp. 268–301). New York: Macmillan.

Schubert, W.H. (1990). The questions of worth as central to curricular empowerment. In J.T. Sears & J.D. Marshall (Eds.), *Teaching and thinking about curriculum: Critical inquiries* (pp. 211–227). New York: Teachers College Press.

Siedentop, D. (Ed.). (1994). *Sport education: Quality physical education through positive sport experiences.* Champaign, IL: Human Kinetics.

Solmon, M.A., Worthy, T., & Carter, J.A. (1993). The interaction of school context and role identity of first-year teachers. *Journal of Teaching in Physical Education, 12,* 313–328.

Stinson, S.W. (1993). Meaning and value: Reflections on what students say about school. *Journal of Curriculum and Supervision, 8,* 216–238.

Taggert, A. (1985). Fitness—Direct instruction. *Journal of Teaching in Physical Education, 4,* 143–150.

Talbert, J.E., McLauglin, M.W., & Rowan, B. (1993). Understanding context effects on secondary school teaching. *Teachers College Record, 95,* 45–68.

Tannehill, D., Romar, J.E., O'Sullivan, M., England, K., & Rosenberg, D. (1994). Attitudes toward physical education: Their impact on how physical education teachers make sense of their work. *Journal of Teaching in Physical Education, 13,* 407–421.

Tannehill, D., & Zakrajsek, D. (1993). Student attitudes toward physical education: A multicultural study. *Journal of Teaching in Physical Education, 13,* 78–84.

Wandzilak, T., Carroll, T., & Ansorge, C.J. (1989). Values development through physical activity: Promoting sportsmanlike behaviors, perceptions, and moral reasoning. *Journal of Teaching in Physical Education, 8,* 13–22.

Wehlage, G.G., Rutter, R.A., Smith, G.A., Lesko, N., & Fernandez, T.R. (1989). *Reducing the risk: Schools as communities of support.* New York: Falmer Press.

Wentzel, K. (1991). Social competence at school: Relation between social responsibility and academic achievement. *Review of Educational Research, 61*(1), 1–24.

CHAPTER 8

Goals and Outcomes

Leslie Lambert

The purpose of this chapter is to explore what we know about the creation of goals and outcomes. What are the theoretical touchstones for the development of curriculum goals and learner outcomes? How have these theoretical underpinnings influenced the curriculum process in practice? As we explore these and other related issues, we will discuss

- dominant and emerging conceptions of learning and their influence on the creation of goals and outcomes,
- the curriculum process—learner outcomes as ends and curriculum goals as means,
- various learner outcome and curriculum goal models in physical education, and
- three frameworks for setting goals and outcomes in physical education.

CURRICULUM DEFINED

There are countless definitions of curriculum, ranging from specific content perspectives to all-inclusive statements of what students are taught and learn (intentionally and vicariously) in school. All are pertinent in various applications, but the one definition that best embraces the intent of this chapter was set forth by Schiller, Schiller & Walberg, "Curriculum is a means of attaining educational ends" (1989, p. 193). Curriculum goals become the programmatic framework (means) that connect disciplinary content and other salient educational experiences with learner outcomes and that guide the teacher and learner toward accomplishing valued learner outcomes. Learner outcomes (educational ends) represent the essential, non-negotiable knowledge and skills we wish students to master as a result of a physical education program. The curriculum process, then, includes the following components:

1. Defining or creating a value-based direction (mission, philosophical base, value orientation) for the program.
2. Outlining learner outcomes consistent with the values set forth.
3. Setting program goals that align with learner outcomes.
4. Selecting and sequencing educational experiences.
5. Assessing student learning.

Depending on the perspective one takes regarding the curriculum process, these five components unfold chronologically in various ways. This chapter will assume that learner outcomes must be determined prior to the setting of curriculum goals and will focus primarily on outlining learner outcomes consistent with the values of the program and setting program goals.

Before we proceed further, I must offer two caveats:

1. Though curriculum, instruction, and assessment are often seen as separate enterprises (particularly among those engaged in scholarly analyses and inquiry), it is awkward and contrived to separate goals and outcomes from instruction and assessment. (Believe me, I have struggled!) It is essential that the three be intimately connected as we think of and implement them. To conceive of them as the three legs of a stool would be helpful—each necessary to create both form and function. At the same time, each should be seen as distinct and should not be confused with the others. So, while this chapter focuses mainly on clarification of goals and outcomes, these components should be seen as integral aspects of the curriculum process.
2. Unless the curriculum process begins with learner outcomes rather than with incremental objectives, it will not work very well. The proverbial notion that if we do not know where we are going, we should not be surprised where we arrive holds true. As a confluent whole, the curriculum process should be guided by the learner outcomes with respect to:
   - setting curriculum goals and educational experiences consistent with the outcomes,
   - deciding on rich assessments of student learning that help validate the accomplishment of the outcomes, and
   - determining the instructional process that will help students/ teachers actualize the outcomes.

Under this set of assumptions, students demonstrate their mastery of learning through assessments that allow them to verify (or not!) a rich integration of knowledge, skills, and practices/behaviors. Learner outcomes and their associated goals and assessments can be quite diverse. Demonstrations of learning may well be idiosyncratic, resistant to normative, standardized instruction and assessment methodologies.

THE PREVAILING EDUCATIONAL CLIMATE: A CONTEXT FOR SITUATING THE DEVELOPMENT OF GOALS AND OUTCOMES

Since the debut of the report entitled "A Nation at Risk" (1983) there have been several waves of educational reform. At the nucleus of the most recent wave (the standards and outcomes wave) are two fundamental premises: (a) goals and outcomes that guide what students should know and be able to do must focus on critical, essential knowledge and skills— these we must make sure our students learn; and (b) reformation of educational programs toward accomplishing these goals and outcomes must be based on what we know about student learning and how to best teach to accomplish it. Adherence to these premises will have a profound effect on the success or failure of any reform initiative. Not surprisingly, however, most reform efforts tiptoe around the periphery and do not attempt "jugular," fundamental changes in the way we think about and create program structures (goals and outcomes) or in the instructional processes that facilitate learning. Indeed, these components of the educational enterprise are the most difficult to change.

The litany of reform initiatives undertaken since the mid-1980s has been staggering. Change-based renewal efforts have been aimed at the manipulation of time (e.g., longer school day, longer school year, redistributing/reconfiguring current time allotments), strategies of governance (e.g., site-based decision making, teacher leadership, parent leadership), ideas to enable learning (e.g., technology, learning environment changes, school-community relations), and so on. While some of these strategies are yielding positive results, most are not aimed at the epicenter of the problem: improvement of student learning. For any reform effort to succeed, it must be grounded in the teaching/learning dynamic— fundamentally, on how students learn and how teachers teach. Accordingly, goals and outcomes must be grounded on these principles as well.

BEHAVIORAL AND COGNITIVE CONCEPTIONS OF LEARNING

What, then, do we know about student learning that provides guidance in determining curriculum goals and learner outcomes? Two conceptions of learning—behavioral and cognitive—provide a theoretical foundation. Before exploring a brief overview of each, let's answer the question: What is learning? Though there are many definitions of learning, this is a synthesis of Shuell's (1986) view: Learning is a process that leads to an enduring change in an individual's knowledge, skill, and/or behavior resulting from practice or experience.

The Behavioral Conception of Learning

Historically, the study of learning has had a behavioral bent (Ebbinghaus, 1913). From the late 1800s to around 1960, the study of learning centered on the memorization of single elements and on the resultant behavior of the learner. This view of learning focuses on the learner as a passive responder to externally imposed factors. This perspective has had a pervasive and resilient impact on curriculum and instruction and typifies conventional educational practice today. From this theoretical base, students are seen as passive accumulators of knowledge, able to learn by listening to lectures and reading or by rote drill and practicing isolated skills out of a realistic context. Progress is measured by the ability of the student to recapitulate what they have heard or read or practiced. As a result of these methodologies, students develop shallow understandings and abilities, which lead to misconceptions, stereotypes, and oversimplification of complex and subtle phenomena (Gardner, 1991).

The behavioral conception of learning gave rise to the elemental, objectives approach to curriculum development that led to homogeneous learning experiences and convergent learner expectations. The curriculum process focused on technical questions of procedure and specificity, not on purposes and what was most valuable to learn (Apple, 1982). Results of this view of learning include programs based on tangible bits and pieces of knowledge; skills that are planned, taught and tested; and curricula that are structured elementally and linearly, in a "layer cake" fashion.

The Cognitive Conception of Learning

As time passed, theorists began to question the validity of simple, stimulus-response conceptions of learning and the relative passivity of the learner (Bruner, 1957; Miller, Galanter, & Pribram, 1960). Learning began to be seen as systematic, involving "mental processes and knowledge structures that can be inferred from behavioral indices" (Shuell, 1986, p. 414). From the 1960s on, there was a sporadic interest in the cognitive conception of learning. Piaget, due to his work in the 1950–60s, is often deemed one of the key figures in reconceptualizing learning theory toward higher order functions. Indeed, various early applications of this school of thought were hewn in what is termed the "progressive era" in education.

The cognitive conception of learning moved the focus on learning away from the learner's behavior following a single element (instructional intervention), and toward the mind and how it functions. Scholars pursuing this avenue of research and thought were more interested in comprehension and understanding than in memorization; more attuned to interrelationships between and among elements than to single, fragmented elements; less intrigued with the resultant behavior of the learner than with the systematic processes that resulted in learning. Not until the 1990s was there a decided shift toward applying and validating the cognitive conception of learning in education.

Implications of the cognitive conception of learning. The cognitive conception of learning is having a transformational effect on current school reform efforts. Some contend (Shuell, 1986) that this concept represents mainstream educational thinking. At the very least it is becoming one of the most provocative and promising reform strategies of the 1990s. The term frequently used by educators to describe this perspective is the *constructivist philosophy of learning* or *constructivist pedagogy*. Educators are tapping into cognitive science as they grapple with constructivist philosophy. Other disciplinary perspectives lend insight as well: sociology (social construction of meaning), psychology (constructivism), and philosophy (phenomenology).

In this view, the learner is seen as one who actively creates his/her own personal "constructions" of what is meaningful. O'Neil (1992) provides a concise description.

> The key tenet of constructivist theory . . . is that people learn by actively constructing knowledge, weighing new information against previous understanding, thinking about and working through discrepencies (on their own and with others) and coming to new understandings. (p. 4)

In Figure 8.1 are propositions of the emerging conception of learning along with their implications. Learning is seen as an active, cumulative, goal-directed process; learners are seen as actively engaged in and responsible for what and that they learn. Learner outcomes are clearly articulated statements that set forth essential (often integrated) learnings. Assessment strategies demand a rich, higher order contextual blending of learner abilities: knowledge, skill, and behavior. It is helpful to visualize the constructivist perspective as an overarching umbrella that situates the learner, not the teacher or the curriculum, on center stage. Ted Sizer (1991) stated:

> Today, most of the teachers, rather than the students, 'do the work.' We present material and expect merely that students will display back to us that to which they have been exposed. Not surprisingly, the kids forget much of what they learned in a matter of months. They were not engaged. They did not have to invent on their own. They saw little meaning to their work. So, . . . we must change

1. Students learn best when actively engaged, not when passively receiving information.

Implications: Goals and outcomes need to be dynamic and confluent—full of energy. Goals and outcomes need to lead to students doing, not just receiving.

2. Students learn best and take responsibility for their learning when given choices about how they learn and how they ultimately demonstrate their learning.

Implications: Goals and outcomes need to be strong, clear guides for learning. However, once the goals and outcomes are set, students should have choices (control of) that lead to the accomplishment of the outcomes. Different students are motivated and learn best from different kinds of learning experiences. Demonstrations of learning should be seen as divergent, not convergent.

3. Students learn best when prior knowledge is connected to new learnings. Learners find meaning as new knowledge intersects with prior knowledge.

Implications: Learning experiences should be based upon building connections between previous learnings and new learnings.

4. Students learn best when learning experiences are relevant and situated in social and cultural contexts.

Implications: Goals and outcomes need to reflect a "living laboratory" approach. Tasks that connect with home, community, workplace, and real life should be used.

5. "Less is more."

Implications: The Bauhaus notion should guide the creation of goals and outcomes. Less time and energy spent on a single element of learning gives way to more time for seeking the connections between and among elements.

6. The teacher is seen as an ally, a partner in learning (facilitator, "guide on the side," coach).

Implications: Goals and outcomes should help set the tone for the learning environment and foster new, more powerful learning relationships among teachers and students.

Figure 8.1.   Emerging conceptions of learning: implications for the development of goals and outcomes

the curriculum from display-of-content to questions-that-ultimately-provoke-content. Press the kids to do their work, to solve the problems presented. The cost? It takes longer to provoke kids to learn for themselves than it does to deliver content to them. (p.33)

Educators need to stop treating facts and isolated skills as outcomes, as ends in themselves, and use them instead as means of developing information processing skills and deep structure understanding and abilities. Facts and isolated skills rarely motivate students—relevant, complex applications and performances do. Imagine for a moment that students were exposed to each of two educational experiences. The first experience is a detailed, biomechanical and physiological lecture on various performance elements related to a particular Olympic event. The second is a group project aimed at analyzing the movement and fitness components necessary for a particular Olympic event and developing a training regimen that would yield high-level performance for a particular athlete. In the first experience, students listen, take notes, and are tested. In the second, students engage in problem setting and solving, concept development, learner generated solutions, negotiation, and so on. Learning is structured around a "big idea" and gradually unfolds and emerges as students seek solutions. Students ultimately demonstrate their learning in an authentic performance indicative of their complex understanding of the task. The first educational experience may engage some students; the second would captivate the attention and curiosity of many more. If the curriculum and its delivery do not challenge and motivate students, students will not learn and will not develop a love for learning.

Current applications of the cognitive conception of learning. In general K–12 educational application, we see various manifestations of the constructionist philosophy in practice—whole language, emergent literacy, hands-on science, personal goal setting, case study approaches, cooperative learning methods, service learning, project-centered education, and so on. Various national standard-setting (learner outcome) groups have grounded their work firmly on these premises (e.g., National Council of Teachers of Mathematics, National Science Teachers Association). The National Council of Teachers of Mathematics views the learner as one who constructs meaning and, in turn, has set forth mathematics standards using real-life problems where more than one answer can be considered correct. (We all remember memorizing procedures and working toward the one correct way to achieve the one right answer!)

The National Association for Sport and Physical Education (NASPE, 1992), through its *Outcomes of Quality Physical Education Programs* document and the subsequent work of the Standards and Assessment Task Force (NASPE, 1995), has kept our profession in step with the perspective of the other subject area standards setting groups. Developers of the document attempted to define what a physically educated person would know and be able to do upon the completion of an appropriately designed and implemented program. There are twenty standards that cluster into five categories. The physically educated person:

- has learned skills necessary to perform a variety of physical activities,
- is physically fit,
- participates regularly in physical activity,
- knows the implications of and benefits from involvement in physical activities, and
- values physical activity and its contributions to a healthy lifestyle.

Notably, the focus of this perspective is squarely on the learner (see chapter 9). Most teacher effectiveness research, however, has centered on determining how effective teachers help students master content learning, particularly of isolated knowledge and skills. As a result, we currently have few insights into how teachers can help students reach levels of understanding that lead to confluent, authentic demonstrations of learning in real, contextual situations. This journey of understanding has just begun.

Where will the cognitive concept of learning lead us?   As we set out to understand learning from the learner's perspective, we are in relatively uncharted waters. Brophy (1992), one of the foremost teacher effectiveness scholars, in referring to constructivist-based research of the 1990s, stated:

> Current research, while building on findings indicating the vital role teachers play in stimulating student learning, also focuses on the role of the student. It recognizes that students do not merely passively receive or copy input from teachers, but instead actively mediate it by trying to make sense of it and relate it to what they already know (or think they know) about the topic. Thus, students develop new knowledge through a process of active construction. In order to get beyond rote memorization to achieve true understanding, they need to develop and integrate a network of associations linking new input to preexisting knowledge and beliefs anchored in concrete experience. Thus, teaching involves inducing conceptual change in students, not infusing knowledge into a vacuum. (p. 5)

The aim of contemporary thought regarding student learning is toward the interrelatedness of learning, seeking the relationships among and between elements of knowledge, skill, and behavior. With an interrelated approach, the results are much greater than meets the eye. Essentially, the whole is greater than the sum of its parts, the relationships created more powerful than the individual and collective elements.

As we travel in the exciting direction of constructivist thought, it is important to remember two things:

1. We need to proceed thoughtfully. The cognitive conception of learning has strong intuitive appeal, but we are just beginning to learn from research and practice.
2. The cognitive conception of learning should not be seen as categorically nullifying traditional processes of curriculum and instruction. It is important to remember that theories do not fade from view because they are "wrong," but because other, more comprehensive views emerge, often perched upon the shoulders of the previous ideas. It would be prudent for us to realize that certain types of learning (e.g., basic skills) may be effectively guided by traditional notions of learning.

Individual learners learn in different ways and at different rates. The taxonomies of Bloom (1956), Krathwohl, Bloom, & Masia (1964), and Harrow (1972) suggest helpful developmental progressions. As one descends or ascends these progressions, various strategies are more or less useful in facilitating student learning. We must find ways to engage the learner at all developmental stages. Likewise, we must aim our educational efforts toward the richest possible learning outcomes for each and every student. As we do so, we must attend to what we know about effective teaching that yields improved student learning.

THE INFLUENCE OF THE TWO CONCEPTIONS OF LEARNING ON THE CURRICULUM PROCESS

The two conceptions of learning just discussed have had a profound effect on the curriculum process. The curriculum process entails the careful setting of learner outcomes and their concommitant curriculum goals and learning experiences that assist in answering the question: What's worth knowing and learning?

THE OBJECTIVES APPROACH AND THE OUTCOMES APPROACH

As we examine the varying effects of the two conceptions of learning on the creation of learner outcomes and curriculum goals, it may be helpful to study Figures 8.2 and 8.3. Figure 8.2 represents the *objectives approach*, which is influenced by the behavioral conception of learning. Figure 8.3 represents the *outcomes approach*, which is influenced by the cognitive conception of learning.

The Objectives Approach

The graphic in Figure 8.2 suggests that the curriculum process begins at the bottom (kindergarten) and progresses to the top (grade 12). This

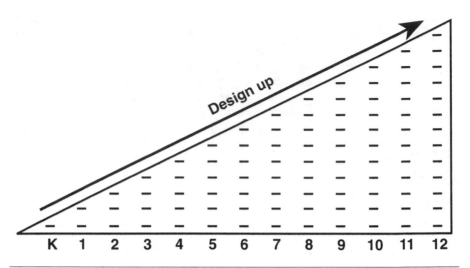

Figure 8.2.   Depiction of the design up curriculum development process

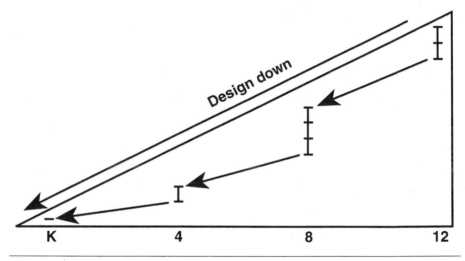

Figure 8.3.   Depiction of the design down curriculum process

depiction shows the classic, behavioral conception of learning that has dominated curriculum work and has shaped ideas of what's worth learning. The
curriculum process typically proceeds from the development of aims and
goals to the setting of specific (often behavioral) objectives from kindergarten
to grade 12. The curriculum is built from the bottom up (usually grade by
grade) adding forward from the most basic, incremental components to the
more complex components, in a "layer cake" fashion. In this process, care is
taken to subsume all of the important content elements to the more advanced
conceptual elements and to create educational experiences aimed at each of
the elements, often in isolation from other elements. In the heyday of the

behavioral objectives movement, curriculum goals and objectives took the form of intricate specifications that led to assessment of discrete, observable, and measureable elements of knowledge and skill.

Often in practice, curriculum writing teams get lost in the minutiae and lose (or never have) focus on a clearly established set of learner outcomes. The curriculum process ends up focusing on the "how tos," the teaching strategies, and not on the outcomes we wish for learners to attain. It is not enough to intuit learner outcomes; they should frame and guide the process of curriculum design.

The objectives approach and curriculum studies. This paradigm has shaped our thinking about planning and implementing educational programs. From policy setting to practice, behavioral assumptions have guided our approach to teaching and learning. Historically, curriculum studies emerged from a need to create a systematic process for selecting and ordering educational experiences (Bobbitt, 1918). The curriculum process became a technical enterprise resulting in goals and objectives that led to rather homogeneous learning expectations. Tyler's (1949) work is most notable.

Tyler's process entailed devising a systematic plan for creating content-derived educational experiences through written objectives indicating the behavior to be developed by the student. His work is seminal in that it led to the dominant curriculum design process of planning the curriculum from the bottom up (K–12). Most curriculum texts and suggested curriculum design protocol reflect this classic notion. Reference to this curriculum process is frequent in the physical education literature (Annarino, Cowell, & Hazelton, 1980; Jewett & Mullan, 1977; Siedel & Resick, 1978; and Siedentop, Mand, & Taggert, 1986). Siedentop, Mand, and Taggert suggested that in physical education we ought to be able to set systematic, behavioral terms for what we want students to be able to do. There are, however, many valued outcomes that do not lend themselves neatly to such analysis due to their ambiguity and complexity (Kirk, 1993).

Kirk (1993) points out various limitations of the objectives approach to curriculum work. Some of these limitations are:

1. The objectives approach has failed to create change in curriculum work or practice. He points out that teachers do not use them as they plan and teach.
2. The objectives approach leads to "compartmentalization, marginalization, trivialization" of qualitative, subjective, and humanistic experiences.
3. This approach has led to the perception in physical education that motor learning can be easily measured due to its overt, performance nature and that other learnings are not deemed as important.

The Outcomes Approach

The graphic in Figure 8.3 depicts a different perspective—a broader, more inclusive process for setting goals that Kirk argues should be considered in physical education. This perspective—that of constructivist pedagogy—emphasizes presenting the "big picture" in order to help students see content and learning experiences in the context of real-life situations and problems. What's worth knowing and learning, from this vantage point, clearly takes on a different face—one that is more inclusive, more complex, and less certain.

Figure 8.3 illustrates that in constructivist pedagogy, the curriculum process begins in the opposite fashion from the objectives approach—from the top down (from 12 through K). Note that there are fewer elements (less is more) than in Figure 8.2 and that elements are interconnected. From this vantage point, content is seen as important but not an end in itself. Rather, it becomes a vehicle for reaching essential learnings and valued learner outcomes.

The outcomes approach and the curriculum process. Since the late 1980s (and more obviously in the curriculum movement of the 1990s), innovative school systems have created curricula based on this perspective. This method of design is often called backward mapping—designing the curriculum "down" from the valued exit outcomes. The process begins with the exit outcomes (usually 10th or 12th grade) and progresses in a backward fashion toward kindergarten. Here, learner outcomes and assessment strategies guide the process—theoretically and in practice. In this process, it is imperative to clearly know the valued learner outcomes in order to create a conceptually sound and meaningful curriculum. The setting of curriculum goals must be focused solely on the valued outcomes set in relevant social and cultural contexts.

The outcomes-based education (OBE) movement, or standards movement, is based on this conception of learning. The actual curriculum design process may well begin with discussions and statements of philosophy, but the process quickly focuses on ends—what students should know and be able to do upon completion of a program. Spady and Marshall (1991), pioneers in the conceptualization and practical implementation of OBE, indicated that an outcome is synonomous with a goal, a purpose, an end. The shift is away from content-driven programs to "outcomes of significance" based on desired learner knowledge and skills. OBE is not without its critics, due to fear of change and the related confusion; but as a curriculum process aimed at rigorous standards of learning, it is conceptually sound and holds great promise.

Resistance to the outcomes approach. Currently, many schools are not devoted to achieving learner outcomes but rather to delivering specific educational programs and "covering the curriculum." Helping educators change the focus of their goals is a mighty task. As we move away from an emphasis on what is taught to an emphasis on what is learned, the perspective is different indeed!

Finn (1990) has said that moving to learner centered outcomes is the greatest reform initiative of all. Teachers can no longer say: "Well, I taught it. If they didn't learn it, it's their fault." Perhaps now we will say and hear: "I taught it, they didn't learn it—what do I need to do differently or in addition to help each student learn?"

What's worth learning is changing. This is becoming obvious in a variety of ways. For example, essentials are not synonomous with the basics (Wiggins, 1989). The basics are often viewed as fragments, while essentials are conceived as rich, meaningful, whole experiences. Lifelong patterns and applications are central. Depth supercedes coverage. Educational experiences generate higher order thinking skills. Facts/concepts/skills/behaviors become enmeshed as students learn and demonstrate their learning and isolated content is overshadowed by larger, conceptual learning.

Types of Learner Outcomes: Content and Process Outcomes

There are two types of learner outcomes: content outcomes and process outcomes.

Content and Process Outcomes Defined

Content outcomes are based on core information or skills that form the base for a discipline. The content outcomes perspective describes information and/or skills essential to the application of a particular discipline or content area. Assessment of content outcomes takes the form of demonstrated mastery of the desired knowledge and/or skills and the appropriate application to real-world situations and problems. Assessments involve meaningful, highly robust tasks that elicit or require the use of important knowledge and skills (Wiggins, 1989). Traditionally, goals and outcomes focused almost exclusively on content.

More recent practices of creating goals and outcomes (the standards and outcome-based view) include process outcomes. Process outcomes are based on cognitive or affective processes (attitudes, beliefs, interpersonal skills) that can be applied when attempting to understand and use information. Assessment of process outcomes occurs via their application to content, not independent of it (teamwork, problem solving, goal setting, communicating).

Factors in Creating Sets of Learner Outcomes

Content and process outcomes come together to create a structure for framing the teaching/learning process.

Values.   When a school sets out to create a set of learner outcomes and program goals, this is necessarily a value-laden task. Experience and research (Chapter 7) suggest that much of a person's belief system operates at an implicit level. One's values and beliefs are not always readily accessible but they do emerge in explicit ways when it comes to the creation of educational programs. In essence, the process of setting learner outcomes and program goals emanate from theoretical and philosophical beliefs about what is worth knowing and doing and what constitutes the best physical education program. Value orientations are discernable in the sets of learner outcomes and program goals (Jewett & Mullan, 1977).

Jewett, Bain, and Ennis (1995) identified five categories of value orientations represented in physical education programs: disciplinary mastery, learning process, social reconstruction, self-actualization, ecological validity. These five categories can be collapsed into two and viewed, from the perspective of guiding program goals and learner outcomes, as: (a) content derived goals and outcomes and (b) learner-needs derived goals and outcomes. Though all goal and outcome articulations of the various value perspectives do not fit cleanly into one category or the other, goals and outcomes generally derive from one dominant perspective. The content-derived perspective includes the disciplinary mastery and learning process value orientation categories. The learner-needs derived perspective includes the individual and social development value orientations: social reconstruction, self-actualization, and ecological validity.

Goal structures. Just as there are variable value orientations that influence program development, there are also varied views of goal structures in physical education. Jewett, Bain, and Ennis (1995) discussed program goals (termed purposes, in their framework) in physical education. They identified 22 purposes which clustered in three domains: fitness, performance, and transcendence (Figure 8.4).

THREE FRAMEWORKS FOR SETTING GOALS AND LEARNER OUTCOMES IN PHYSICAL EDUCATION

As teachers and other educational leaders endeavor to construct curricula, a design framework should be used. Without a lens through which to view the creation of curriculum, the tendency is to replicate old curriculum content and processes or to "borrow" the ideas and structures of another already existing document.These common strategies often result in a curriculum that does not challenge and motivate students, and so does not contribute to student learning or to developing a love of learning.

It may be helpful to understand how the curriculum process unfolds in practice. One can ascertain a program's value orientation and dominant goal derivation by examining curriculum guides or frameworks. Most

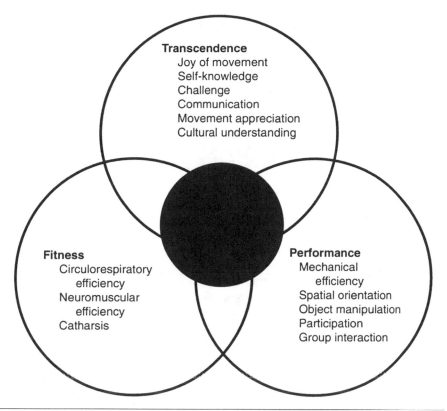

Figure 8.4.   Personal meaning value clusters
From "The Status of Physical Education Curriculum Theory," by A.E. Jewett, 1980, *Quest,*
32(2), p. 170. Copyright 1981 by the National Association for Physical Education in Higher
Education. Reprinted with permission.

physical education programs derive from the discipline of physical education and include content foci of fitness, motor skill, and movement forms
(Bain, 1988). The curriculum process commonly focuses on setting goals
and learning experiences aimed at the accomplishment of specific movement, fitness, and motor skill objectives. Chapters 11 and 12 reflect program emphases that are predominantly content-derived, *predominantly*
being the operative word. Clearly, various process outcomes are also included but the dominant framework is motor skill or fitness, in these
cases. The educational end is mastery of disciplinary content.

While most physical education programs are content derived, others are
learner-needs derived. As a result, the learner outcomes and program goals
are aimed at processes and learner needs, not disciplinary content. The
predominant focus is upon the learner. Chapter 13 sets forth the personal
and social responsibility perspective of Hellison as a notable example. In
Hellison's view, learner needs are not subjugated to content. Content serves
as a means to the end of developing personal and social responsibility.

Three frameworks for setting goals and outcomes in physical education will be shared in this section: traditional, transitional, and transformational. Spady and Marshall (1991), in their work related to OBE, categorized various program efforts aimed at OBE. Using the terms *traditional*, *transitional*, and *transformational*, they distinguished each of the three approaches. I will use these terms to clarify the frameworks for guiding the curriculum process in practice in physical education. I shall briefly explain each framework and will focus on the following: (a) What's worth learning?; (b) What "lens" is helpful in creating a curriculum within this framework?; and (c) What characterizes this framework?

TRADITIONAL FRAMEWORK: CONTENT DERIVED

This framework is the one most often used in curriculum design in physical education. The focus of the curriculum process is on the acquisition of disciplinary content (knowledge and skills, primarily) in physical education. The curricula that result from this process are often highly fragmented, objectives-based programs.

What's Worth Learning?

The focus in this framework is upon acquiring existing disciplinary knowledge. Most often, a single content focus is taken (e.g., volleyball). The activity is broken down into elemental pieces (e.g., basic skills, rules, strategies), and these elements determine what's worth learning. In this case the skills and knowledge of the sport of volleyball would be the valued learner outcomes. Occasionally, multiple content foci may be used. For example, the teacher may focus on disciplinary mastery of the sport of volleyball but also integrate various components of health related physical fitness. The student would then be taught (and, we hope learn) the motor skill and physical fitness disciplinary content pertinent to volleyball.

What "Lens" is Helpful in Creating a Curriculum Within This Framework?

Curricula most often are viewed through an objectives-based lens, resulting in a typical scope and sequence chart articulating the various skills and knowledge of the specific content area. Usually, the curriculum is created from the bottom up (as in Figure 8.2), but it could just as easily be developed from an outcomes-based perspective (as in Figure 8.3). All connections are content, disciplinary based. This framework is not difficult to grasp. Visualize a typical unit approach to designing a curriculum— three weeks of volleyball, three weeks of aerobics, three weeks of tennis, etc. Each unit stands alone and is composed of its own unique content and skills. There are no connections between the units of instruction.

What Characterizes This Framework?

This curriculum is often prescriptive, and the curriculum document is extensive, including many elements that are assumed to add up to a complete skill or mastery performance. An apt characterization would be skills/drills/team play. Goals and outcomes derive from the disciplinary content. Knowledge, skill, and behavior goals and outcomes are most frequently separate and not integrated. Student assessment methods center on mastery of the skills and knowledge of the content. Skill tests, often out of realistic gamelike contexts (e.g., wall volley test) would be used.

TRANSITIONAL FRAMEWORK: LEARNER/SOCIETY-NEEDS DERIVED

In this framework, disciplinary content can be seen as an end in itself (as in the traditional framework), but more often it is also seen as a means of helping students develop competencies that carry beyond the gymnasium. Students are viewed as having a variety of needs, including intellectual, physical, emotional, and social. Hellison's work fits most closely within this framework.

What's Worth Learning?

The major thrust of this view of the curriculum process is helping students develop skills (e.g., decision making, problem solving, personal and social responsibility, etc.) that will assist them in their lives outside the school. Disciplinary content is less central than in the traditional framework and is used as a vehicle for attaining the affective life skills. Learner needs supercede content coverage, and meeting these needs contributes to fulfilling social needs as well.

What "Lens" Is Helpful in Creating a Curriculum Within This Framework?

This framework converges around an affective skill or group of skills. If, for example, personal and social responsibility is our learner outcome, what curriculum goals and content do we wish to create that will enable the accomplishment of this outcome? Sport, dance, and fitness experiences aim at the development of skill and fitness, but the major purpose of the learning experiences is to help students develop personal and social responsibility. The affective skill, then, is seen as the primary organizer across the curriculum in physical education (or beyond). Visualize an affective skill in the hub of a wheel with various content components emanating out like spokes from that center. All content experiences are aimed at the accomplishment of the life skill. If the content is not useful in elaborating upon the life skill, it is not used.

What Characterizes This Framework?

In this framework, outcomes and goals are often less concrete than in the traditional framework. The curriculum is focused on bigger questions, questions that transcend content and strive toward different human and societal needs. The lines between knowledge, skill, and behavior goals and outcomes blur and, in many cases, disappear. Assessment of student learning includes demonstrations of in-class and real-life application of the life skills.

TRANSFORMATIONAL FRAMEWORK: SOCIETY/LEARNER-NEEDS DERIVED

You will note the reversal of "learner" and "society" in the transitional and transformational captions. The transformational framework assumes that the purpose of education is to prepare the learner for an uncertain, global, integrated future. While the individual student is central in this framework, the thrust is the development of each individual to be prepared for and make a difference in both the present and the future.

What's Worth Learning?

Content emerges from relevant, meaningful, real-life contexts that require relevant, meaningful, real-life competencies and solutions. Students and teachers work together to determine broad, higher order, life role performances that blend past, present, and future. For example, if physical fitness was seen as an important concept or learning focus, it would be studied from a variety of angles—historical, political, economic, legal, sociological, environmental, mass media, and so on. Instead of teaching the discipline of physical education, the importance of physical activity to survival would be examined. Efforts to make sense of the human condition would be prominent, and learning that is essential to life now and in the future would be central.

What "Lens" Is Helpful in Creating a Curriculum Within This Framework?

The best way to conceive of the curriculum process within this framework is to visualize a common, encompassing theme or concept in the center of a circle. Instead of spokes (as in the transitional framework), concentric circles cluster around the circle. All circles connect with the central concept and with each other. All connections are based on real life, or the way life is projected to be, and aim at the development of skills for living a meaningful, productive life.

What Characterizes This Framework?

This framework transcends content boundaries and aims at seeking meaning and relevance through life-centered experiences. Content is determined by student and teacher collaboration, not by predetermined curriculum. Knowledge is seen as interconnected and value-laden, not fragmented and value-less. More large-scale connections and essential learning experiences seen by the teacher and the learners as vital to the future are apparent. Learning is validated by the ability of the learners to create a learning journey. Assessment of learning is necessarily performance based, with students demonstrating deep understanding of those things they and their teacher deemed "essential."

SUMMARY

Learner outcomes are valued educational ends—what students should know and be able to do upon the completion of a course of study. Curriculum goals comprise the programmatic framework for content and learning experiences aimed at the realization of learner outcomes. Both derive from philosophical beliefs about what is worth learning. The creation of goals and outcomes is situated in a particular environmental and temporal context. Historically, most programs have been developed from a developmental, elemental perspective influenced primarily by the behavioral conception of learning. The current standards and outcomes reform initiative in education is pushing the curriculum process toward a constructivist pedagogy, emerging from a cognitive conception of learning. Further, the curriculum process may unfold in practice in a variety of ways. Frameworks for traditional, transitional, and transformational processes were provided.

REFERENCES

Annarino, A.A., Cowell, C.C., & Hazelton, H.W. (1980). *Curriculum theory and design in physical education* (2nd ed.). St. Louis: Mosby.

Apple, M. (1982). Curricular form and the logic of technical control: Building the possessive individual. In M. Apple & L. Weiss (Eds.), *Cultural and economic reproduction of education* (pp. 247–270). New York: Routledge & Kegan Paul.

Bain, L.L. (1988). Curriculum for critical reflection in physical education. In R. Brandt (Ed.), *Content of the curriculum* (pp. 133–147). Alexandria, VA: Association for Supervision and Curriculum Development.

Bloom, B. (1956). *Taxonomy of educational objectives. Handbook I: The cognitive domain.* New York: David McKay.

Bobbitt, F. (1918). *The curriculum.* Boston: Houghton Mifflin.

Brophy, J. (1992, April). Probing the subtleties of subject-matter teaching, *Educational Leadership, 49*(7), 10.

Bruner, J. (1957). Going beyond the information given. In J.S. Bruner, E. Brunswick, L. Festinger, F. Heider, K. Muenzinger, C. Osgood, & D. Rapport (Eds.), *Contemporary approaches to cognition* (pp. 41–69). Cambridge, MA: Harvard University Press.

Ebbinghaus, H. (1913). *Memory* (H.A. Rugert and C.E. Bussenius, Trans.). New York: Teachers College. (Original work published 1885.)

Finn, C. (1990, April). The biggest reform of all. *Phi Delta Kappan, 71*(8), 584–92.

Gardner, H. (1991). *The unschooled mind: How children think and how schools should teach.* New York: Basic Books.

Harrow, A.J. (1972). *A taxonomy of the psychomotor domain: A guide for developing behavioral objectives.* New York: David McKay.

Hellison, P. (1985). *Goals and strategies for teaching physical education.* Champaign, IL: Human Kinetics.

Jewett, A.E., Bain, L.L., & Ennis, C.D. (1995). *The curriculum process in physical education.* Dubuque, IA: Brown and Benchmark.

Jewett, A.E., & Mullan, M. (1977). *Curriculum design: Purposes and processes in physical education teaching-learning.* Washington, DC: AAHPERD.

Kirk, D. (1993). Curriculum work in physical education: Beyond the objectives approach? *Journal of Teaching in Physical Education, 12*, 244–265.

Krathwohl, D.R., Bloom, B., & Masia, B. (1964). *Taxonomy of educational objectives, Handbook II: Affective domain.* New York: David McKay.

Miller, G.A., Galanter, E., & Pribram, K.L. (1960). *Plans and the structure of behavior.* New York: Holt, Rinehart & Winston.

National Association for Sport and Physical Education. (1992). *Outcomes of Quality Physical Education.* Reston, VA: American Alliance for Health, Physical Education, Recreation and Dance.

National Association for Sport and Physical Education. (1995). *Moving into the future: National standards for physical education.* Reston, VA: American Alliance for Health, Physical Education, Recreation and Dance.

O'Neil, J. (1992, March). Wanted: Deep understanding: Constructivism posits new conceptions of learning. *ASCD Update, 34*(3), 1, 4–5, 8.

Schiller, D.P., Schiller, W.J., & Walberg H.J. (1989). Ralph Tyler: 20th century patriot. *Vitae Scholasticae: The Bulletin of Educational Biography, 7*(1), 193–206.

Shuell, T.J. (1986). Cognitive conceptions of learning. *Review of Educational Research, 56*, 411–436.

Siedel, B., & Resick, M. (1978). *Physical education. An overview* (2nd ed). Reading, MA: Addison-Wesley.

Siedentop, D., Mand, C., & Taggart, A. (1986). *Physical education: Teaching and curriculum strategies for grades 5-12.* Mountain View, CA: Mayfield.

Sizer, T.R. (1984). *Horace's compromise: The dilemma of the American high school.* Boston: Houghton Mifflin.

Sizer, T.R. (1991). No pain, no gain. *Educational Leadership, 48*(8), 32–34.

Spady, W.G., & Marshall, K. (1991). Beyond traditional outcome-based education. *Educational Leadership, 49*(2), 67–72.

Tyler, R. (1949). *Basic principles of curriculum and instruction.* Chicago: University of Chicago Press.

United States Department of Education. (1983). *A nation at risk: The imperative for educational reform.* Washington, DC: United States Government Printing Office.

Wiggins, G. (1989). The futility of trying to teach everything important. *Educational Leadership, 47*(3), 44–48, 57–59.

CHAPTER 9

Effective Instruction in Physical Education

Judith E. Rink

Identifying good teaching has always been a problem for educators. There has been a tendency to say that good teaching is something that you cannot describe or define, let alone prescribe.

The problem is that if you cannot describe good teaching, then any teaching is as good as any other. We need to be able to describe good teaching so that we can help teachers to become better at what they do and so that we have a knowledge base from which to train and educate new teachers. The increasing research base on teacher effectiveness has helped us to describe more fully than ever before "good teaching."

WHAT IS EFFECTIVE TEACHING?

Although the terms *effective teaching* and *good teaching* have been used interchangeably at times, more often the former has been used to describe teaching that results in intended learning (Berliner, 1987; Brophy, 1979; Rosenshine, 1987). Students learn a lot as a result of experience. They learn a lot in schools that is not intended, some of it desirable and some not desirable, but the primary function of schools is to produce intended learning. Effective teaching, then, is teaching that results in more intended learning than does less effective teaching (Gage, 1978).

Most of what we know about effective teaching comes to us from well conducted classroom research studies that identify what teachers do who produce the most learning (Brophy & Evertson, 1974; Brophy & Good, 1986; Good & Grouws, 1975; McDonald & Elias, 1976; Stallings & Kaskowitz, 1974). These efforts were large, correlational studies conducted primarily in a process-product research design. Process-product research designs examine the relationship between characteristics of the teaching process and the products of teaching (most often student learning). These studies utilized primarily highly structured subject matter and short-term teaching objectives. These studies were very consistent in the variables they identified as important to effective classroom teaching. Most of these variables have been studied in the physical education literature with similar findings. A set of teaching principles that describe what effective teachers do has evolved from this research base (Berliner, 1987; Brophy & Good, 1986; Gage, 1978).

As you read this material you will need to keep in mind that we are talking about studies based on highly structured content and short-term objectives. Highly structured subject matter lends itself to being broken down into small parts. The effective teaching literature has identified primarily generic variables related to teacher effectiveness; that is, those variables that seem to discriminate effective teaching across content and settings. More recent research has been concerned primarily with the identification of context-specific ideas that describe in detail how effective teachers teach particular content to particular learners in particular settings.

The problem, of course, in defining effective teaching in terms of what students learn is that goals for student learning are often complex, long-term, multidimensional, and not easily measured. What makes a multiobjective setting complex from a measurement perspective is that teachers can be effective in meeting one objective and ineffective in meeting another. The multi-objective problem is compounded by the idea that there may be real differences in what is effective in the short run and what is effective with time. There is the possibility that teachers may accomplish short-term objectives in a way that jeopardizes the usually more important long-term objectives of teaching (e.g., making students fit but destroying their love for activity; acquiring motor skills as opposed to retaining motor skills).

It has been suggested that some teachers do not have as the goal of their teaching student learning (Ennis, 1994). Under those conditions the concept of effective teaching is a moot point. Most educators accept the idea that it is their responsibility to facilitate student learning in some way. The National Association for Sport and Physical Education (NASPE) Outcomes Project (1992) and the NASPE Standards and Assessment Project (1995) reinforce the multifaceted goals of a comprehensive physical education program. In these materials skill development, fitness, physical activity, cognitive, and affective concerns directly related to the development of a physically active lifestyle are described.

PROPOSITIONAL RULES AND PRINCIPLED PRACTICE

In spite of the complexity of trying to sort out issues related to what effective teachers actually do, it is important to try and understand the teaching/learning process in depth. A search for rigid prescriptions of the right way to teach has largely been replaced with the search for propositional rules and principles to guide practice. Principles of teaching represent ideas on how to teach that are general guidelines for practice to be applied situationally (Berliner, 1987; Ornstein & Levine, 1981; Rosenshine & Stevens, 1986).

In this perspective, what the teacher does is seen in terms of the function of a particular teaching act in a particular setting. Teaching functions have been identified at three domains in terms of the preactive, interactive, and postactive decisions teachers have to make (Rosenshine & Stevens, 1986). More specifically, teaching functions for physical education have been described in terms of

- identifying intended outcomes for learning;
- planning learning experiences to accomplish those outcomes;
- presenting tasks to learners;
- organizing and managing the learning environment;
- monitoring the learning environment;
- developing the content; and
- evaluating the effectiveness of the instructional/curricular process (Rink, 1993).

Principles of teaching can describe in broad terms the characteristics of these functions when they are performed well. Principles of teaching cannot be used to prescribe particular behaviors because many behaviors can perform the same function and the same behavior can perform different functions in different settings. For example, providing learners the information they need on how to perform a skill can be done through teacher explanation, student or teacher demonstration, media, or peers. Expertise involves knowing when and how to apply a principle of teaching to accomplish particular objectives in particular settings.

TEACHER EFFECTIVENESS IN PHYSICAL EDUCATION

Because physical education is concerned with the psychomotor domain it has a unique position in the educational community. Principles of teaching physical education are drawn from the effective teaching literature in

ı and the classroom and, to some extent, from motor
nd research. The rest of this chapter outlines the critical
ıe effective teaching research in physical education. This
ı been organized as principles of practice and is discussed
of the limitations of the knowledge base as well as the
ıf that knowledge base for teaching physical education.

STUDENTS WHO SPEND MORE TIME IN GOOD PRACTICE LEARN MORE

The fact that students learn more when they practice more should not surprise anyone, particularly when it comes to learning motor skills. Initially this variable was investigated in terms of the amount of time a teacher allocated for practice (Anderson, 1980; Metzler, DePaepe, & Reif, 1985). Gradually the construct has been refined to the idea that if you want students to learn a motor skill they have to be engaged at a high level and successful at an appropriate task for a sufficient amount of time to produce learning (Cousineau & Luke, 1990; Goldberger & Gerney, 1990; Metzler, 1989; Silverman, 1985, 1990; Silverman, Devillier, & Ramírez, 1991).

Research

The first descriptive studies in physical education outlined a rather dismal picture. Students in physical education classes were actually active only about a third of the class time (Anderson, 1980; Costello, 1977). Newer descriptive studies using an instrument called Academic Learning Time-Physical Education (ALT-PE) (Metzler, 1979) describe the amount of time students were engaged in activity at an appropriate level of difficulty. The results of these studies have not changed the fact that students in physical education classes are not spending a great deal of time engaged in appropriate practice of physical skills and therefore do not have much of an opportunity to become skillful.

More specific measures of practice that look at the number of actual practice trials, as opposed to time only, and attempts to look at the quality of the practice have been more productive in identifying a strong, positive relationship between practice and learning (Ashy, Lee, & Landin, 1988; Buck, Harrison, & Bryce, 1991; Silverman, 1990; Werner & Rink, 1989). A relationship exists between the motor appropriate variable in the ALT-PE instrument (as well as other measures of time) and the content and learning, although this relationship is not as close as might have been anticipated (Godbout, Burnelle, & Tousignant, 1983; Silverman et al., 1991). The idea that time in practice is not a sufficient predictor of effectiveness is most likely due to the fact that there are other factors of engagement that influence the quality of practice and determine whether or not a student learns.

Implications

The message from most process-product studies using complex motor skills, such as those most frequently taught in physical education, is that learning takes time. It is not uncommon to see physical education units planned for a period of three weeks that assign one class period to the development of each skill. If students are to learn a skill well enough to use it in game situations or to participate in a given activity, sufficient time must be allocated for learning, particularly if the goal is competence in sports that involve complex and difficult motor skills. This idea has serious implications for curriculum planning in physical education. Either teachers must increase the time spent teaching one activity and teach fewer of them, or, they must change the activities taught so that it is possible to master a skill or activity in the time allowed. This curricular issue, which has been identified from primarily instructional research, is perhaps the most significant issue facing physical educators with limited program time who continue to try and teach a comprehensive curriculum.

PRACTICE SHOULD BE APPROPRIATE TO THE GOAL OF LEARNING AND THE INDIVIDUAL STUDENT

Tasks must be appropriate in order for students to learn them. First, the tasks students are asked to do must relate to an objective or measurement. If, for instance, you are interested in teaching students how to use a forearm pass in volleyball and the practice never gets beyond a soft toss from the partner, it is unlikely that you will see much progress if you look at how well students execute a forearm pass in a game. Transfer of practice to game conditions depends on the extent to which the practice resembles the game (Magill, 1993). A key question teachers should ask themselves about student tasks is, "Will this task develop the objective I want to develop?" If the answer to this question is "No," the next question is, "How can I make the task and the practice more appropriate?" or, "How can I gradually move students from where they are to where I want them to be?"

A second factor related to appropriateness is the characteristics of the individual learner. If students do not have the prerequisites to learn a skill, they could practice forever and probably not make a great deal of progress. Students who do not have the abdominal strength cannot do a hip circle on a bar no matter how hard they try.

Research

Research on teaching volleyball in high school/middle school identified the fact that about one third of the student population from the studies made no progress over six days of practice in their ability to use a forearm pass or an overhand serve pattern in rather simple conditions. (French,

Rink, Rickard, Mays, Lynn, & Werner, 1991; French, Rink, & Werner, 1990; Rink, French, Werner, Lynn, & Mays, 1992). A simple to complex progression of tasks was used but low-skilled students were not able to generate enough force in the testing conditions which were more gamelike. What are the long-term implications of presenting to learners tasks that are not within their capabilities?

Implications

If students do not practice in gamelike conditions, they will not be able to play the game. If practice conditions are *too* gamelike beginning learners may not improve because the practice conditions may be too difficult for them. These two statements present the major problem physical education teachers have in trying to teach the skills of complex games and sports to students in a typical physical education class. Practice needs to occur at a level that incorporates as much of the "game" as students can manage successfully.

STUDENTS WHO PRACTICE AT A REASONABLY HIGH SUCCESS LEVEL LEARN MORE

The issue of success rate is related to task appropriateness. The students in the volleyball example above were not successful at even minimal levels. From the classroom literature we have learned that students should be engaged in the content with a high level of success approaching 80% (Berliner, 1987). Although the physical education research supports the importance of successful practice, there are several indications that the application of an 80% success rate for motor skills may be inappropriate for many motor tasks.

Issues and Research

The type of motor skill being practiced is a factor in determining an appropriate success rate for practice. Consider for example basketball shooting. The expectation that beginners should have an 80% success rate would not be appropriate. An 80% success rate in many shots would be unheard of even for professional players who have high degrees of skill. We are less able to be consistent when we are performing skills in a changing environment and when we are performing complex skills that require a great deal of eye-hand or eye-foot coordination, such as tennis serves, golf drives, volleyball spikes, and so on. As discussed in a later section on progressions, teachers can reduce the level of complexity of skills to increase the likelihood of greater success.

A more recent issue related to success rate has been raised in the motor learning literature: Does more successful practice always mean more learning (Magill, 1993)? In order to fully understand the implications of this idea the distinction between acquisition and retention must be made. Acquisition refers to the success of learners while they are learning a motor skill. Retention refers to their ability to perform after they have learned a motor skill. There is some support for the idea that a very high success rate during the acquisition phase of learning does not always lead to increased retention or learning. From a motor skill perspective, "errorless practice and rote repetition are poor learning strategies" (Lee, Swinnen, & Serrien, 1994, p. 338). Although work in this area is still at beginning stages, theorists suspect that the reason for this may be related to cognitive processing, as discussed in the next section.

Physical educators often talk about trying to find the balance between tasks that are not challenging enough for students and those that are too difficult to sustain practice. Finding the balance in motor activities that approaches an appropriate level of challenge for all students is difficult because the appropriate level of challenge is likely to be different for different students and performance in many motor skills is much more variable than cognitive learning. In addition, some students are more willing to practice at lower success rates than other students. This willingness is most likely related to the age of the learner, the particular skill they are practicing, and personality characteristics.

Implications

Most educators believe that students will not continue to do that at which they are not successful. This is true for both short-term practice of skills and long-term program goals. A good guideline for teachers to use in determining whether task difficulty is appropriate is probably, if the learner can be successful with effort then the task is appropriate. If it takes no effort and if learners try hard but cannot be successful then the task is probably not appropriate. Although teachers work with groups, success rate is related to the appropriateness of the task for an individual. Effective teachers find ways to help individual students be successful by manipulating the demands of motor tasks. In many instances teachers can break down skills (e.g., starting with the toss in the tennis serve); change the conditions of practice (e.g., move partners closer together); or, modify the equipment (e.g., use lighter volleyballs or shorter rackets). Developing the ability to design learning experiences within your class so that different students can be working at different levels takes preparation and a real commitment to the importance of student success rate in learning.

STUDENTS WHO PRACTICE AT A HIGHER LEVEL OF PROCESSING LEARN MORE

One of the characteristics of quality practice is related to the learner's level of cognitive effort. Learner attention to the task was identified early

on as an important ingredient in learning. Fitts and Posner (1967) identified the first stage of motor learning as being cognitive, which means that
the learner must translate information on how to perform into a motor
program. The last stage of motor learning is automatic, which means that
the movement response is reduced to a lower level of cognitive functioning.
Students cannot get to the later stages of learning without processing
responses and attending to their actions.

Research

The importance of cognition becomes apparent at the point where the
learner is trying to determine how to attempt the skill (the initial motor
program) as well as during practice. Although we do not have a great deal
of consensus on the specific, underlying cognitive mechanisms governing
motor performance, the importance of cognitive processes in anticipating,
planning, regulating, and interpreting motor performances has received
increased attention from researchers in both motor leaning theory and
pedagogy (French et. al., 1990; Housner & French, 1994; Lee, et. al., 1994;
Sweeting & Rink, 1994).

The critical role of learner cognition has long been the justification for
many of the variables we have identified as important to instructing
learners on how to perform (Magill, 1993; Rink, 1993). The intent has
been to present information on performing a task to learners in such a
way as to help them design an accurate motor plan for a movement
response. If a student has the prerequisites to perform a motor skill
correctly and does not, the assumption is that the learner does not have
a clear idea of how to perform that skill. It is not the muscular-skeletal
system that is not functioning correctly, it is the cognitive plan being
executed that is not correct. Obviously, the nature and manner in which
information is communicated to learners can facilitate the development
of accurate motor plans. This information is presented later in this chapter
(see the section on task presentation).

Teachers facilitate cognitive processing not only by the manner in which
they present tasks but also by the way in which they arrange practice
(Good & Magill, 1986; Lee, et. al., 1994). Mere repetition of responses
without processing is unlikely to be as effective for learning as practice
where the student must continue to process or review their actions during
each trial.

Implications

The idea that students should be engaged at a high level with the content
for prolonged periods should surprise no one. When practice fails to produce student learning we can only suggest that what was practiced, or
how it was practiced, is not appropriate, assuming the measure of learning
and the learning objective was appropriate. In one sense, the ability of

the teacher to increase the quantity and quality of practice is the ultimate teaching skill. As Silverman and Tyson (1994) have identified, most other teaching skills affect learning through their influence on practice. Student engagement is the goal—not only the quantity of time a student spends engaged with the content but the quality of that time. Until we know more about how to engage students appropriately we will not know enough to be of help to teachers. Many of the variables which follow provide insight into how to engage students appropriately with the content.

EFFECTIVE TEACHERS CREATE AN ENVIRONMENT FOR LEARNING

Although management is often contrasted with the substantive content of instruction, the two are integrally related. Good managers are not necessarily effective teachers, but effective teachers must be good managers. Management was an early focus of research on teaching, both in the classroom as well as in the gymnasium, and is a continuous concern for practicing teachers in public school settings.

Research

Management has come to be thought of as a process of obtaining and maintaining order (Doyle, 1986). Management usually involves two dimensions: The first is related to the ability of the teacher to develop and maintain a learning climate, and the second is related to the teacher's organizational skills (Emmer, Evertson, & Anderson, 1980; Evertson & Emmer, 1982; Soar & Soar, 1979). A positive learning climate is one in which students are focused and motivated to learn. The classroom climates of effective teachers are task-oriented, businesslike, and slightly warm in their affective tone. Effective learning environments are not necessarily high affect. The teacher must motivate students to engage in academic content at a high level of engagement and avoid criticism (which is negative affect), but this does not necessarily mean that the environment created is totally student centered.

Studies describing the classrooms of effective managers identified the critical role of teaching students rules and procedures and using these in a consistent fashion. Effective managers monitor student behavior, develop systems and methods of holding students accountable for their work, present information clearly, and organize instruction so that more time is spent on academic tasks rather than nonacademic tasks (Emmer et al., 1980; Evertson & Emmer, 1982).

Early work on teacher management probably spent too much time concerned with the teacher's responsibility for behavior and student compliance with rules. More recent efforts in studying teacher management have focused on trying to understand differences between settings and individual students as well as ways to transfer the responsibility for student behavior to the student (McCaslin & Good, 1992). Motivating students to learn requires that the teacher develop sympathy with the abilities and needs of particular students in particular settings without abandoning the comprehensive goals of the physical education program or the broader curricular goals of a school.

Implications

Management is important because time spent managing behavior or learning experiences is time taken away from substantive content. Teachers who are good managers organize for high levels of practice and develop a learning environment that maintains a high level of student engagement in that practice. Effective managers are in charge. Students are not simply let go; they are held accountable for their work and are on task during class time. Teachers who teach and maintain rules and procedures in their class, use stop and start signals, and respond to inattentive and disruptive behavior quickly are more likely to be effective teachers.

Management continues to be a major problem and concern for many physical education teachers who have not been able to develop a learning environment that enables them to focus students on learning. Many physical education environments are characterized by a great deal of student off-task behavior or a predominant teacher focus on student compliance. Many physical education environments have no learning expectations. Students are not off-task—they are simply not engaged in learning. In some cases teachers have lost their belief that students can learn or want to learn physical education content, which has produced subtle but substantial changes in curriculum (Ennis, 1994). Teachers have been unable to create an environment that enables them to teach motor or fitness content, which may be why they are looking elsewhere for program justification.

When teachers have not produced a learning environment conducive to learning, the teacher's choice of learning experiences is very limited. Many of the exciting teaching strategies and curriculum approaches that are often recommended for physical education require a degree of student independence not developed in most physical education teaching environments. Students need a degree of independence to work in cooperative learning environments or to work independently at their own level with tasks. Teachers who do not develop a learning environment that minimally supports a level of student self-control (Hellison, 1995) will not be able to use many alternative teaching strategies critical to the development of many important goals of physical education.

EFFECTIVE TEACHERS ARE GOOD COMMUNICATORS

Much of the classroom research related to communication has taken the form of investigations of teacher clarity (Kennedy, Cruickshank, Bush, & Meyers, 1978; Land, 1981). The teacher's ability to communicate with the learner is critical to effective physical education. In terms of instructional events, the presentation of the instructional task is critical. The teacher must be able to select important information for the learner, organize that information, and communicate it to the learner.

Research

Rosenshine and Stevens (1986) have described several aspects of clear presentations from the classroom research. These ideas are summarized in Table 9.1. There is no reason to assume that these generic aspects of clarity are not appropriate for physical education. Teachers need to have explicit goals for their classes that are clearly communicated. They need to organize and present material logically, in step-by-step progressions. They need to take material to concrete levels and check to make sure students understand what they are saying (Rink, 1994).

Almost all the work on task presentation in physical education has assumed a direct approach to teaching, the assumption being that the

Table 9.1   Rosenshine and Stevens' Aspects of Clear Presentations

1. Clarity of goals and main points

    a. State the goals and objectives of the presentation.
    b. Focus on one thought, point, or direction at a time.
    c. Avoid digressions.
    d. Avoid ambiguous phrases and pronouns.

2. Step-by-step presentations

    a. Present the material in small steps.
    b. Organize and present the material so that one point is mastered before the next point is given.
    c. Give explicit step-by-step directions (when possible).
    d. Present an outline when the material is complex.

3. Specific and concrete procedures

    a. Model the skill or process (when appropriate).
    b. Give detailed and redundant information for difficult points.
    c. Provide students with concrete and varied examples.

4. Checking for students' understanding

    a. Be sure that students understand one point before proceeding to the next point.
    b. Ask the students questions to monitor their comprehension of what has been presented.
    c. Have students summarize the main points in their own words.
    d. Reteach the parts of the presentation that the students have difficulty comprehending, either by further teacher explanation or by students tutoring other students.

learner must be given explicit information on what to do and how to do it. What differentiates physical education from the classroom is it's emphasis on presenting motor skills. Several instruments for use in a physical education setting have been developed to describe task presentation characteristics. The Qualitative Measures of Teaching Performance Scale (QMTPS) (Rink & Werner, 1989) was primarily designed to describe the manner in which the teacher presents tasks to learners. The categories of the scale are described in Table 9.2. The initial work validating the relationship between this instrument and student learning has been most encouraging. The total score on the QMTPS was highly correlated with student learning in a middle school volleyball setting, supporting earlier studies with elementary children (Gusthart, Kelly, & Rink, in press). Task explicitness— including communicating to the learner the situation, the criterion for performance, and the outcome of the desired performance—has been identified and supported by Silverman and his colleagues as a critical dimension of effective teaching as well (Silverman, Kulinna, & Crull, 1995).

One recent study providing a great deal of support for a direct approach to task presentation was done by Kwak (1993). Five different task presentations were compared in terms of their effects on process characteristics (form), the product characteristics of learning, and the learner's ability to verbalize how to perform an unfamiliar, complex, gross motor skill (lacrosse throw). The five different treatments were:

1. Verbal explanation with partial demonstration.
2. Full demonstration only.
3. Overload explanation with partial demonstration.
4. Verbal explanation with full demonstrations and summary cues, visual/verbal rehearsal task presentation.
5. Control group—no task presentation.

The results of the study strongly support the use of full demonstration, summary cues, and student rehearsal. The students in the last group had higher product and process scores and were better able to verbalize how to perform the skill.

Graham and her colleagues (Graham, 1988; Graham, Hussey, Taylor, & Werner, 1993) have studied the task presentations of effective teachers in physical education and have identified eight dimensions of effective task presentations:

1. Making instruction explicit.
2. Emphasizing the usefulness of the content being presented.
3. Structuring new content.
4. Signaling student's attention.
5. Summarizing and repeating information.
6. Checking for understanding.
7. Creating a productive climate for learning.
8. Presenting accountability measures.

Table 9.2 QMTPS Task Presentation Categories

1. Clarity

   Teacher's verbal explanation/directions communicated a clear idea of what to do and how to do it. This judgment is confirmed on the basis of student movement response to the presentation and is relative to the situation.

   Yes: Students proceed to work in a focused way on what the teacher asked them to do.

   No: Students exhibited confusion, questions, off-task behavior, or lack of intent to deal with the specifics of the task.

2. Demonstration

   Visual information modeling desired performance executed by teacher, student(s), and/or visual aids.

   Yes: Full model of the desired movement.

   Partial: Incomplete model of task performance exhibiting only part of the desired movement.

   No: No attempt to model the movement task.

3. Appropriate Number of Cues

   The degree to which the teacher presented sufficient information useful to the performance about the movement task without overloading the learner.

   Appropriate: Three or fewer new learning cues related to the performance of the movement task.

   Inappropriate: More than three new learning cues related to the performance of the movement, or none given when needed.

   None Given: No attempt at providing learning cues was made.

4. Accuracy of Cues

   The degree to which the information presented was technically correct and reflected accurate mechanical principles.

   Accurate: All information present was correct.

   Inaccurate: One or more instances of incorrect information.

   None Given: No cues given.

5. Qualitative Cues Provided

   Verbal information provided to the learner on the process or mechanics of movement.

   Yes: Teacher's explanation or direction included at least one aspect of the process of performance.

   No: Teacher's explanation or direction included no information on the process of performance.

(continued)

Table 9.2   *(continued)*

---

6. Appropriate to the Focus

   The degree to which student responses reflected an intent to perform the task as stated by the teacher.

All:	One—no more than two students viewed on the screen exhibited inappropriate responses.
Partial:	Two—three or more students viewed on the screen exhibited inappropriate behavior.
None:	Three—no students exhibited appropriate behavior.

7. Specific Congruent Feedback

   The degree to which teacher feedback during activity was congruent with (matched) the focus of the task.

Yes:	More than two instances were evident of teacher feedback being congruent with the task.
Partial:	One or two instances of congruent feedback were evident.
No:	No congruent feedback was given.

The reader will recognize the overlap of teaching functions in this list. It is not only the clarity of the information that these authors have identified as being important to task presentation, but also the need to structure content and organize and motivate learners.

Demonstration.   Demonstration (modeling) has received a great deal of research support in social learning, classroom research, motor learning laboratory research, and research on teaching physical education. It has long been recognized as a critical aspect of presenting information to learners (Martens, Burwitz, & Zuckerman, 1976; McCullagh, Stiehl, & Weiss, 1990). In spite of the evidence supporting the use of demonstration in physical education settings, a large percentage of motor tasks are presented to learners without the help of a visual demonstration of the movement (Gusthart & Sprigings, 1989; Gusthart et. al., in press; Werner & Rink, 1989).

Some effort has gone into trying to define the characteristics of good demonstrations in both laboratory and physical education settings. Most experts support the idea that the model should be accurate and suggest that a high-status model of the same gender as the learner is more likely to be an effective demonstrator (Gould & Roberts, 1982). If tasks need to be broken down, they should be demonstrated in sequence, and complex movements need to be seen more than one time by a learner. In reviewing this research, Lee et. al. (1994) suggest that rather than search for expert models of a movement, there may be merit in using a learner to demonstrate, suggesting that while the expert model produces "learning by imitation" the "learner" model is more likely to promote more cognitive processing of the skill by the learner. Unless the learner already has a clear idea of how to perform, however, it is not likely he or she will be able to contrast his or her attempts with how the motor response can be performed accurately. The use of demonstration is part of a larger issue related to presenting information clearly to learners and is better understood as part of a process of communication. In this respect, the combination of verbal and visual information and the use of verbal rehearsal are most effective when the objective is to give the learner a clear idea of how to perform a motor task.

Verbal cues.   The use of verbal learning cues is another aspect of presenting information to learners that has received a great deal of support in the motor learning literature (Landin, 1994; Magill, 1993) and encouraging support in the pedagogy literature (Kwak, 1993; Masser, 1993). Learning cues are verbal words or phrases that describe the critical features of a skill, such as the term *squash* for the giving action in landing from height, or the phrase *sit into it* for the ready position for a volleyball forearm pass. The theoretical support for learning cues comes primarily from research on attention and information processing (Housner & French, 1994; Landin, 1994). Learning cues help the learner to sort out and attend to what is relevant in a response and to compress many parts of a movement skill into a single response. *Squash* for instance, might replace a description of how to land that involves remembering how to reach with the toes and give gradually with the ankles, knees, and hips. The use of the term *squash* helps to produce the combined response.

There is also ample support in the literature that student involvement in the learning process and therefore student learning is increased if the learner verbalizes rehearsal strategies. Verbal rehearsal strategies (Madigan, Frey, & Matlock, 1992) and self-talk regimens (Landin, 1994) involve the learner in using spoken verbal cues to rehearse the sequence either before or during performance. A student learning a tennis serve might say, for instance, "stretch-down and back-stretch" as he or she practices the serve.

Implications

Selecting good learning cues is part of the art of teaching. Expertise is knowing how to break down, organize, and present content for particular learners . For most physical education tasks, teachers will want to communicate not only the sequence of action but the characteristics of good performance. Good learning cues accurately reflect the movement characteristics they want to convey and are rich in the amount of information they convey. It is possible to use a learning cue that merely phases parts of a skill, such as 1-2-3, which is often used in teaching dance steps to cue the timing as well as the sequence of actions. Numbers or words are useful if they help the learner to perform a skill accurately. Most students find it more meaningful for teachers to use words or expressions that communicate effectively. The teacher who says "make like a chicken" for "keep your elbows out" is likely to receive a better response from more motivated learners.

The selection of learning cues depends on the age of the learner, the stage of the learner, and type of task to be performed. Learning cues break down a skill into phases, which is useful for the beginning stages of most tasks. Continued reliance on sequenced practice, however, might interfere with skills that need to be performed without clear breaks, which means that the teacher may want to change the learning cues for some motor skills according to the stage of learning. For example, if the teacher is trying to teach a jumping action, initial cues for the preparation, execution, and recovery of the action might be replaced with the simple cue, "explode," to produce a more holistic response.

Summary on effective communication. A major conclusion of the work on presenting information to learners—particularly the work on initially instructing learners on what they are to do—is that the teacher must select and organize learning cues and demonstrate the skill to be acquired. Most teachers would not have difficulty with these ideas, and yet a very large percentage of movement tasks that are presented to learners in physical education classes are not presented with selected cues or a demonstration of what is to be done. The result is that, even though the teacher intends that the learners replicate a movement response in a particular way, they end up practicing movement responses without a clear idea of what they are trying to do. A useful technique used by effective teachers is to check to see if students understand what they were asked to do before they practice it. Or the teacher can determine the clarity of the information presented by noting as the students practice how many of them are using the information the teacher presented.

We do not have a great deal of information on how to present tasks when it is not the teacher's intent that learners replicate a movement response. The issue is, "How much information do learners need and when do they need it?" There are several orientations to teaching movement skill and sport that suggest there are times when the learner should not be given detailed information on how to perform (process characteristics of performance). These orientations include "inner game" strategies, a games-for-understanding approach, and environmental approaches to teaching motor skills and games. (Bunker & Thorpe, 1982; Madden & McGowen, 1989; Sweeting & Rink, 1994). All of these strategies approach learning a motor skill without focusing the learner on how to do a movement. They are indirect teaching strategies. We simply do not know a great deal on how to effectively orchestrate more indirect strategies of teaching and learning, and there is very little support for their effectiveness at this time. There is no reason to believe, however, that there is not just as great a need for clarity in terms of communicating the intent of the response in this situation. The important criterion for good communication is whether the learners have a clear idea of what they are trying to do after the teacher has asked them to do it. When the teacher is presenting information to learners and the intent is not a motor response, classroom research guidelines on teacher clarity would seem most appropriate.

TEACHER FEEDBACK

Teacher feedback was identified by physical educators early on as a critical variable in learning motor skills. Learning was assumed to be enhanced if the learner was given information on performance. The justification for this variable came initially from work in motor learning laboratory settings and was reinforced by much of the classroom literature on the use of teacher feedback. Virtually all motor learning and teaching methodology textbooks in physical education identified teacher feedback as critical to learning.

Research

The research support for teacher feedback in physical education settings has not been strong (Rink, 1993; Silverman & Tyson, 1994). We do not have any support for a direct link of this variable with student learning. There are probably many reasons for this, including the idea that most students in physical education classes actually receive very little skill related feedback (Toby, 1974; Yerg, 1978). For skill feedback to appropriately change student movement responses, the teacher would have to observe several movement trials of a single student to identify consistent errors, and then would have to stay with that student long enough to insure that the student understood the feedback and was able to make the necessary changes. A teacher faced with large groups of students finds it impossible to give effective individual feedback.

Classroom research has explored the effects of different kinds of teacher feedback on learners with different characteristics. The idea of teacher feedback in this literature reflects a broad concept of reactions to student behavior beyond the correctness of the response, such as teacher praise and criticism. Brophy (1982) indicated that for the most part students assume they are correct unless told otherwise. Criticism and praise have an affective dimension attached to knowledge of performance. Teacher criticism has consistently been shown to have negative effects on student learning, and most educators would agree that criticism does not have a place in an educational setting. There was a time when most educators thought that the more praise (positive evaluative comments to the learner) the teacher gave the more effective that teacher would be. Brophy (1982) summarized the literature in his description on how teachers should use praise, which is presented in Table 9.3. Educators today suggest a more

Table 9.3   How Teachers Should Use Praise

- The teacher should praise genuine progress or accomplishment. (Quality, credibility, and the individualized nature of the accomplishment are more important than quantity.)
- The teacher should praise students when they may not realize their accomplishment.
- The teacher should praise students who respond well to praise.
- Praise should be informative or appreciative but not controlling. (The focus should be on task-relevant aspects, not on pleasing the teacher.)
- Praise should be contingent on objective accomplishment.
- Praise should be specific.
- Praise should show variety and other signs of credibility.
- Praise should be natural rather than theatrical or intrusive.
- Most praise should be private.
- Praise should be individualized.
- Praise should attribute success to effort and ability.
- Praise should attribute effort expenditure to intrinsic motivation.

---

sparing use of teacher praise because of its controlling nature (i.e., the giving or withdrawing of teacher affect).

Feedback is a form of teacher attention. Several studies have focused on the amount of feedback given to different types of learners and its effects on them. To a low-skilled or insecure learner, feedback can be assuring and motivating. To a high-skilled or self-assured learner, too much teacher feedback can be detrimental to learning. There is some evidence that even though low-skilled students may profit from more teacher praise and feedback, more highly skilled students may be adversely affected by the feedback (Berliner, 1987; Brophy, 1981; Rickard, 1991; Silverman, Tyson, & Krampitz, 1993). There is also evidence that teachers do not dispense attention to students in an equitable fashion. Teachers in physical education tend to give more attention to the students that they like, high achievers, and boys (Allard, 1979; Crowe, 1979; Martinek, Crowe, & Rejeski, 1982).

Motor learning theorists have been interested primarily in the use of teacher feedback to provide information to the learner on performance. Magill (1994) suggests that the influence of augmented teacher feedback on skill learning depends on the characteristics of the skill and the learner. According to Magill, augmented feedback is necessary for skills in which the learner is not able to access sensory information. There are many complex skills in physical education settings for which the learner does not have visual information on where different parts of the body are at different points in a movement and therefore can not profit from feedback on limb position. Although all learners have kinesthetic information on limb position available at all times, the beginner usually cannot access this information. Magill also suggests that if the learner does not have prior information on the relationship of the movements required to reach a goal, then teacher feedback would be necessary (speed of performance). Teacher feedback may not be necessary if the learner receives feedback directly from performance or has a clear enough idea of how to perform (through demonstration) so that they may compare their own performance with correct performance. Magill goes on to suggest that there are times when feedback, although not necessary for learning, can enhance learning. In situations where learners receive feedback from the task itself, learning can be enhanced if the teacher also gives learners feedback that causes them to change some aspect of their response. There are also situations in which feedback can actually hinder learning; for instance if given to the point where learners become dependent on that feedback and do not learn to use feedback that is intrinsic to the task.

In terms of Magill's classification, most learners in most physical education settings would profit from teacher-augmented feedback. The fact that pedagogy research has not been able to establish direct links between teacher feedback and learning probably has more to do with teaching situations than it does with learner needs. Giving accurate and well timed feedback to individual learners in large groups on their skill performance is not possible for many teaching settings.

Implications

The use of specific feedback to learners continues to be recommended by most experts in pedagogy. This is probably due to a recognition that specific feedback in a teaching setting is thought to provide learners with more than merely information on performance (van der Mars, 1989). Teacher feedback is also used to motivate and keep practice focused in large group instruction, which is a valid and important function of the teacher. Settings with large numbers of learners and one teacher necessitate that teachers look for alternative ways to provide learners with information on performance when this kind of information can enhance learning. The refining task (corrective feedback to the total class) is just one alternative to the teacher moving quickly from one student to another. A second alternative is to look toward other teaching strategies for ways to provide individual learner feedback.

If, for most tasks in physical education, learning is enhanced if students can make use of the feedback intrinsic to the task then pedagogy needs to focus on ways in which learners can be helped to use the feedback intrinsic to the task—either external or internal. If external feedback is critical to the task, then teachers need to focus on ways in which this kind of feedback can be provided in group settings, for example through the use of peer feedback strategies or videotapes of performance to be viewed immediately after performance (or later) time by the learner.

GOOD CONTENT DEVELOPMENT
CAN INCREASE LEARNING

One of the characteristics of expertise in teaching is the ability to organize content for learners and develop that content through a process of interactive decision making. The process of development as it plays out in a class has been referred to as *content development* (Rink, 1993). As part of this process, teachers can establish a sequence of tasks or learning experiences that increase or decrease in complexity. Teachers can also refine what students do by putting an emphasis on the quality of the response. Or they can apply learning to a game or performance. Developing content includes giving information on how to perform a task; changing the complexity or difficulty of that task; refining performance; and applying what has been learned. When teachers add a player, increase distance between players, or change the rules they are manipulating the difficulty of movement tasks (extending tasks). When teachers focus the learner on an aspect of performance, such as "Keep your shoulders square" or "Stay with the player who has the ball," they are refining performance (refining task). There are not many studies in this area, but those we do have seem to support the use of progressions that move from simple to complex and the use of tasks with a refining focus.

One of the more difficult decisions teachers have to make regarding the content they want to teach is about when and how to break down content into smaller, progressive units for students. Many teachers continue to believe that students will learn the complex motor skills of many games by playing the game despite the evidence that this is not so (Buck & Harrison, 1990; Earls, 1983; French & Thomas, 1987; Parker & O'Sullivan, 1983). Ordering appropriate progressions for learners is a critical function of effective teaching. There is not a great deal of research on progressions in physical education, but in the skills studied there seems to be ample evidence that students do profit from progressions of content going from simple to complex (French, et al., 1990, 1991; Masser, 1985; Rink et al., 1992). Not only do students not profit from progressions that are inappropriate for them, but this may actually cause a regression in performance (Earls, 1983).

Even fewer studies have investigated the use of the refining task in content development. Teachers who use the refining task select a prescriptive focus for practice based on observation of what the class as a whole needs to correct their practice, such as "When you go back to practice, make sure your weight is on the forward foot by stepping into your swing." Masser (1985) studied the use of the refining task in an elementary school skill and found that students who received refining tasks did better than students who did not. Rink et al. (1992) found that the use of the progression with the refining task was most effective in producing student skill acquisition. There seem to be times when a good progression is sufficient to maintain student success at increasing levels of difficulty. There also seem to be times when the learner does not adjust adequately to more complex conditions without the help of the teacher refining performance. In other words, appropriate progressions are most important, but there are times when students need more specific help in adjusting their movement to increased task demands.

In dealing with the problem of trying to maintain accountability and focus on skill performance, Rink (1993) has suggested that the refining task in which the teacher provides corrective feedback to the class is a useful strategy for large group instruction. Students are focused when the teacher asks a class to adjust some aspect of their response, and the class can be observed actually working on the substantive content of the refining task. Although refining tasks do help a teacher maintain accountability for performance, they can only improve skill performance to the degree that their focus is appropriate—when a large majority of the students can profit from the same information. When this assumption cannot be made, feedback of this nature can be inappropriate.

Implications

The issue of content development is related to the issue of appropriate practice. The progression a teacher uses and the refining focus determines the success rate of the learner and the relationship of the practice to the teaching objective. Most of the complex skills in a physical education program should be taught in a progressive manner. The teacher can break down skills either into parts of the skill itself such as the toss, swing and execution of the tennis serve, or in terms of the conditions of practice (from a toss; from a hit; to particular areas of the court). Although there are some skills that should not be broken down for extensive practice because the timing of the movement is destroyed if it is divided into parts, most complex motor skills in the physical education program can profit from being broken down into parts for beginners at an initial stage of learning.

Progressions for open skills—particularly complex open sport skills— need to occur in gradually more gamelike conditions. If for instance you want a learner to be able to use the forearm volleyball pass to receive a serve, eventually practice will have to include a ball coming across the net at a speed and force equal to a serve and the player will have to be able to place a pass to different parts of the court. Practice from a soft toss to a partner is many steps away from game conditions.

One question teachers always ask regarding the issue of progression is, "How do I know when to move on to the next step, particularly when I have a variety of skill levels within one class?" If we had a definitive answer to the success rate question we would be able to tell the teacher when to move on. A study by French et. al. (1991) compared groups of students who were required to reach an 80% success rate before moving on to the next step in a progression with those students who moved on when they had a particular number of practice trials. There was no difference between the groups on a final test in this situation, which kept the amount of practice trials consistent for both groups. We simply do not know enough about how much success learners need at lower levels of movement tasks before we can expect them to profit from more advanced levels of movement tasks.

Issues regarding teaching progressions have a great deal of significance for both instruction and curriculum. How refined do progressions for skill learning have to be? When can the learner expect to take "leaps" from one level to another? What would be the long-term curricular effects of physical education programs if teachers actually taught less content more effectively at each grade? Even though we lack answers to many of these questions, we suspect that students would be far more skillful if progressions that helped learners to be successful were chosen, and if teachers taught all students for success. Teachers often respond that if they stay on skills too long the students get bored. Interestingly enough, in the volleyball studies on content development it was the highly skilled students who quickly decreased their effort when confronted with a situation in which they were not immediately successful (French et. al., 1990, 1991). The low-skilled student met with even less success, yet persevered. It is important that teachers know what drives the decision to move on. The teacher must not only be able to plan progressions that go from simple to complex, but must also be able to design many ways to practice skills at the same level.

DIRECT INSTRUCTION

We began this chapter with an introduction that described the research base for effective teaching as having its foundation in a group of research studies on highly structured content and rather short-term objectives. The collection of teaching behaviors identified by this research have come to be associated with the construct of direct instruction or explicit teaching. Direct instruction usually means that the teacher teaches in small steps; gives explicit directions or instructions on what the student is to do; maintains a task-oriented, teacher-monitored environment with high student engagement with the content; and provides immediate feedback to students.

Most of the principles identified in this chapter are associated with direct instruction. Direct instruction is appropriate when subject matter is highly structured and when teachers can describe specifically what they want students to learn (Peterson, 1979a, 1979b) Most of the process-product research in physical education has identified direct instruction as an effective way to teach motor skills, which should not surprise anyone. It is the intent of most physical education instructional lessons for students to perform in a particular way that is identified by the teacher. Under these conditions, teachers would be most effective if they utilized the principles of teaching described in this chapter. More students would successfully learn skills if teachers developed and used these skills. What we are less clear about in physical education is describing our intent for student learning when we may not want every student doing the same thing in the same way.

SUMMARY

This chapter has provided a set of basic and generic principles for teaching. Research on the teaching process has continued to identify contextual variables that affect relationships between what we do as teachers and effects on different learners in different contexts with different content. The material in this chapter has been presented with the intent to help the reader develop an understanding of the more generic principles of teaching. The research presented is stronger in some areas than in others, but represents the best information we have at this time. There is more to learn, but the principles we have established can provide guidance for teaching in a motor context. Thoughtful practitioners will carefully select what they will teach and will select just as carefully the manner in which they will teach it.

REFERENCES

Allard, R. (1979). A need to look at dyadic interactions. In American Alliance for Health, Physical Education, Recreation and Dance, Research Consortium Symposium Papers: *Teaching behavior and women in sports* (vol. 2, book 1). Washington, DC: American Alliance for Health, Physical Education, Recreation and Dance.

Anderson, W. (1980). *Analysis of teaching physical education.* St. Louis, MO: The C.V. Mosby Co.

Ashy, M., Lee, A., & Landin, D. (1988). Relationship of practice using correct technique to achievement in a motor skill. *Journal of Teaching in Physical Education* , 7, 115–120.

Berliner, D. (1987). Simple views of classroom teaching and a simple theory of classroom instruction. In D. Berliner & B. Rosenshine (Eds.), *Talks to teachers,* (pp. 93–110), New York: Random House.

Brophy, J. (1979). Teacher behavior and its effects. *Journal of Educational Psychology, 71,* 733–750.

Brophy, J. (1981). Teacher praise: a functional analysis. *Review of Educational Research, 51,* 5–32.

Brophy, J. (1982, January). On praising effectively. *The Education Digest,* 16–19.

Brophy, J., & Evertson, C. (1974). *Process product correlations in the Texas teacher effectiveness study* (final report). Austin, TX: The University of Texas at Austin, Research & Development Center for Teacher Education.

Brophy, J., & Good, T. (1986). Teacher behavior and student achievement. In M. Wittrock, (Ed.), *Handbook of research on teaching* (3rd ed., pp. 328–375). New York: MacMillan.

Buck, M., & Harrison, J. (1990). An analysis of game play in volleyball. *Journal of Teaching in Physical Education, 10,* 38–48.

Buck, M., Harrison, J., & Bryce, G. (1991). An analysis of learning trials and their relationship to achievement. *Journal of Teaching in Physical Education, 10,* 134–152.

Bunker, D., & Thorpe, R. (1982). A model for the teaching of games in secondary schools. *Bulletin of Physical Education, 18,* 5–8.

Costello, J. (1977). *A descriptive analysis of student behavior in elementary school physical education classes.* Unpublished doctoral dissertation, Columbia University, NY.

Cousineau, W., & Luke, M. (1990). Relationships between teacher expectations and academic learning time in sixth grade physical education basketball classes. *Journal of Teaching in Physical Education, 9,* 262–271.

Crowe, P. (1979). An observational study of teachers' expectancy effects and their mediating mechanisms. In American Alliance for Health, Physical Education, and Recreation, Research Consortium Symposium Papers: *Teaching behavior and women in sport* (vol. 2, book 1). Washington, DC: American Alliance for Health, Physical Education, Recreation and Dance.

Doyle, W. (1986). Classroom organization and management. In M. Wittrock, (Ed.), *Handbook of research on teaching* (3rd ed., pp. 392–441). New York: MacMillan Publishing.

Earls, N. (1983). Research on the immediate effects of instructional variables. In T. Templin, & J. Olson (Eds.), *Teaching in physical education* (pp. 254–264). Champaign, IL: Human Kinetics.

Emmer, E., Evertson, C., & Anderson, L. (1980). Effective classroom management at the beginning of the school year. *Elementary School Journal, 80,* 219–231.

Ennis, C. (1994, April*). They just don't want to learn anymore. What can you do?: Teachers' resistance to curricular change.* Paper presented at the annual meeting of the American Educational Research Association, New Orleans.

Evertson, C., & Emmer, E.T. (1982). Effective management at the beginning of the year in junior high school classes. *Journal of Educational Psychology, 74,* 485–498.

Fitts, P.M., & Posner, M.I. (1967). *Human performance.* Belmont, CA: Brooks/Cole.

French, K., Rink, J., Rickard, L., Mays, A., Lynn, S., & Werner, P. (1991). The effects of practice progressions on learning two volleyball skills. *Journal of Teaching in Physical Education, 10,* 261–275.

French, K.E., Rink, J.E., & Werner, P.H. (1990). Effects of contextual interference on retention of three volleyball skills. *Perceptual and Motor Skills, 71,* 179–186.

French, K., & Thomas, G. (1987). The relation of knowledge development to children's basketball performance. *Journal of Sport Psychology, 9,* 15–32.

Gage, N.L. (1978, November). The yield of research on teaching. *Phi Delta Kappan,* 230–235.

Godbout, P., Burnelle, J., & Tousignant, M. (1983). Academic learning time in elementary and secondary physical education. *Research Quarterly for Exercise and Sport, 54,* 11–19.

Goldberger, M., & Gerney, P. (1990). Effects of learner use of practice time on skill acquisition. *Journal of Teaching in Physical Education, 10,* 84–95.

Good, S., & Magill, R.A. (1986). Contextual interference effects in learning three badminton serves. *Research Quarterly for Exercise and Sport, 57,* 308–315.

Good, T., & Grouws, D. (1975). *Process-product relationships in fourth grade mathematics classrooms: Final Report of National Institute of Education Grant* (NE-G-00-0123). Columbia: University of Missouri.

Gould, D., & Roberts, G. (1982). Modeling and motor skill acquisition. *Quest, 33,* 214–230.

Graham, K.C. (1988). A qualitative analysis of an effective teacher's movement task presentations during a unit of instruction. *The Physical Educator, 11,* 187–195.

Graham, K.C., Hussey, K., Taylor, K., & Werner, P. (1993). A study of verbal presentations of three effective teachers. *Research Quarterly for Exercise and Sport, 64,* 87A (Abstract).

Gusthart, J., & Sprigings, E. (1989). Student learning as a measure of teacher effectiveness. *Journal of Teaching in Physical Education, 8,* 298–311.

Gusthart, L., Kelly, I., & Rink, J. (in press). The validity of the Qualitative Measures of Teacher Performance Scale (QMTPS) as a process measure of achievement. *Journal of Teaching in Physical Education.*

Hellison, D. (1995). *Teaching responsibility through physical activity.* Champaign, IL: Human Kinetics.

Housner, L.D., & French, K.E. (Eds.) (1994). Expertise in learning, performance, and instruction in sport and physical activity [Monograph]. *Quest, 46,* 2.

Kennedy, J., Cruickshank, D., Bush, A., & Meyers, B. (1978). Additional investigations into the nature of teacher clarity. *Journal of Educational Research, 2,* 3–10.

Kwak, C. (1993). *The initial effects of various task presentation conditions on students' performance of the lacrosse throw.* Unpublished doctoral dissertation, University of South Carolina, Columbia.

Land, M. (1981). Combined effect of two teacher clarity variables on student achievement. *Journal of Experimental Education, 50,* 14–17.

Landin, D. (1994). The role of verbal cues in skill learning. *Quest, 46,* 299–313.

Lee, T., Swinnen, S., & Serrien, D. (1994). Cognitive effort and motor learning. *Quest, 46,* 328–344.

Madden, G., & McGowan, C. (1989). The effect of the inner game method versus the progressive method on learning motor skills. *Journal of Teaching in Physical Education, 9,* 39–48.

Madigan, R., Frey, R., & Matlock, T. (1992). Cognitive strategies of university athletes. *Canadian Journal of Sport Science, 17,* 135–140.

Magill, R.A. (1993). *Motor learning: Concepts and applications.* Dubuque, IA: Wm. C. Brown.

Magill, R.A. (1994). The influence of augmented feedback during skill learning depends on characteristics of the skill and the learner. *Quest, 46,* 314–327.

Martens, R., Burwitz, L., & Zuckerman, J. (1976). Modeling effects on motor performance. *Research Quarterly, 47,* 277–291.

Martinek, T., Crowe, P., & Rejeski, W. (1982). *Pygmalion in the gym: Causes and effects of expectations in teaching and coaching.* West Point, NY: Leisure Press.

Masser, L. (1985). The effect of refinement on student achievement in a fundamental motor skill in grades K-6. *Journal of Teaching in Physical Education, 6,* 174–182.

Masser, L. (1993). Critical cues help first grade students' achievement in handstands and forward rolls. *Journal of Teaching in Physical Education, 12,* 301–312.

McCaslin, M., & Good, T. (1992). Compliant cognition: The misalliance of management and instructional goals in current school reform. *Educational Researcher, 21,* 4–16.

McCullagh, P., Stiehl, J., & Weiss, M. (1990). Developmental modeling effects on the quantitative and qualitative aspects of motor performance. *Research Quarterly for Exercise and Sport, 61,* 344–350.

McDonald, F., & Elias, P. (1976). *The effects of teacher performance on student learning: Beginning teacher evaluation study—phase II final report* (Vol. 1). Princeton, NJ: Educational Testing Service.

Metzler, M. (1979). The measurement of academic learning time in physical education. *Dissertation Abstracts International, 40,* 5365A. (University Microfilms No. 8009314)

Metzler, M. (1989). A review of research on time in sport pedagogy. *Journal of Teaching in Physical Education, 8,* 87–103.

Metzler, M., DePaepe, J., & Reif, G. (1985). Alternative technologies for measuring academic learning time in physical education. *Journal of Teaching in Physical Education, 6,* 271–285.

National Association for Sport and Physical Education. (1992). *Outcomes of quality physical education.* Reston, VA: American Alliance for Health, Physical Education, Recreation and Dance.

National Association for Sport and Physical Education. (1995). *Moving into the future: National standards for physical education.* Reston, VA: American Alliance for Health, Physical Education, Recreation and Dance.

Ornstein, A., & Levine, D. (1981, April). Teacher behavior research: Overview and outlook. *Phi Delta Kappan,* 592–596.

Parker, M., & O'Sullivan, M. (1983). Modifying ALT-PE for game play contexts and other reflections [Monograph]. *Journal of Teaching Physical Education, 1,* 8–10.

Peterson, P. (1979a, October). Direct instruction: effective for what and for whom? *Educational Leadership,* 46–48.

Peterson, P. (1979b). Direct instruction reconsidered. In P. Peterson, & H. Walberg (Eds.), *Research on teaching: Concepts, findings, and implications* (pp. 57–69). Berkeley, CA: McCutchan.

Rickard, L. (1991). The short term relationship of teacher feedback and student practice. *Journal of Teaching in Physical Education, 10,* 275–285.

Rink, J. (1993). *Teaching physical education for learning.* St. Louis: Mosby Year Book.

Rink, J. (1994). Task presentation in pedagogy. *Quest, 46,* 270–280.

Rink, J., French, K., Werner, P., Lynn, S., & Mays, A. (1992). The influence of content development on the effectiveness of instruction. *Journal of Teaching in Physical Education, 11,* 139.

Rink, J., & Werner, P. (1989). Qualitative measures of teaching performance scale (QMTPS). In P. Darst, D. Zakrajsek, & V. Mancini (Eds.), *Analyzing physical education and sport instruction* (2nd ed., pp. 269-276). Champaign, IL: Human Kinetics.

Rosenshine, B. (1987). Explicit teaching. In D. Berliner, & B. Rosenshine (Eds.), *Talks to teachers* (pp. 75–92). New York: Random House.

Rosenshine, B., & Stevens, R. (1986). Teaching functions. In M. Wittrock (Ed.), *Handbook of research on teaching* (3rd ed., pp. 376–391). New York: MacMillan.

Sheffield, F.D. (1961). Theoretical considerations in the learning of complex sequential tasks from demonstration and practice. In A.A. Lumsdaine (Ed.), *Student response in programmed instruction* (National Research Council Publication 943, pp. 13–32). Washington, DC: National Academy of Sciences.

Silverman, S. (1985). Relationship of engagement and practice trials to student achievement. *Journal of Teaching in Physical Education, 5,* 13–21.

Silverman, S. (1990). Linear and curvilinear relationships between student practice and achievement in physical education. *Teaching and Teacher Education, 6,* 305–314.

Silverman, S., Devillier, R., & Ramírez, T. (1991). The validity of academic learning time -physical education (ALT-PE) as a process measure of student achievement. *Research Quarterly for Exercise and Sport, 62,* 319–325.

Silverman, S., Kulinna, P., & Crull, G. (1995). Skill-related task structures, explicitness, and accountability: Relationships with student achievement. *Research Quarterly for Exercise and Sport, 66,* 32-40.

Silverman, S., & Tyson, L. (1994, April). *Modeling the teaching learning process in physical education.* Paper presented at the annual meeting of the American Educational Research Association, New Orleans.

Silverman, S., Tyson, L., & Krampitz, J. (1993). Teacher feedback and achievement: Mediating effects of initial skill and sex. *Journal of Human Movement Studies, 24,* 97–118.

Soar, R., & Soar, R.M. (1979). Emotional climate and management. In P. Peterson, & H. Walberg (Eds.), *Research on teaching: concepts, findings and implications* (pp. 97–119). Berkeley, CA: McCutchan.

Stallings, J., & Kaskowitz, D. (1974). *Follow through classroom observation evaluation, 1972-1973* (Office of Education contract OEC 08522480-4633[100]). Menlo Park, CA: Stanford Research Institute.

Sweeting, T., & Rink, J. (1994). *Effects of a direct instructional and environmental instructional strategy on learning the standing broad jump for 5- and 7- year-olds.* Manuscript submitted for publication.

Toby, C. (1974). *A descriptive analysis of the occurrence of augmented feedback in physical education classes.* Unpublished doctoral dissertation, Columbia University Teacher's College, NY.

Van der Mars, H. (1989). Effects of specific verbal praise on off-task behavior of second grade students in physical education. *Journal of Teaching in Physical Education, 8,* 162–169.

Werner, P., & Rink, J. (1989). Case studies of teacher effectiveness in physical education. *Journal of Teaching in Physical Education, 4,* 280–297.

Yerg, B. (1978). Identifying teacher behavior correlates of student achievement. In AAHPERD Research Consortium Symposium Papers: *Teaching behavior and sport history* (vol. 1, book 1). Washington, DC: American Alliance for Health, Physical Education and Recreation.

CHAPTER 10

Evaluation and Testing: The Road Less Traveled

Terry M. Wood

Life is difficult. This is the great truth, one of the greatest truths. It is a great truth because once we really see this truth, we transcend it. Once we truly know that life is difficult—once we truly understand and accept it—then life is no longer difficult. Because once it is accepted, the fact that life is difficult no longer matters.

M. Scott Peck, *The Road Less Traveled,* (1978, p. 15)

INTRODUCTION

At no other time in recent history has public school physical education been under such siege. Calls for national educational reform in science, math, English, history, and the arts, coupled with increased emphasis on accountability in the classroom and severe budgetary shortages, have forced school administrators to make difficult choices. Increasingly, physical education has carried the burden of program and staff reduction during budgetary crises, particularly at the elementary and middle school levels. In this new era of educational reform and accountability, the very survival of physical education in the public school system will depend, in part, on how well we define the purposes and outcomes of our programs and the methods we use to document the successes of our students and teachers within those programs.

Measurement and evaluation (M&E) is an integral component of the current wave of educational reform. To measure higher order objectives such as critical thinking and problem-solving skills, to enhance integrated learning across the curriculum, and to improve the accountability of teachers and programs, a plethora of alternative assessment procedures—such as portfolios and event tasks—are being advocated for both classroom and high-stakes standardized testing. Physical educators and teacher educators cannot afford to ignore these changes. Our survival depends on our ability to catch this new wave of reform and use it to reflect on what we assess and how we assess it. The purposes of this chapter are to

1. Outline and contrast recommended M&E practices with practices being employed in the field.
2. Examine the roots of the current assessment revolution, with particular emphasis on M&E practices in physical education.
3. Provide a brief description of alternative assessment procedures, their promise for public school physical education, and potential pitfalls in their implementation.

DISCLAIMER

This chapter focuses on current issues in M&E. Readers interested in the "nuts and bolts" of measurement theory and practice for physical education are encouraged to read the many useful M&E textbooks such as Safrit and Wood (1995), Baumgartner and Jackson (1995), Miller (1994), and the myriad of professional and research journals (e.g., *Journal of Teaching in Physical Education, Journal of Educational Measurement, Teaching Elementary Physical Education, Applied Measurement in Education, Schools in the Middle, Instructor, Phi Delta Kappan, Educational Leadership, Principal, Childhood Education,* and *Middle School Journal*).

Similarly, in the space provided it is impossible to provide a comprehensive and detailed review of the voluminous literature concerning current M&E practices and the burgeoning knowledge base concerning alternative assessment. Where possible, I will point readers in the direction of others who provide more complete discussions of relevant topics.

To avoid misinterpretation and maximize the clarity of the discussion, the following definitions are employed:

- *Measurement* and *testing* are used interchangeably to describe the process of obtaining a score.
- *Evaluation* is the process of making judgments regarding the worth of scores. For example, we test/measure students in a class to obtain scores on a knowledge test and use those scores to evaluate student progress toward meeting course objectives.

- *Assessment* is an often used but problematic term. For the purposes of this discussion, assessment refers to the combined processes of M&E. Student assessment, therefore, involves collecting accurate and reliable information through informal and formal testing and then using those data to make judgments about student progress.

TRADITIONALLY RECOMMENDED M&E PRACTICE IN PUBLIC SCHOOL PHYSICAL EDUCATION: THE ROAD LESS TRAVELED

M&E practice currently advocated in both teacher preparation programs and the literature stresses a traditional model of assessment which involves

- formally stating the objectives of instruction (typically cognitive, affective, and psychomotor objectives) (Hensley, 1990; Safrit & Wood, 1995);
- pre-assessing students;
- after appropriate instructional activities, measuring achievement of objectives using valid, reliable standardized or teacher-made tests; and
- a formative framework using a criterion-referenced grading system, for evaluating student progress toward meeting stated objectives (see Safrit & Wood, 1995, or Lambert's chapter on curriculum models).

Preferably, M&E should be systematically delivered as an integral part of the instructional process (Dunham, 1986). In addition, while informal assessment (Ornstein, 1994) is recommended to enhance day-to-day instruction, formal assessment using valid and reliable tests is recommended for grading purposes. That is, grades should be based on low-inference criteria (e.g., skills tests and cognitive tests) which demand a low degree of subjectivity to link criterion performance to achievement in physical education, rather than on high-inference criteria (e.g., attendance, effort, participation) which demand a high degree of subjectivity to link criterion performance to achievement in physical education (Wood, Ritson, & Hensley, 1989).

The traditional model of assessment is relevant for all grade levels and permits a high degree of flexibility in the types of tests that can be used. The overriding goal of the model, however, is development of an accountability system that defines the objectives of instruction and uses appropriate measurement devices to evaluate how well students have met those objectives.

FOUNDATION OF THE TRADITIONAL MODEL

Three primary principles provide a foundation for the assessment model, as described below.

Establish Appropriate Instructional Objectives

Historically, physical education has included objectives from three behavioral domains: psychomotor (e.g., attainment of competency in fundamental movement patterns, selected sport skills, and physical fitness activities), cognitive (e.g., knowledge of game rules, biomechanical principles, principles of training and physical fitness), and affective (e.g., appreciation of cooperation, fairness, following the rules of games, and the social and cultural value of dance). Objectives for physical education programs are typically found in documents at the national (e.g., the National Association for Sport and Physical Education, Moving Into the Future: National Standards for Physical Education, 1995) and state (e.g., Oregon Department of Education Physical Education Common Curriculum Goals, 1988) levels. The number of objectives listed in such documents is intimidating. Therefore, teachers must be very selective in choosing objectives from each domain, with primary emphasis placed on the psychomotor and cognitive domains. In addition, objectives should be stated as instructional objectives; that is, they should describe what a student should be able to do to meet the objective.

Use Appropriate Tests to Measure Characteristics Related to Instructional Objectives

Measurement can take many different forms. For example, tennis serving ability can be measured by recording the accuracy, velocity, and trajectory of the ball or by an analysis of student form using a rating scale or checklist. Understanding of the mechanics of kicking a soccer ball could be tested by an essay exam, asking students to critically evaluate videotaped performance, or by a project which challenges students to develop demonstrations of the effects of violating the biomechanical principles. No matter what the method of measurement, the guiding principles should be: that tests should measure characteristics which lead to achievement of specified course objectives (validity) and provide measurement which is relatively error free (reliability). The degree to which tests should be valid and reliable is in direct proportion to the importance of the decisions made based on test scores. For example, if a multiple choice exam is to account for 50% of a grade in physical education, the test should be developed with careful attention paid to content validity. A short, nongraded, "pop quiz" administered at the end of a class and designed to assess student understanding of a class discussion, however, requires only minimal evidence for validity. The same holds true for subjective assessments of motor skill. Day-to-day assessment of progress can be accomplished with quick, visual assessment; however, measurement of skill for the purposes of grading should be achieved with structured, purposeful assessment via valid and reliable sport skills tests or formalized rating scales and checklists (Hensley, 1990; Hensley, Morrow, & East, 1990).

Develop an Evaluation Scheme That Reflects Attainment of Instructional Objectives

The criteria which make up grades in a physical education class should reflect the important instructional objectives. A grading plan should reflect both the teacher's choice of objectives and the emphasis placed on each objective. If mastery of selected psychomotor skills and knowledge of rules, biomechanical principles, and methods for training are specified as the primary objectives of a middle school soccer class, the grading scheme should reflect assessment of each of those elements.

PROBLEMATIC ASSESSMENT AREAS

Assessment of physical fitness, M&E in the affective domain, and cognitive testing have proven to be particularly troublesome for physical education and thus deserve special consideration.

Assessing Physical Fitness

The past two decades have witnessed remarkable changes in the assessment of youth physical fitness, such as the development of health-related physical fitness tests with criterion-referenced standards (Safrit & Wood, 1995). Most notably, however, the focus in the delivery of physical fitness education has shifted from a primary emphasis on assessment of physical fitness components to providing students with knowledge and concepts about fitness and helping them develop positive attitudes toward participating in a healthy, active lifestyle over their life span. Nationally recognized youth fitness tests, such as the Prudential FITNESSGRAM (Cooper Institute for Aerobics Research, 1992), incorporate fitness tests as one component in a comprehensive fitness program which emphasizes knowledge, motivation, and assessment. This change in focus is the result of a body of research that condemned inappropriate uses of fitness test scores (e.g., Fox, 1991; Fox & Biddle, 1988; Whitehead, 1993). Current recommended practice advocates using fitness test scores to aid students in understanding fitness concepts rather than as a grading criteria. Moreover, for many students, individualized goal setting, rather than insistence on meeting criterion-referenced standards, will better serve to meet the objective of motivating students to participate in health-enhancing physical activity.

Assessing the Affective Domain

Controversy over assessment in the affective domain has plagued physical educators for years (e.g., see the feature concerning this controversy in the February 1982 issue of the *Journal of Physical Education, Recreation and Dance*). The affective domain, nevertheless, has been and continues to be included in physical education objectives. Most recently, the 1995 National Standards for Physical Education published by the National Association for Sport and Physical Education (NASPE) includes affective components.

The assessment controversy surrounding the affective domain centers on two issues: (a) should affective characteristics be measured and (b) should affective objectives be evaluated.

Should affective characteristics be measured? Few educators would disagree that affective characteristics, such as fairness, honesty, discipline, self-esteem, kindness, and social responsibility are important characteristics that should be fostered in public school settings. To what extent, however, should physical education teachers focus on measuring such attributes? Arguments against measuring affective characteristics (see Mood, 1982) include lack of valid, reliable, objective measurement instruments; lack of time to measure the myriad potential affective components; lack of appropriate training to administer and interpret scores from available instruments; unethical use of affective test scores; invasion of student privacy; and the criticism that affective teaching properly belongs with all formal and informal instructional units in a school and not primarily with physical education.

Arguments for measuring affect center around the historical inclusion of the domain in education (Wentzel, 1991) and the unique nature of physical education in contributing to positive affective development. Moreover, there is some evidence that positive affective behavior, such as student social responsibility, contributes to classroom achievement through fostering a more positive learning environment (Wentzel, 1991). Affective development is a substantial component of several physical education curriculum models, such as the personal and social responsibility model (Hellison & Templin, 1991; Young, Klesius, & Hoffman, 1994). These models use physical education as a medium for learning positive affective characteristics, such as self-control and caring/helping behavior.

Perhaps a reasonable middle ground between the two camps is to recognize the significance of the affective domain and the responsibility of teachers to (a) monitor overall classroom behavior with the aim of adjusting instruction to help students understand and exhibit positive affective behavior and (b) observe and report extreme negative behavior to administrators and counselors. Monitoring classroom behavior and developing instructional strategies can be accomplished through direct observation and with the help of more structured models of curriculum, such as Hellison's levels of self- and social responsibility (Hellison & Templin, 1991, and Hellison's chapter in this book).

Should affective characteristics be evaluated?   Evaluation of affective behavior also has its pitfalls. Should measurements of affect be used in grading? A common practice is to grade students based on effort, participation, and attitude and/or to lower grades in physical education if students accrue too many "demerit" points for lack of effort, participation, or positive attitude. Such practices are not recommended for several reasons.

A grade based largely on criteria such as attitude, effort, and participation ignores student achievement in the psychomotor and cognitive domains. Are physical education teachers being accountable for teaching the body of knowledge known as physical education if an individual who tries hard and participates receives an "A" in physical education? It is impossible to determine if that individual has mastered the appropriate motor/fitness skills and knowledge if the grading criteria are based solely on affective criteria.

If grades in physical education are lowered for demonstration of inappropriate behavior, then behavior is used to penalize students and teachers must begin to question if grades are being used to manage student behavior rather than to reflect student achievement. Moreover, if inappropriate student behavior is being penalized teachers must determine if they are judging students fairly. Specifically, is a teacher's observation of student behavior correctly interpreted; is it fair to penalize students based on one or two instances over a period of several weeks; does penalizing behavior serve to change the behavior? These arguments are not intended to dismiss the importance of monitoring affective behavior and developing appropriate teaching strategies to foster positive affect.

A more balanced approach to evaluation that recognizes the importance of affective behavior is to (a) monitor affective behavior using an appropriate model, such as the model of personal and social responsibility (Hellison & Templin, 1991) and (b) provide an evaluation for affect separate from a grade which combines the psychomotor and cognitive domains to represent achievement in physical education. Such evaluation schemes are common in elementary schools and include an evaluation of "citizenship" separate from evaluation of achievement in academic areas (Parsons, 1994).

Assessing in the Cognitive Domain

If a primary goal of physical education is to provide individuals with the knowledge, understanding, and motivation to participate in a healthy, active lifestyle over their life span, then we do our students and our profession a disservice by failing to assess the extent to which students have mastered the knowledge base associated with physical education. Moreover, mastery of the knowledge of physical education provides a means for those few students unable to achieve movement competency to excel in physical education. Mastery of knowledge can be assessed in many different ways, including traditional multiple choice and essay tests, term projects, oral presentations, and portfolios (see Melograno, 1994, for a discussion of portfolios in K-12 physical education). Appropriate procedures for constructing such tests can be found in most M&E textbooks.

CURRENT M&E PRACTICE IN PHYSICAL EDUCATION: THE ROAD TOO TRAVELED

The M&E practices of physical educators have been examined extensively over the past three decades (e.g., Hensley et al., 1989; Imwold, Rider, & Johnson, 1982; Kneer, 1986; Matanin & Tannehill, 1994; Morrow, 1978; Veal, 1992; Wood & Cusimano, 1992; Wood et al., 1989). Early work employed written surveys of teachers and student teachers to determine current M&E practices (e.g., Hensley et al., 1989; Imwold et al., 1982; Morrow, 1978; Wood et al., 1989). More recent efforts have used case studies (e.g., Veal, 1992), structured interviews (Kneer, 1986), and a combination of written surveys, interviews, and observation (e.g., Matanin & Tannehill, 1994; Wood & Cusimano, 1992) to describe and extract the underlying reasons for current practice. Three major conclusions can be drawn from this body of literature:

- There is incongruity between the M&E practices advocated in teacher preparation programs and the M&E practices of inservice teachers. This incongruity is most often labeled the "theory/practice gap" (see Kneer, 1986, and Wood & Safrit, 1990, for a description and etiology of the theory/practice gap).
- Judged by the persistent reporting of the theory/practice gap since 1978, the incongruity between preferred and actual M&E practice is a durable trait.
- The factors which contribute to and exacerbate the incongruity are numerous, often complex, and not easily remedied.

THE WIDTH OF THE THEORY/PRACTICE GAP

Research has shown conclusively that M&E practices of inservice physical education teachers are not congruent with the preferred practice. Early studies by Matthews (1968) and Morrow (1978) questioned student teachers concerning the grading practices in the public school physical education classes which provided the student teaching experience. Matthews' student teachers reported that grades in physical education were based primarily on attendance and proper attire in 80% of the schools investigated. More than 66% of Morrow's 29 student teachers reported that their mentor teachers seldom or never used measurement in the classroom; skills tests were seldom or never used; and dressing appropriately, participation, conduct, and attendance were most often used in determining grades.

Numerous mail surveys of the M&E practices of inservice teachers support the findings of Morrow and Matthews. Imwold et al. (1982) surveyed 500 Florida public school physical educators at all levels (elementary, middle, junior high, and high school) concerning the types of tests administered in physical education classes, grading methods, and grade reporting methods. Almost 20% of respondents failed to use any tests in their program, while approximately 53% used skill tests and less than 40% used knowledge tests to examine students. Moreover, Imwold et al. reported that "a large percentage" of teachers based their grades on attendance and subjective assessments of such factors as effort, sportsmanship, and citizenship.

The most comprehensive mail survey of public school physical education practices was reported by Hensley et al. (1989). Of 5,000 physical education teachers surveyed in six states (Georgia, Illinois, Iowa, Kansas, Tennessee, and Wyoming) 2,202 returned completed questionnaires concerning grading criteria, test use, grade reporting, sources of tests, and opinions regarding use of skills tests and microcomputers. On a positive note, Hensley et al. concluded that "it appears that public school physical education teachers in the states surveyed are more involved in some type of systematic evaluation process than has been reported previously" (p. 39). Their findings, however, also confirmed that subjective evaluation and participation/effort were the primary factors in determining grades for 36% of the respondents. These results were supported by Wood, Ritson, and Hensley (1989) in a similar survey of 662 certified public school physical educators in Oregon.

More recently, Matanin and Tannehill (1994) investigated (via questionnaire and interview) the congruency between teachers' perceptions of the assessment process and actual procedures used to assess students (determined by direct observation and review of appropriate documentation) by 11 high school teachers. While the purpose of assessment for these teachers was "to test student skill levels, understanding, and knowledge and to teach students to appreciate physical education" (p. 403), actual assessment practice indicated that proper attire and participation were emphasized to students as the primary grading criteria; only 30% of the grade on average was based on knowledge and skill testing; and attendance, appropriate attire, behavior, and effort were the most consistent grading criteria used by teachers. Matanin and Tannehill concluded that "these programs displayed characteristics of structured recreation, rather than physical education. From an assessment point of view, it appears that these teachers gained little knowledge about what students accomplished in their classrooms or what they accomplished as teachers" (p. 404).

REASONS UNDERLYING THE THEORY/PRACTICE GAP

It is clear that the grading practices of public school physical educators do not meet the expectations of teacher educators. Recently, researchers have focused their attention on the reasons underlying the theory/practice gap (e.g., Matanin & Tannehill, 1994; Veal, 1988a, 1990; Wood & Cusimano, 1992). Figure 10.1 presents a summary of what the literature reveals about factors contributing to the lack of preferred M&E practices in public school physical education.

Teacher Preparation

The issue of teacher preparation falls along two dimensions—lack of M& E preparation; and insufficient or inappropriate M&E preparation. There is little evidence that physical education teachers fail to receive preservice training in M&E. It has been argued, however, that teacher preparation programs fail to adequately prepare preservice classroom teachers (e.g., Schafer & Lissitz, 1987; Stiggins, 1988) and preservice physical education teachers (e.g., Veal, 1992; Wood, 1990) for the realities of public school teaching. Veal (1992) recommended that (a) assessment and accountability systems be modeled in preservice activity classes, (b) theory and practice be integrated more fully in M&E classes by including realistic field

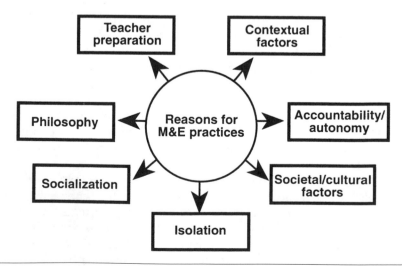

Figure 10.1.   Factors contributing to the theory/practice gap in M&E

experiences, and (c) assessment be properly modeled during the student teaching experience. In addition, Wood (1990) encouraged M&E specialists in teacher training programs to become more involved in the realities of public school teaching in order to more effectively integrate measurement theory and practice in preservice M&E instruction.

Contextual Factors

On the surface, contextual factors such as large class sizes, infrequent class meetings, short class duration, outside responsibilities (e.g., coaching), and lack of sufficient equipment and facilities appear to be contributing factors to the theory/practice gap (Kneer, 1986; Veal, 1988a; Wood & Cusimano, 1992). Matanin and Tannehill (1994) discovered, however, that the only significant contextual factor that affected grading practices reported by secondary school teachers was how their colleagues graded. Moreover, as Veal (1988b) pointed out, "if those [contextual] were the only factors that relate to the lack of formal assessment, we would not find the exceptions to the rule who manage to teach and coach while still maintaining the integrity of accountability" (p. 3).

Accountability/Autonomy

A question of some interest is why an apparent lack of accountability in public school physical education classes is allowed to persist in the schools. To shed some light on this issue, Wood and Cusimano (1992) employed structured interviews and questionnaires to examine the measurement and evaluation practices of 14 physical education teachers in rural school settings (6 high school, 2 middle school, 4 K-8, and 2 elementary classroom teachers). To further delineate the factors contributing to M&E practices 9 administrators were surveyed (7 principal/superintendents, 1 superintendent, and the state coordinator of physical education). It became very clear that, in general, physical education teachers were not held accountable for their M&E practices. All teachers were given complete autonomy in determining the criteria used in formulating a grade. Moreover, the annual formal assessment of teachers by the school principal did not include evaluation of M&E practices. These findings are supported by Veal (1988a), who noted lack of administrative support as a roadblock to effective assessment among secondary school physical educators.

Isolation

Wood and Cusimano (1992) reported that teachers in rural settings feel isolated in their teaching environment and out of touch with new teaching strategies in general and new M&E practices in particular. Moreover, professional isolation described by beginning teachers (Stroot, Faucette, & Schwager, 1993) limits interaction with experienced teachers who may be able to provide positive mentoring. At first glance, an antidote to feelings of isolation might be inservice training. The research evidence concerning the effect of inservice training, however, is mixed. For example, Kneer (1986) reported that amount of inservice education was positively associated with use of proper instructional practices by physical education teachers, while Brookhart (1993) discovered that a group of practicing teachers recently enrolled in a graduate level M&E class showed no difference in their thinking about grade interpretation and use compared to a matched group of practicing teachers who received no additional M&E instruction.

Philosophy

One of the most intriguing factors influencing M&E practices of teachers is the philosophy of teachers regarding the purpose of the physical education program and usefulness of M&E in the teaching/learning process. Kneer (1986) reported that 42% of the teachers she surveyed who failed to use proper planning, practice, and evaluation procedures believed "it wasn't necessary," while Veal (1988c) described a "deep-seated mistrust of testing by some teachers" (p. 154). More recently, Matanin and Tannehill (1994) concluded that many teachers perceived M&E to be "impractical and unimportant to what they were trying to achieve" (p. 404). Why? Part of the answer lies in teachers' perceptions of the purpose of the physical education program and what should be assessed. For many teachers the purpose of the physical education program is to keep students active and enjoying physical activity. The primary responsibility of the teacher is seen as managing student behavior rather than achievement of knowledge and skill, and the primary criteria for evaluation purposes is effort and participation (Veal 1988c). In contrast, a philosophy of the teacher as responsible for student learning, coupled with an emphasis on measuring achievement of a body of knowledge and skill, may seem impractical and unnecessary to these teachers. Teacher preparation programs need to impart to their students the importance of assessing achievement in their classes. More important, teacher preparation programs need to provide strategies for accomplishing this task in the realities of the public school setting.

Socialization

No matter how hard we try to be individuals, many of us, for better or worse, acquire the traits of our parents. Lortie (1975) hypothesized a similar process for public school teachers. That is, personal experiences as students in the public school and higher education systems coupled with experiences as full-time teachers had a greater influence in shaping the philosophy and practices of teachers than formal education. Crum (1993) hypothesized that Lortie's ideas are especially applicable to physical education, hence we see what he termed "the vicious circle of the self-reproducing failure of PE" (p. 346). That is, today's teachers provide the model for tomorrow's teachers, resulting in the perpetuation of questionable practice. Lortie's disturbing assertions provided the impetus for two decades of research into the socialization of teachers (see Volume 12 Number 4 of the *Journal of Teaching in Physical Education*) and the creation of a more formal technology of teaching (Lawson, 1993). The implications of socialization for the development of M&E practices are significant. If teachers are influenced by their experiences as students (what Lortie, 1975, termed the "apprenticeship of observation"), then it is imperative that preservice programs not only deliver appropriate content but also model appropriate practice (Veal, 1992).

A second area of concern is the socialization of teachers as they enter the professional ranks. For example, Matanin and Tannehill (1994) reported that most of their teachers used the grading procedures advocated by their colleagues. Breaking the cycle of "self-reproducing failure" has not proven to be an easy task. However, a greater emphasis on the development of "reflective thinking" skills in preservice programs may help new teachers cope more effectively with the realities and changing contexts of the public school experience (e.g., Crum, 1993; Sebren, 1994).

Societal/Cultural Factors

Wood and Cusimano (1992) discovered that some teachers resisted testing because parents and students held negative attitudes toward it. The prevailing attitude among some parents and students was that testing in the cognitive or psychomotor domains detracted from the perceived primary purposes of physical education—exercise, fun, and recreation.

THE ROAD AHEAD:
ALTERNATIVE ASSESSMENT STRATEGIES

It is clear that the current path of M&E in public school physical education is really two paths—one advocated by teacher educators and one followed by teachers. Perhaps what is required to make these paths converge is a change in the perspective of what we teach, how we teach, and how we assess in physical education. Such a "paradigm shift" is occurring in other subject areas, with the current emphasis on outcomes-based education, integrated learning, and alternative assessment strategies. In fact, educational measurement and evaluation is in the throes of a major revolution. Dissatisfaction and frustration with traditional M&E practices at the grassroots level coupled with an educational reform movement at the local, state, and federal levels is being reflected in an increasing emphasis on alternative M&E procedures in public school education. A look at the major research and professional journals in education over the past few years will reveal entire issues or parts of issues dedicated to topics such as performance assessment, authentic assessment, and outcomes-based education (e.g., *Journal of Educational Measurement*, 30(3), 1993; *Applied Measurement in Education*, 4(4), 1991; *Middle School Journal*, 25(2), 1993; *Principal*, 73(3), 1994). Physical education has not responded as quickly or definitively to educational reform as other subject areas, yet similar trends are beginning to impact on M&E in the gymnasium.

GENESIS OF THE EDUCATIONAL REFORM MOVEMENT

On April 26, 1983, the results of an 18-month, federally funded, nation-wide study of the quality of American education was released under the title "A Nation at Risk" (National Commission on Excellence in Education, 1983). The results of the report painted a bleak picture of American education and can be summed up by such memorable quotes as "a rising tide of mediocrity" (p. 5) and "if an unfriendly foreign power had attempted to impose on America the mediocre educational performance that exists today, we might well have viewed it as an act of war" (p. 5).

The response to "A Nation at Risk" was immediate. Commissions developed at the state level amplified a growing demand for the development of content standards for subject areas and increased accountability of teachers for student learning. In 1989, President Bush met with state governors at an Education Summit. Six national goals of education were drafted, including the establishment of content standards for five subject areas. This summit marked the official beginning of the current outcomes movement in education. The task for each subject area was to develop a portrait of what students should know and be able to do at each grade level. The task for teachers was to implement the content standards and assess the degree to which students were meeting them. M&E thus became a cornerstone of the outcomes movement. Although physical education was not identified at the Education Summit as one of the five core subject areas, a task force sponsored by the National Association for Sport and Physical Education began in 1986 to develop learning outcomes for physical education. Completed in 1992, the NASPE "Outcomes of Quality Physical Education" described 20 outcomes necessary for the development of a physically educated person.

"Goals 2000: Educate America Act" was enacted in 1994, codifying the national goals as a framework for federal involvement in education. Federal funding was linked to the establishment of voluntary standards and assessment in eight core subject areas. Again, although physical education was not identified in the Act as one of the eight core subject areas, NASPE responded to the intent of the legislation by funding in 1992 a Standards and Assessment Task Force. The task force further clarified the content standards for physical education (reducing the standards from 20 to 7) and added guidelines for assessing the standards at each grade level (K, 2, 4, 6, 8, 10, 12). The culminating document from the task force, released in

June of 1995, represents physical education's most recent contribution to the national outcomes movement (NASPE, 1995).

The educational reform movement has reached beyond development of content standards. Other significant changes advocated by the movement include upgrading the use of current technology, particularly computer technology, increasing the development and assessment of higher order cognitive skills, such as problem solving and critical thinking, and promoting integrated learning across subject areas (see chapters 4 and 14).

IMPLICATIONS FOR M&E IN PHYSICAL EDUCATION

The implications of the educational reform movement and its emphasis on assessment for physical education in general and M&E in particular are far-reaching. If the response from other subject areas is any indication, physical education may be on the verge of an assessment revolution characterized by greater integration of assessment into the instructional process and development of alternative assessment strategies. At the very least, the increased emphasis on accountability in the classroom demands that physical education teachers and researchers critically evaluate current assessment practices.

ALTERNATIVE ASSESSMENT STRATEGIES

Traditional psychometric assessment devices (e.g., multiple choice tests, sport skills tests) may no longer be sufficient for assessment in the quickly changing educational landscape characterized by emphasis on learning outcomes, higher order cognitive skills, and integrated learning. Traditional assessment devices tend to measure narrowly defined cognitive, affective, and psychomotor characteristics; treat the three behavioral domains separately; and often fail to measure higher order performance processes under realistic or authentic conditions. An increased emphasis on assessing what students know and can actually do as they exit various grade levels and integrating higher order cognitive, affective, and psychomotor processes has led to dissatisfaction with traditional tests, resulting in the development of various alternative assessment strategies. The term alternative assessment includes a wide range of assessment options, such as portfolios (Collins & Dana, 1993; Melograno, 1994), discussions and debates, event tasks, case studies, student logs, role playing, and oral presentations (see Bartz, Anderson-Robinson, & Hillman, 1994; Feuer & Fulton, 1993; and Ornstein, 1994). Alternative assessments are often characterized as "performance assessments" or assessments in which "the student completes or demonstrates the same behavior that the assessor desires to measure" (Meyer, 1992, p. 40) and "authentic assessments," which are best described as performance assessments conducted in real-life contexts (Meyer, 1992). Performance assessments are characterized by direct assessment of desired behavior, focus on product and process or quality of performance, assessment of a single performance or performance over time, criterion-referenced scoring, and assessment criteria which are delineated to students in advance (Bartz et al., 1994).

An Alternative Assessment Example

To contrast the differences between traditional and alternative assessment, we can look at the example of assessing high school students enrolled in a physical fitness unit. Traditional assessment might include (a) a written test (typically of the multiple choice or essay variety) assessing students' mastery of knowledge concerning such areas as the components of fitness and how one assesses, achieves, and maintains adequate levels of each component and (b) assessment of health-related fitness status and improvement relative to criterion-referenced standards. In contrast, an authentic assessment task might direct students individually or as a group to develop a staff fitness program for volunteer teachers in the school. The assignment might include instructions for students to develop strategies for determining the fitness needs and recreation patterns of participating teachers, assess present fitness status, and develop an appropriate fitness program. In addition, students might be expected to present their project orally to the class and/or develop a detailed, written report of the project which includes reflective thinking about the worth of the project at each stage.

Advantages of Alternative Assessments

Alternative assessments, particularly authentic assessments, tend to engage students in the learning process; allow for the assessment of higher order cognitive processes; permit assessment of a combination of cognitive, psychomotor, and affective behaviors; permit the assessment of what students know and what they can do in real-life contexts; and provide an assessment method for integrated learning across subject areas. Moreover, because they can involve students in the development and critique of the assessment process and encourage them to be reflective "self-learners," alternative assessments provide a means for linking teaching, learning, and assessment.

Much of the psychomotor assessment in physical education tends to be "authentic" in the sense that student performance is assessed in real-life performance settings. The greatest potential of alternative assessments for physical education lies in using the physical education setting to foster integrated learning in an environment that is naturally engaging for most students. For example, an analysis/demonstration of popular dance can lead to large- or small-scale projects integrating the historical and cultural roots of dance (history, social studies, geography), the physical and psychological benefits of dance (health, biology), and the aesthetics of dance (music, art). By focusing attention on topics of relevance to students, creating opportunities for students to formulate their own questions and reflect upon their responses, and allowing self-, peer-, and teacher evaluation of progress and product, alternative assessment strategies focus on the process as well as the product of learning.

Challenges of Alternative Assessments

From a M&E perspective, alternative assessments raise a number of issues concerning reliability, objectivity, and validity. The subjective nature of these assessments requires the construction of detailed and precise scoring criteria or *rubrics* (Pate, Homestead, & McGinnis, 1993) and sufficient teacher training in using these criteria to maximize reliability of scoring. Content validity must be emphasized to maximize the degree to which the assessments measure important learning outcomes and that the time devoted to material covered in class is represented proportionally in the assessment (Pierson & Beck, 1993). Another important measurement issue is one of bias—Do alternative assessments adequately consider the cultural background and previous education (i.e., opportunity to learn) of students (Linn, Baker, & Dunbar, 1991)? From a practical perspective, the time required to organize, deliver, and score alternative assessments may be prohibitive (Madaus & Kellaghan, 1993; Nuttal, 1992) unless we change the way teachers teach. For example, a teacher implementing a large-scale authentic assessment project may find the role of facilitator rather than teacher more conducive to success. Successful implementation of alternative assessments also will require significant retraining of inservice teachers, significant changes in the M&E content of teacher education programs, and consideration of how alternative assessments will be used in the grading process (Pierson & Beck, 1993).

Alternative Assessment in Physical Education

Ironically, the formal assessment of performance is not emphasized by a large percentage of physical education teachers, yet the assessment of performance in physical education appears to be more natural than in other subject areas such as history, math, and science. Moreover, little has been written to date concerning the nature, application, and effectiveness of alternative assessments in physical education (Melograno, 1994; Veal, 1992). Several states (e.g., Kentucky, Vermont, California), however, are beginning to mandate the use of performance assessments as part of educational reform. Alternative assessments are not the panacea for problems of M&E in physical education. Physical educators and teacher educators must continue to grapple with the problems of the theory/practice gap and encourage accountability and adherence to the basic model of assessment in the physical education class. The educational reform movement and its emphasis on accountability and alternative assessment, however, can provide the impetus for moving into a new era of assessment in physical education (e.g., see Vickers, 1992, for a vision of a dynamic and integrated physical education curriculum using alternative assessment strategies combined with traditional tests).

SUMMARY

Student assessment is an integral component of the teaching/learning process. However, incongruity between assessment procedures advocated in teacher education programs and the assessment practices of inservice teachers undermines the effectiveness of assessment in physical education. It also threatens the very existence of physical education in the public schools. Current educational reform movements—with their emphasis on accountability, integrated learning, higher order cognitive processes, outcomes-based education, and alternative assessment strategies—can be viewed as a catalyst for revolutionizing assessment in physical education. Choosing to change our ways for the betterment of our profession and those we serve is "the road less traveled," and the path of change often is uncertain and at times frightening.

> Yet it is in this whole process of meeting and solving problems that life has its meaning . . . Problems call forth our courage and our wisdom; indeed, they create our courage and our wisdom. . . . It is through the pain of confronting and resolving our problems that we learn.
>
>   M. Scott Peck, *The Road Less Traveled,* (1978, p. 16)

REFERENCES

Bartz, D., Anderson-Robinson, S., & Hillman, L. (1994). Performance assessment: Make them show what they know. *Principal, 73*(3), 11–14.

Baumgartner, T.A., & Jackson, A.S. (1995). *Measurement for evaluation in physical education and exercise science* (5th ed.). Dubuque, IA: Wm. C. Brown.

Brookhart, S.M. (1993). Teachers' grading practices: Meaning and values. *Journal of Educational Measurement, 30,* 123–142.

Collins, A., & Dana, T.M. (1993). Using portfolios with middle grades students. *Middle School Journal, 25*(2), 14–19.

Cooper Institute for Aerobics Research. (1992). *The Prudential FITNESSGRAM test administration manual.* Dallas: Cooper Institute for Aerobics Research.

Crum, B.J. (1993). Conventional thought and practice in physical education: Problems of teaching and implications for change. *Quest, 45,* 339–356.

Dunham, P., Jr. (1986). Evaluation for excellence: A systematic approach. *Journal of Physical Education, Recreation and Dance, 57*(6), 34–36.

Feuer, M.J., & Fulton, K. (1993). The many faces of performance assessment. *Phi Delta Kappan, 74,* 478.

Fox, K. (1991). Motivating children for physical activity: Towards a healthier future. *Journal of Physical Education, Recreation and Dance, 62*(7), 34–38.

Fox, K., & Biddle, S.J.H. (1988). The use of fitness tests: Educational and psychological considerations. *Journal of Physical Education, Recreation and Dance, 59*(2), 47–53.

Hellison, D.R., & Templin, T.J. (1991). *A reflective approach to teaching physical education.* Champaign, IL: Human Kinetics.

Hensley, L.D. (1990). Current measurement and evaluation practices in professional PE. *Journal of Physical Education, Recreation and Dance, 61*(3), 32–33.

Hensley, L.D., Aten, R., Baumgartner, T.A., East, W.B., Lambert, L.T., & Stillwell, J.L. (1989). A survey of grading practices in public school physical education. *Journal of Research and Development in Education, 22*(4), 37–42.

Hensley, L.D., Morrow, J.R., Jr., & East, W.B. (1990). Practical measurement to solve practical problems. *Journal of Physical Education, Recreation and Dance, 61*(3), 42–44.

Imwold, C.H., Rider, R.A., & Johnson, D.J. (1982). The use of evaluation in public school physical education programs. *Journal of Teaching in Physical Education, 2*(1), 13–18.

Kneer, M. (1986). Description of physical education instructional theory/practice gap in selected secondary schools. *Journal of Teaching in Physical Education, 5,* 91–106.

Lawson, H.A. (1993). Teachers' uses of research in practice: A literature review. *Journal of Teaching in Physical Education, 12,* 366–374.

Linn, R., Baker, E., & Dunbar, S. (1991). Complex, performance-based assessment: Expectations and validation criteria. *Educational Researcher, 20*(8), 15–21.

Lortie, D. (1975). *Schoolteacher: A sociological study.* Chicago: University of Chicago Press.

Madaus, G.F., & Kellaghan, T. (1993). The British experience with 'authentic' testing. *Phi Delta Kappan, 74,* 458–469.

Matanin, M., & Tannehill, D. (1994). Assessment and grading in physical education. *Journal of Teaching in Physical Education, 13,* 395–405.

Matthews, D.K. (1968). *Measurement in physical education* (3rd ed.). Philadelphia, PA: W.B. Saunders.

Melograno, V.J. (1994). Portfolio assessment: Documenting authentic student learning. *Journal of Physical Education, Recreation and Dance, 65*(8), 50–55, 58–61.

Meyer, C.A. (1992). What's the difference between authentic and performance assessment? *Educational Leadership, 49*(8), 39.

Miller, D.K. (1994). *Measurement by the physical educator: Why and how* (2nd ed.). Dubuque, IA: Brown and Benchmark.

Mood, D. (1982). Evaluation in the affective domain? No! *Journal of Physical Education, Recreation and Dance, 53*(2), 18–20.

Morrow, J.R., Jr. (1978). Measurement techniques—Who uses them? *Journal of Physical Education & Recreation, 49*(9), 66–67.

National Association for Sport and Physical Education. (1992). *Outcomes of quality physical education.* Reston, VA: American Alliance for Health, Physical Education, Recreation and Dance.

National Association for Sport and Physical Education. (1995). *Moving into the future: National standards for physical education.* Reston, VA: American Alliance for Health, Physical Education, Recreation and Dance.

National Commission on Excellence in Education. (1983). *A nation at risk: The imperative for educational reform.* Washington, DC: U.S. Government Printing Office.

Nuttall, D.L. (1992). Performance assessment: The message from England. *Educational Leadership, 49*(8), 54–57.

Oregon Department of Education. (1988). *Physical education: Common curriculum goals.* Salem, OR: Oregon Department of Education.

Ornstein, A.C. (1994). Assessing without testing. *Principal, 73*(3), 16–18.

Parsons, R.B. (1994). Grading how we grade. *Principal, 73*(3), 24–26.

Pate, P.E., Homestead, E., & McGinnis, K. (1993). Designing rubrics for authentic assessment. *Middle School Journal, 25*(2), 25–27.

Peck, M.S. (1978). *The road less traveled: A new psychology of love, traditional values, and spiritual growth.* New York: Simon and Schuster.

Pierson, C.A., & Beck, S.S. (1993). Performance assessment: The realities that will influence the rewards. *Childhood Education, 70*(1), 29–32.

Safrit, M.J., & Wood, T.M. (1995). *Introduction to measurement in physical education and exercise science* (3rd ed.). St. Louis, MO: Mosby.

Schafer, W.D., & Lissitz, R.W. (1987). Measurement training for school personnel: Recommendations and reality. *Journal of Teacher Education, 38*(3), 57–63.

Sebren, A. (1994). Reflective thinking—Integrating theory and practice in teacher preparation. *Journal of Physical Education, Recreation and Dance, 65*(6), 23–24, 57–59.

Stiggins, R.J. (1988). Revitalizing classroom assessment: The highest instructional priority. *Phi Delta Kappan, 68*, 363–368.

Stroot, S.A., Faucette, N., & Schwager, S. (1993). In the beginning: The induction of physical educators. *Journal of Teaching in Physical Education, 12*, 375–385.

Veal, M.L. (1988a). Pupil assessment practices and perceptions of secondary school teachers. *Journal of Teaching in Physical Education, 7*, 327–342.

Veal, M.L. (1988b, April). *Generic coursework in undergraduate measurement and evaluation from the perspective of the practitioner/teacher educator.* Paper presented at the National Convention of the American Alliance for Health, Physical Education, Recreation and Dance, Kansas City, MO.

Veal, M.L. (1988c). Pupil assessment issues: A teacher educator's perspective. *Quest, 40,* 151–161.

Veal, M.L. (1990). Measurement and evaluation curricula in professional physical education preparation programs: A view from the practitioner. *Journal of Physical Education, Recreation and Dance, 61*(3), 36–38.

Veal, M.L. (1992). School-based theories of pupil assessment: A case study. *Research Quarterly for Exercise and Sport, 63,* 48–59.

Vickers, J. (1992). While Rome burns: Meeting the challenge of the reform movement in education. *Journal of Physical Education, Recreation and Dance, 63*(7), 80–87.

Wentzel, K.R. (1991). Social competence at school: Relation between social responsibility and academic achievement. *Review of Educational Research, 61,* 1–24.

Whitehead, J.R. (1993, May). Physical activity and intrinsic motivation. President's Council on Physical Fitness and Sports, *Physical Activity and Fitness Research Digest, Series 1*(2), 1-7.

Wood, T.M. (Speaker). (1990). *Evaluation practices in public school physical education: A theoretician's perspective* (Cassette Recording No. 9015 Tape 16). Paper presented at the National Convention of the American Alliance for Health, Physical Education, Recreation and Dance, New Orleans.

Wood, T.M., & Cusimano, B. (1992). *Oregon school physical education measurement and evaluation project.* Poster session presented as part of a 1/2 day workshop/symposium titled "Measurement and Evaluation in the School Physical Education Program: A View from the Inside" at the AAHPERD National Convention, Indianapolis.

Wood, T.M., Ritson, B., & Hensley, L. (1989). Grading practices in physical education: The Oregon experience. *Oregon Journal of Health, Physical Education, Recreation and Dance, 23*(2), 18–19, 24.

Wood, T.M., & Safrit, M.J. (1990). Measurement and evaluation in professional physical education—A view from the measurement specialists. *Journal of Physical Education, Recreation and Dance, 61*(3), 29–31.

Young, J., Klesius, S., & Hoffman, H. (1994). *Meaningful movement: A developmental approach to children's physical education.* Dubuque, IA: Kendall/Hunt.

PART 4

Promoting Valued Outcomes and Attitudes

CHAPTER 11

Physical Activity, Fitness, and Health-Related Physical Education

Thomas L. McKenzie

James F. Sallis

$\mathbf{P}$hysical activity, physical fitness, and health are inextricably connected. Physical fitness has long been a primary goal of physical education and is the component that is most frequently assessed. Physical fitness is extremely important in sport skill performance and it is related to improved health. Because physical fitness is achieved and maintained through participation in physical activity, the primary focus of this chapter is how to promote physical activity through school physical education.

WARMING UP: AN INTRODUCTION

Physical inactivity has recently been recognized as a risk factor for cardiovascular disease (CVD), which accounts for more than half of the adult deaths in the United States each year. Approximately 24% of the population is sedentary (U.S. Department of Health and Human Services [USDHHS], 1991), and many deaths could be prevented if individuals made changes in their physical activity habits. Engaging children and adolescents in physical activity and teaching them behavioral skills related to developing and maintaining appropriate physical activity could help prevent future generations of adults from becoming so sedentary.

Because most students have about nine years of required physical education, schools are the institutions with primary responsibility for physical activity promotion (Sallis & McKenzie, 1991). Reorienting school programs to promote physical activity could have a major impact on public health. Therefore, the notion of health-related physical education (HRPE) has been advanced (Pate & Hohn, 1994; Sallis & McKenzie, 1991). The main goal of HRPE is to prepare children and adolescents for a lifetime of physical activity. While this is not a new goal for physical education, reaching it will require the implementation of both curricular and instructional strategies that are substantially different from those in traditional fitness and sport-oriented programs.

The second section of this chapter, Serious Preparation: A Review of Related Literature, provides an overview of research related to physical activity and fitness and describes the current status of HRPE in schools. The third section, Exercising Opinions: A Health-Related View, discusses the conduct of physical education and the preparation of teachers from a health-related viewpoint. The fourth, SPARKing up Physical Education, describes Sports, Play, and Active Recreation for Kids (SPARK), an experimental elementary school physical education program designed with a health-related focus. The fifth section, Cooling Down, summarizes the chapter and encourages teachers to redirect physical education and physical fitness instruction toward reaching public health objectives.

SERIOUS PREPARATION: A REVIEW OF RELATED LITERATURE

This section describes the current status of HRPE in schools and provides a brief overview of research related to physical activity and fitness in youth. Connections between physical activity, physical fitness, and health are identified, and several questions related to the appropriateness of current levels of physical activity in youth are answered.

STATUS OF THE FIELD

Although sports typically dominate school programs after the third grade, physical fitness is usually advanced as the primary goal of physical education, particularly during threats of program elimination. Yet state, district, and school regulations for the content and delivery of physical education vary tremendously, with individual teachers being the major decision makers for what happens during classes. Most physical educators at least provide lip service to physical fitness and use various approaches to include it in their curricula. Some incorporate a few minutes of general fitness activities into each class, some match the fitness activities to the sport unit being instructed, some offer specialized fitness units, and some conduct obligatory, annual fitness tests. One state, Florida, requires that high school graduates complete one-half credit in physical education that focuses on the assessment, improvement, and maintenance of physical fitness (Johnson & Haragones, 1994). In 1992, only 25% of states reported mandatory testing in physical education, and these consisted primarily of physical fitness assessments conducted only at designated grade levels (Bennett & Peel, 1994).

Most popular general texts on elementary and secondary school physical education include sections or chapters on physical fitness, and there are numerous books specifically written on teaching physical fitness. *Fitness for Life* (Corbin & Lindsey, 1989), a textbook for junior and senior high schools, and *Teaching Strategies for Improving Youth Fitness* (Pangrazi & Corbin, 1994), which is geared for all grades, are two examples. The latter text includes information on the new FITNESSGRAM, recognition systems to motivate physical activity, and family involvement in students' fitness activities. Additionally, Pate and Hohn (1994) include several chapters on physical fitness curriculum and methods, as well as descriptions of special school programs. Although many theoretically sound curricula and instructional strategies have been promoted, few have been examined empirically, and none have been investigated for their long-term effects. As a result, the effects of different physical education programs on either students' out-of-school physical activity or their future physical fitness essentially have been untested.

Historically, being physically fit has been associated with being good at sports. A distinction is now made among the various components of physical fitness, and they are classified according to whether they develop skill or health-related fitness. Skill fitness is considered to be activity- or sport-specific and includes components such as accuracy, agility, balance, coordination, power, reaction time, and speed. Health-related physical fitness is more general and encompasses components directly related to reduced risk of hypokinetic disease, including cardiovascular fitness, muscular strength and endurance, flexibility, and body composition. The most widely used fitness testing programs at schools now measure health-related components (Pate & Shephard, 1989). While the various components of fitness are distinct and can be measured separately, they do affect one another—health-related fitness aids sports performance, and participation in sports contributes to health-related physical fitness.

PHYSICAL FITNESS, PHYSICAL ACTIVITY, AND HEALTH CONNECTIONS

Physical fitness, physical activity, and health are interconnected, but the full relationship remains unclear. Physical fitness is typically viewed as one of the variables that have an impact on how physical activity affects health (Bouchard, Shephard, & Stephens, 1994). Children's habitual physical activity is significantly related to multiple health-related fitness components, including cardiovascular endurance and muscular strength and endurance (Malina, 1994; Sallis, McKenzie, & Alcaraz, 1993). Increases in both physical activity and physical fitness are also associated with improved health measurements (Malina, 1994). However, the effects of physical activity on health appear to have multiple mechanisms, some of which do not depend upon fitness (Bouchard et al., 1994). Additionally, all three are influenced by other factors, including heredity, environment, and general lifestyle behaviors.

There is no doubt that training programs specifically designed to influence one or more components of health-related physical fitness can be successful (Malina, 1994). Resistance training programs have been shown to bring about substantial gains in static and functional strength measures in both prepubescent and adolescent boys and girls, although the data on girls are limited. Endurance training programs affect both boys and girls; however, the data suggest even intensive programs do little to change the maximal aerobic power of children under 10 years of age. Though there are design problems with these studies, it is generally agreed that structured and vigorous training programs can improve most fitness components in children. Because children have relatively high levels of fitness compared to adults (Simons-Morton, O'Hara, Simons-Morton, & Parcel, 1987), health professionals considered it more important that they maintain a good level of fitness rather than reach even higher levels.

HEALTH BENEFITS OF PHYSICAL ACTIVITY IN YOUTH

Physical activity seems to have beneficial effects on many bodily systems (Bouchard et al., 1994), but the effects on youth are just beginning to be understood. Recent reviews of the scientific literature have shown that physical activity in adolescence (defined as ages 11 to 21) reduces the risk of obesity and aids in its treatment (Bar-Or & Baranowski, 1994). Activities that work against gravity help increase the density of bones, which may prevent osteoporosis later in life (Bailey & Martin, 1994). Another important effect is that vigorous exercise improves psychological health and mood (Calfas & Taylor, 1994). Among high-risk youth, physical activity can reduce blood pressure (Alpert & Wilmore, 1994) and increase HDL-cholesterol (Armstrong & Simons-Morton, 1994).

Improvement in children's flexibility, muscular strength, and bone health is thought to be related to reduced occurrences of back pain and fractures in adulthood. The strongest reason for health related physical education, however, appears to be the prevention of CVD. Cardiovascular risk in childhood predicts risk in young adulthood (Cresanta, Burke, Downey, Freedman, & Berenson, 1986), so decreasing risk factors in children is important.

The CVD risk associations are similar for children and adults (Sallis, Patterson, Buono, & Nader, 1988), and it is possible that children can reduce their risk of future heart disease through regular physical activity.

ARE STUDENTS PHYSICALLY FIT AND ACTIVE ENOUGH?

There has been substantial public concern about how physically inactive and unfit American children are becoming. Despite the negative press, there is little scientific information available to indicate that today's children are either less fit than those of previous generations or that they compare badly to age-matched youth in other industrialized nations (Falls & Pate, 1993). Levels of obesity in both children (Gortmaker, Dietz, Sobol, & Wehler, 1987) and adults are increasing, however, this health problem could be partially solved if individuals were more active. Simons-Morton et al. (1987) found children to be substantially more fit than adults and concluded that increasing cardiopulmonary fitness was not a health priority for children. They recommended that the programs for children should focus on promoting regular physical activity habits that would carry over from childhood to adulthood, rather than emphasizing physical fitness.

To be able to judge whether children are active enough, there must be a standard to which they are compared. Recently, a consensus statement was developed for physical activity guidelines for adolescents (Sallis & Patrick, 1994). Following these guidelines should produce important health effects in adolescents. The first recommendation is that they should do some activity, regardless of intensity, daily or nearly every day. A reasonable guideline is 30 minutes per day. National surveys of adolescents indicate that the vast majority are meeting this guideline (Pate, Long, & Heath, 1994). The second recommendation is that they should engage in vigorous exercise, three or more times a week, for 20 minutes or more at a time. Unfortunately, only about one half of adolescent boys and one quarter of adolescent girls are meeting this standard (Pate et al., 1994).

Sallis (1993) found variations in both physical activity and aerobic power related to age and gender. Aerobic power remained stable from ages 6 to 16 for boys, but declined about 2% per year in girls. Overall, boys were about 25% more fit than girls. Reviews of studies using both self-reports and objective measures revealed that boys were from 15 to 25% more physically active than girls. A constant decline in physical activity engagement over time was seen, with boys decreasing about 2.7% per year and girls decreasing 7.4% per year. These results suggest that older students and females are at increased risk because of a more sedentary lifestyle. Minority and economically disadvantaged adults are relatively inactive compared to majority and more affluent adults. This pattern may start in childhood. Four-year-old Mexican-American boys and girls were found to be less physically active than their Anglo-American counterparts, both at home and during school recess (McKenzie, Sallis, Nader, Broyles, & Nelson, 1992).

OBSERVATIONS OF PHYSICAL ACTIVITY IN ELEMENTARY SCHOOLS

When elementary physical education classes are actually observed, relatively little physical activity is seen. Several studies have shown that children, particularly boys, may be more active during recess than during physical education classes (e.g., Sarkin, McKenzie, & Sallis, 1994). One study found the average child in 30-minute classes taught by specialists was vigorously active for only 2 minutes (Parcel et al., 1987). Faucette, McKenzie, and Patterson (1990) found PE classes of classroom teachers consisted mainly of game play in which a few children were active while the remainder waited for a turn. Only 5% of the classes had fitness activities as the major focus. In a study of third-grade physical education in 95 schools in four states, children engaged in moderate to vigorous physical activity (MVPA) 36% of class time, far short of the 50% recommended by the *Healthy People 2000* objectives (McKenzie et al., 1995). Classes conducted outdoors provided significantly more physical activity than those held indoors. For children in this study, physical education classes provided only 25% of the vigorous activity and 12% of the MVPA recommended per week for health purposes by national objectives.

DO CURRENT PHYSICAL EDUCATION AND ATHLETIC PROGRAMS MOTIVATE YOUTH TO ENGAGE IN PHYSICAL ACTIVITY AS ADULTS?

Only a few studies have attempted to answer this question, and they have produced conflicting findings (Powell & Dysinger, 1987). One study found participation in physical activities during childhood and adolescence to be one of the lowest of 25 correlates of adult vigorous activity (Sallis et al., 1989). Because most adult physical activities are solitary and noncompetitive, one might not expect too much carryover from physical education programs that emphasize team sports. This is recognized by *Healthy People 2000* Objective 1.9, which recommends (in part) that students in physical education classes spend more time being active, preferably "engaged in lifetime activities" (USDHHS, 1991). Along the same lines, both the American Academy of Pediatrics (1987) and the American College of Sports Medicine (1988) support physical education adopting more health-related goals.

HEALTH GOALS FOR THE NATION

Public health objectives designed to reduce preventable death, disease, and disability in the United States have recently been established and are likely to influence the conduct of school physical education in the future. The objectives and their rationale are described in the document *Healthy People 2000: National Health Promotion and Disease Prevention*

Objectives (USDHHS, 1991). Developed by 22 working groups of health experts that represented over 300 national and state organizations, the objectives were intended as outcomes that could be met realistically by the year 2000. The objectives related to physical activity are prominently listed first in *Healthy People 2000*, and those objectives that are pertinent to the conduct of physical education in schools are included in Table 11.1 in abbreviated form. The number preceding the objective in the table provides a reference for the complete objective in the *Healthy People 2000* document.

HEALTH-RELATED PHYSICAL ACTIVITY INTERVENTIONS: SCHOOL-BASED PROGRAMS

Controlled studies have shown that physical education programs emphasizing health-related physical activity and cardiovascular fitness can be

Table 11.1   Year 2000 Objectives Relevant to the Conduct of Physical Education in Schools

Health Status Objective

1.2   Reduce the prevalence of over-fatness among adolescent and adult populations.

Risk Reduction Objectives

1.3   Increase the proportion of people who engage in physical activity regularly, preferably daily.

1.4   Increase the proportion of people who engage in regular physical activity for cardiovascular fitness.

1.5   Decrease the proportion of people who do no leisure-time physical activity.

1.6   Increase the proportion of people who do regular physical activity for strength, muscular endurance, and flexibility.

1.7   Increase the proportion of overweight people who use physical activity to attain desirable body fatness.

4.11 Reduce the proportion of male adolescents who use anabolic steroids.

Services and Protection Objectives

1.8   Increase the proportion of children and adolescents in grades 1 through 12 who participate daily in school physical education.

1.9   Increase the proportion of school physical education class time that students spend being physically active, preferably engaged in lifetime physical activities.

1.10 Increase employer-sponsored worksite physical activity and fitness programs.

1.11 Increase community availability and accessibility of physical activity and fitness facilities.

From "Children's Activity Levels and Lesson Context During Third-Grade Physical Education," by T.L. McKenzie et al., 1995, *Research Quarterly for Exercise and Sport*, **66**(3), pp. 184-193. Copyright 1995. Reproduced with permission from the American Alliance for Health, Physical Education, Recreation and Dance, Reston, VA 22091.

implemented successfully at elementary schools (Sallis & McKenzie, 1991). Increases in physical activity at school have been documented by self-report, direct observation, and heart rate monitoring. At least five studies found that children who participated in health-related PE improved their cardiovascular fitness, and several showed that children reduced their skinfold thickness. It appears that if programs are implemented as planned, improvements in health-related outcomes do result.

Simons-Morton, Parcel, and O'Hara (1988) provided training to help PE specialists implement health-related PE. The amount of class time spent in fitness activities during the first year of intervention almost doubled that provided in control schools. This indicates that experienced specialists can be retrained to make substantial changes in their teaching practices. Similarly, elementary school classroom teachers can make substantial improvements in the quality and quantity of physical education if they are provided with an active, teacher-friendly curriculum accompanied by training and follow-up (McKenzie, Sallis, Faucette, Roby, Kolody, 1993). Over a three-year period, trained classroom teachers conducted significantly more classes and provided children almost twice as much MVPA as their untrained peers (Sallis et al., 1994).

A major barrier to improving physical education is the concern by administrators that spending more time in physical education take time away from scholastic work. A Canadian study, however, has shown that this concern is not justified. Even when more time is allocated for physical education in the school day, it does not result in a decline in academic performance (Shephard, Lavallee, Volle, LaBarre, & Beaucage, 1994).

It appears that health promotion programs that target children's physical activity without directly influencing physical education classes are somewhat unsuccessful. Coates, Jeffery, and Slinkard (1981) reported the results of a classroom-based diet and physical activity change program designed to reduce CVD risk factors in fourth- and fifth-grade students. Behavioral self-management procedures were used to help children change health-related behaviors, and the program produced significant effects on dietary behavior. However, the six-session physical activity component targeted at increasing physical activity during the daily recess produced no observed effects. Similarly, the five-year, classroom-based, "Know Your Body" program produced significant changes in total cholesterol, dietary intake, and health knowledge, but not physical fitness (Walter, Hofman, Vaughan, & Wynder, 1988). From these data it appears that school efforts to successfully modify children's physical activity and fitness must target physical education directly.

Several multidisciplinary and multifaceted programs that have included physical activity as a target have been implemented. Many of these programs have been funded by the National Institutes of Health, and several are currently still in operation.

Child and Adolescent Trial for Cardiovascular Health (CATCH).   This intervention is being studied in third through fifth grades in 96 schools in California, Louisiana, Minnesota, and Texas (Stone, McGraw, Osganian, & Elder, 1994). The program targets physical activity, eating, and smoking behavior and includes classroom curricula, school environment changes involving physical education and food service, and family involvement components.

Go for Health Program.   This program was implemented in several elementary schools in Texas and was designed to produce changes in physical education, classroom health education, and school lunch (Simons-Morton et al., 1988).

Heart Smart.   This health education intervention for grades kindergarten through six was implemented in Louisiana and included eating habits, physical fitness and exercise, and saying "no" to tobacco and drugs. Heart Smart employs the Superkids-Superfit model for physical education (Virgilio & Berenson, 1988).

Know Your Body.   This comprehensive, classroom-based program with diet, physical activity, and smoking components was implemented by classroom teachers in grades K–6. Physical education classes were not targeted directly (Walter et al., 1988).

Sports, Play, and Active Recreation for Kids (SPARK).   This randomized intervention, being tested in California, focuses exclusively on promoting physical activity. In addition to a physical education program designed to provide ample amounts of activity, fourth- and fifth-grade children participate in weekly self-management workshops where they learn to plan and be responsible for out-of-school physical activity. The SPARK curricula are described more fully later in this chapter.

EXERCISING OPINIONS: A HEALTH-RELATED VIEW OF PHYSICAL EDUCATION

New research on the benefits of physical activity has produced a conceptual shift regarding the relative importance of physical fitness and physical activity. Physical activity has been recognized as a CVD risk factor, although physical fitness has not. Physical fitness is transitory and can only be maintained by regular physical activity. As a result, several reviewers argue from a public health perspective that increasing the physical activity of children is more important than improving their physical fitness (Sallis & McKenzie, 1991; Simons-Morton et al., 1987). This notion has many implications for the conduct of physical education, with a major distinction being whether the primary outcome of programs should be a behavior (physical activity engagement) or a biological (physical fitness) characteristic. This section discusses various aspects of the conduct of physical education and the preparation of teachers from a health-related viewpoint.

MODERATE VERSUS VIGOROUS INTENSITY ACTIVITIES

Improvements in physical fitness and sport performances (especially those involving cardiovascular endurance) require that physical activity be done at a high-intensity or vigorous level. On the other hand, the clear message from recent research and put forth in *Healthy People 2000* objectives is that it is not necessary to exercise vigorously to receive health benefits. Cardiovascular, musculoskeletal, and mental health improvement also result from engaging in lower or moderate-intensity physical activity.

In both developing programs and conducting classes, physical educators should consider the implications of the results from a large number of studies that have demonstrated the lack of adherence by adults to high-intensity exercise programs (Dishman & Sallis, 1994). Compliance to low-intensity exercise is higher than that to high-intensity exercise, and a public health benefit is more likely to result from getting the sedentary to move rather than from increasing the activity levels of those already physically active (Blair, Kohl, Gordon, & Paffenbarger, 1992). Studies of obese children suggest that moderate-intensity activities that can be incorporated into one's daily lifestyle are more effective at maintaining weight loss than vigorous exercise (Epstein, Wing, Koeske, & Valoski, 1985). At least one study has reported that upper-elementary school children preferred moderate-intensity physical activity units of instruction to more strenuous ones (McKenzie, Alcaraz, & Sallis, 1994). These studies suggest that for long-term public health impact, regular, moderate-intensity activity may in some ways be a more appropriate goal in schools than vigorous exercise. It may be possible that some students are turned off to physical education (and physical activity) because classes demand high-intensity exercise.

The recommendation that teachers include lower-intensity activities does not mean that physical education should be devoid of strenuous activity or that programs should not strive for students to become fit and highly skilled in sports. Becoming physically fit and highly skilled are important outcomes that provide substantial personal benefits (see chapter 12 by Siedentop), but these may not be important goals for all students. Alternative programs and activities are needed if public health objectives are to be met.

TIME FOR PHYSICAL ACTIVITY AND FITNESS

The health benefits from low-intensity activity do not accrue as quickly as those from high-intensity activity. It takes longer, for example, to achieve a weight loss from walking than running, and subsequent modifications in the frequency and duration of physical education classes might be necessary if health objectives are to be met. This is particularly true for programs that strive to reach all the standard objectives of physical education (such as the 20 promoted by NASPE).

Students do not have enough time in physical education to meet fitness and physical activity objectives, let alone reach the vast number of other objectives assigned to PE programs. Most fifth- and sixth-grade students have some physical education, with approximately 100 minutes being allocated each week (Ross & Gilbert, 1985; Ross & Pate, 1987). Enrollment declines with each successive grade, however, and only about 40% of boys and girls take physical education in grade 12 (Centers for Disease Control, 1993).

Although it is clear that elementary school physical education classes are not particularly active, fewer data are available for secondary schools. Classes at this level, however, typically allocate large amounts of time for dressing and showering (often 20 minutes of a 55-minute class). After the lesson starts, students spend a substantial amount of time in sedentary activities, including being managed, waiting a turn, and receiving knowledge. It is not unusual for students at the beginning of classes to warm up in preparation for skill learning, only to cool down while they have to sit and listen. This is probably not only medically unsound, but could also turn students off to physical education. This would be evidenced in measures of enrollment, absenteeism, and tardiness.

A PLACE FOR FITNESS KNOWLEDGE

As Lambert has noted in her chapter, fitness and health knowledge are important aspects of physical education. Most knowledge could be taught in an environment that is much more conducive to learning than a gymnasium or playing field. Classrooms are more suitable for engaging in cognitive learning. They are more comfortable, provide fewer distractions, have more instructional aids, and expectations for student knowledge gains are already present. Classes conducted in gymnasia and on playing fields should be primarily reserved for students to engage in physical activity and develop motor skills.

With the newly available evidence of the benefits of lower intensity physical activity, it would also be appropriate to teach students how much time they should spend being active for health purposes. The general standards established for adolescents include 30 minutes of activity daily and at least three 20-minute bouts of MVPA weekly (Sallis & Patrick, 1994). Additionally, it would be appropriate to teach advanced high school students about how energy expenditure is expressed in calories, and that they, as adults, can substantially improve their health and reduce risk of death from cardiovascular disease by expending more calories per week in physical activity.

Physical education and athletic programs are also important vehicles for delivering relevant messages about steroids, eating disorders, and other sport and exercise practices related to health. This includes teaching secondary school students to be informed consumers, so they can make appropriate decisions about sports drinks, exercise equipment, and exercise clubs.

It is important to remember that knowledge in and of itself is insufficient to change behavior. Knowledge dissemination should be accompanied by prompts and reinforcement for engaging in appropriate health-related behavior. This is rarely done. We recommend using school settings to teach behavior change skills, such as how to plan and set goals to be physically active outside of school and how to resist peer pressure to engage in unhealthy habits.

INVOLVING THE FAMILY IN PHYSICAL EDUCATION

Family members influence each other's physical activity in many different ways (Sallis & Nader, 1988). School programs that promote physical activity and fitness would do well to involve the entire family. One successful family-based program identified fourth- through sixth-grade students with low fitness levels and involved their parents in a 12-week home reinforcement program (Taggart, Taggart, & Siedentop, 1986). Parents worked with behavioral consultants who trained and assisted them to develop individualized programs to promote their children's physical activity. Almost all of the children increased both their physical activity and fitness, and it was noted that the availability of appropriate facilities for activity and weekly contact with consultants were felt to enhance the program's effectiveness. Some of the methods of this intensive, individualized treatment could be implemented more broadly in schools.

There are several ways school could involve families in physical education, such as offering special events and evening programs, sending home newsletters, and prompting parents to encourage and reward their children's physical activity. Although these strategies have been described in different publications, data on their effectiveness are limited. Meanwhile, many impediments to family-oriented programs exist that need to be considered and overcome. Money, time, and staff training are the most conspicuous barriers, but programs also must be perceived as relevant to parents or they will not participate. Families are more likely to participate in programs for younger children, and it is questionable whether many adolescents would appreciate being involved with their parents in programs that are conducted on the school site.

ASSESSING PHYSICAL FITNESS

About 25% of the United States mandate some physical fitness testing in schools (Bennett & Peel, 1994). Regular fitness testing is useful in determining the effectiveness of programs and it can aid in assessing how students compare both to health-related standards and to the performance of others. Fitness testing in schools is controversial, however, with some leading professionals proposing more of it and others suggesting that it be abolished completely. Using physical fitness test results in determining physical education grades is a problem. Heredity plays a major role in the level of performance on fitness tests, and students may not reach either their own expectations or health-related standards no matter how hard they try or how long they practice.

Unless administered judiciously, fitness testing could discourage students from participating in physical activity. To take a valid measure of fitness, such tests require that students must do their best—in school, this means performing publicly in front of peers. Rarely do people look, smell, or sound good when "going all out" on a physical test, and this may be embarrassing, particularly for adolescents in coeducational classes. Little effort is made to be discrete about how well students are performing on tests; results are frequently posted publicly; and rewards are sometimes distributed at assemblies.

For health purposes, fitness tests should be administered periodically and in a humane manner; for example, measures of adiposity should be taken privately for sensitive individuals. Students should be told that their scores are personal and highly affected by heredity, practice, and effort. They should be encouraged to meet standards for good health and make individual improvements rather than be compared to others. Students should also be taught how to assess themselves and be given chances to practice any school-administered tests. Prior to testing, they should also receive information on tactics proven to be successful. After testing, students should receive feedback on how their scores correlate to health-related standards and suggestions on how to overcome any performance deficits. Computerized feedback is now available to assist teachers who use some of the widely available, standard test batteries.

ASSESSING PHYSICAL ACTIVITY

While physical educators are typically knowledgeable about field-based measures of physical fitness, they are generally less informed about how they can assess students' physical activity levels or how much activity is provided by their school programs. A variety of methods and techniques for measuring physical activity are available, including self-report, electronic motion sensors and heart rate monitors, and direct observation. The purpose, validity, and reliability of various instruments, as well as guidelines for their use, are described in a special issue of the *Journal of School Health* (1991).

Although some techniques were designed for use in large-scale epidemiology studies, most can be adapted for assessing the amount or intensity of students' physical activity. Self-reports are reasonably reliable with children over age 10 and can be used to assess the out-of-school physical activity of adolescents, including that done on weekends and vacations. Use of this technique could provide a measure of the generalizability of programs to promote physical activity beyond the physical education class.

Heart rate monitors and accelerometers, such as the Caltrac, could provide more objective measures of out-of-school activity, but they are likely to be too expensive and burdensome for widespread use in schools. Nonetheless, Caltracs and heart rate monitors could be placed on randomly selected students during class time to provide feedback to instructors on how active their classes are.

A number of direct observation instruments, including System for Observing Fitness Instruction Time (SOFIT) (McKenzie, Sallis, & Nader, 1991), have been used to assess physical education interventions. These tools are particularly useful because they can provide simultaneous measures of student activity, lesson context, and teacher behavior. Trained observers use the instruments in research studies; but with the increased availability of videotaping, conscientious physical educators could assess their own classes. An easier but less sophisticated method to assess activity levels in ongoing classes would be for teachers to use placheck (momentary time-sampling) recording (Siedentop, 1991) and periodically record the number of students being sedentary versus being physically active. Teachers could also use checklists to assess periodically whether their own behavior matches proposed goals. In one of our studies, elementary students were observed to be prompted or rewarded for out-of-school physical activity during less than 5% of the lessons, even though this was a stated goal of the teachers.

ASSESSING THE PULSE OF THE CLASS

The heart rate is the most frequent method for determining the intensity of student engagement in cardiovascular exercise, and various target zones have been set. Physical education curricula frequently call for students to learn about the Frequency, Intensity, Time, Type (FITT) principle and to exercise a minimum of three times per week, at 60 to 80% of their maximum heart rate, for at least 20 minutes at a time. Students are commonly taught how to take pulse rates and calculate how well they are doing during fitness classes. This exercise is best reserved for older students. Elementary school students can be taught these skills, but they are not particularly accurate. The time it takes to teach and use the procedures could probably be better spent engaging children in activity. More global and less time-consuming indicators of intensity, such as sweating and breathing hard, are likely more useful in elementary schools.

STRENGTH TRAINING

Many high schools and some junior high schools offer specialized units targeted at producing increases in strength and power. These courses are particularly popular with male adolescents interested in athletic performance and body building, although information and practice in strength development activities are important for all students. A recent study indicated that weightlifting was the most prevalent physical activity engaged in by male adolescents (Sallis, Zakarian, Hovell, & Hofstetter, 1994). Strength training not only improves the function of muscles, but also strengthens bones, ligaments, and tendons which might help decrease risk of injuries, poor posture, and lower back pain.

The efficient development of strength through progressive resistance training requires substantial amounts of equipment. Only a limited number of schools have the newly developed, sophisticated, and expensive variable resistance machines; free weights and constant resistance machines are more common. Strength development equipment requires that a special place (i.e., weight room) be set aside so that it can be both properly monitored and secured when supervision is not available. Interscholastic teams often receive priority in the use of these facilities. Because weight training equipment is usually limited, a substantial percent of students may be inactive during class time. Circuit training has been used as a means to accommodate more users, and some schools are able to use private fitness facilities during off-peak hours. Using off-campus exercise facilities should promote the generalization of physical activity beyond graduation.

There is substantial evidence that some athletes and body builders use illegally obtained anabolic steroids to produce rapid gains in strength and muscle size. Junior and senior high school students may be generally aware of some of these benefits of steroids, but they do not necessarily know about accompanying, undesirable side effects. Reducing the proportion of male high school seniors who use anabolic steroids is one of the objectives of *Healthy People 2000*.

PREPARING TEACHERS

Are current teacher preparation practices meeting the current and future needs of students regarding physical activity and fitness? A vast number of elementary school students receive their only physical education instruction from classroom teachers, many of whom have had little or no training in elementary school physical education. Additionally, the trend to require potential physical education specialists to take more theoretical and scientific courses while reducing their exposure to instructional methods, program development and assessment, and physical activities is not necessarily positive. Graduates who complete these courses of study are often better prepared to teach sedentary, cognitive-focused classes than they are to teach students to be physically active. Though a goal of physical education should be to promote regular physical activity as a habit, only a small number of physical educators are required to take courses in behavior analysis and behavior change. No wonder the cry from graduating teachers facing the responsibility of getting students to be active is frequently "Don't tell me why, tell me how!"

Schools do not hire enough physical education specialists so that all students can receive physical education daily or even three times per week. To better serve elementary school pupils, schools might consider modifying the role of specialists to take on new duties—as consultants. In this revised role, specialists would teach fewer physical education classes but would have added responsibilities for planning, coordinating, and supervising the physical education classes of generalists. Another consultant function would be to help structure the entire school environment to promote physical activity, including supervising morning, recess, and after-school programs. These tasks would require specialized training that is currently not usually offered in teacher preparation programs, but the reorientation of the physical education teacher's role would likely improve the quality of classes that students receive.

A survey of teacher licensing practices across the United States between 1988 and 1992 indicated a tendency to increase the separation between health and physical education certifications (Bennett & Peel, 1994). During this time, there was a significant reduction in the number of states that issued combined health and physical education certifications (n=13 in 1992). Meanwhile, 48% of the states permit certified physical educators to teach health classes, and 24% permit health educators to teach physical education classes (Bennett & Peel, 1994). This is unfortunate because different skills and training are needed for each of these disciplines.

PE: A PLACE TO BE

To successfully promote physical activity in both the short and long term, the physical education class needs to become a nice place to be. There are few data on how students view physical education, but low enrollments and high rates of tardiness and absenteeism in classes at secondary schools present an unfavorable picture. Physical educators need to begin to think about students as consumers. Consumers do not all want or need the same product. Events and activities that motivate the highly skilled and highly fit in physical education are not necessarily effective with those who are inactive or unfit. Some students do not enjoy competing against others, so the role of competition in classes needs to be examined. Support from friends and peers is known to reinforce exercise maintenance, so it would seem to be appropriate for teachers to allow friends to participate together. But what effect does allowing students to work in self-determined groups have on other class goals? Success enhances activity maintenance, but does exposure to large numbers of activities/sports in a curriculum enhance the generalization of physical activity out of school? Is generalization hindered because students are not skilled enough to be successful and feel comfortable in any one activity area? Answers to curricular questions such as these need to be debated and subjected to empirical study. In the meantime, it is reasonable to expect that consumers of physical education would like to participate in a clean, friendly environment and would enjoy participating in classes that are small enough to allow teachers to both recognize them and plan an activity program that meets their individual needs.

SPARKING UP PHYSICAL EDUCATION: A SAMPLE PROGRAM

Sports, Play, and Active Recreation for Kids (SPARK) is a health-oriented physical education program that teaches carry-over activities and behavioral skills to upper elementary school children.[1] SPARK is funded by the Heart, Lung, and Blood Institute of the National Institutes of Health and has been validated as a "program that works" by the Program Effectiveness Panel of the National Diffusion Network, U. S. Department of Education. SPARK consists of two curricula, the SPARK Physical Education Program and the SPARK Self-Management Program. These curricula blend science and theory into practical programs that can be implemented in schools. Because 36 states do not require that physical education be taught by specialists (National Association for Sport and Physical Education, 1993), the curricula were written for and tested by both classroom teachers and physical education specialists.

SPARK PHYSICAL EDUCATION PROGRAM

The SPARK physical education curriculum is a comprehensive program with the student goal of learning to enjoy and to seek out physical activity. SPARK PE classes are designed to promote high levels of physical activity which will improve health-related fitness, promote movement skills that add to success and enjoyment in physical activity, and engender positive socialization.

Maximum student participation during class time is promoted both by the selection of activities and the way they are taught. Inactive sports and drills, elimination games, and activities that require either specialized and expensive equipment (e.g., formal gymnastics) or demand inordinate amounts of time to set up are excluded from the program.

The curriculum promotes individual improvement, and students are encouraged to monitor their own progress over time. Eight times per year, students participate in "Personal Best Day" in order to self-assess and track their cardiovascular fitness and upper-body and abdominal strength and endurance.

A standard SPARK lesson is 30 minutes in length and has two parts: (a) a health-fitness activity, which includes an introduction (warm-up) with a transition to a health-fitness activity (15 min.) and (b) a skill-fitness activity with a transition to closure (cool down) (15 min.).

Health-Fitness Activities

This portion of the lesson focuses on developing health-related fitness and locomotor skills. The SPARK PE curriculum includes 10 different units, including aerobic dance, aerobic games, and jump rope. Progression is developed by modifying the intensity, duration, and complexity of the activities selected. While the main focus is on developing cardiovascular endurance, activities to develop abdominal and upper body strength are also included.

Sport-Fitness Activities

The second part of the lesson focuses on developing skill-related fitness, particularly as it relates to the development of body/limb/object coordination and specialized sport skills (e.g., basketball, soccer). The SPARK PE curriculum includes a limited number of sports units, but these are the ones that have the most potential for cardiovascular development and teaching movement skills that will carry over into the child's community.

SPARK SELF-MANAGEMENT PROGRAM

The goal of the self-management component of SPARK is to provide children with cognitive and behavioral skills that will help them stay physically active on their own and to promote parental support for the children's activity. Children are taught specific methods to help themselves achieve personal goals. Because multiple studies show that knowledge gains are usually insufficient to produce changes in behavior, teaching behavior change skills related to physical activity is emphasized with students, rather than teaching them knowledge. The effectiveness of self-management skills is supported by hundreds of studies (e.g., Kanfer & Goldstein, 1980), and these skills can be used to enhance the generalization and maintenance of physical activity.

Self-management skills and related topics are taught in weekly classroom sessions. A beginning and advanced curricula, each with 22 scripted lessons, has been developed and implemented with fourth and fifth grades.

A standard, 30-minute self-management session begins with a brief review of the skills or information presented during the previous session and a discussion of the students' progress on activity goals during the previous week. Goal attainment is praised and lack of progress is approached as a problem-solving opportunity. After the review, approximately 15 to 20 minutes are spent on the presentation of a new topic. Students usually spend much of this time working in small groups or playing games designed to convey the information and provide them with practice using the targeted skills. The next 4 to 5 minutes are spent setting physical activity goals for the coming week. On occasion, homework designed to reinforce the skill or information provided during the session is assigned. At the end of the session, rewards for goal achievement are provided to those students who have earned them.

Students are reinforced for meeting weekly activity goals. They are provided with a chart that indicates the points they can receive for specific amounts of time spent in various physical activities. Limited points can be earned each day and each week, so moderate levels of regular physical activity are encouraged, instead of excessive amounts. The reward system continues throughout most of the first year (fourth grade). However, because the aim is to prepare students to be active on their own, the reward system is faded out approximately halfway through the second year (fifth grade).

Family involvement is strongly encouraged in the self-management program. Students are instructed to share and discuss handouts and homework assignments with their parents. A parent signature is required on each goal sheet to receive points for activities, and many homework assignments require family participation. Students can receive extra points for having family members be active with them. Monthly newsletters to families encourage this behavior and instruct family members how to effectively promote children's physical activity.

COOLING DOWN:
A SUMMARY

This chapter has introduced the notion of health-related physical education; provided an overview of research related to physical activity and fitness; described the current status of health-related physical education in schools; discussed various aspects of the conduct of physical education and the preparation of teachers from a health-related viewpoint; and described one experimental elementary school physical education program designed with a health-related focus. This final section reorients the reader to the purpose of health-related physical education and the place it might play in reaching public health objectives.

The goal of HRPE is to prepare children and adolescents to develop and maintain physically active lifestyles. It goes beyond the traditional notion of getting students fit and teaching them physical fitness concepts. In addition, it includes arranging the entire school environment to ensure all students are provided with ample opportunities to participate in physical activity and that they learn the behavioral and cognitive skills necessary for maintaining physical activity outside the school setting. A reorientation of physical education to make it a vehicle for physical activity promotion would go a long way toward reaching the public health goals of the nation.

The goals of physical education in promoting physical activity are closely aligned to public health priorities. These common purposes can lead to increased appreciation for, and support of, school physical education. It is unknown how the *Healthy People 2000* objectives will impact physical education, but many policy makers now are aware of the benefits of regular physical activity. Meanwhile, it is clear from the data that if schools are to carry the major responsibility for activity promotion for youth, changes will need to be made. There simply is not enough time allocated to physical education for it to be able to reach physical activity promotion goals, let alone all the other outcomes expected of it. More opportunities for students to be active could be created by increasing the frequency and length of physical education classes and by increasing the proportion of time students are physically active during them. These changes would still not provide enough physical activity for students to reach recommended standards for health purposes, so additional early-morning, noontime, and after-school programs will need to be provided.

A primary question at this time is how—not whether—schools should become involved in health-related physical education. The content of health-related physical education and how it is best taught is still to be determined. There are no clear-cut answers as to what an effective, health-oriented physical education program at either the elementary or secondary level looks like. How much will current practices have to change? How will traditional goals of physical education be accommodated? Will students like health-related physical education? Will it be well received by athletic coaches? Will the movement and behavioral skills taught in these classes generalize to out-of-school settings during the holidays and summers, let alone be maintained into adulthood? Questions such as these need to be seriously discussed by practitioners and scientists alike, and sample programs need to be developed and subjected to empirical tests. In the interim, it is the responsibility of all physical educators to assess each class they teach to determine whether or not what they did today is likely to increase the probability that their students will be physically active tomorrow and in the future.

---

[1]Additional information on the SPARK physical education, self-management, and teacher training programs may be obtained from: SPARK, San Diego State University, 6363 Alvarado Court, Suite 250, San Diego, California, 92120 (619-594-4815).

REFERENCES

Alpert, B.S., & Wilmore, J.H. (1994). Physical activity and blood pressure in adolescents. *Pediatric Exercise Science, 6,* 361–380.

American Academy of Pediatrics. (1987). Physical fitness and the schools. *Pediatrics, 80,* 449–450.

American College of Sports Medicine. (1988). Physical fitness in children and youth. *Medicine and Science in Sports and Exercise, 20,* 422–423.

Armstrong, N., & Simons-Morton, B. (1994). Physical activity and blood lipids in adolescents. *Pediatric Exercise Science, 6,* 381–405.

Bailey, D.A., & Martin, A.D. (1994). Physical activity and skeletal health in adolescents. *Pediatric Exercise Science, 6,* 330–347.

Bar-Or, O., & Baranowski, T. (1994). Physical activity, adiposity, and obesity in adolescents. *Pediatric Exercise Science, 6,* 348–360.

Bennett, J.P., & Peel, J.C. (1994). Health and physical education teacher certification practices in the United States 1988–1992. *Journal of Health Education, 25,* 239–243.

Blair, S.N., Kohl, H.W., Gordon, N.F., & Paffenbarger, R.S. (1992). How much physical activity is good for health? *Annual Review of Public Health, 13,* 99–126.

Bouchard, C., Shephard, R., & Stephens, T. (1994). *Physical activity, fitness, and health: International proceedings and consensus statement.* Champaign, IL: Human Kinetics.

Calfas, K.J., & Taylor, W.C. (1994). Physical activity and psychological health in adolescents. *Pediatric Exercise Science, 6,* 406–423.

Centers for Disease Control and Prevention. (1993). Prevalence of sedentary lifestyle: Behavioral risk factor surveillance system, United States, 1991. *Morbidity and Mortality Weekly Report, 42,* 576–579.

Coates, T.J., Jeffery, R.W., & Slinkard, L.A. (1981). Heart healthy eating and exercise: Introducing and maintaining changes in health behaviors. *American Journal of Public Health, 71,* 15–23.

Corbin, C.B., & Lindsey, R. (1989). *Fitness for life* (3rd ed.). Glenview, IL: Scott, Foresman.

Cresanta, J.L., Burke, G.L., Downey, A.M., Freedman, D.S., & Berenson, G.S. (1986). Prevention of atherosclerosis in childhood: Prevention in primary care. *Pediatric Clinics of North America, 33,* 835–858.

Dishman, R.K., & Sallis, J.F. (1994). Determinants and interventions for physical activity and exercise. In C. Bouchard, R. Shephard, & T. Stephens (Eds.), *Physical activity, fitness, and health* (pp. 214–238). Champaign, IL: Human Kinetics.

Epstein, L.H., Wing, R.R., Koeski, R., & Valoski, A. (1985). A comparison of lifestyle exercise, aerobic exercise, and calisthenics on weight loss in obese children. *Behavior Therapy, 16,* 345–356.

Falls, H.B., & Pate, R.R. (1993). Status of physical fitness in U. S. children. In M. Leppo (Ed.), *Healthy from the start: New perspectives on childhood fitness* (pp. 3–23). Washington, DC: ERIC Clearinghouse on Teacher Education.

Faucette, N., McKenzie, T.L., & Patterson, P. (1990). Descriptive analysis of nonspecialist elementary physical education teachers' curricular choices and class organization. *Journal of Teaching in Physical Education, 9,* 284–293.

Gortmaker, S.L., Dietz, W.H., Sobol, A.N., & Wehler, C.A. (1987). Increasing pediatric obesity in the U.S. *American Journal of Diseases of Children, 14,* 535–540.

Johnson, D.J., & Harageones, E.G. (1994). A health-fitness course in secondary physical education: The Florida experience. In R. Pate & R. Hohn (Eds.), *Health and fitness through physical education* (pp. 165–175). Champaign, IL: Human Kinetics.

Kanfer, F.H., & Goldstein, A.P. (1980). *Helping people change.* New York: Pergamon.

Malina, R.M. (1994). Physical activity: Relationship to growth, maturation, and physical fitness. In C. Bouchard, R. Shephard, & T. Stephens (Eds.), *Physical activity, fitness, and health* (pp. 918–930). Champaign, IL: Human Kinetics.

McKenzie, T.L., Alcaraz, J., & Sallis, J.F. (1994). Assessing children's liking for activity units in an elementary physical education curriculum. *Journal of Teaching in Physical Education, 13,* 206–215.

McKenzie, T.L., Feldman, H., Woods, S., Romero, K., Dahlstrom, V., Stone, E., Strikmiller, P., Williston, J., & Harsha, D. (1995). Student activity levels and lesson context during third grade physical education. *Research Quarterly for Exercise and Sport, 66,* 184–193.

McKenzie, T.L., Sallis, J.F., Faucette, N., Roby, J.J., & Kolody, B. (1993). Effects of a curriculum and inservice program on the quantity and quality of elementary physical education classes. *Research Quarterly for Exercise and Sport, 64,* 178–187.

McKenzie, T.L., Sallis, J.F., & Nader, P.R. (1991). SOFIT: System for observing fitness instruction time. *Journal of Teaching in Physical Education, 11,* 195–205.

McKenzie, T.L., Sallis, J.F., Nader, P.R., Broyles, S.L., & Nelson, J.E. (1992). Anglo- and Mexican-American preschoolers at home and at recess: Activity patterns and environmental influences. *Developmental and Behavioral Pediatrics, 13,* 173–180.

National Association for Sport and Physical Education. (1993). *Shape of the nation 1993: A survey of state physical education requirements.* Reston, VA.: Author.

Pangrazi, R.P., & Corbin, C.C. (1994). *Teaching strategies for improving youth fitness* (2nd ed.). Reston, VA: AAHPERD.

Parcel, G.S., Simons-Morton, B.G., O'Hara, N.M., Baranowski, T., Kolbe, L.J., & Bee, D.E. (1987). School promotion of healthful diet and exercise behavior: An integration of organizational change and social learning theory interventions. *Journal of School Health, 57,* 150–156.

Pate, R.R., & Hohn, R.C. (Eds.). (1994). *Health and fitness through physical education.* Champaign, IL: Human Kinetics.

Pate, R.R., Long, B.J., & Heath, G. (1994). Descriptive epidemiology of physical activity in adolescents. *Pediatric Exercise Sciences, 6,* 434–447.

Pate, R.R., & Shephard, R.J. (1989). Characteristics of physical fitness in youth. In C.V. Gisolfi, & D.R. Lamb (Eds.), *Perspectives in exercise science and sports medicine: Vol. 2. Youth, exercise, and sport* (pp. 1–46). Indianapolis, IN: Benchmark.

Powell, K.E., & Dysinger, W. (1987). Childhood participation in organized school sports and physical education as precursors of adult physical activity. *American Journal of Preventive Medicine, 3,* 276–281.

Ross, J.G., & Gilbert, G.G. (1985). The National Children and Youth Fitness Study: A summary of findings. *Journal of Physical Education, Recreation and Dance, 56*(1), 45–50.

Ross, J.G., & Pate, R.R. (1987). The National Children and Youth Fitness Study II: A summary of findings. *Journal of Physical Education, Recreation and Dance, 58*(9), 51–56.

Sallis, J.F. (1993). Epidemiology of physical activity and fitness in children and adolescents. *Critical Reviews in Food Science and Nutrition, 33,* 403–408.

Sallis, J.F., Hovell, M.F., Hofstetter, C.R., Faucher, P., Elder, J.P., Blanchard, J., Casparsen, C.J., Powell, K.E., & Christenson, G.M. (1989). A multivariate study of exercise determinants in a community sample. *Preventive Medicine, 18,* 20–34.

Sallis, J.F., & McKenzie, T.L. (1991). Physical education's role in public health. *Research Quarterly for Exercise and Sport, 62,* 124–137.

Sallis, J.F., McKenzie, T.L., & Alcaraz, J.E. (1993). Habitual physical activity and health related physical fitness in fourth-grade children. *American Journal of Diseases of Children, 147,* 890–896.

Sallis, J.F., McKenzie, T.L., Alcaraz, J.E., Kolody, B., Faucette, N., Roby, J.J., Hovell, M.F. (1994). *The effects of health related physical education on physical fitness and activity in elementary school students: Project SPARK.* Manuscript submitted for publication.

Sallis, J.F., & Nader, P.R. (1988). Family determinants of health behavior. In D.S. Gochman (Ed.), *Health behavior: Emerging research perspectives* (pp. 107–124). New York: Plenum.

Sallis, J.F., & Patrick, K. (1994). Physical activity guidelines for adolescents: Consensus statement. *Pediatric Exercise Sciences, 6,* 302–314.

Sallis, J.F., Patterson, T.L., Buono, M.J., & Nader, P.R. (1988). Relation of cardiovascular fitness and physical activity to cardiovascular disease risk factors in children and adults. *American Journal of Epidemiology, 127,* 933–941.

Sallis, J.F., Zakarian, J.M., Hovell, M.F., & Hofstetter, C.R. (1994). *Ethnic, socioeconomic, and sex differences in physical activity among adolescents.* Manuscript submitted for publication.

Sarkin, J.A., McKenzie, T.L., & Sallis, J.F. (1994). Gender differences in children's physical activity levels in a structured and unstructured setting. *Medicine and Science in Sports and Exercise Abstracts, 26*(Suppl. 5), 143.

Shephard, R.J., Lavallee, H., Volle, M., LaBarre, R., & Beaucage, C. (1994). Academic skills and required physical education: The Trois Rivières experience. *CAHPER/ACSEPL Research Supplement, 1*(1), 1–12.

Siedentop, D. (1991). *Developing teaching skills in physical education.* Mountain View, CA: Mayfield.

Simons-Morton, B., O'Hara, N.M., Simons-Morton, D., & Parcel, G.S. (1987). Children and fitness: A public health perspective. *Research Quarterly for Exercise and Sport, 58,* 295–302.

Simons-Morton, B.G., Parcel, G.S., & O'Hara, N.M. (1988). Implementing organizational changes to promote healthful diet and physical activity at school. *Health Education Quarterly, 15,* 115–130.

Stone, E., McGraw, S., Osganian, S., & Elder, J. (Eds.). (1994). Process evaluation in the multicenter child and adolescent trial for cardiovascular health (CATCH). *Health Education Quarterly,* (Suppl. 2), S-1–S-144.

Taggart, A.C., Taggart, J., & Siedentop, D. (1986). Effects of a home-based activity program: A study with low fitness elementary school children. *Behavior Modification, 10,* 487–507.

U. S. Department of Health and Human Services. (1991). *Healthy people 2000: National health promotion and disease prevention objectives* (DHHS Publication No. 91-50212). Washington, DC: Author.

Virgilio, S.J., & Berenson, G.S. (1988). Super kids-super fit: A comprehensive fitness intervention model for elementary schools. *JOPERD, 59*(8), 19–25.

Walter, H.J., Hofman, A., Vaughan, R.D., & Wynder, E.L. (1988). Modification of risk factors for coronary heart disease: Five-year results of a school-based intervention trial. *New England Journal of Medicine, 18,* 1093–1100.

CHAPTER 12

Physical Education and Education Reform:
The Case of Sport Education

Daryl Siedentop

Physical educators have recently expressed concern about the status and vitality of school physical education programs, especially those in secondary schools (Locke, 1992; Siedentop, 1987a, 1992; Tinning & Fitzclarence, 1992). It is also obvious that education reform is a major issue as we face environmental and economic uncertainties in a multicultural, high-technology world. This chapter focuses on one aspect of education reform and what it might mean for physical education.

Physical education has been part of the school curriculum in the United States since universal education became a reality in the late 19th century (Siedentop, 1994b). Physical education in America developed from a medical tradition emphasizing formal systems of gymnastics (Weston, 1962). Sport entered the physical education curriculum early in the 20th century as the field became more closely tied to education, resulting in a "new" physical education, conceptualized as part of the emerging progressive education movement. This "developmental" model has been the primary influence on curriculum and teaching for most of this century, with occasional changes to assimilate curricular revisions, based on lifetime sports and movement education, and periodic concerns expressed about children's and youth fitness (Siedentop, 1994b).

This chapter describes and analyzes current issues related to the enduring questions of what students should learn in the name of physical education and what are the most effective ways for teachers to help them achieve those learning outcomes. The material for this chapter is taken primarily from current theory and research in education reform and physical education teacher education. The argument will develop using the language of outcomes-based education and authentic assessment, with special reference to what those concepts imply for a subject matter that will be voluntarily pursued by students once they leave school. The implications of this conceptualization for establishing goals and providing an appropriate pedagogy for achieving them will be discussed. The curriculum and instruction model called Sport Education (Siedentop, 1994a) will be used as an example of how physical education might be organized and implemented more authentically.

TOWARD AN AUTHENTIC PHYSICAL EDUCATION

Two of the major reform agendas in education in the 1990s have been outcomes-based education and authentic assessment (see Lambert's discussion in chapter 8). There are many variations on these themes and many different labels used to describe the variations, some of which have become politically volatile. However, their core ideas have been developing for some time, representing a major shift in how we conceptualize and organize curriculum and teaching (Spady & Marshall, 1991).

AUTHENTIC OUTCOMES

What constitutes an authentic outcome in physical education? First of all, it represents a performance: It is defined as the capability to do something to completion, to "execute a task or process and to bring it to completion" (Wiggins, 1993, p. 202); it is a "culminating demonstration of learning" (Brandt, 1992–93, p. 66). Secondly, the completed task should have a contextual meaning that is directly related to the eventual use of the skill as an adult. Authentic outcomes, as outcomes of significance, "require substance of significance, applied through processes of significance in settings of significance" (Spady & Marshall, 1991, p. 67). What constitutes "significance" will become clear as this chapter progresses.

THE OBJECT OF CURRENT REFORM

Outcomes-based education and authentic assessment are "hot topics" in education. It would be a mistake to pass them off as educational fads. The buzz-words may change, but the content of this reform agenda has been evolving for some time and represents a major shift in how education is perceived. When public schools took hold in the United States in the latter part of the 19th century, the students who attended them came from experience-rich, information-poor households (Coleman, 1987). Common schools were designed to complement households, to deliver what they could not do well. As our society has gradually changed, schools have remained largely the same, still organized primarily to provide information to students. American society today is in some ways opposite to the mostly agrarian culture of the late 19th century. Many students today come from information-rich and experience-poor households. In the late 19th century many households had few books, magazines, or newspapers. Of course they didn't have radio or television, let alone interactive computers! Children's sense of their world was often limited to what they could see in their immediate area and what adults in their household told them. Yet these same children were expected to participate in household chores, often worked nearly full-time at a young age, married early, and began their own families early. Today that world has been turned around. Providing meaningful, contextually rich experiences involving students as active agents is one direction of current education reform. This represents an evolutionary change in the role school plays in society.

THE VOLUNTARY NATURE OF LEISURE, FITNESS, AND SPORT INVOLVEMENT

Every subject matter in schools can be thought of as a group of related, authentic performance capabilities. With physical education, however, there is an added dimension of fundamental importance.[1] When adults decide to take a brisk walk after dinner, join a fitness club, complete a summer cycling holiday, play tennis regularly, join a summer softball team, or buy a boat to water ski, they do so voluntarily. There are no requirements for participation as an adult! Adults choose to make time to participate in these activities and regard them as leisure. In contrast, while mathematics, astronomy, or chemistry (or any subject, for that matter) can be approached voluntarily as leisure activity, most people will use these skills in work situations. If adults wish to have jobs, they have no choice about using certain skills.

Physical educators, therefore, can not only organize their teaching around authentic outcomes but at the same time can work to help students develop the predisposition leading to voluntary participation. As a profession, we have talked about the many benefits—health, social, and mental—of regular participation in sport, leisure, fitness, and dance activities. I have no doubt that these benefits are important, but all of them depend on a common factor; namely, that people voluntarily choose to participate regularly in some form of physical activity.

Why do people choose to do some things rather than others? Why do some people organize their daily lives to allow for a good workout, a golf game, or a tennis match? Because for them it has become an adult form of play, activity which is valued in and of itself for what it provides to the quality of the moment and the quality of life. For this and other reasons, I have argued that physical education should be understood as a form of play education (Siedentop, 1972; 1976; 1980; 1990; 1994b). Play is an irreducible form of human behavior, common to all cultures, albeit playful activity is institutionalized differently in different cultures (Caillois, 1961; Huizinga, 1962).

Adult play is very different from child's play (Caillois, 1961). Adult play is characterized by competence, ritual, a taste for imposed difficulty, organization, and affiliation, rather than the spontaneity, lack of ongoing organization, and turbulence that characterize the play of children. Children are gradually educated and socialized into adult forms of play, in schools, on teams, in clubs, in dance studios, and the like. What goes on in those places is education, the dual focus of which is increasing performance capabilities and predisposition to participate. When that education is successful, adults develop a lifetime commitment to a particular form of institutionalized, playful physical activity.

TACTICAL APPROACHES TO TEACHING SPORT/GAME SKILLS

If the ability to play the game is a major outcome of physical education, then sport activity should be taught and evaluated based on that outcome. It is interesting to note that several of the major proponents of outcomes-based education have used sport as the primary analogy in explaining their positions. As Wiggins (1993) has said: "What we must keep asking is, what is the equivalent of the game in each subject?" (p. 202).

Research suggests, however, that most teaching in physical education emphasizes skill development tasks, often isolated from their contextual performance in contests (Siedentop, 1991; Siedentop, Doutis, Tsangaridou, Ward, & Rauschenbach, 1994). Students are often taught skills, then put into games with very little attention paid to the tactical strategies of competition. Students learn to forearm pass and overhead pass in skill drills, but they often cannot play volleyball with sufficient tactical skills to make it a satisfying game experience, even if the game is modified for novice learners. Fortunately, there is an emerging literature about the teaching of tactics (Doolittle & Girard, 1991; Griffin & Mitchell, in press; Thorpe, Bunker, & Almond, 1986; Werner & Almond, 1990) which should help to remedy this situation for the next generation of physical educators.

Contextualized performance, as in a game setting, requires a repertoire of skills which can be applied automatically to the changing nuances of the game setting. In a game, the competent performer is always anticipating, thinking ahead, letting the performance itself fill in automatically (Erricson, Krampe, & Tesch-Romer, 1993). This has important implications for how physical educators should think about their curricular goals and instructional planning. One implication is that skill practice should be organized with a tactical application in mind. Another is that sufficient time has to be allocated for the development of tactical awareness and competence, which is a much more complicated outcome than isolated skill development.

AUTHENTIC ASSESSMENT AND INSTRUCTIONAL ALIGNMENT

Doyle (1979) suggested that accountability drives the tasks teachers use for instruction, and without accountability learning suffers. When accountability is suspended, educational outcomes are based only on the motivation students bring to an activity. Research in physical education supports this conclusion (Alexander, 1982; Lund, 1992; Siedentop, 1990; Tousignant & Siedentop, 1983). It appears that formal assessment is not a major accountability factor in physical education (Lund, 1992; Matanin & Tannehill, 1994; Siedentop, et al., 1994; Stroot & Morton, 1989). Yet these same studies have found that imaginative physical educators find diverse ways to sustain accountability, through challenges, public recognition, competitions, timings, and the like.

When outcomes are defined as contextualized performance capabilities (i.e., authentic outcomes), the legitimate assessment of goal achievement is the contextualized performance itself, which is often referred to as an "exhibition" (Wiggins, 1987).

> . . . we speak of such a final challenge as an "exhibition." It is a "test" in the sense that the big game on opening night is a "test." Unlike the conventional "final," the exhibition—like a piano recital or a play—lets a performer show off or "exhibit" what he or she knows. (p. 15)

Thus, playing games competently, completing a planned floor exercise routine, performing a folk dance in costume to an audience, and completing a planned double-Dutch rope routine would all provide opportunities for authentic assessments.

Two desirable pedagogical principles are related to authentic outcomes and authentic assessment. First, if the goal is a contextualized performance (e.g., performing a complete folk dance to an audience) the goal should be made clear to the learner from the outset of instruction. Secondly, if the goal is known in advance and the assessment is the contextualized performance itself, instruction and practice become highly focused on learning the knowledge, skills, and tactics necessary to perform competently. This situation, where the aim of the stated goals, instruction, and assessment are united, is called "aligned instruction" (Siedentop, 1991). Cohen (1987) has shown that aligned instruction produces substantially greater achievement gains than situations where goals, instruction, and assessment are less well aligned; for example, where volleyball game play might be a goal, but much practice is devoted to isolated skill development and the formal assessment is a partner-toss forearm pass test or a wall-volley overhead pass test.

WHAT SHOULD STUDENTS LEARN IN MOTOR SKILL AND SPORT EDUCATION?

The goals for physical education have remained remarkably similar for most of this century (Siedentop, 1980). Although the language varies, the goals are typically categorized into motor skill, fitness, cognitive, and social outcomes. Recent evidence (Siedentop, et al., 1994) suggests that these categories are still the most commonly used in formal curriculum syllabi in physical education. It should also be noted that most of these goals are articulated as personal educational outcomes and it is only in the rather vague area of "citizenship" that one might see outcomes that are structural or cultural rather than personal.

How then might we think about broad goals for physical education that would lead to authentic outcomes and satisfy the profession's long-standing desire that physical education contribute not only to physical goals but also to mental and social goals? The following goals derive from my commitments to play education and sport education, and my belief that structural/cultural goals are as important as personal goals.

I refer to sport in its broadest sense, as in the Sport for All movement, rather than in the more narrow sense of elite, institutionalized sport that is common in the United States. Sport for All was launched in 1966 by the Council of Europe. By 1978 it had developed sufficiently that UNESCO ratified an International Charter of Physical Education and Sport. In this tradition, the term "sport" covers a variety of recreational and competitive pursuits, and it is in this tradition that I discuss sport education.

PROPOSED GOALS FOR PHYSICAL EDUCATION

I understand that regular participation in moderate to vigorous physical activity is now clearly associated with reduced all-cause mortality (Blair, 1992). I understand that the health benefits of regular activity involvement can reduce the increasing burden of national health costs (Pritchard & Potter, 1990). I believe that in the next several decades equally strong evidence will show that regular physical activity has ameliorative and prophylactic effects for stress reduction (Dishman, 1988). The importance of these benefits and programs that might help to achieve them are reviewed in chapter 11 of this text. To secure these benefits, however, more adults must participate regularly. For this to happen, sport and activity cultures must become more accessible and people must value activity sufficiently to take advantage of that accessibility, to seek it out or demand it when necessary. I believe that the goals described in this section are those most likely to secure the health benefits for more adult citizens.

Valuing sport involvement. Valuing is a strong term. It suggests that persons organize their lives in order to assure regular, lifelong participation in a given activity. Valuing is evidenced in the choices we make. It is not just that we talk about fitness or sport as important, but that we show our commitment through our actions. Students who experience anywhere from 4–12 years of physical education should emerge valuing sport involvement. The best evidence of that valuing would be their participation habits, particularly as demonstrated by their remaining committed to that involvement. It should also be noted that a goal of valuing sport involvement requires that we think carefully about helping students become independent and responsible in their participation habits.

Competent and confident performance. If we want students to value activity, we need to help them become competent, confident performers. Although valuing is clearly a complex phenomenon, it is generally accepted that we tend to value what we can do well. This goal reflects the difference between a "skills" approach to physical education teaching and a more authentic approach where competence in performing in a contextualized activity is emphasized. Competent performance relates more to tactics and modified games and games progressions than it does to isolated skill development.

Becoming a literate sportsperson. I use the term literate to describe the person who knows and values the traditions and rituals associated with a sport and has learned to distinguish between helpful and harmful practices related to that sport. A literate sportsperson knows where the sport is played, how to gain access to participation opportunities, how the sport is governed, and is sensitive to how children and novices should be educated and socialized into the sport practice.

Protecting evolving sport cultures. Sport practices are constantly evolving. Some changes are good; others are harmful either to participants or to the sport itself. Who is responsible to ensure that soccer for children is developmentally sensitive? Who protects the interests of pubescent children in sport? Who is to ensure that sport competition for adults is organized primarily for the benefit of participants? My view is that a literate sportsperson also has the responsibility to be an activist in preserving the best in a sport and helping to ensure that the sport evolves in positive directions. This goal unites knowledge and attitude. Knowledge of an inappropriate sport practice for youth is not useful unless a person is inclined to act on that knowledge. The predisposition to act is not helpful if it is not informed by appropriate knowledge. Being educated in a sport, then, means being activist in the sense I have described here.

Reducing barriers to sport involvement. An activist, literate sportsperson will work to make more sport available to more people, as in the Sport for All tradition described earlier in this chapter. I have argued that play is a fundamental form of human behavior and social life. People of all sorts in all cultures play, regardless of race, gender, or social status within the culture. They may play differently because of constraints in the culture, but they nonetheless play. Therefore, in a sport education model based on play education, characteristics such as gender, race, socioeconomic status, and motoric giftedness (talent) are irrelevant attributes. In our culture, however, these attributes have been relevant in the world of sports. A physically educated person will adhere to the slogan "sport in all its forms for all the people" and will work locally, regionally, and nationally to ensure that sport is made more available to more persons in ways that are sensitive to the contexts of those persons' lives.

TEACHING EFFECTIVENESS RELATED TO SPORT EDUCATION

We have learned a great deal about teaching effectiveness in physical education over the past quarter century. Much of that information is reviewed in this text by Rink in chapter 9. My purpose in this section is to emphasize the elements of teacher effectiveness that are particularly salient to an authentic physical education.

THE STUDENT AS WORKER, TEACHER AS COACH

In one important respect teaching research and curriculum theory have converged in the past several decades. This convergence has developed around the notion that outcomes in education can best be understood by examining the quantity and quality of work performed by students; that is, the student-as-worker has become a central focus of both research and theory.

Developing Theories of Teacher Effectiveness

Early teacher effectiveness research described teaching and correlated teacher actions with student outcomes, typically standardized achievement tests (Rosenshine, 1979). As the research field developed, content-valid achievement tests became more frequent and attitude and self-growth outcomes were also measured, most often through psychometric instrumentation. In the late 1970s researchers began to focus their observational lenses on student actions as completely as teacher actions, in what was called the mediating-process paradigm (Berliner, 1979). The underlying conceptual shift was to recognize that teachers do not affect student achievement directly, but instead affect the work students accomplish; it is the amount and quality of student work that influences achievement. Doyle's (1979; 1986) ecological model further emphasized student work and emphasized the dual-directional influence between teachers and students with the notion that student work developed across time through negotiation of the instructional tasks that define the work accomplished by students.

Although the slogan "student as worker, teacher as coach" is associated most clearly with the Coalition of Essential Schools, an organization devoted to reforming the content and delivery of curriculum in schools (Sizer, 1984), the concepts underlying the slogan are widely accepted in current educational reform. The general view in the reform literature is that students have traditionally been too passive, spending too much time memorizing "facts," and reporting those facts on decontextualized "achievement" tests (Wiggins, 1993).

Teaching for "Authentic Outcomes"

Refocusing education research and reform on the work of students does not reduce the importance of effective teaching skills; rather, it recasts them in a different contextual relationship to student work. Using the term *coach* rather than *teacher* underscores this conceptual shift, and it should be more than a little interesting to us that sport metaphors dominate this reform literature.

> Coaches should help performers to know and internalize the standards of good performance . . . There is nothing inherently more ambiguous about the standards of "good" writing than those of good defensive work in basketball. But coaches know that the abstract teaching and learning of criteria has little effect on the athlete's performance; they must show their players what "good" defense feels and looks like in concrete terms. (Wiggins, 1987, p. 15)

If you keep in mind that contextualized performance is the authentic outcome sought, then it becomes easier to see how coaching rather than teaching has become a favored descriptor. The contextualized performance goal allows students to know in advance what they are working toward. Since that final performance, classwork leading up to it is seen as practice. Practice implies active student involvement rather than passive involvement (i.e., listening to a lecture). A major "purpose" of each practice (lesson) is to prepare students to do the final performance as well as possible.

Less Is More—Time and Opportunity to Learn

If education is directed more toward authentic performance capabilities, teachers will have to be allowed to cover less than they now do in most curricula. The multi-activity curriculum model has dominated American physical education for more than 60 years (Siedentop, 1980). It is now often referred to as a "smorgasbord" or "exposure" curriculum. Recent research shows that physical education teachers believe that exposing students to a variety of activities allows them to "discover" the activity they are suited for and starts them on the way to a lifetime commitment to that activity (Siedentop, et al., 1994). There is no evidence to support this logic; indeed, what evidence exists suggests an opposite view (Dishman, 1990).

Research in classrooms (Rosenshine & Stevens, 1986) and in physical education (Siedentop, 1991; Silverman, 1991) supports the contention that the number and quality of opportunities to respond to tasks related to the desired outcome are the key variables in achievement and learning in schools.[2] Authentic performance goals require a more complex learning environment and more time to develop than traditional goals.

An Example of an Authentic Performance Experience

The meaning of the less-is-more slogan becomes apparent if you consider the time necessary for an 8th grade basketball unit to reach the goal of a well played three versus three game. In most basketball units, students learn a variety of passes, dribbling, and shooting with perhaps some emphasis on individual defense and rebounding. They then play a game, but the game is not well played in the sense that team play is evident and specific offensive and defensive tactics are recognizably present. What if you not only had to review basic skills, but gradually contextualize them in game-like drills as well as introduce and refine at least one defensive tactic (switching person-to-person defense or a three-person zone defense) and one offensive tactic (a simple, rule-based, passing-game offense or a ball-movement, three-person offense against a zone). Your "teams" must have time to practice and refine their skills in "scrimmages" and also to learn the coordinated team movements necessary to properly execute the three-person defensive and offensive tactics. Could you accomplish all of this in a 6-lesson unit? 10 lessons? 20 lessons? And, if you completed 4 such units in a typical school year, would you be accomplishing less or more than if you completed 12 units? In answering these questions you will see the rationale underlying the less-is-more argument.

BALANCING SUCCESS AND CHALLENGE

One of the most often-cited findings in physical education teaching research is Placek's (1983) conclusion that the main goal of some physical educators is to keep students "busy, happy, and good" (BHG). It is important to recognize that BHG is not in and of itself negative. Researchers and practitioners agree that students should enjoy physical education. They also agree that a well managed class in which students cooperate with the teacher and among themselves and active student involvement for a substantial portion of class time are necessary ingredients for effective teaching. However, I would raise some points of contention with the "busy" and "happy" portions of the BHG characterization.

So What's Wrong With Busy?

What does it mean for students to be kept busy? Busy with what? The implication of the Placek conclusion was that too many physical educators created what amounts to periods of supervised recreation in which students behaved well and actively participated, albeit often at a very low intensity level and not in activities that led to serious learning outcomes. A substantial amount of descriptive research in physical education suggests that this characterization is too often true (Metzler, 1989; Siedentop, et al., 1994; Tousignant & Siedentop, 1983).

My view is that some kinds of busy are better than others. What is most missing from the BHG approach is student success in important learning activities. Success has been shown to be a crucial factor in achievement (Rosenshine & Stevens, 1986; Siedentop, 1991; Silverman, 1991). The concept of success implies several instructional features that are typically absent in BHG settings. Success requires instruction with clear descriptions and demonstrations of the critical elements of skills and strategies. Success results from frequent practice opportunities under the scrutiny of the teacher (coach?) to immediately correct major errors. Success also requires abundant practice at a high success rate to ensure sufficient learning to make the skill useful. Success is based on a progression of practice tasks through which the skill is refined and extended toward its contextualized form. Success is encouraged in modified games where students get more performance opportunities under conditions more conducive to progress than an adult form of a game allows. None of these features is typically present in settings where students are merely kept busy.

What About Happy?

Now let's examine the notion of happy. You would have to look long and hard to find any researcher or practitioner who would argue that physical education shouldn't be enjoyable or that students shouldn't have fun in PE. Some kinds of fun, however, are different than other kinds of fun (Griffin, Chandler, & Sariscsany, 1993). What is left out of most discussions of student enjoyment is the degree of challenge in the activities and the degree to which the activities lead to some valued outcome. Challenge is an essential component of success. When activities lack challenge they become boring. When the challenge is too great relative to skills, students become anxious and try to avoid the activity or reduce the demands (Csikszentmikhalyi, 1975; Doyle, 1986). When students take on a significant challenge and experience success, a satisfaction ensues that represents a sustaining source of fun and happiness. Trying to balance challenge and success for a heterogeneous group of students in a physical education class remains one of the most difficult tasks for effective teachers.

GROUPING AND AFFILIATION

A much neglected yet powerful pedagogical factor in learning communities is grouping and affiliation. Research has consistently shown that small groups exert strong influence on their members (Johnson & Johnson, 1991; Slavin, 1991; Wynne & Walberg, 1994). Recently, this principle, so long understood in families, the military, and in sport, has begun to be more widely adopted in business and education.

Group Longevity

It is not uncommon in education for students to be put on teams or in cooperative learning groups. Some physical educators have used squads as grouping devices for years. These groupings, however, are often transitory, which greatly reduces the potential positive influence of the strategy. For small groups to exert positive influence they must persist; that is, students must develop and sustain an affiliation to the group (Siedentop, 1994a). The sport club model, common to sport systems in most of the world, is an important example of sustained affiliation in sport.

Positive Groupings

There are examples of imaginative grouping and affiliation in education. Sizer (1984) has argued for dividing large high schools into smaller "schools" with ongoing teams of students and teachers. Many in education now look back longingly at the benefits of the one-room schoolhouse. Schools have used "homerooms" for this purpose for years (Wynne & Walberg, 1994). In some Japanese high schools, teachers in each subject area stay with the same class for four years; for example, the same class and teacher would go through an entire curriculum in math or language (Rohlen, 1983). Darnell (1994) has described an elementary sport education program where students are members of the same team throughout the school year. One might argue that the sometimes extraordinary accomplishments of elementary physical education programs (Siedentop, 1989) is partially attributable to groups of children having one teacher for six years in the same subject. Recent research on the sport education model, of which team affiliation is one guiding principle, suggests that favorable teacher and student reactions are partially attributable to that feature (Grant, 1994). The potential positive influence of persisting small groups seems sufficiently powerful that ways to better implement this pedagogical strategy should be explored at all levels in physical education.

SPORT EDUCATION

Sport education is a curriculum and instruction model that I have developed, with the help of physical education practitioners, over the past decade (Siedentop, 1987b; Siedentop, 1994a; Siedentop, Mand, & Taggart, 1986). It represents one example of an authentic approach to physical education, incorporating most of the features discussed in this chapter.

THE SPORT EDUCATION MODEL

Let me first describe what sport education looks like and how it differs from typical multi-activity approaches to curriculum and instruction in physical education. In sport education teachers plan for seasons rather than units. Seasons are longer than units in a multi-activity program. For example, one elementary program has five seasons per year (Darnell, 1994) and one secondary sport education model has four seasons per year (Dugas, 1994).

Students are placed on teams for the duration of the season, and sometimes for an entire school year. A formal schedule of competition is arranged (round robin, dual meets, required and optional gymnastics meets, etc.). Every student in every sport education season will learn to perform, referee, and score the particular sport. In addition, each team will have diverse roles that students will fill; manager, coach, trainer, publicist, and the like. Throughout the course of a school year and across multiple school years, all students will experience all roles. Most of these roles require students to exert leadership and behave responsibly for their group. To build and sustain an effective team requires that students learn to subordinate their interests to the overall goals of the team; therefore, both leader and follower roles are practiced.

Students choose a team name and often a team uniform. Many teachers take team pictures and post them on bulletin boards. Every effort is made to make the sport season festive. The history and rituals of the sport are taught; the rituals are practiced as part of the practice and competition. Students are informed when local competition in the sport is available outside of school and are told how they might become involved. A festive, culminating event concludes the sport education season.

Small-sided games are favored, with rules and equipment modified to match the experience and skills of the students. Tactics and playing the game confidently are stressed as much or more than individual skills. For example, in a soccer sport education season for children (Bell & Darnell, 1994), the initial competition is one versus one, with dribbling, tackling, defensive space, and goal kicking emphasized. When that competition is finished, a two versus two competition begins in which passing, trapping, and tandem defense are added. In ensuing three versus three and five versus five competitions, more sophisticated strategy is developed and skills and rules become more complex (corner kicks, offensive spacing, centering, etc.). Starting with the simplest competition (one versus one) each game has a student referee and scorekeeper. The scorekeeper not only keeps score but also tallies simple statistics (shots on goal, steals, etc.). As the competitions become more sophisticated, so too does the scorekeeping.

In each competition there is an overall team winner (for example, in two versus two competition, each team in the class must organize three or four two-person teams; the victory or loss accrues to the larger team unit). Teams are encouraged to practice together at recess or outside of physical education class. Fair play is emphasized throughout the season. Many teachers incorporate fair play points in their championship scoring and bestow an end-of-season fair play award. Eventually, an overall soccer champion is recognized, but there are sufficient ways for students to "win" that all students experience success within the context of the soccer season.

SPORT EDUCATION GOALS AND OBJECTIVES

Education is always provided for the immediate benefit of students, but education also has long-term implications, not only for the students but for the well being of the society. Sport education has the following objectives which students achieve through their participation (Siedentop, 1994a):

- Develop skills and fitness specific to the sport.
- Appreciate and be able to execute strategic play.
- Participate at a level appropriate to their skill and experience.
- Share in the planning and administration of the sport experience.
- Provide responsible leadership in the sport context.
- Work effectively within the team toward common goals.
- Appreciate the rituals and conventions that give particular sports their unique meanings.
- Develop the capacity to make reasoned decisions about sport issues.
- Develop and apply knowledge about refereeing and training.
- Decide voluntarily to become involved in nonschool sport.

It is through the achievement of these immediate objectives, repeated for each sport season, that the longer term goals of sport education get fulfilled. Sport education seeks to educate students to be players in the fullest sense and to help them develop as competent, literate, and enthusiastic sportspersons.

A competent sportsperson has sufficient skills to participate satisfactorily, is competent in strategic play approp ate to the complexity of the game, and is a knowledgeable gameplayer. A literate sportsperson understands and values the traditions of the sport and can distinguish between good and bad practices related to a specific sport, whether at a children's level or an elite level. An enthusiastic sportsperson values participation, seeks actively to maintain participation, and behaves in ways that serve to preserve, protect, and enhance the sport practice.[3] Sport education is a model designed to bring the benefits of sport to all students; an inclusionary model rather than the exclusionary model common to interscholastic and intercollegiate sport.

TEACHER AND STUDENT REACTIONS TO SPORT EDUCATION

The sport education model has been used for many sports (volleyball, tennis, touch rugby, gymnastics, acrosport, soccer, etc.) as well as for fitness activities (such as strength training and aerobics) (Tannehill, 1994). Both teachers and students have reacted positively to initial efforts at sport education (Alexander, 1994; Grant, 1992; Pope, 1992). Some physical education teachers thought sport to be too competitive, too elitist, and not appropriate for physical education, but their perceptions changed when they experienced students in their classes taking responsibility, valuing fair play and even competition, and trying hard to improve themselves and their teammates (Grant, 1992).

Students tend to like sport education because it provides more time for them to learn skills and strategies. They also report that they like learning from their own teammates and appreciate the chance to act responsibly and be more "in charge" of their own sport education experience (Brine, 1994). The relationship between teachers and their students seems to change somewhat when sport education is implemented (Grant, 1992). The typical relationship in physical education seems to be students complying with the teacher's requests and cooperating with the teacher's agenda (Siedentop, 1991; Tousignant & Siedentop, 1983). Sport education puts more responsibility on students, leading to a more educationally functional relationship between them and their teacher. One secondary physical education teacher observed:

Initially I found it quite hard to get away from my dictatorial approach. I got frustrated by this and started to interfere. I actually got told to "back off" by one of the teams. . . . Their case was eventually proved by their vast improvement in skills. . . . Their willingness to be part of a group with a purpose was so evident. (Grant, 1994, p. 90)

Once students are given responsibilities and held accountable by their teacher and teammates, a new kind of relationship is possible, one which is characterized by coaching, counseling, and supporting.

TOWARD AN AUTHENTIC PHYSICAL EDUCATION

The sport education model is one example of authentic physical education. When a 6th grade student has to create a balance beam routine within guidelines provided for the competition, practice the skills included in the routine, gradually blend the separate skills together into a smooth routine through purposive practice, then perform the routine in a competition in which that performance counts for a team score, you have an authentic outcome. When the learning and practice for this event is done within a team context, with team members each having specific responsibilities; when the practice and competition have been modified to fit the skills and experiences of the students; and when the practice and competition are made festive, then the chances of a positive experience leading to self-sustaining activity involvement have been optimized. When the balance beam performance is evaluated by judges, with each element of the routine scored, an authentic assessment has taken place. When class time and nonattached time is used primarily for the creation, practice, and refinement of the routine, the goals, practice, and assessment have been fully aligned. When fair play and responsible team membership are also goals, continuously emphasized during class sessions and included in team points or awards, then that part of the education is also aligned.

Sport education represents one approach to an authentic physical education. There certainly are many other ways to organize and deliver our subject matter which are consistent with the education reform principles cited in this chapter.

Students in a high school in Toulouse, France (Cottet & Pontello, 1994) planned, trained for, and implemented a 5-day cycling-camping trip from Toulouse to Spain, a distance of 130 miles. The crossdisciplinary activity included elements of biology, mathematics, physics, and physical education. Cycling safety and care, noninvasive camping, and the like formed the core of the physical education component, along with regular cycling training sessions.

A personal fitness course with student developed goals relating to activity, body composition, nutrition, and weight would be another example.

Adventure education courses, particularly those in the Outward Bound model, would certainly qualify as authentic approaches to physical education. When students have to study and train for a trek or a climbing experience, learn about the safety and dynamics of working with a group in such ventures, organize and plan for the travel required, and then actually do it, an authentic physical education is taking place.

SUMMARY

A major shift in how school curriculums are planned and delivered is taking place, with outcomes-based education and authentic assessment the current popular manifestations of an evolution emphasizing the quality and quantity of student work at the center of curriculum and instruction theory and research. Sport education is one example of how physical education can be modified to provide a more authentic experience.

It is important to underscore that thinking about physical education as an outcomes-based, authentically assessed enterprise is still evolving. Questions abound. What is a significant outcome? What happens if students do not "pass" the authentic assessment? Is the cost/benefit ratio of authentic assessment worthwhile? Does the subject matter training of teachers make it impossible to move to what has been called "transformational" outcomes-based education (Spady, 1994), where life performance roles define the curriculum and traditional subject matter distinctions are blurred? Can the political opposition to outcomes-based education be reduced (Zitterkopf, 1994)?

On the other hand, one also needs to face squarely the marginalized status of physical education in schools. How much longer can it survive in its current forms? Do we need to "think differently" (Siedentop, 1992) about how physical education is delivered to students? If so, are the examples shown in this chapter different enough? Nobody has the answers to these questions. What is most important now is that the profession supports a healthy dialogue searching for answers.

---

[1]The same could be said for art, drama, and music education.

[2]A criterion task is the learning goal and is defined operationally by how the learning goal is measured; e.g., a final test, a standardized test, or an authentic assessment of a contextualized performance.

[3]These short- and long-term goals make sport education appropriate for elementary aged children. Sport education is for all students. It eschews elitism. It is clearly within the guidelines set forth by the Council on Physical Education for Children of AAHPERD.

REFERENCES

Alexander, K. (1982). *Behavior analysis of tasks and accountability.* Unpublished doctoral dissertation, The Ohio State University, Columbus, OH.

Alexander, K. (1994). Developing sport education in Western Australia. *Aussie Sport Action, 5*(1), 8–9.

Bell, C., & Darnell, J. (1994). Elementary soccer. In D. Siedentop (Ed.), *Sport education: Quality PE through positive sport experiences* (pp. 37–46). Champaign, IL: Human Kinetics.

Berliner, D. (1979). Tempus educare. In P. Peterson & H. Walberg (Eds.), *Research on teaching: Concepts, findings, and implications* (pp. 120–135). Berkeley, CA: McCutchan.

Blair, S. (1992). Are American children and youth fit? *Research Quarterly for Exercise and Sport, 63*(2), 120–123.

Brandt, R. (1992–93). On outcomes based education: A conversation with Bill Spady. *Educational Leadership, 50*(4), 66–70.

Brine, K. (1994). Sport education is a winner. *Aussie Sport Action, 5*(1), 10.

Caillois, R. (1961). *Man, play, and games.* New York: Free Press of Glencoe.

Cohen, S. (1987). Instructional alignment. *Educational Researcher, 16*(8), 16–20.

Coleman, J. (1987). Families and schools. *Educational Researcher, 16*(6), 32–38.

Cottet, J., & Pontello, C. (1994). Raid VTT Toulouse-Espagne. *Revue Education Physique et Sport, 246,* 54–56.

Csikszentmikhalyi, M. (1975). *Beyond boredom and anxiety.* San Francisco: Jossey-Bass.

Darnell, J. (1994). Sport education in the elementary curriculum. In D. Siedentop (Ed.), *Sport education: Quality PE through positive sport experiences* (pp. 61–72). Champaign, IL: Human Kinetics.

Dishman, R. (1988). *Exercise adherence.* Champaign, IL: Human Kinetics.

Dishman, R. (1990). Determinants of participation in physical activity. In C. Bouchard, R. Shephard, T. Stephens, J. Sutton, & B. McPherson (Eds.), *Exercise, fitness, and health: A consensus of current knowledge* (pp. 75–101). Champaign, IL: Human Kinetics.

Doolittle, S., & Girard, K. (1991). A dynamic approach to teaching games in elementary PE. *Journal of Physical Education, Recreation and Dance, 62*(4), 57–62.

Doyle, W. (1979). Classroom tasks and students' abilities. In P. Peterson & H. Walberg (Eds.), *Research on teaching: Concepts, findings, and implications.* Berkeley, CA: McCutchan.

Doyle, W. (1986). Classroom organization and management. In M. Wittrock (Ed.), *Handbook of research on teaching* (3rd. cd., pp. 392–431). New York: Macmillan.

Dugas, D. (1994). Sport education in the secondary curriculum. In D. Siedentop (Ed.), *Sport education: Quality PE through positive sport experiences* (pp. 105–112). Champaign, IL: Human Kinetics.

Erricson, K., Krampe, R., & Tesch-Romer, C. (1993). The role of deliberate practice in the acquisition of expert performance. *Psychological Review, 100*(3), 363–406.

Grant, B. (1992). Integrating sport into the physical education curriculum in New Zealand secondary schools. *Quest, 44*(3), 304–316.

Grant, B. (1994). High school touch rugby and tennis. In D. Siedentop (Ed.), *Sport education: Quality PE through positive sport experiences* (pp. 83–92). Champaign, IL: Human Kinetics.

Griffin, L., Chandler, T., & Sariscsany, M. (1993). What does "fun" mean in physical education? *Journal of Physical Education, Recreation and Dance, 64*(9), 63–66.

Griffin, L., & Mitchell, S. (in press). A tactical approach to teaching softball. *Journal of Physical Education, Recreation and Dance.*

Huizinga, J. (1962). *Homo ludens: A study of the play element in culture.* Boston: Beacon Press.

Johnson, D., & Johnson, R. (1991). Cooperative learning and classroom and school climate. In B. Fraser & H. Walberg (Eds.), Educational environments: Evaluation, antecedents, and consequences (pp. 55–74). Oxford, England: Pergamon Press.

Locke, L. (1992). Changing secondary school physical education. *Quest, 44*(3), 361–372.

Lund, J. (1992). Assessment and accountability in secondary physical education. *Quest, 44*(3), 352–360.

Matanin, M., & Tannehill, D. (1994). Assessment and grading in physical education. In M. O'Sullivan (Ed.), High school physical education teachers: Their world of work [Monograph]. *Journal of Teaching in Physical Education, 13*(4), 395–405.

Metzler, M. (1989). A review of research on time in sport pedagogy. *Journal of Teaching in Physical Education, 8*(2), 87–103.

Placek, J. (1983). Concepts of success in teaching: Busy, happy and good? In T. Templin & J. Olson (Eds.), *Teaching in physical education* (pp. 46–56). Champaign, IL: Human Kinetics.

Pope, C. (1992). *A sport education curriculum model: An ethnographic investigation to student and teacher response.* Unpublished thesis, School of Education, University of Waikato, New Zealand.

Pritchard, R., & Potter, G. (1990). *Fitness Inc.: A guide to corporate health and wellness programs.* Homewood, IL: Dow-Jones-Irwin.

Rohlen, T. (1983). *Japanese high schools.* Berkeley, CA: University of California Press.

Rosenshine, B. (1979). Content, time, and direct instruction. In P. Peterson & H. Walberg (Eds.), *Research on teaching: Concepts, findings, and implications* (pp. 28–56). Berkeley, CA: McCutchan.

Rosenshine, B., & Stevens, R. (1986). Teaching functions. In M. Wittrock (Ed.), *Handbook of research on teaching* (3rd. ed., pp. 376–391). New York: Macmillan.

Siedentop, D. (1972). *Physical education: Introductory analysis.* Dubuque, IA: Wm. C. Brown.

Siedentop, D. (1976). *Physical education: Introductory analysis* (2nd ed.). Dubuque, IA: Wm. C. Brown.

Siedentop, D. (1980). *Physical education: Introductory analysis* (3rd ed.). Dubuque, IA: Wm. C. Brown.

Siedentop, D. (1987a). High school physical education: Still an endangered species. *Journal of Physical Education, Recreation and Dance, 58*(2), 24–25.

Siedentop, D. (1987b). The theory and practice of sport education. In G. Barrette, R. Feingold, R. Rees, & M. Piéron (Eds.), *Myths, models, and methods in sport pedagogy* (pp. 79–86). Champaign, IL: Human Kinetics.

Siedentop, D. (Ed.). (1989). The effective elementary specialist study [Monograph]. *Journal of Teaching in Physical Education, 8*(3).

Siedentop, D. (1990). An ecological model for understanding teaching/learning in physical education. In *New horizons of human movement* (pp. 111–124). Dankook, Korea: Sport Science Institute.

Siedentop, D. (1991). *Developing teaching skills in physical education* (3rd ed.). Mountain View, CA: Mayfield.

Siedentop, D. (1992). Thinking differently about secondary physical education. *Journal of Physical Education, Recreation and Dance, 63*(7), 69–72, 77.

Siedentop, D. (1994a). *Sport education: Quality PE through positive sport experiences.* Champaign, IL: Human Kinetics.

Siedentop, D. (1994b). *Introduction to physical education, fitness, and sport* (2nd ed.). Mountain View, CA: Mayfield.

Siedentop, D., Doutis, P., Tsangaridou, N., Ward, P., & Rauschenbach, J. (1994). Don't sweat gym! An analysis of curriculum and instruction. In M. O'Sullivan (Ed.), High school physical educators: Their world of work [Monograph]. *Journal of Teaching in Physical Education, 13,* 375–395.

Siedentop, D., Mand, C., & Taggart, A. (1986). *Physical education: Teaching and curriculum strategies for grades 5–12.* Mountain View, CA: Mayfield.

Silverman, S. (1991). Research on teaching physical education. *Research Quarterly for Exercise and Sport, 62,* 352–364.

Sizer, T. (1984). *Horace's compromise.* Boston: Houghton Mifflin.

Slavin, R. (1991). Synthesis of research on cooperative learning. *Educational Leadership, 48*(5), 71–82.

Spady, W. (1994). Choosing outcomes of significance. *Educational Leadership 51*(6), 18–22.

Spady, W., & Marshall, K. (1991). Beyond traditional outcome-based education. *Educational Leadership, 49*(2), 67–72.

Stroot, S., & Morton, P. (1989). Blueprints for learning. In D. Siedentop (Ed.), The effective elementary specialist study [Monograph]. *Journal of Teaching in Physical Education, 8*(3), 213–222.

Tannehill, D. (1994). High school fitness applications. In D. Siedentop, *Sport education: Quality PE through positive sport experiences* (pp. 93–104). Champaign, IL: Human Kinetics.

Thorpe, R., Bunker, D., & Almond, L. (1986). A change in focus for the teaching of games. In M. Piéron & G. Graham (Eds.), *Sport pedagogy: The 1984 Olympic Scientific Congress Proceedings. Vol. 6.* Champaign, IL: Human Kinetics.

Tinning, R., & Fitzclarence, L. (1992). Postmodern youth culture and the crisis in Australian secondary school physical education. *Quest, 44*(3), 287–303.

Tousignant, M., & Siedentop, D. (1983). A qualitative analysis of task structures in required secondary physical education classes. *Journal of Teaching in Physical Education, 3*(1), 47–57.

Werner, P., & Almond, L. (1990). Models of games education. *Journal of Physical Education, Recreation and Dance, 61*(4), 23–27.

Weston, A. (1962). *The making of American physical education.* New York: Appleton-Century-Crofts.

Wiggins, G. (1987, Winter). Creating a thought-provoking curriculum. *American Educator*, 10–17.

Wiggins, G. (1993). Assessment: Authenticity, context, and validity. *Phi Delta Kappan, 75*(3), 200–214.

Wynne, E., & Walberg, H. (1994). Persisting groups: An overlooked force for learning. *Phi Delta Kappan, 75*(7), 527–530.

Zitterkopf, R. (1994). A fundamentalist's defense of OBE. *Educational Leadership, 51*(6), 76–78.

CHAPTER 13

Teaching Personal and Social Responsibility in Physical Education

Don Hellison

"**K**ids aren't the same anymore," a veteran physical education teacher recently lamented. He is right, of course. As LeaAnn Tyson points out in chapter 4, changes in the diversity of student backgrounds, family structure, the inclusion of special education students (see also chapter 6 by Karen DePauw), and at-risk behaviors such as drug use, violence, and dropping out (or staying in school and "cruisin' in neutral") have created problems for teachers and students alike. Students have more unsupervised discretionary time, more access to guns and drugs, and more exposure to the electronic media (including the music industry), which bombards them with messages about dress, money, fame, and violence at a time when they are perhaps most vulnerable, most interested in being "cool" and "looking good." These problems are exacerbated for kids who live in inner city "war zones" (Garbarino, Dubrow, Kostelny, & Pardo, 1991), face poverty and racism every day, and are not well served by bureaucratic, unresponsive schools (Weiner, 1993). Although the inner city has special needs, the problems this nation's children and youth face are by no means confined to minority groups in urban settings. For example, data on white youth ages 15 to 19 show a rise in illegitimate births, homicides, and suicides in recent years (Nucci, 1989).

Children and youth today need more guidance, yet not only urban schools but schools in general (Des Dixon, 1994) and community agencies ("Free time presents," 1993; McLaughlin & Heath, 1993) are being criticized for failing to meet student needs, and many teachers are frustrated by student problems and behaviors and afraid for their own safety, according to a recent poll reported in *USA Today* (October 23, 1993, p. 3A).

WHAT IS OUR RESPONSIBILITY?

In chapter 4, LeaAnn Tyson describes changes in education which attempt to respond to these trends. While many current social problems are rooted in social, economic, and political policy and are beyond the purview of the school (Mesa, 1992), education can help prepare students for the problems they face and, in the long run, can change society (Cuban, 1993).

The question that confronts physical education is whether to respond to these social problem trends by making these kinds of changes. A popular alternative to doing so has been to implement classroom management strategies in order to both control and motivate students who bring their problems into the gym. This approach focuses on reducing discipline and motivation problems rather than dealing with the underlying personal and social needs of students. Moreover, McCaslin and Good (1992) argue that classroom management strategies conflict with some personal and social development goals, such as helping students to think critically and make decisions.

Polish scholar Krzysztof Zuchora (1987, p. 79) believes that more than stop-gap measures are needed in physical education. He contends that the personal and social needs of students ought to be the starting point for building a physical education curriculum:

The starting point of this conception [of contributing to the common good] can no longer be, as [has been] the case so far, a catalogue of physical exercises and exaggerated control of motoric development, but a catalogue of human problems, reaching back to tradition and reflecting the state of today's social needs.

Of course, interest in character and social development is nothing new in physical education and sport (Miller & Jarman, 1988), but curriculum guides rarely deal with these issues in substantive ways, preferring to concentrate on the development of motor skills and fitness (Ennis, 1993). Fortunately, physical education teachers are not above departing from curriculum guide dictums. Recent research shows that some physical education teachers have shown considerable interest in prioritizing the personal and social needs of their students (Ennis, 1992).

This chapter describes one approach to addressing students' personal and social needs. Although this approach attempts to take into account the whole child, integrated education, cooperative learning, and reflective thinking, it is not the only way. Such approaches as cooperative games (Orlick, 1978), moral education (Romance, Weiss, & Bokoven, 1986), adventure and wilderness education (Siedentop, Mand, & Taggart, 1986), and sport education (see chapter 12 by Daryl Siedentop) also hold promise for addressing some of the personal and social problems children and youth face today.

GOALS FOR TEACHING PERSONAL AND SOCIAL RESPONSIBILITY IN PHYSICAL EDUCATION

This approach, which I will call teaching personal and social responsibility (or TPSR), first emerged during my first few years as a part-time teacher in inner city schools in Portland, Oregon, based on my own values, my experiences with students, and a good deal of reflection. (Recovery and reflection are two of the benefits of shuttling back and forth between the roles of part-time teacher and university professor.) While I could not change the experiences my students brought to the gym—the poverty, racism, violence, access to drugs, and so on—I could teach them to be more reflective in the personal and social decisions they were making. Now, in my 24th year of doing this work, I look back and realize how naive I was and how daunting a task I had taken on.

TPSR requires, at the minimum, thinking about responsibility in such a way that it means more than doing what the teacher says to do (e.g., "Please be responsible and do what I say!"). Instead, responsibility encompasses both *learning to become more responsible* and *learning to take responsibility* within the context of physical education instruction and its transfer outside the gym.

BECOMING MORE RESPONSIBLE: THE FIVE TPSR GOALS

The five TPSR goals shown in Figure 13.1 provide guidelines for *becoming more responsible* by describing areas of responsibility. Two of these goals, effort and self-direction, address the students' responsibility for personal development; and two, respect for the rights and feelings of others and being sensitive and responsive to the well being of others, address the students' social and moral responsibility for their relationships with others and as members of groups. The fifth goal focuses on transfer of responsibility from physical education to the rest of school, the playground, "the street," and home.

The Goals as a Progression

These five goals are often presented to students as a loose progression of levels to represent both a teaching-learning progression and a hierarchy

I. Respect for the rights and feelings of others
   a. Maintaining self-control
   b. Respecting everyone's right to be included
   c. Respecting everyone's right to a peaceful conflict resolution

II. Participation and effort
   a. Exploring effort
   b. Trying new things
   c. Developing a personal definition of success

III. Self-direction
   a. Demonstrating on-task independence
   b. Developing a sound knowledge base
   c. Developing, carrying out, and evaluating a personal plan
   d. Balancing current and future needs
   e. "Striving against external forces" (deCharms, 1976)

IV. Sensitivity and responsiveness to the well-being of others
   a. Developing prerequisite interpersonal skills
   b. Becoming sensitive and compassionate
   c. Contributing to the community and beyond
   d. Helping others without rewards

V. Outside the gym
   a. Trying out the levels in the classroom, on the playground and street, and at home
   b. Making decisions about the usefulness of the levels outside the gym

Figure 13.1. The TPSR levels

of values, as shown in Figure 13.1. As a teaching-learning progression, the respect issue is introduced first, because the class is a community which requires minimal protection of the rights of its members. Participation in physical activity instruction and the exploration of effort are intended to be addressed after dealing with the respect issue, although in practice Level I, Respect, must be revisited often. When this occurs, students learn that respect is the number one concern and that it must be addressed right away. Giving students time for self-direction comes later in the progression, because it assumes that respect and motivation issues have been more or less resolved. Caring is perhaps the most difficult level to reach, unless students are socialized to do so at an early age, for three reasons:

- It requires taking one's own time away from personal interests and goals.
- It is not usually perceived as being the "in" thing to do (especially with people who aren't friends).
- It is to be done without rewards (virtue is its own reward!).

This progression also represents a hierarchy of values: respect is the least one can do for another, caring perhaps the most. Putting effort into a personal task or challenge is the least one can do for one's self, while being self-directed is more complex and of higher value.

Using the Goals as Levels

Turning goals into levels gives teachers an accessible vocabulary for talking about responsibility, such as "Are you ready for some Level III time?" The levels can also be converted into "shorthand" so that students can more easily visualize goals toward which to work and can more easily evaluate their progress. This is accomplished by presenting them as cumulative levels, as shown in Figure 13.2.

While the idea of presenting goals as levels has been implemented in many physical education classes (and other programs) across the country, in Canada, and elsewhere in the world, some physical education teachers have used TPSR without the levels. They simply introduce the five goals

---

Level 0, Irresponsibility: Students who operate at Level 0 make excuses and blame others for their behavior and deny personal responsibility for what they do or fail to do.

Level I, Respect: Students at Level I may not participate in the day's activities or show much mastery or improvement, but they are able to control their behavior enough so that they don't interfere with other students' right to learn or the teacher's right to teach. And they do this without being prompted by the teacher very without constant supervision.

Level II, Participation: Students at Level II not only show minimal respect to others but also participate in the subject matter. They willingly, even enthusiastically play, accept challenges, practice motor skills, and train for fitness under the teacher's supervision.

Level III, Self-Direction: Students at Level III not only show respect and participation, but they are also able to work without direct supervision. They can identify their own needs and can begin to plan and execute their own physical education programs.

Level IV, Caring: Students at Level IV, in addition to respecting others, participating, and being self-directed, are motivated to extend their sense of responsibility beyond themselves by cooperating, giving support, showing concern, and helping.

Figure 13.2.   The cumulative levels
From *Goals and Strategies for Teaching Physical Education* (pp. 6-8), by D. Hellison, 1985, Champaign, IL: Human Kinetics. Copyright 1985 by Donald R. Hellison. Adapted with permission.

as goals without the progression and use words such as respect, effort, self-direction, and caring to replace Level I, II, III, and IV as the vocabulary of TPSR. As you will see, this and many other adaptations of TPSR are not only permissible but an integral part of the implementation process.

Definition of Responsibility

The definition of responsibility that we want to convey to students goes something like this: "You are personally responsible if you are willing to try and to experience new things, and if you can work on your own and develop and carry out a plan for yourself that will enhance your well being. You are socially responsible if you respect the rights and feelings of others and are sensitive and responsive to the well being of others. To fully carry out these responsibilities you need to attempt to put them into practice outside PE."

LEARNING TO TAKE RESPONSIBILITY

The definiiton above identifies the substance of responsibility, the "what." However, it is one-sided; it does not address the "how." To become responsible, students must also *learn to take responsibility*. However, they cannot take responsibility if they are not *given some responsibility*.

Approaching Instructional Strategies

That means implementing instructional strategies that emphasize sharing power with students, allowing them to make and reflect upon decisions, and negotiating issues with them. Taken to their logical conclusion, these strategies encompass an evaluation and perhaps modification of the above definition of becoming more responsible, so that the levels become provisional goals, to be learned, experienced, reflected upon, and eventually validated, changed, or even rejected.

Figure 13.3 shows seven strategies that attempt to give some responsibility to students. Awareness talks and experiencing are necessary prerequisites; students must first be aware of, and try out, the levels before they can decide whether they "work" for them or not. By evaluating their own attitudes and behaviors in relation to the levels during reflection time at the end of each lesson, they can begin to judge not only how they are doing, but also whether it matters to them. Individual decision making, including negotiation when problems arise, is an advanced strategy designed to shift some responsibility to individual students, while group meetings provide occasional opportunities for the whole class or smaller groups to problem solve; to evaluate the class, the teacher, and TPSR; and to discuss issues relevant to Level V, Outside the Gym. Counseling time is designed for one-to-one meetings with all students, not just

Awareness Talks	Group Meetings
Experiencing the Levels	Counseling Time
Reflection Time	Teacher Qualities
Individual Decision Making	

Figure 13.3.   TPSR strategies

those in trouble or those who stand out, in order to check in and co-evaluate what has been (or not been) going on. Counseling time can be conducted before and after class and, as the class progresses, during Level III (self-direction) time. If one or two students are "counseled" every lesson, all students will eventually get their turn at a few minutes of one-on-one time. Teacher qualities remind us that as teachers we have to live the levels the best we can. We have to treat kids with respect, to include everyone, to solve problems peacefully, to show effort, to engage in self-improvement, to care, to do these things outside the gym, and so on. While they are not instructional strategies as such, they are very influential in making this approach work. As Bill Ayers (1989) writes:

> . . . there is no clear line delineating the person and the teacher. Rather, there is a seamless web between teaching and being, between teacher and person. Teaching is not simply what one does, it is who one is. (p. 130)

Despite the simplicity of Figures 13.1 and 13.2 (which, by the way, need to be simple enough to enable teachers, including me, to memorize completely), conceptualizing responsibility is no easy task. It is a reflective, interpretive activity, and as such, teachers must be free to modify these ideas and substitute some of their own. (For this approach to really work, they must be given responsibility, too!)

SPECIFIC STRATEGIES FOR TEACHING RESPONSIBILITY

Once responsibility has been conceptualized, as shown in Figures 13.1 and 13.2, it needs to be included in each physical education lesson. To do this, TPSR must become the framework for the program, so that, as far as possible, everything that goes on in the gym is related back to taking responsibility. In actuality, I would guess that my classes spend about 70 percent of their time in activities related to TPSR (including physical activities). The rest is learning and being involved in activity for the intrinsic meaning of those experiences (including having fun).

•

AWARENESS TALKS AND REFLECTION TIME

The instructional strategies shown in Figure 13.3 provide guidelines for infusing responsibility into each lesson. Brief awareness talks can be held at the beginning of class, or the levels (or their equivalent) can be posted. Brief reflection time can be allocated at the end of class, for example by asking students to raise their hands for each level they were "at" during the period. There are many variations of reflection time. For example, Kit Cody uses a target with Level IV in the center, Level III in the next ring, and so on. Students simply touch whichever cumulative level they think they reached that day on the way out of class, and if Kit disagrees, he takes the student aside and they negotiate. I've used journals so students can do a bit more self-reflection, and some teachers have modified the workload inherent in this approach by having one of their classes keep daily journals.

EXPERIENCING STRATEGIES

Experiencing strategies involve anything directly associated with teaching physical activities that give students experience in respecting, trying, being self-directed, or caring. Here is an example for each level (for other examples, see Hellison, 1995):

For Level IV, Mosston's (Mosston & Ashworth, 1986) reciprocal teaching, in which students learn to give feedback to each other during a skill drill, helps all students to experience helping each other.

For Level III, setting aside a few minutes for Level III self-direction time gives students an opportunity to experiment with working on their own.

For Level II, developing a lesson around self-paced challenges—for example, a progression of basketball dribbling tasks that students work their way through at their own pace—emphasizes the experience of effort and improvement rather than winning or being the best (especially if accompanied by an awareness talk).

For Level I, game rules, such as requiring two hits before returning the ball to the other team in volleyball or requiring all players on a basketball team to touch the ball before it is shot, help students experience all-inclusive activities.

INDIVIDUAL DECISION MAKING

Infusing individual decision-making skills is more difficult for teachers who have not experienced much empowerment as students, athletes, or preservice teachers and who have therefore not taught that way either (with notable exceptions, of course). As with experiencing strategies, the list of possibilities is lengthy and can be found elsewhere (Hellison, 1995). Some examples: For Level IV, teachers can offer students the choice of voluntarily coaching their team, and for Level III, of moving from teacher-directed time (where the teacher selects, teaches, and evaluates the activity) to self-direction. For Level II, having students choose their own intensity level—for example, by offering competitive, recreational, and practice options in class—shifts the effort decision to the students. Coupled with a brief reflection time, this strategy and others like it encourage students to decide how much effort they want to put into an activity and whether their decision worked for them. For Level I, negotiating a plan to deal with a recurring respect issue or giving students who lose self-control the option of sitting out in order to regain control (and coming back in on their own) as part of a sit-out progression can empower students to handle their own problems.

GROUP MEETINGS

Group meetings empower students as well by allowing them to define what respecting others' rights and feelings means to them (e.g., "What *don't* you want others, including me, doing to you?"). They can evaluate the class (e.g., "What was one thing you liked or disliked today?") or the teacher (to me last year: "You've got to be tougher on us"... "Yeah, make us do pushups when we're bad"). They can suggest changes (e.g., "Passing the ball all around is okay, except when we got a fast break"). They can discuss the *possibility* of taking the ideas being presented to them in physical education outside the gym (e.g., "You mean do this stuff on the street??!").

IMPLEMENTATION

A recent study (Georgiadis, 1992) refers to this approach as a model, as do Jewett and Bain (1985), and even the present authors (Hellison & Templin, 1991). Joyce and Weil (1986) define a model as an approach that has theoretical coherence, has been refined in practice, and is supported by evidence, but the term is limiting in that, as Sizer (1992) puts it,

> We share ideas, not models; we believe that these convictions should be apparent in the functioning of our schools, even as the ways in which we choose to express these ideas differ from school to school and from year to year. (p. xi)

VARIETY OF SETTINGS

Implementation of TPSR has taken place in a variety of settings, including elementary and secondary public schools in the inner city, suburbs, and rural towns; diversion and detention schools for so-called at-risk students (e.g., students who are court-referred, perpetually truant, and "behaviorally disordered"); public school elementary and secondary classrooms; after-school programs in schools and social agencies; organized sport; at the school level in a few elementary and secondary schools; even in university classrooms and in Dean of Students meetings with university students. This diversity, as well as the diversity within each of these kinds of settings, precludes the implementation of one model; rather, the "convictions" integral to *becoming* personally and socially responsible and *being given* such responsibility "should be apparent" in the program, as Sizer suggests.

SAMPLE LESSON PLAN

Having said that, the following lesson plan provides some ideas for implementing TPSR in school physical education programs, with the caveat that modifications be made for the teacher's style (within the confines of teacher qualities, as described above), setting, and students. Young kids, for example, may only be introduced to the ideas of being responsible and taking responsibility; on the other hand, some teachers have shifted considerable responsibility to first graders. For example, Suzanne Marter asks her first graders to make and carry out their own personal plans, and Nelson and Frederick (1994) describe first graders devising their own curriculum using a three-step process. Class size is another variable. Although some controversy surrounds the class size issue (Robinson, 1990), I have found that so much more can be done in diversion and after-school programs, because class size typically does not exceed 15 (e.g., Hellison, 1986, 1993). In inner-city school physical education classes of 30 and more, I have been forced to resort to more structure, including behavior modification (Hellison, 1978).

Opening

The lesson can open with a brief awareness talk or reminder, sometimes using an incident of the previous lesson to show the relevance of the levels. Once awareness is firmly established and students have had some experience with the levels, they can come into the gym before class and begin their Level III Personal Plan (typically a goal to improve in a specific skill or fitness component, but many variations are possible [see Hellison, 1985]). The teacher can take attendance, help students whose plan is not well formed or whose motivation is low, and conduct counseling time with a few students. If Level III time is going well, it can be extended into the period.

Fitness Component

If fitness is part of the physical education curriculum (and it often is in TPSR because of its potential for noncompetitive individualization), a 10-

to 15-minute fitness routine can be conducted next. In this part of the lesson, students are taught the concepts underlying the exercises for future use at Level III—for example, that overload is necessary to improve one's performance in situps and pushups—and are permitted to select their own intensity for each exercise (rather than have all students do 15 pushups). Once students have learned this routine, they can be asked to do it on their own, seeking help from other students if they forget something and only consulting the teacher as a last resort. Once most of them can do the routine independently, they can be asked to devise their own 10- to 15-minute fitness routine, deleting those exercises that they don't want to do, doing more of what they do want to do, and so on.

As responsibility is increasingly shifted to students, some of them may struggle. Counseling time sometimes helps, but if students refuse to take responsibility, they can *choose* to become a member of a teacher-directed group and receive direct instruction from the teacher or a Level IV student. This is not using fitness as punishment, because everyone is doing fitness. This option simply takes the student(s) through the original routine.

Skill Component

If skill development is part of the physical education curriculum, a practice session can be held next, using such strategies as a progression of self-paced challenges and reciprocal teaching. Then, if desired, a game can be played, using such strategies as game modifications to include everybody; options for less intense, less motivated, or less skilled students; and student coaches.

Dealing With Problems and Closing

When Level I problems arise during the lesson, several strategies are available, including counseling time, the sit-out option and progression, making a Level I plan, invoking an NBA time-out (even if the skill or game is not basketball), adjusting the extent of responsibility being shifted to students or a particular student, and inviting the student to join the teacher-directed group.

The lesson can close with a group meeting, at least from time to time, and reflection time (at the end of every lesson).

EFFECTIVE PROGRAMS

A number of programs are described in some detail in the literature—for example, a middle school program (Hellison, 1983), an inner-city high school program (Hellison, 1978), several after-school programs (Georgiadis, 1990; Hellison, 1988, 1993; Lifka, 1990; Williamson & Georgiadis,

1992), an alternative high school program (Hellison, 1986); an alternative elementary in-school program (DeBusk & Hellison, 1989), and several organized sport programs (Hellison, 1995). These cases are exemplars of TPSR; they reflect both the promise of this approach and the struggle to make it work.

THE DIFFICULTY OF EVALUATION

This collection of cases does not readily reveal what is effective in every circumstance. As McLaughlin and Heath (1993, p. 230) point out, however, it is exceedingly difficult to measure the effectiveness of approaches such as TPSR:

The "softer" outcomes, such as improved self-concept, an expanded sense of possible futures, a connection with a coherent system of values and beliefs, and a sense of personal and emotional safety, elude typical evaluation instruments and so do not "count." According to Wally Shabazz, for a program to be effective, "something [must be] changed inside them that's going to remain different over a long time" (Ascher, 1992, p. 781). The elusive nature of these kinds of "softer" outcomes is compounded by the "sleeper effect," which suggests that sometimes the impact of a program is not felt until years later (Lickona, 1991).

EVIDENCE OF SUCCESS

Fortunately, recent (and not-so-recent) developments in program evaluation have opened education (and physical education) to more interpretative forms of inquiry. According to Schon (1990), the "swamp of practice" differs enormously from what goes on on the "high hard ground" of scientific research, so that more reflective and less positivistic forms of inquiry are required. Both Carter (1993) and Schubert and Ayers (1992) justify the use of story-telling in such inquiry, and about 100 years ago William James viewed conscious experience as data (McDonagh, 1973). Both Tom (1984) and Kliebard (1993) offer compelling arguments for approaching curriculum work as a craft, and Kirk (1993, p. 262) applies this notion to my work, praising the reflective, craft-oriented process of developing and field testing TPSR, and saying "It is not necessarily the substance but the spirit of Hellison's work we need to attend to in approaching curriculum work." Georgiadis (1992) argues in considerable detail (a 201-page dissertation!) that my work is practical inquiry in the tradition of John Dewey and Joseph Schwab.

Therefore, a variety of evaluation approaches, taken together, hold promise for gaining some insight into the effectiveness of TPSR. Based on these kinds of evaluation, there is considerable evidence that students in TPSR programs learn, experience, and practice the levels and the empowerment process in the programs (DeBusk & Hellison, 1989; Hellison, 1978; Keramidas, 1991;

Lifka, 1989; Mulaudzi, 1995; Williamson & Georgiadis, 1992). Outside the gym, some evidence, while not so strong, suggests that students have felt the impact of TPRS (DeBusk & Hellison, 1989; Lifka, 1989; Mulaudzi, 1995). From many letters I have received and conversations I have had, it is clear that teachers perceive this approach to be helpful to them and to their students (Hellison, 1983; Hellison, 1985). Ennis (1992), who used TPSR with teachers whose values were oriented toward social development, found that their response was positive, as indicated by this quote: "This was the first time in 30 years of teaching that I felt good about my own personal goals for teaching physical education. It was nice to get strategies for what I believe" (p. 327). However, whether students truly change inside themselves as Shabazz (Ascher, 1992) calls for is open to question. Their journals and interviews with them suggest some changes (see above references), and I have received a few letters from former students who, in their mid-20s, comment at length on how my program helped them. I have no idea, however, how generalizable or even how valid their comments are. One African-American PE major who helped with one of my inner-city programs seemed certain that, whether we see results or not, "it sticks in their minds."

Despite the very applied nature of TPSR and the reflective, interpretive character of much of the writing about it, scholars have been quite supportive. It has been identified as an exemplary curriculum model (Bain, 1988; Jewett & Bain, 1985; Steinhardt, 1992); one of the few applications of critical theory (Bain, 1986), although flawed (Bain & Jewett, 1987); an alternative approach to discipline problems (Graham, Holt/Hale, & Parker, 1993; Rink, 1993); and an exemplary approach for special populations (Siedentop, Mand, & Taggart, 1986; Winnick, 1990). Kirk (1992, p. 4) makes this point about the contribution of TPSR to social problems: "Hellison . . . [offers] genuinely alternative forms of social organization in physical education classes in an attempt to constructively redress the social conditions placing some young people's well-being at risk." The very successful Northern Fly-In Sports Camps, serving native Canadians in northern Manitoba, bases its work in part on TPSR:

> . . . the conceptual framework for the [NFISC] program is in part rooted in the work of Dr. Don Hellison . . . [whose] community work, research, and . . . humanistic curriculum models became a framework for NFISC programs. (Searle, Winther, & Reed, 1994, p. 1)

Taken together, these various strands of evidence, ranging from storytelling and interviews with students to the judgments of recognized scholars, provide some range and depth of support for the effectiveness of TPSR. This is not to argue that TPSR is without flaws. For example, I have had doubts about its effectiveness (Hellison, 1990), and Shields and Bredemeier (1994) find the levels themselves to be problematic to some extent.

SUMMARY

Classroom management and rhetoric about building character through
sport and exercise are not enough to effectively address the social problems
and needs of kids today. TPSR is one of several approaches that holds
promise for doing more to help youngsters grow socially. Based on over
two decades of experience and numerous studies and reflections by teachers, youth workers, and scholars, TPSR offers a specific set of goals (or
levels) and strategies for teaching kids to take more responsibility for
their own well-being and their relationships with others. Putting TPSR
into practice, however, demands more than how-to knowledge. It requires
reflecting on the question "What's worth doing?"

WHAT'S WORTH DOING?

TPSR attempts to delicately balance a set of values to assist students in
becoming responsible (the levels) and provide an empowerment process
to assist in *giving students responsibility*. At some points, sparks fly. What
would have happened in my after-school basketball program, for example,
if I had denied my students' request in a group meeting to play trash-
talk/in-your-face basketball? Worse, after I told them it was their decision,
what would have happened if they liked playing that way? Would I have
spent the year "presiding over" a trash-talking basketball program? (Fortunately for me, they tried trash talking briefly and decided to go back
to our "old" way.) Trying to maintain the balance requires continual refocusing, and sometimes the issues outstrip my ability to do justice to
both sides.

The constraints and potentialities of human agency (e.g., empowerment) in relation to social context have been addressed in the education
literature (e.g., Levinson, 1992). Although students clearly have the ability to rise above their environment (Taylor, 1991), the odds are overwhelm-
ingly against such empowerment in some settings, especially without a
community "youth charter" (Ianni, 1989) or an integration of education
and social services (Lawson, 1993). Certainly, fundamental social, economic, and political changes are necessary to create a more hospitable
environment for teaching responsibility.

However, it may well be that some of us, whether such changes are
forthcoming or not, will continue to press our case with kids. For us, it's
what's worth doing. As Kenny Moore (1992, p. 26) wrote about Arthur
Ashe and his commitment to working with kids despite having AIDS,
shortly before his untimely and tragic death:

The logical question, then, is, What good are good works to him now?
. . . Ashe's sporting answer is that you play out your match, you
pound away as hard as you can at what you care about until it's
over, for the very practical reason that we are not here in a vacuum.
. . . There are, he insists, only two alternatives. If enough human
beings do not advance the common good, we cannot go on . . .
Well said, Arthur.

REFERENCES

Ascher, C. (1992). School programs for African-American males . . . and females.
Phi Delta Kappan, 73, 777–782.

Ayers, W. (1989). *The good preschool teacher: Six teachers reflect on their lives.*
New York: Teachers College Press.

Bain, L.L. (1986). *Present status and future directions in research on teaching and
teacher education in physical education.* Paper presented at the International
Conference on Teaching and Teacher Education in Physical Education, Vancouver, BC.

Bain, L.L. (1988).Curriculum for critical reflection in physical education. In R.S.
Brandt (Ed.), *Content of the curriculum: 1988 ASCD yearbook* (pp. 133–147).
Washington, DC: Association for Supervision and Curriculum Development.

Bain, L.L., & Jewett, A.E. (1987). Future research and theory-building. *Journal
of Teaching in Physical Education, 6,* 346–362.

Carter, K. (1993). The place of story in the study of teaching and teacher education.
Educational Researcher, 22, 5–12.

Cuban, L. (1993). Reforming again, again, and again. *Educational Researcher,
19,* 3–13.

DeBusk, M., & Hellison, D. (1989). Implementing a physical education self-responsibility model for delinquency-prone youth. *Journal of Teaching in Physical
Education, 8,* 104–112.

deCharms, R. (1976). *Enhancing motivation.* New York: Irvington.

Des Dixon, R.G. (1994). Future schools and how to get there from here. *Phi Delta
Kappan, 75,* 360–365.

Ennis, C.D. (1992). The influence of value orientations in curriculum decision-making. *Quest, 44,* 317–329.

Ennis, C.D. (1993). Can we do it all? Making curriculum choices in middle and high
school programs. *Proceedings of the NASPE Critical Crossroads Conference for
Middle and Secondary Physical Education.* Reston, VA: AAHPERD.

Free time presents opportunity and risk for adolescents (1993, March). *Update,*
p. 7.

Garbarino, J., Dubrow, N., Kostelny, K., & Pardo, C. (1991). *Children in danger:
Coping with the consequences of community violence.* San Francisco: Jossey-Bass.

Georgiadis, N. (1990). Does basketball have to be all W's and L's? An alternative program at a residential boys' home. *Journal of Physical Education, Recreation and Dance, 61,* 42–43.

Georgiadis, N. (1992). *Practical inquiry in physical education: The case of Hellison's personal and social responsibility model.* Unpublished PhD dissertation, University of Illinois at Chicago.

Graham, G., Holt/Hale, S., & Parker, M. (1993). *Children moving: A reflective approach to teaching physical education* (3rd ed.). Mountain View, CA: Mayfield.

Hellison, D. (1978). *Beyond balls and bats: Alienated (and other) youth in the gym.* Washington, DC: AAHPERD.

Hellison, D. (1983). Teaching self-responsibility (and more). *Journal of Physical Education, Recreation and Dance, 54,* 23, 28.

Hellison, D. (1985). *Goals and strategies for teaching physical education.* Champaign, IL: Human Kinetics.

Hellison, D. (1986). Cause of death: Physical education. *Journal of Physical Education, Recreation and Dance, 57,* 27–28.

Hellison, D. (1988). Cause of death: Physical education—a sequel. *Journal of Physical Education, Recreation and Dance, 59,* 18–21.

Hellison, D. (1990). Making a difference—reflections on teaching urban at-risk youth. *Journal of Physical Education, Recreation and Dance, 61,* 44–45.

Hellison, D. (1993). The coaching club: Teaching responsibility to inner city students. *Journal of Physical Education, Recreation and Dance, 64,* 66–70.

Hellison, D. (1995). *Teaching responsibility through physical activity.* Champaign, IL: Human Kinetics.

Hellison, D., & Templin, T. (1991). *A reflective approach to teaching physical education.* Champaign, IL: Human Kinetics.

Ianni, F.A.J. (1989). *The search for structure: A report on American youth today.* New York: The Free Press.

Jewett, A.E., & Bain, L.L. (1985). *The curriculum process in physical education.* Dubuque, IA: Wm. C. Brown.

Joyce, B., & Weil, M. (1986). *Models of teaching* (3rd ed.). Englewood Cliffs, NJ: Prentice-Hall.

Keramidas, K. (1991). *Strategies to increase the individual motivation and cohesiveness of a junior male basketball team.* Unpublished master's thesis, University of Illinois at Chicago.

Kirk, D. (1992). *Articulations and silences in socially critical research on physical education: Towards a new agenda.* Paper presented at the AARE Annual Conference, Geelong, Australia.

Kirk, D. (1993). Curriculum work in physical education: Beyond the objectives approach? *Journal of Teaching in Physical Education, 12,* 244–265.

Kliebard, H.M. (1993). What is a knowledge base, and who would use it if we had one? *Review of Educational Research, 63,* 295–303.

Lawson, H.A. (1993). School reform, families, and health in the emergent national agenda for economic and social improvement: Implications. *Quest, 45,* 289–307.

Levinson, B.A. (1992). Ogbu's anthropology and the critical ethnography of education: A reciprocal interrogation. *Qualitative Studies in Education, 5,* 205–225.

Lickona, T. (1991). *Educating for character: How our schools can teach respect and responsibility.* New York: Bantam.

Lifka, R. (1989). *Implementing an after-school alternative wellness / activities program for at-risk Hispanic youth.* Unpublished master's thesis, University of Illinois at Chicago.

Lifka, R. (1990). Hiding beneath the stairwell: A dropout prevention program for Hispanic youth. *Journal of Physical Education, Recreation and Dance, 61,* 60–61.

McCaslin, M., & Good, T.L. (1992). Compliant cognition: The misalliance of management and instructional goals in current school reform. *Educational Researcher, 21,* 4–17.

McDonagh, J. (1973). The open-ended psychology of William James. *Journal of Humanistic Psychology, 13,* 49–54.

McLaughlin, M.W., & Heath, S.B. (1993). Casting the self: Frames for identity and dilemmas for policy. In S.B. Heath & M.W. McLaughlin (Eds.), *Identity and inner-city youth: Beyond ethnicity and gender* (pp. 210–239). New York: Teachers College Press.

Mesa, P. (1992, November). *Keynote address.* First Annual At-Risk Youth Conference, Lake Tahoe, NV.

Miller, R.F., & Jarmon, B.O. (1988). Moral and ethical character development— views from past decades. *Journal of Physical Education, Recreation and Dance, 59,* 72–78.

Moore, K. (1992). The eternal example. *Sports Illustrated, 77,* 15–26.

Mosston, M., & Ashworth, S. (1986). *Physical education: From intent to action.* Columbus, OH: Merrill.

Mulaudzi, L. (1995). *A program evaluation of the implementation of a responsibility model for inner-city youth.* Unpublished master's thesis, University of Illinois at Chicago.

Nelson, J.R., & Frederick, L. (1994). Can children design curriculum? *Educational Leadership, 51,* 71–74.

Nucci, L. (Ed.) (1989). *Moral development and character.* Berkeley, CA: McCutchan.

Orlick, T. (1978). *Winning through cooperation.* Washington, DC: Hawkins.

Rink, J. (1993). *Teaching physical education for learning* (2nd ed.). St Louis: Times Mirror/Mosby.

Robinson, G.E. (1990). Synthesis of research on the effects of class size. *Educational Leadership, 47,* 80–90.

Romance, T.J., Weiss, M.R., & Bokoven, J. (1986). A program to promote moral development through elementary physical education. *Journal of Teaching in Physical Education, 5,* 126–136.

Schon, D.A. (1990). *Educating the reflective practitioner: Toward a new design for teaching and learning in the professions.* San Francisco: Jossey-Bass.

Schubert, W.H., & Ayers, W.C. (Eds.). (1992). *Teacher lore: Learning from our own experience.* Albany, NY: State University of New York Press.

Searle, M.S., Winther, N.R., & Reed, M. (1994). *An assessment of the daily life experiences of Native youth: Implications for Northern Fly-In Sports Camps, Inc.* Winnipeg, Manitoba: Health, Leisure, and Human Performance Research Institute, University of Manitoba.

Shields, D.L.L., & Bredemeier, B.J.L. (1994). *Moral development and action in physical activity contexts.* Champaign, IL: Human Kinetics.

Siedentop, D., Mand, C., & Taggart, A. (1986*). Physical education: Curriculum and instruction strategies for grades 5-12.* Palo Alto, CA: Mayfield.

Sizer, T.R. (1992). *Horace's school: Redesigning the American high school.* Boston: Houghton Mifflin.

Steinhardt, M. (1992). Physical education. In P.W. Jackson (Ed*.), Handbook of research on curriculum* (pp. 964–1001). New York: Macmillan.

Taylor, A.R. (1991). *The disadvantaged child: From "risk" to "resilience."* Paper presented at the Conference on Perspectives on Diversity: Lines of Vision, California State University, Chico, CA.

Tom, A.R. (1984). *Teaching as a moral craft.* New York: Longman.

Weiner, L. (1993). *Preparing teachers for urban schools: Lessons from thirty years of school reform.* New York: Teachers College Press.

Williamson, K.M., & Georgiadis, N. (1992). Teaching an inner-city after-school program. *Journal of Physical Education, Recreation and Dance, 63,* 14–18.

Winnick, J. (1990). *Adapted physical education and sport.* Champaign, IL: Human Kinetics.

Zuchora, K. (1987). Physical culture and education in schools. *Scientific Yearbook, Academy of Physical Education in Warsaw, 1,* 79–96.

CHAPTER 14

Integration as a Curriculum Model in Physical Education:
Possibilities and Problems

Judith H. Placek

When we think of integration as a curriculum model in physical education (PE) what do we really mean? Consider the following examples:

- Teaching a Russian folk dance in a 5th grade social studies unit on Russia.
- Examining the role sport played in ancient Greece in a 9th grade world history class.
- Using prominent sports figures as examples in a middle school interdisciplinary unit on heroes and heroines.
- Teaching biomechanical principles in a PE basketball unit.
- Co-teaching a unit on orienteering with the math and science teachers instructing students in pacing and map reading.
- Using games explicitly to teach 2nd grade students how to cooperate and share.
- Requiring students to complete a research project on a sport related topic.
- Teaching reading as a part of a fundamental movement unit.
- Making sure students understand that similar tactics can be used in basketball and soccer, as both are examples of invasion games.

Are these all examples of integration? The answer could be yes depending on three factors: how the word integration is defined; beliefs about the appropriate subject matter of PE for the schools; and beliefs about the appropriateness of either integrating PE topics into other subjects in the school or integrating other subject matter into PE. This chapter will examine integration as a curricular model for school PE, including the development of a framework for thinking about integration in PE, a review of selected literature and research on integration, and a discussion of the possibilities and potential problems arising from the adoption of an integrative model.[1]

DEVELOPMENT OF AN INTEGRATIVE FRAMEWORK

The following section discusses the terms *interdisciplinary* and *integrative* and offers a brief review of integrative efforts in education and physical education.

DEFINING INTEGRATION

A literature review reveals that two terms, *interdisciplinary* and *integrative,* are used indiscriminately in the education literature. While sometimes considered synonymous and often used interchangeably, the two terms have different meanings. Interdisciplinary denotes the use of more than one discipline in pursuing a particular topic; that is, the linking of existing categories or disciplines. Integrative, on the other hand, describes a higher, more powerful conceptual synthesis or unity between forms of knowledge and their respective disciplines. Two metaphors help make the distinction clear—bridge building and restructuring. Bridge building, or interdisciplinary work, is more common and less difficult, as it "takes place between complete and firm disciplines . . . [and] preserves disciplinary identities. Restructuring is more radical . . . [and] usually assumes the need for new organizing concepts and the methodologies or skills common to more than one discipline" (Klein, 1990, p. 28–29). A truly integrative curriculum helps learners understand new relationships themselves, thus realizing that the traditional academic disciplines are but one way of organizing knowledge (Harter & Gehrke, 1989).

A BRIEF HISTORY

Although the concept of interdisciplinarity can be traced to Plato (Klein, 1990), the term itself did not emerge until the 20th century, and the brief review that follows will be limited to this latter time period.

Developments in General Education

Tanner, using the term integrative, describes the ebb and flow of the integrative tide over the years—calls for integration alternating with proposals for a return to basics (Tanner, 1989, 1992). In the early 20th century, influential progressives such as John Dewey and Alfred North Whitehead saw the need for integrative education. Shortly thereafter, the results of the Eight-Year Study (from 1933 to 1941) found that students with an integrative education—based, for example, on a problem-focused core curriculum—scored better on a number of factors (e.g., attitude toward learning, success in college) than students pursuing a traditional college preparation program (Aikin, 1942).

Post World War II America, however, saw a back-to-basics movement and then, as a result of Soviet achievements, the 1950s and 60s emphasized math, science, and foreign languages. Educators eventually realized these efforts at "new math" and "new physics" had not produced the promised results and again began thinking of integrative formats. In the 1960s, campus unrest related to the civil rights movement and the Vietnam War sparked a call for curriculum "relevance." While elective courses in both colleges and high schools were added in response to these demands, the additions did not change the basic offerings and allowed the disciplines to remain as the primary basis for curriculum structure in secondary schools. The mid-1970s saw dwindling concern for relevance, and the perceived "Japanese challenge" lent new energy to the isolation of disciplines in the back-to-basics movement through the 1980s and into the 90s.

Of course, many elementary teachers in self-contained classrooms always have integrated parts of their curriculum, and over the last 30 years the developers of middle schools have helped keep integrative education alive in the literature by proposing an integrative core curriculum. With these few exceptions, however, schools have been dominated by a traditional, discipline-based curriculum.

Developments in PE

A small but steady interest in integrating PE with other subjects has been evidenced in the PE literature since the 1970s. Several books (Gallahue, Werner, & Luedke, 1975; Gilbert, 1977; Humphrey, 1990) and numerous articles give ideas for PE's contribution to integrated education. Specialists who develop integrative curriculum have included PE in such diverse topic areas as aging education (Myers, 1979), multicultural education (Nethery, 1980), winter outdoor education (Matthews, 1975), the oceans (Hall, 1985), and even pottery (Counts, 1976)! As might be expected, the quality of the suggestions for PE varies widely. Unfortunately, middle school curriculum writers, who have begun serious integrative work toward a core curriculum, have not included PE as one of the core subjects (Placek, 1992).

LITERATURE, PRACTICE, AND
RESEARCH ON INTEGRATION

The following section proposes two ways of thinking about integration in PE. The first, internal integration, discusses integrating traditionally taught game and sport skills with concepts drawn from the disciplinary base of PE in addition to social and thinking skills. The second, external integration, integrates PE with other school subjects. Examples of the available descriptive literature and research on these two types of integration will be reviewed.

DEFINITIONS

I will use the term integrative throughout this chapter even though some of the examples provided have characteristics of interdisciplinary curriculum; it is difficult in practice to separate perfectly integrative efforts from those that are interdisciplinary. Accordingly, integrative PE is defined as a curriculum in which (a) subject matter from other subjects (e.g., math or English) is included in PE classes, (b) PE subject matter is included in other classes, (c) PE concepts from the disciplinary base of PE are taught, or (d) social or thinking skills are consciously selected and specifically taught. In other words, integrative PE makes a conscious and deliberate effort to go beyond teaching students motor skills, games, sports, and fitness activities.

MODELS FOR INTEGRATION

Most models present integration as a continuum beginning with nonintegration (i.e., subjects taught as separate disciplines) and continuing to complete integration of all subjects (Fogarty, 1991; Jacobs, 1989; Vars, 1987). The models differ considerably in their complexity, suggesting a varying number of intermediate stages between the two poles. For example, Vars' model (1987) suggests 3 stages (correlation, fusion, and core); Jacobs (1989) has 6 stages (disciplines, parallel, complementary, interdisciplinary, integrated day, and complete day); Fogarty (1991) tops the list with 10 (fragmented, connected, nested, sequenced, shared, webbed, threaded, integrated, immersed, and networked).

All three models above begin with the disciplines as a source of knowledge for learners. Harter and Gehrke (1989) suggest that, to the contrary, the disciplines provide only one way of organizing knowledge. Knowledge also can be structured around topics, concepts, great ideas, life problems, or mind constructs in order to promote integration. Regardless of the organizing structure, Fogarty (1991) asserts that, "Both integration within a discipline and integration across disciplines are necessary to fully integrate the curricula" (p. xiv). Before addressing the integration of PE with other subjects (external integration), the next part of this chapter develops a framework for thinking about integrating PE within itself, that is, what I will call internal integration.

INTERNAL INTEGRATION OF PHYSICAL EDUCATION

What does it mean to integrate our own subject? Fogarty (1991) suggests three areas which may be integrated within a subject: content-specific skills, social skills, and thinking skills. Although goals for these three skills have been included in various forms in the PE literature, Fogarty's division provides a clear way to reorganize them conceptually. I have modified two of the names to match terms used in the PE literature more closely (i.e., concepts rather than content, and social interaction/personal development rather than social). Certainly all three areas overlap in the world of teaching, but for the sake of clarity each will be discussed separately.

Integration of Concepts

During the past 30 years, enormous changes have taken place in PE departments in colleges and universities. PE evolved from a major that focused on sports skill instruction and training PE teachers to a multifaceted configuration that includes specialized study in subdisciplines (e.g., sport psychology, biomechanics) and a variety of career options, such as athletic training and sport management.

Lack of implementation. With the exception of an increased emphasis on fitness, PE in the schools has remained virtually untouched by this evolution. Although elementary PE has explored a number of different models (e.g., movement education, skill themes, teaching for understanding) in addition to sports and games, secondary PE largely has retained a multi-activity model (Siedentop, Mand, & Taggart, 1986); that is, a curriculum organized around a series of short units in which the skills and strategies of sports and games are taught. Although different models for thinking about how to teach these sports have been proposed (e.g., Rink, 1993; Vickers, 1990), sport skill classes in secondary schools today look much the same as they did 20 years ago.

   Material promoting and suggesting ways of integrating the disciplinary base of PE into elementary and secondary PE, often called a conceptual or kinesiological model, has been available for more than 20 years from books (e.g., Dodds, 1987; Hoffman, Young, & Klesius, 1981; Kneer, 1981; Lawson & Placek, 1981) and articles (see Placek's annotated bibliography in Carr, 1987). The application of disciplinary knowledge from exercise physiology can be seen most readily in the fitness-based offerings at all levels of K–12 schooling (e.g., Smith & Cestaro, 1992; Wescott, 1992). While K–12 PE has expanded to offer courses such as fundamentals of fitness, cross training, aerobics, and personal fitness development, the other "disciplines" have had limited impact on school programs.

Proposals for integration of concepts.   Although the integration of concepts into school PE has been limited (Placek, 1989), recent interest in integrating disciplinary material has become apparent. Student textbooks with accompanying teacher's editions have been published which include a great deal of integrative material (e.g., Means, Taylor, & Zanin, 1988; Spindt, Weinberg, Hennessy, Holyoak, & Monti, 1993a, 1993b, 1993c; Stokes, Moore, & Schultz, 1993). For example, the Spindt et al. text (1993b) includes student objectives such as, "describe how PE relates to other subjects you are studying in school" (p. 3), "define individual excellence and peak experience" (p. 15), "describe the differences and similarities of the basic skills and how they can be used in sports and dance" (p. 55), "and explain what motivates people to excel in physical activities" (p. 97).

In fact, a careful reading of AAHPERD's most recent goals for PE, *Outcomes of Quality Physical Education Programs* (National Association for Sport and Physical Education, 1992), shows that performance outcomes make up only one half of the total number. The benchmarks, examples of appropriate skills for seven different grade levels, have a significant component of conceptual material. Kindergartners, for example, should be able to "identify selected body parts, skills, and movement concepts" (p. 10), and sixth graders should be able to "recognize the role of games, sports, and dance in getting to know and understand others of like and different cultures" (p. 13).

Integration of concepts in Australia and Great Britain.   The integration of disciplinary material into school PE also is occurring in Australia and, to a lesser extent, in Great Britain (Macdonald & Leitch, 1994; Smith, 1993). The Queensland Senior PE course, for example, which counts toward entrance in Australian colleges, includes both performance and analysis. That is, students must be both competent thinkers and competent performers. Three core content themes are required:

- The complex processes involved in the learning and performance of physical skills (e.g., skills, strategies, controlling aggression).
- Physical fitness as a concept of social and biological significance (e.g., energy systems, the place of strength and flexibility in basketball).
- Physical activity as an institutionalized and formalized component of Australian society (e.g., gender equity and the media, the growth pattern of basketball) (Macdonald & Leitch, 1994).

Research on concept integration.[1]   Although over 20 years of suggestions on how to integrate conceptual content into PE exist, almost no research has been done on this type of curriculum. We are left to ask, therefore, the most fundamental questions about integration. First, can students learn conceptual material in PE? Even with only one study to help answer this question (Blood, 1984), the logical answer is yes—if PE teachers choose to teach this material, students can learn it. Beyond this basic level of inquiry, however, lies a series of vital and as yet unaddressed problems. Can concepts be taught without detriment to the development of psychomotor skills? Will students use the conceptual material later in life (e.g., to design their own exercise program, to detect fraudulent claims about fitness programs, to understand the role sport plays in our society)? What is the best way to teach concepts in different settings? Are teachers willing to change their teaching to include concepts? How will students respond to the integration of concepts into PE? Given the recent emphasis on conceptual skills by textbook authors and curriculum developers, questions such as these need answers.

Integration of Social Interaction/Personal Development Goals

PE has long promoted the inclusion of goals related to what Fogarty (1991) calls social skills. In addition to social goals such as teamwork, cooperation, and fair play, PE has touted its ability to enhance personal goals such as self-esteem and confidence (Lumpkin, 1986; Wuest & Bucher, 1991). In many cases, however, these goals were assumed to accrue through osmosis or incidental learning; that is, from students' participation and instruction in sports and games rather than direct instruction (Espiritu, 1987; Hellison, 1987). While realizing that teachers consider these skills to be important (Ennis, 1985) and students indeed may serendipitously learn some of them, I will not address such incidental learning in this chapter. Instead, I will examine two models from the literature which make an explicit effort to teach these social/personal skills: Hellison's model for teaching personal and social responsibility, and Adventure Education.

Hellison's teaching self-responsibility.   The best known example in the literature for teaching personal development skills is Hellison's blueprint for teaching self-responsibility (Hellison, 1985). The five levels, progressing from Level 0: Irresponsibility, to Level IV: Caring, were designed originally for use with high-risk youth, and have been adopted in schools from Montana to Michigan (Hellison, 1987; Masser, 1990). This model is one example of how teaching a specific personal/social skill can be integrated into PE. Other physical educators also advocate teaching responsibility in PE, although not necessarily using Hellison's model. For example, Pica (1993) uses a problem-solving approach, while Stiehl (1993) suggests using a three-step strategy of awareness, practice, and choice to teach students responsibility.

Adventure Education.   Another well known model for teaching social/ personal skills is Adventure Education (Rohnke, 1984, 1989). Goals such as increasing participants' sense of personal confidence, increasing mutual support within a group, and developing an increased joy in one's physical self and in being with others are pursued through various individual and group physical activities (games, stunts, initiative problems, trust activities, rope courses). The model, while developed as an alternative PE curriculum, has been adapted and used in a number of different settings, including traditional academic settings, marriage and family therapy, and corporate training (Bronson, Gibson, Kichar, & Priest, 1992; Gillis, 1985; Gillis & Gass, 1993; Paling, 1984–85).

Research on social/personal skills. Limited research on these models has been reported in the literature. Although Hellison's model is widely circulated and written about, insufficient research has been conducted to evaluate its effectiveness. Hellison discusses both the problems inherent in evaluating this model and the generally positive results from implementing his model in a variety of settings (Hellison, 1978, 1995). Most of the research on this model has been conducted in out-of-school settings, such as sport teams and after-school programs (see Hellison, 1996; Williamson & Georgiadis, 1992) or pull out programs (DeBusk & Hellison, 1989). While this research reported some increases in students' acceptance of responsibility, Georgiadis (1992) suggests that this model is better explained and justified through a paradigm of practical inquiry rather than traditional, formal research designs.

Research on Adventure Education was reported in the late 1970s after two years of implementation at a single high school (Fersch & Smith, 1978). While cautioning that the findings might be the result of many different factors, the evaluation at the end of both years showed a number of positive changes in students' attitudes toward school, self-concept, and willingness to try new things. While subsequent studies on the effects of Adventure Education in PE are lacking, a recent study (Dyson, 1994) examined two magnet elementary schools in which the entire school curriculum was integrated around the five concepts of Adventure Education (risk, trust, cooperation, challenge, problem solving). PE and the PE teachers played a central and important role in these schools rather than being marginalized, as in many schools.

The results of a study by Giebink and McKenzie (1985) indicate the need for caution in generalizing from any such limited and often context-specific studies. Although not specifically referring to either of the two models, these researchers examined the effects of intervention strategies on the social/personal skill of sportsmanship, finding that sportsmanship behaviors could be improved but the behaviors did not transfer to another setting. Similar questions about transfer surely must be examined with regard to social/personal skills as part of integrative PE.

Integration of Thinking Skills

Teaching thinking skills, such as problem solving and critical thinking, is considered the job of all school subjects, although it is generally reported on in regard to academic subjects. Although PE claims to engender those skills, they usually are assumed to be instilled through incidental learning (after all, you must use your mind in order to play a game!). Recently, interest has been shown in using PE directly to teach thinking skills, either as teaching strategies (ask open-ended questions), as part of sport and game curriculum (e.g., game strategies), or as part of a conceptual model of curriculum (e.g., using knowledge to create fitness programs, solving movement problems) (McBride, 1989; Miller, 1987; Schwager & Labate, 1993).

McBride (1992) presented an overview of this topic, discussing the difficulty of defining critical thinking and presenting a schema representing critical thinking in physical education. He also suggested research is needed to examine appropriate ways of teaching critical thinking in PE and explored the question of whether such skills can transfer within PE and across different subject matters.

A model for integration of thinking skills. One specific model for teaching students to think about the games they are learning to play is present in the PE literature. Teaching Games for Understanding (Bunker & Thorpe, 1982; Doolittle & Girard, 1991; Werner, 1989; Werner & Almond, 1990) approaches games teaching through a conceptual model in which games are divided into four categories—invasion, net/wall, fielding/run-scoring, and target games. Students learn basic offensive and defensive strategies applicable to each game category and then are asked to transfer this knowledge to other games in the same category. Students are asked to confront the question, "What should I do in this situation?" For example, in games such as badminton, tennis, or volleyball students should understand that one offensive strategy common to net games is to try and make your opponent move up, back, and side to side (Werner, 1989).

Research on thinking skills. As with the concepts and social/personal types of internal integration, little research data are available to show the effects of teaching thinking skills, including the Teaching Games for Understanding model (Chandler & Mitchell, 1990; Werner & Almond, 1990). Although a study by Rink, Werner, Hohn, Ward, and Timmermans (1986) reports that a traditional approach to teaching volleyball did not significantly improve students' knowledge of strategies, no direct research evidence yet indicates that students who are taught through this model are better game players than students who are not. A beginning step has been made by Mitchell, Griffin, and Oslin (1994) to identify and assess possible student outcomes. The first research to actually examine the type of thinking skills PE teachers asked students to use in their classes has been conducted by Ennis (1991). We need to clarify what we mean by thinking skills and conduct research on PE's effectiveness in producing these skills.

Means of Internal Integration

To this point, three types of content which could be integrated have been discussed, but not how a teacher might actually integrate this material.

Fogarty (1991)[2] suggests two ways to integrate within a subject: connected and nested. In a connected curriculum, course material is connected topic to topic, concept to concept, and each year's material to the next. Teaching for Understanding, where similar strategies are used across different types of games, is an example of this type of curricular integration. A nested curriculum addresses multiple skills. For example, a teacher directly teaches both a content specific skill, such as target heart rate, and self-responsibility in designing and participating in one's own exercise program.

Summary of Internal Integration

If internal integration is taken seriously by teachers and teacher educators, the potential exists for a revolution in the curricula of school PE in the United States. This type of integration has the potential to initiate a fundamental change in school-based PE curriculum similar to the change from various gymnastics systems to sport in the early 20th century (Spears & Swanson, 1983). Although the PE literature has always portrayed PE as contributing to a great number of objectives, in reality, minimal instruction in fundamental movement, games, and sport has been the norm. A change to an organized, integrated curriculum—which purposefully plans and teaches the skills necessary for students to become skilled players and to learn concepts as well as social, personal, and thinking skills—would indeed be a revolution.

EXTERNAL INTEGRATION: PE AND OTHER SCHOOL SUBJECTS

Integration of PE and other subjects may be thought about in two ways— first, the integration of PE content (however defined) into other subjects, and second, the integration of material from other subjects into PE. The distinction between these two categories, though somewhat artificial, is important to consider. Is integration defined as teaching PE related material in other subject areas or using the PE environment as a means of teaching concepts from math, science, or language arts? The literature reviewed in this section is more interdisciplinary than integrative because bridges are built between subjects, but fundamental restructuring of curriculum does not occur.

Teaching Content From Other Areas in PE

Certainly there is no lack of literature written by physical educators showcasing ideas about how PE can help teach content from other subjects. Authors suggest ways of incorporating other subjects into a movement environment, and their ideas range from helping students learn the alphabet by making letters with their bodies to understanding fractions through the use of a parachute. This review is not intended to be exhaustive, but it provides a representative sampling of the available literature. Most writing focuses on the elementary level and encompasses ideas about integrating material from language arts (including reading and writing), math, science, geography, history, social studies, art, health, music, biology, and career education (Bennett & Hastad, 1981; Gallahue, et al., 1975; Gilbert, 1977; Jensen, G.D., 1985; Jensen, T.M., 1971; Marston, 1980; Moore, 1992; New York State Education Department, 1986; Saccone, 1984; Savoy, 1971; Tenoschok, 1978; Werner 1981, 1982; Werner, Simmons, & Bowling, 1989).

Although the ideas presented in this literature use concepts from other subjects, many suggestions (as might be expected) have a distinctly PE flavor. For example, math skills include keeping score in games and calculating heart rate (Bennett & Hastad, 1981) and measuring playing areas (Werner, 1982). Teaching math concepts, such as estimation, prediction, and graphing, in fitness-focused PE classes is suggested by non-physical educators Pereira-Mendoza and May (1983). Many concepts to be integrated from science are based on biomechanics and include studying flight trajectories (Bennett & Hastad, 1981; Jensen, G.D., 1985; Savoy, 1971), the use of levers in movement (Bennett & Hastad, 1981; Gallahue, et al., 1975; Gilbert, 1977; Werner, et al., 1989), and Newton's Laws of Motion (Marston, 1980; New York State Education Department, 1986; Werner, et al., 1989). Suggestions for incorporating social studies into PE include teaching games and dances from holidays or other time periods or cultures (Gallahue, et al., 1975; Gilbert, 1977; New York State Education Department, 1986; Werner, et al., 1989), comparing the physical activities of ancient Greeks and Romans with those of contemporary Americans (New York State Education Department, 1986), examining attitudes, behaviors, and personal values of athletes (Moore, 1992), and learning facts about a city or area when charting jogging mileage (Saccone, 1984; Tenoschok, 1978).

Integrating PE Material Into Other Subjects

When considering the integration of PE material into other courses, it is important to note the PE topics chosen. The operative definition of the PE subject matter will dictate the topics. If the main subject matter is sports and games, integrative opportunities are fairly narrow (e.g., early American sports and games in a unit on colonial America; sports and dance from other countries in social studies units). If PE is viewed as encompassing not only traditional games and sport, but also concepts, social/personal development, and thinking skills, as discussed earlier in this chapter, totally different avenues become available.

Physical educators have written a great deal about the possibilities of including classroom concepts in PE, but have published very little about the contributions PE could make to other subjects. Thus, the following section, although including references to a few physical educators, mainly samples non-physical educators' views of the potential contributions of PE to other subjects in an integrated curriculum.

Some of the suggestions are rather traditional; others stretch the imagination:

- The ubiquitous use of games and dances from other time periods or countries is a favorite suggestion (Colorado State Department of Education, 1987; Hall, 1985; Kirman, 1988; Murphy, 1983).
- The teaching of fitness and fitness knowledge by elementary classroom teachers was reported in two studies (Pissanos & Temple, 1990; Sander, Harageones, Ratliffe, & Pizarro, 1993).
- Incorporating language arts skills, such as reading and writing about sports topics, is another common idea (Carter, 1985; Diamond, Haugen, & Kean, 1980; Myers, 1984; Parrish, 1984).
- Environmental educators suggest that PE has become a subject in which topics in outdoor ethics and consumptive versus nonconsumptive outdoor activities are covered (Monroe, 1991).
- The inclusion of PE in an interdisciplinary, building-construction project led to objectives for PE such as, the student will perform the most efficient method of lifting and carrying large heavy objects (i.e., a 90-lb. bag of cement), and the student will describe the possible effects of improper nutrition and rest on a physical laborer (Armstrong, 1976).
- A teacher's guide focusing on wildlife (Harmon, 1987) suggests such activities as performing dances named after animals, conducting a trust walk, and playing predator/prey games.

Research on external integration. The limited amount of research on the effects of integrating PE and other subjects shows mixed results. The results are difficult to generalize because many different academic and PE related variables in various settings were measured. No attempt will be made in this section to discriminate between the two types of integration. Integration of PE and a number of different subjects have been studied. Two studies which integrated math and PE found no significant difference between experimental and control groups in the learning of fractions (Shields, 1974) and multiplication tables (Carleton, 1982).

Studies of science (Werner, 1971), language arts (Earle, 1981; Penman, Christopher, & Wood, 1977), and music (Brown, Sherrill, & Gench, 1981) showed positive effects for integration of the subject matter and PE. Two studies in which elementary classroom teachers included fitness activities and fitness concepts in the curriculum showed positive effects on measures of fitness (Pissanos & Temple, 1990) and increases in children's motivation to exercise, participation in fitness activity outside of school, and fitness knowledge (Sander, et al., 1993). Milner and Hancock (1980) reported mixed results with students enrolled in a two-week environmental science program. Students showed positive growth in individual responsibility, awareness of individual differences, and a sense of belonging, which the authors credit to the students working together and sharing in PE activities such as canoeing, backpacking, and skin and SCUBA diving. Other outcomes were not confirmed, however, and some attitude measures showed negative changes.

The need for more studies seems clear. For example, in what ways does the subject matter affect its integration with PE? Why was math less successful than science, language arts, and music? Will results differ depending on where the integration takes place (PE or the classroom)? The major problem in this type of research, however, may prove to be methodological. It may be impossible to confirm differences based on standard forms of experimental research for a multifaceted problem like integration.

Summary of External Integration

Beginning in the 1970s, both physical educators and non-physical educators were writing about the integration of PE and other subjects. A number of observations seem appropriate about this body of literature. First, its authors clearly believe that a wide variety of classroom concepts can be taught in PE and, to a lesser extent, that PE can enrich other subjects. Second, many similarities are apparent in the choice of material to be integrated from both approaches. Third, with the exception of some rather bizarre interpretations of PE by non-physical educators, games, sport, and dance are seen as PE's contribution to the curriculum. Fourth, although some of the contributions by physical educators come from an internal integration of subject matter from such areas as biomechanics and exercise physiology, there appears to be no clear attempt to incorporate other areas, such as the meaning of play and sport in our society or aspects of motor learning. The authors have taken the discrete disciplines offered in school and tried to adapt PE to fit these disciplinary bases; they do not suggest that concepts related to PE can help enrich the academic curriculum. To achieve that end, both physical educators and classroom teachers have to work together to understand the contributions each field can make to the other and the ways they can combine their subjects to enhance student learning in new ways.

APPROACHES TO INTEGRATION

Fogarty (1991) suggests several ways to integrate two or more different subject matters: sequenced, shared, webbed, and threaded.

A *sequenced integration* requires teachers to arrange topics or units to be taught at the same time. For example, the PE teacher has students form the letters of the alphabet with their bodies at the same time the classroom teacher is teaching the alphabet. Another example is the coordination of environmental science concepts with lifetime/outdoor fitness concepts; for example, students go on field trips to apply their skills (Smith & Cestaro, 1992).

A *shared integration* uses overlapping concepts or ideas as organizing elements. Team teachers may plan a unit of study which focuses on key concepts, skills, or attitudes traditionally taught in the individual subjects. For example, home economics, health, and PE may organize a unit on wellness in which nutrition, exercise, stress reduction, and healthy lifestyles are key components. This type of integration is more complex than simply sequencing topics to correspond with another subject. The next two types of integration, webbed and threaded, make a significant step toward a truly integrated curriculum.

A *webbed curriculum* is organized around themes. The themes could be concepts, such as caring or cooperation; topics, such as institutions or the mind; categories, such as science fiction or great books; great ideas, such as "knowledge is power"; or problems, such as "how do humans survive?" (Beane, 1990; Fogarty, 1991, 1994; Harter & Gehrke, 1989). Ideas for PE have been included in curricular themes, such as the Constitution (Colorado State Department of Education, 1987), a Japanese cultural festival (Murphy, 1983), and the oceans (Hall, 1985). The use of shared concepts, such as space, force, and time, are suggested as means of integrating movement with art and music (Werner, 1982; Werner, Sins, & DeBusch, 1987) and computers (Burton & Lane, 1989). Although the themes suggested above are designed to integrate several subject areas, the PE literature has proposed the use of other themes, such as becoming independent and experiencing joy and success, to internally integrate our field (Catelli, 1990; Hoffman, et al., 1981). Clearly, these themes could also be used for external integration with other subjects.

A *threaded curricular approach* is a metacurriculum in which thinking skills or social skills, for example, thread through all the disciplines. For example, the idea of multiple intelligences or ways of knowing could be infused into language arts (verbal/linguistic intelligence), math (logical/mathematical intelligence), music (musical/rhythmic intelligence), and PE (body/kinesthetic intelligence) (Fogarty, 1991). A truly integrated model finds overlapping skills and concepts in the subjects involved and plans curriculum with the learner, rather than the content, as the focus. The whole language approach to literacy is an example of this model.

Although each type of integration has been presented as a discrete model, actual school curricula show many different versions of integration. Clearly, models such as connected and sequenced integration are easier to design and implement than formats that are webbed or threaded. Thus, a curriculum integrating fitness in health and PE (Petray & Cortese,

1988) is more common than a truly integrated science and PE class (Howell & Jordan, 1984) or a curriculum that embeds PE throughout an entire elementary school (Stroot, Carpenter, & Eisnaugle, 1991).

POSSIBILITIES AND PROBLEMS IN INTEGRATION

Integration as a model of curriculum for PE is in its infancy. Internal integration appears to be gaining advocates in the profession, but it is still at the beginning phase. PE is included in external integration, but often in rather limited ways (e.g., dances from other countries). The kinds of true integration represented by the core curriculum in middle schools and Fogarty's integrated model usually include only the subjects of math, science, language arts, and social studies.

REASONS FOR INTEGRATION

Given the long tradition of discrete disciplines and the enormous effort required to design, implement, and evaluate any type of integrated curriculum, what arguments can be used to convince teachers, administrators, and curriculum developers to take on the task?

First, the rate of knowledge growth and the finite time available to teach that knowledge in schools requires us to rethink the way we select what and how students study. If new knowledge is to be added to the curriculum, we are faced with the decision of what to eliminate (Jacobs, 1989). An integrated curriculum should "condense" the subject matter and thus provide a significant improvement in economy.

Second, the isolation and fragmentation of knowledge represented by a traditional curriculum does not match real life. The world outside school doesn't exist in discrete, disciplinary chunks, and real problems don't come in neat, discipline-bound packages which require a change of location and mind-set every 40 minutes (Jacobs, 1989; Tanner, 1989).

Third, an integrated curriculum may help overcome the common complaint of students that school is irrelevant to their lives. Integrating school subjects and emphasizing their connection to the larger world will help students see the value of school and learning (Jacobs, 1989).

Finally, an integrated curriculum will not only give students an exemplar of integration at the time material is taught, but should provide a model for achieving their own integrated thinking. That is, integration of school curriculum should prepare children with skills necessary to transfer knowledge/skills from one area or problem to another (Dressel, 1958; Nielsen, 1989). It should be noted that although the sincerity of these arguments cannot be doubted, their veracity has been little tested in schools.

POSSIBILITIES

What possibilities does integration open for PE? Are there reasons, in addition to the above arguments, why PE should integrate either internally or externally with other subjects? One rationale may be found in the fact that PE is considered a marginal subject in the schools by both teachers and students (Carlson, 1994; Pinkham, 1994). In a previous paper (Placek, 1992), I suggested that one way of alleviating some of the marginal status of PE in middle schools is by working toward an integrated curriculum. Dyson's (1994) recent research supports this view.

How might this work? Integration, both internal and external, may force us to examine our subject matter and define to ourselves and others both our unique contribution to the schools and areas in which we reinforce common school goals. In some ways external integration may force this self-examination more readily than internal integration, because we will be compelled to work with teachers of other subjects. We may fool ourselves into thinking we have revised our curriculum by adding a new activity, but being forced to examine and explain the basic assumptions behind our curriculum to others will eliminate self-delusions. Not only will other teachers see what we have to offer, but students may come to see "gym" as an important and legitimate part of the school curriculum and of life, rather than as a subject they don't consider "real" (Carlson, 1994).

In addition to providing the impetus for serious consideration of our subject matter (i.e., what do we really have to offer in the education of children and youth?), an externally integrated curriculum will help reinforce PE subject matter through its inclusion with other subjects (e.g., PE taught in an all-school unit on outdoor education). If internal integration is done deliberately and consciously, students will be provided richer learning experiences as they increase their knowledge about PE subject matter.

POTENTIAL PROBLEMS

This section considers potential problems for PE teachers, teacher education programs and teacher educators, preservice teachers, and students attempting to integrate PE, either internally or externally.

For Teachers

Today's teachers have a number of obstacles to overcome in developing an integrated curriculum. They must be convinced that it is in their interest to do so, and they must be allowed the time to accomplish it. Many PE teachers coach and, indeed, became teachers because that is the only route to coaching. Therefore, coaching receives the majority of their time and attention, and PE is relegated to a secondary status. Second, most PE teachers have little experience in designing and teaching an internally integrated curriculum. It seems optimistic, therefore, to expect a level of sophistication beyond a rudimentary integration (e.g., dances of other countries) when working with other subjects. Third, given the knowledge obsolescence which occurs (Kelly & Lindsay, 1980; Kneer, 1986) and the new knowledge constantly being developed, teachers must be willing to stay at the forefront of PE. Finally, the fact that teachers have not been trained to think about, develop, or teach an integrated curriculum (internal or external) presents a formidable set of constraints. For example, the skills necessary to work with other teachers and learn new ways of teaching present substantial problems of inservice development.

For Teacher Education Programs

Teacher education programs would need significant modifications to enable preservice teachers to learn to think about and teach either an internally or externally integrated PE curriculum. In addition to changes in teacher education programs, teacher educators would need additional training. How many teacher educators are knowledgeable about integrative curriculum, much less how to teach preservice teachers to develop, teach, and evaluate an integrative curriculum (Lawson, 1993)?

Preservice teachers perceive a number of the disciplinary-based classes (in particular, sociocultural courses) as not relevant to their future roles as teachers because knowledge from these courses is not easily applied to performance (Dewar, 1987). In addition, these classes usually are not taught in a manner which allows easy transfer of their content knowledge to pedagogical content knowledge. In other words, how are preservice students expected to figure out how to teach biomechanics to K–12 students, much less conceive of how to integrate it with other subject matter in the schools? Given what we know about why students choose to teach PE (e.g., stay close to sport, coach, continued association with sport), what is the likelihood they would accept or be interested in teaching this different, integrated version of PE? One discouraging clue comes from a study by O'Brien & Stewart (1990) which indicates that PE majors may resist teaching subject matter other than PE.

Student Issues

Even if such problems can be solved, student expectation of PE as a nonacademic subject may be the most difficult barrier to overcome. Students who view PE as requiring only participation and effort may resist an academic component to the program, whether through internal or external integration (Lawson & Placek, 1981; Macdonald & Leitch, 1994). We know teachers view students as a major influence on their teaching. Thus, if students are unhappy with an integrated curriculum, teachers may abandon it rather quickly as unworkable. Ironically, student resistance may be less if academic topics from PE are integrated into other subjects rather than internally integrated into PE.

Perhaps the above scenario is too pessimistic. Given the many examples of integration cited in this chapter, a number of teachers and curriculum developers have been enthusiastic about developing integrated curricula. The picture is much less clear if we ask for proof that such curricula actually have been implemented and accepted by students and teachers, and even more opaque if we want evidence that they have been effective in producing student learning.

SUMMARY

If teachers or teacher educators who are inexperienced in integration decide to design and teach an integrated curriculum, what recommendations might help such novices? Such advice might take this form. First, many types of integration are available. An appropriate, initial step is to become knowledgeable by reading and talking to experienced integrators. Begin slowly and carefully with familiar topics. Search the literature for ready-made ideas. Be flexible, and change unsuccessful ideas or teaching strategies. Be persistent and willing to explain to students, parents, and other teachers why this type of curriculum is important.

Make natural connections between subject areas. Not every subject integrates well in every case—don't force something that isn't there. For example, natural connections between health and PE will be easier than figuring out how PE connects with American government. The middle school, with its emphasis on team teaching and core curriculum, may provide an easy access point for a teacher interested in integrating PE with other subjects. Finally, PE teachers must leave the isolation of their locker-room-bound offices and gyms and build alliances among themselves and with other teachers in their schools. It is hard to begin the process of integration if one is only talking to one's self.

---

[1]The reader is referred to a bibliography by Vars (1991) for research dealing with integration of subject matter other than physical education.

[2]For a detailed explanation of each type of integration, see Fogarty (1991).

REFERENCES

Aikin, Q.A. (1942). The story of the eight-year study. New York: Harper & Row.

Armstrong, H. (1976). *Interdisciplinary approach to building construction.* Amity, OR: Amity School District No. 4-J. (ERIC Document Reproduction Service No. ED 215 805)

Beane, J. (1990). *A middle school curriculum: From rhetoric to reality.* Columbus, OH: National Middle School Association.

Bennett, J.P., & Hastad, D. (1981). Interdisciplinary teaching. *Journal of Physical Education and Recreation, 52*(2), 23.

Blood, D.G. (1984). An investigation of the effects of implementing 'Basic Stuff' in secondary school physical education classes. *Dissertation Abstracts International, 46,* 98A. (University Microfilms No. 8504999)

Bronson, J., Gibson, S., Kichar, R., & Priest, S. (1992). Evaluation of team development in a corporate adventure training program. *The Journal of Experiential Education, 15*(2), 50–53.

Brown, J., Sherrill, C., & Gench, B. (1981). Effects of an integrated physical education/music program in changing early childhood perceptual-motor performance. *Perceptual and Motor Skills, 53,* 151–154.

Bunker, D., & Thorpe, R. (1982). A model for the teaching of games in secondary schools. *Bulletin of Physical Education, 18*(1), 5–8.

Burton, E.C., & Lane, C.C. (1989). Using computers to facilitate the integration of art, music and movement. *Journal of Physical Education, Recreation and Dance, 60*(7), 58–61.

Carleton, N.L. (1982). Implications of physical education activities as reinforcement in learning multiplication tables. *Dissertation Abstracts International, 43,* 107A. (University Microfilms No. 8213015)

Carlson, T.B. (1994). *Why students hate, tolerate, or love gym: A study of attitude formation and associated behaviors in physical education.* Unpublished doctoral dissertation, University of Massachusetts, Amherst, MA.

Carr, N.J. (Ed.) (1987). *Basic Stuff Series II* (2nd ed.). Reston, VA: American Alliance for Health, Physical Education, Recreation and Dance.

Carter, J.M. (1985). Writing games in the Bayeux Tapestry. *English Journal, 74*(7), 31–34.

Catelli, L. (1990). School-college partnership: Developing a working model for an inner-city physical education curriculum. *Middle School Journal, 21*(4), 36–39.

Chandler, T.J.L., & Mitchell, S.A. (1990). Reflections on "models of games education." *Journal of Physical Education, Recreation and Dance, 61*(6), 19–21.

Colorado State Department of Education. (1987). *The Constitution: Experiencing democracy. A curriculum guide for elementary schools.* Denver, CO: Author. (ERIC Document Reproduction Service No. ED 269 185)

Counts, R. (1976). *Pottery.* Walker County, GA: Walker County Board of Education. (ERIC Document Reproduction Service No. ED 132 259)

DeBusk, M., & Hellison, D. (1989). Implementing a physical education self-responsibility model for delinquency-prone youth. *Journal of Teaching in Physical Education, 8,* 104–112.

Dewar, A. (1987). Knowledge and gender in physical education. In J. Gaskell & A. McLaren (Eds.), *Women and education: A Canadian perspective* (pp. 265–288). Calgary: Detselig Enterprises.

Diamond, I.M., Haugen, N.S., & Kean, J.M. (1980). *Interdisciplinary writing: A guide to writing across the curriculum.* Madison, WI: University of Wisconsin. (ERIC Document Reproduction Service No. ED 193 855)

Dodds, P. (Ed.). (1987). *Basic Stuff Series I* (2nd ed.). Reston, VA: American Alliance for Health, Physical Education, Recreation and Dance.

Doolittle, S.A., & Girard, K.T. (1991). A dynamic approach to teaching games in elementary PE. *Journal of Physical Education, Recreation and Dance, 62*(4), 57–62.

Dressel, P.L. (1958). The meaning and significance of integration. In N.G. Henry (Ed.), *The integration of educational experiences: The fifty-seventh yearbook of the National Society for the Study of Education, Part III.* (pp. 3–25). Chicago: The University of Chicago Press.

Dyson, B. (1994). *A case study of two alternative elementary physical education programs.* Unpublished doctoral dissertation, Ohio State University, Columbus.

Earle, J.A. (1981). The effect of the integration of language arts objectives with motor development objectives in the physical education curriculum: Kindergarten through second grade. *Dissertation Abstracts International, 42,* 2558A. (University Microfilms No. 8127583)

Ennis, C.D. (1985). Purpose concepts in an existing physical education curriculum. *Research Quarterly for Exercise and Sport, 56,* 323–333.

Ennis, C.D. (1991). Discrete thinking skills in two teachers' physical education classes. *The Elementary School Journal, 91,* 473–487.

Espiritu, J.E. (1987). Quality physical education programs—cognitive emphases. *Journal of Physical Education, Recreation and Dance, 58*(6), 38–40.

Fersch, E., & Smith, M. (1978). *Project Adventure, year II, Final quantitative evaluation for 1972-73.* Washington, DC: Bureau of Elementary and Secondary Education. (ERIC Document Reproduction Service No. ED 173 060)

Fogarty, R. (1991). *The mindful school: How to integrate the curricula.* Palatine, IL: Skylight.

Fogarty, R. (1994). Thinking about themes: Hundreds of themes. *Middle School Journal, 25*(4), 30–31.

Gallahue, D.L., Werner, P.H., & Luedke, G.C. (1975*). A conceptual approach to moving and learning.* New York: John Wiley & Sons.

Georgiadis, N.S. (1992). Practical inquiry in physical education: The case of Hellison's personal and social responsibility model. *Dissertation Abstracts International, 53,* 2742A. (University Microfilms No. 9238324)

Giebink, M.P., & McKenzie, T.L. (1985). Teaching sportsmanship in physical education and recreation: An analysis of interventions and generalization effects. *Journal of Teaching in Physical Education, 4,* 167–177.

Gilbert, A.G. (1977). *Teaching the three Rs through movement experiences.* Minneapolis: Burgess.

Gillis, H.L. (1985, July). *An active adventure for groups.* Paper presented at the Georgia School Counselors Institute, St. Simons Island, GA. (ERIC Document Reproduction Service No. ED 260 879)

Gillis, H.L., & Gass, M.A. (1993). Bringing adventure into marriage and family therapy: An innovative experiential approach. *Journal of Marital and Family Therapy, 19*(3), 273–286.

Hall, W.D. (1985). *Oceans: A multi-age, integrated subjects curriculum unit.* Bozeman, MT: Montana State University. (ERIC Document Reproduction Service No. ED 269 184)

Harmon, J. (1987). *Home is where the habitat is. Teacher's guide and student's guide, grade 6.* Kansas State Department of Wildlife and Parks. (ERIC Document Reproduction Service No. ED 323 105)

Harter, P.D., & Gehrke, N.J. (1989). Integrative curriculum: A kaleidoscope of alternatives. *Educational Horizons, 68*(1), 12–17.

Hellison, D. (1978). *Beyond balls and bats.* Washington, DC: AAHPERD.

Hellison, D. (1985). *Goals and strategies for teaching physical education.* Champaign, IL: Human Kinetics.

Hellison, D. (1987). The affective domain in physical education: Let's do some housecleaning. *Journal of Health, Physical Education, Recreation and Dance, 58*(6), 41–43.

Hellison, D. (1996). Teaching personal and social responsibility in physical education. In S. Silverman & C. Ennis (Eds.), *Student learning in physical education: Applying research to enhance instruction* (pp. 269-286). Champaign, IL: Human Kinetics.

Hoffman, H.A., Young, J., & Klesius, S.T. (1981). *Meaningful movement for children.* Boston: Allyn & Bacon.

Howell, M., & Jordan, B.J. (1984). Body/mind research: An integrated physical education and science class. *Journal of Health, Physical Education, Recreation and Dance, 55*(3), 80–81.

Humphrey, J.H. (1990). *Integration of physical education in the elementary school curriculum.* Springfield, IL: Charles C. Thomas.

Jacobs, H.H. (1989). Design options for an integrated curriculum. In H.H. Jacobs (Ed.), *Interdisciplinary curriculum: Design and implementation* (pp. 13–24). Alexandria, VA: Association for Supervision and Curriculum Development.

Jensen, G.D. (1985). *A guide to curriculum planning in physical education.* Madison, WI: Wisconsin State Department of Public Instruction. (ERIC Document Reproduction Service No. ED 267 024)

Jensen, T.M. (1971). Creative ropes. *Journal of Physical Education and Recreation, 42*(5), 56–57.

Kelly, E., & Lindsay, C. (1980). A comparison of knowledge obsolescence of graduating seniors and practitioners in the field of physical education. *Research Quarterly for Exercise and Sport, 54,* 636–644.

Kirman, J.M. (1988). Integrating geography with other school subjects. *Journal of Geography, 87*(3), 104–106.

Klein, J.T. (1990). *Interdisciplinarity: History, theory, and practice.* Detroit: Wayne State University Press.

Kneer, M.E. (Ed.). (1981). *Basic Stuff Series I.* Reston, VA: American Alliance for Health, Physical Education, Recreation and Dance.

Kneer, M.E. (1986). Description of physical education instructional theory/practice gap in selected secondary schools. *Journal of Teaching in Physical Education, 5,* 91–106.

Lawson, H.A. (1993). School reform, families, and health in the emergent national agenda for economic and social improvement: Implications. *Quest, 45,* 289–307.

Lawson, H.A., & Placek, J.H. (1981). *Physical education in the secondary schools: Curricular alternatives.* Boston: Allyn & Bacon.

Lumpkin, A. (1986). *Physical education: A contemporary introduction.* St. Louis: Times Mirror/Mosby.

Macdonald, D., & Leitch, S. (1994). Praxis in PE: The Queensland senior physical education syllabus on trial. *Journal of Physical Education New Zealand, 27*(2), 17–21.

Marston, R.E. (1980). Chutes and learners. *Teacher, 98*(3), 64, 66.

Masser, L.S. (1990). Teaching for affective learning in elementary physical education. *Journal of Health, Physical Education, Recreation and Dance, 62*(7), 18–19.

Matthews, B.E. (1975). *Winter outdoor education activities: Snowshoes and exploring the winter environment.* Cortland, NY: Cortland-Madison Board of Cooperative Educational Services. (ERIC Document Reproduction Service No. ED 161 579)

McBride, R. (1989). Teaching critical thinking in the psycho-motor learning environment—A possibility or passing phase? *The Physical Educator, 46,* 170–173.

McBride, R. (1992). Critical thinking—an overview with implications for physical education. *Journal of Teaching in Physical Education, 11,* 112–125.

Means, C., Taylor, B., & Zanin, E. (1988*). The new physical education and me!* Winston-Salem, NC: Hunter.

Miller, D.M. (1987). Energizing the thinking dimensions of physical education. *Journal of Physical Education, Recreation and Dance, 58*(8), 76–79.

Milner, E.K., & Hancock, P.A. (1980). *The effects of an interdisciplinary collegiate program for secondary school students on their attitudes toward selected physical education and social concepts.* Paper presented at the annual meeting of the American Alliance for Health, Physical Education, Recreation and Dance, Detroit. (ERIC Document Reproduction Service No. ED 195 518)

Mitchell, S.A., Griffin, L.L., & Oslin, J.L. (1994). Tactical awareness as a developmentally appropriate focus for the teaching of games in elementary and secondary physical education. *Physical Educator, 51*(1), 21–28.

Monroe, M.C. (1991). Meeting the mandate: Integrating environmental education. *Clearing, 71,* 8–11.

Moore, C. (1992). *Learn & play Olympic sports: Curriculum guide for teachers grades 3, 4, and 5.* Los Angeles: Amateur Athletic Foundation of Los Angeles. (ERIC Document Reproduction Service No. ED 356 167)

Murphy, C. (1983). *A step by step guide for planning a Japanese cultural festival.* (ERIC Document Reproduction Service No. ED 238 748)

Myers, J.W. (1979). *Aging education for the junior high/middle school years.* Cookeville, TN: Tennessee Technological University. (ERIC Reproduction Service No. ED 204 251)

Myers, J.W. (1984). *Writing to learn across the curriculum. Fastback 209.* Bloomington, IN: Phi Delta Kappa Educational Foundation.

National Association for Sport and Physical Education. (1992). *Outcomes of quality physical education*. Reston, VA: American Alliance for Health, Physical Education, Recreation and Dance.

Nethery, M. (1980). *The cultural exchange: A cross-cultural and interdisciplinary multicultural education curriculum for grades 4-8*. Eureka, CA: Humboldt County Office of Education. (ERIC Reproduction Service No. ED 202 781)

New York State Education Department. (1986). *Physical education syllabus, grades K - 12*. Albany, NY: Bureau of Curriculum Development. (ERIC Document Reproduction Service No. ED 272 461)

Nielsen, M.E. (1989). Integrative learning for young children: A thematic approach. *Educational Horizons, 68*(1), 18–24.

O'Brien, D.G., & Stewart, R.A. (1990). Preservice teachers' perspective on why every teacher is not a teacher of reading: A qualitative analysis. *Journal of Reading Behavior, 22*(2), 101–129.

Paling, D. (1984-1985). Project Adventure. *The College Board Review, 134*, 21–24, 31.

Parrish, B. (1984). Reading practices and possibilities in physical education. *Journal of Physical Education, Recreation and Dance, 55*(3), 73–77.

Penman, K.A., Christopher, J.R., & Wood, G.S. (1977). Using gross motor activity to improve language arts concepts by third grade students. *Research Quarterly, 48*, 134–137.

Pereira-Mendoza, L., & May, S. (1983). The environment—A teaching aid. *School Science and Mathematics, 83*(1), 54–60.

Petray, C.K., & Cortese, P.A. (1988). Physical fitness: A vital component of the school health education curriculum. *Health Education, 19*(5), 4–7.

Pica, R. (1993). Responsibility and young children—what does physical education have to do with it? *Journal of Health, Physical Education, Recreation and Dance, 64*(5), 72–75.

Pinkham, K.M. (1994). *Perspectives of secondary school physical educators on the school as a workplace*. Unpublished doctoral dissertation, University of Massachusetts, Amherst, MA.

Pissanos, B.W., & Temple, I.G. (1990). Fitting together—physical education specialists and classroom teachers. *Journal of Physical Education, Recreation and Dance, 62*(7), 55–61.

Placek, J.H. (1989). An evaluation of the implementation of basic stuff. *Journal of Teaching in Physical Education, 8*, 152–161.

Placek, J.H. (1992). Rethinking middle school physical education curriculum: An integrated, thematic approach. *Quest, 44*, 330–341.

Rink, J. (1993). *Teaching physical education for learning*. St. Louis: Mosby.

Rink, J.E., Werner, P.H., Hohn, R.C., Ward, D.S., & Timmermans, H.M. (1986). Differential effects of three teachers over a unit of instruction. *Research Quarterly for Exercise and Sport, 57*, 132–138.

Rohnke, K. (1984). *Silver bullets: A guide to initiative problems, adventure games, and trust activities*. Hamilton, MA: Project Adventure.

Rohnke, K. (1989). *Cowstails and cobras II: A guide to games, initiatives, ropes courses, & adventure curriculum.* Dubuque, IA: Kendall/Hunt.

Saccone, P.P. (1984). *It's 'funner' to be a runner physical education/classroom program.* El Cajon, CA: Cajon Valley Union School District. (ERIC Document Reproduction Service No. ED 242 660)

Sander, A.N., Harageones, M., Ratliffe, T., & Pizarro, D. (1993, March). *A survey assessment of Florida's Fit to Achieve program.* Paper presented at the Annual Meeting of the American Alliance for Health, Physical Education, Recreation and Dance, Washington, DC. (ERIC Document Reproduction Service No. ED 356 228)

Savoy, G.H. (1971). *Archery—a catalyst for subject integration.* Atikodan, Ontario: Marks Street School. (ERIC Document Reproduction Service No. ED 085 149)

Schwager, S., & Labate, C. (1993). Teaching for critical thinking in physical education. *Journal of Physical Education, Recreation and Dance, 64*(5), 24–26.

Shields, S.L. (1974). A functional curriculum of interdisciplinary team teaching in the areas of mathematics and physical education and the effect of such a program upon the achievement of sixth-grade students in mathematics. *Masters Abstracts International, 12,* 231. (University Microfilms No. 1305822)

Siedentop, D., Mand, C., & Taggart, A. (1986). *Physical education teaching and curriculum strategies for grades 5-12.* Palo Alto, CA: Mayfield.

Smith, M.D. (1993). Physical education in the British national curriculum. *Journal of Physical Education, Recreation and Dance, 64*(9), 21–32.

Smith, T.K., & Cestaro, N. (1992). Saving future generations—The role of physical education. *Journal of Physical Education, Recreation and Dance, 63*(8), 75–79.

Spears, B., & Swanson, R.A. (1983). *History of sport and physical activity in the United States.* Dubuque, IA: Brown.

Spindt, G.B., Weinberg, G., Hennessy, B., Holyoak, C., & Monti, W.H. (1993a). *Moving as a team.* Dubuque, IA: Kendall/Hunt.

Spindt, G.B., Weinberg, G., Hennessy, B., Holyoak, C., & Monti, W.H. (1993b). *Moving with confidence.* Dubuque, IA: Kendall/Hunt.

Spindt, G.B., Weinberg, G., Hennessy, B., Holyoak, C., & Monti, W.H. (1993c). *Moving with skill.* Dubuque, IA: Kendall/Hunt.

Stiehl, J. (1993). Becoming responsible—theoretical and practical considerations. *Journal of Physical Education, Recreation and Dance, 64*(5), 38–40, 57–59, 70–71.

Stokes, R., Moore, C., & Schultz, S.L. (1993). *Personal fitness and you.* Winston-Salem, NC: Hunter Textbooks.

Stroot, S.A., Carpenter, M., & Eisnaugle, K. (1991). Focus on physical education: Academic and physical excellence at Westgate Alternative School. *Journal of Physical Education, Recreation and Dance, 67*(2), 49–53.

Tanner, D. (1989). A brief historical perspective of the struggle for an integrative curriculum. *Educational Horizons, 68*(1), 7–11.

Tanner, D. (1992). Synthesis versus fragmentation: The way out of curriculum confusion. In J.M. Jenkins & D. Tanner (Eds.), *Restructuring for an interdisciplinary curriculum* (pp. 1–14). Reston, VA: National Association of Secondary School Principals.

Tenoschok, M. (1978). Jogging geography. *Journal of Physical Education and Recreation, 49*(6), p. 68.

Vars, G.F. (1987). *Interdisciplinary teaching in the middle grades: Why & how.* Columbus, OH: National Middle School Association.

Vars, G.F. (1991). *A bibliography of research on the effectiveness of block-time, core, and interdisciplinary team teaching programs.* Kent, OH: National Association for Core Curriculum.

Vickers, J.N. (1990). *Instructional design for teaching physical activities.* Champaign, IL: Human Kinetics.

Werner, P. (1971). Effects of integration of physical education with selected science concepts upon science knowledge and selected physical performance skills of boys and girls at the fourth-, fifth-, and sixth-grade levels. *Dissertation Abstracts International, 32,* 5601A. (University Microfilms No. 72-9743)

Werner, P. (1981). Teaching language through movement. *Journal of Physical Education and Recreation, 52*(2), 24–25.

Werner, P. (1982). Interdisciplinary experiences through child designed games. *Journal of Physical Education, Recreation and Dance, 53*(7), 50, 55.

Werner, P. (1989). Teaching games—A tactical perspective. *Journal of Physical Education, Recreation and Dance, 60*(3), 97–101.

Werner, P., & Almond, L. (1990). Models of games education. *Journal of Physical Education, Recreation and Dance, 61*(4), 23–27.

Werner, P., Simmons, M., & Bowling, T. (1989). Combining the arts and academics. *Journal of Physical Education, Recreation and Dance, 60*(7), 55–57.

Werner, P., Sins, N., & DeBusch, L. (1987). Creating with art, music, and movement. *Physical Educator, 44,* 291–295.

Wescott, W.L. (1992). High school physical education: A fitness professional's perspective. *Quest, 44*(3), 342–351.

Williamson, K.M., & Georgiadis, N. (1992). Teaching an inner-city after-school program. *Journal of Physical Education, Recreation and Dance, 63*(8), 14–18.

Wuest, D.A., & Bucher, C.A. (1991). *Foundations of physical education and sport.* St. Louis: Mosby.

PART 5

Learning to Teach:
An Ongoing Process

CHAPTER 15

What Do We Know About the Professional Preparation of Teachers?

Mary O'Sullivan

Calls for reform in teacher education have been frequent in recent years. Although most critics and educational reformers agree on the need for a major overhaul of how we prepare the next generation of teachers, there is little consensus on the nature and scope of the problems to be addressed or strategies for solving them. For some, the focus of teacher education reform has been mainly political, aimed at changing conditions in schools, the nature of the teaching profession, and the nature of the training program (Carnegie, 1986; Holmes, 1986). Such advocates support post-baccalaureate teacher preparation and expanding the time devoted to general education courses as strategies that will increase the status of the teaching profession. The tacit assumption of this position is that if teachers are to address contemporary social issues in schools proactively and successfully, they require a broader based general education in addition to subject matter expertise and education coursework. The Holmes and Carnegie reports also recommended improving (read increasing the time allowed for) prospective teachers' subject matter knowledge and spending more time teaching in schools during preservice education.

While other educational critics recognize the limitations of teacher preparation, they are less convinced that the solution lies in increasing the length of current programs. Tom (1987) argued that the problem in

developing better qualified teachers is not the length of teacher preparation but its coherence and quality. He noted that the rethinking of general
education and subject matter preparation may be a far more significant
reform than the expansion of either of these areas of study. Still others
consider the key problem in professional preparation to be an overcrowded
teacher education curriculum; they suggest that a five-year program could
provide more time to cover the content, allow students the opportunity
to gain more practical experience, and integrate theoretical and practical
experience into a coherent, personal philosophy of teaching.

This chapter begins with a discussion of criteria for quality programs
of professional preparation and presents a series of conceptual orientations to teacher preparation that must be considered when judging the
scope and quality of teacher education programs. The chapter reviews
literature on attributes for—and considers the problematic concept of—
quality teacher education programs in physical education. It discusses
the content, scope, and sequence of such programs. It summarizes the
main findings of that research, suggesting there is little empirical work
to support many of the programmatic decisions of teacher educators. The
chapter ends with a call for the intensive study of the effectiveness of
different types of teacher education programs in preparing physical education teachers and respect for multiple perspectives on the role of a physical
education teacher in today's schools.

QUALITY TEACHER
EDUCATION PROGRAMS

In a recent study, Howey and Zimpher (1989) conducted an in-depth,
cross-institutional analysis of teacher preparation in six highly regarded
elementary teacher education programs. They identified a set of conditions
and characteristics that appeared to contribute in substantial ways to
the education of teachers, but cautioned readers that the nature of their
descriptive research did not allow them to "speak with any confidence
about [program] effectiveness, however defined" (p. 246). The teacher
education programs studied demonstrated the following attributes:

1. Programs were driven by clear conceptions of schooling and teaching. Faculty contributed to and supported a shared set of beliefs
   about what was valued in a teacher and what should be expected of
   a prospective teacher and shared in designing the scope, sequence,
   integration, and articulation of the curriculum.
2. Faculty coalesced around a set of planned variations, sharing a
   specific agenda for instruction and joint ownership and responsibility for the program.

3. Program goals were clear and reasonable and could be clearly articulated by students of the programs.
4. Programs were rigorous and academically challenging communicating to students that quality work and a commitment to the program were expected.
5. Key concepts ran through the programs, providing students a framework to assist in developing their perspective on learning to teach. The key here was that several such concepts existed within programs and students had a choice in where they would align themselves.
6. There was a balance between time and respect for learning content knowledge, learning about pedagogy, pedagogical knowledge, and experience in learning to teach.
7. Cohort groups of students were identified as a strength of these programs. Faculty indicated a greater sense of accountability when interacting with a group they knew over long periods of time.
8. Each program had a curricular event which served to socialize students to their teaching career and reinforce their commitment to teaching. Howey and Zimpher (1989) advocated that such milestones be purposefully built into programs at key points.
9. Each program had a well conceived set of laboratory and clinical experiences. One such scope and sequence study in physical education teacher preparation has been described by Taggart (1988).
10. Each program had a systematic plan for program evaluation and direct linkage to research and development in teacher education.

FEIMAN-NEMSER'S "CONCEPTUAL ORIENTATIONS"

To understand and evaluate the effectiveness and coherence of teacher preparation programs, Feiman-Nemser (1990) suggested we must be aware of various ways of thinking that influence both the form and structure of how teachers learn to teach. She suggested that there exist several different perspectives among teacher educators about what it means to successfully prepare a teacher to teach. Each of these perspectives emphasizes particular ways of thinking about teacher education, which Feiman-Nemser (1990) referred to as "conceptual orientations" and defined as:

a set of ideas about the goals of teacher preparation and the means for achieving them. Ideally, a conceptual orientation includes a view of teaching and learning and a theory about learning to teach. Such ideas should give direction to the practical activities of teacher preparation such as program planning, course development, instruction, supervision, and evaluation. (p. 220)

Feiman-Nemser described five orientations that exist in teacher preparation: (a) academic, (b) practical, (c) technological, (d) personal, and (e) critical/social. She cautioned that while such orientations often reflect only theory as opposed to practice in teacher education curriculum, the framework is useful in providing insight into the diversity of what is valued in the preparation of beginning teachers.

The academic orientation focuses on teaching as "the transmission of knowledge and the development of understanding" (Feiman-Nemser, 1990, p. 221). Researchers in this orientation are trying to determine what it means to know one's subject matter in order to teach it and how teachers' knowledge of their subject influences teaching and learning in their classrooms. Lee Shulman's (1986, 1987) work, and that of his students and colleagues (Grossman, 1991; Gudmundsdottir, 1990), on teachers' pedagogical content knowledge (which I will address later in the chapter) are among the more recent examples of this orientation in teacher education.

The practical orientation endorses the "primacy of experiences as a source of knowledge about teaching and a means of learning to teach" (Feiman-Nemser, 1990, p. 222) and focuses on the techniques and artistry skillful teachers demonstrate in their work. "The technological orientation focuses attention on the knowledge and skills of teaching. . . . Learning to teach involves the acquisition of principles and practices derived from the scientific study of teaching" (p. 223). Research on effective teaching, specifically the process-product research of the 1970s and 1980s (Brophy & Good, 1986; Waxman & Walberg, 1991) is viewed as the substantive content in teacher preparation programs with this orientation.

The personal orientation views learning to teach "as a process of learning to understand, develop, and use oneself effectively . . . [and] advocate field experiences, in which students can learn what they need to know and try their wings in encounters with real professional problems" (p. 225). The critical orientation "highlights the teacher's obligations to students and society, challenging teacher educators to help novices learn to align school practices with democratic principles of justice and equality" (Feiman-Nemser, 1990, p. 227). The work of Ken Zeichner and his colleagues (Zeichner & Liston, 1987) in the elementary teacher education program at the University of Wisconsin and the works of Richard Tinning (1992) and Allison Dewar (1989) in physical education teacher education (PETE) are examples of a critical orientation to teacher preparation.

ORIENTATIONS IN PETE

Rink (1993) adapted and applied these orientations to physical education teacher education (PETE). These orientations for PETE programs included

- an academic orientation (a focus on the subject matter of games, sport, dance, fitness, etc.),

- a practical orientation (heavy reliance on field experience and practice),
- a technological orientation (emphasis on teacher effectiveness skills and research-based teaching skill development),
- a personal orientation (emphasis on personal-meaning-based orientations to growth as a teacher), and
- a critical/social orientation (emphasis on the moral basis of teaching and on the issues of equity and the social dimensions of teaching).

In contrast to Feiman-Nemser, Rink (1993) suggested the orientations "can and do coexist in different aspects of the same program and perhaps should all be a consideration in program design" (p. 316) and do not necessarily have to compete. Rink argues that we have spent too much energy in recent years debating the relative merits of what have been presented as competing conceptual orientations to teacher education in physical education and not enough energy presenting our visions of teacher education and how well those visions are realized. However, others take a more purist stance and suggest many of these visions of teacher education in physical education are mutually exclusive (Sparkes, 1989). Indeed, Sparkes (1992) looks on this positively from both a research and programmatic viewpoint, noting that such new visions and voices encourage us to consider different perspectives "in a spirit of intellectual curiosity and respect [and] is essential if theoretical vitality is to be nurtured within the PE community. In broadening our perspectives and becoming more aware of research paradigms that offer alternatives to our own, even if we disagree with them, we become far less parochial" (p. 49).

Depending on one's beliefs about teaching and learning to teach, one or more orientations may be emphasized at the expense of others, and thus a judgment about the scope and content of the curriculum for teacher education is made. Graham (1991), in a review of the general education and PETE literature, identified "four dimensions of teacher preparation that appeared to positively influence the development of preservice students' perspectives toward teaching" (p. 6) regardless of the conceptual orientation brought to bear on a PETE program. These included:

1. A shared vision of teacher education held jointly by university and school personnel (cooperating teachers, clinical faculty, and university supervisors) who worked hard to establish and maintain a relationship with practicing teachers, an effort which was seen as central to the operation of teacher education.
2. The presence of an inquiry approach to teaching where students, in a nonthreatening, safe environment, were provided various types of "assignments" at different times during their programs to reflect on teaching (their own and others) and critically examine the nature of their values and beliefs about teaching and learning.
3. The structure and content of such experiences "were wed inextricably to the theoretical perspective undergirding the program" (p. 8).

4. A final feature of the programs, especially in social studies and
   elementary education as distinct from physical education, was the
   promotion of a critical approach to curriculum and instruction
   where school was viewed as a place for questioning and transforming existing societal injustices and inequalities. According to
   Graham (1991) a critical approach to curriculum and instruction
   tends to reject "the traditional, rational or means-ends approach
   to curriculum . . . [which] is generally consistent with a focus on
   the technical aspects of teaching" (p. 9).

Graham suggested two implications of this work for the practice of
teacher education in physical education. First was that the development
of critical, inquiring teachers must become a primary goal of all PETE
programs, and she suggested works by Van Manen (1977), Schon (1987),
and Zeichner and Liston (1987) as a guide in the developments of these
efforts. More recent works in physical education by Sebren (1995) and
Tsangaridou and O'Sullivan (1994) may also be useful here. Graham
challenged teacher educators to determine at what stage in PETE programs each of the dimensions of reflection (technical as distinct from
critical) might be emphasized. Graham's second implication was that
personnel can make or break a program. While there is little likelihood
that what happens in one quality program can be generalized to another,
knowledge of the literature can "serve as a stimulus for discussions by
teacher educators about the purpose, process, and intended outcomes of
their own programs" (p. 13).

A FRAMEWORK FOR THINKING ABOUT
TEACHER EDUCATION CURRICULUM

Regardless of one's position on the key issues in reforming teacher education, an important question remains as to what makes for coherent or
effective professional preparation programs for prospective physical education teachers? Let us start with the question, "What do we know about
how to prepare teachers who will conduct quality instructional programs
in schools?"

EVALUATING THE QUALITY
OF PETE PROGRAMS

Any discussion of quality must first address the question, "What or who
determines quality?" My view is that the quality of any teacher education
program should be judged against the specific goals articulated for that

program. In other words, a program that emphasizes an academic orientation ought to be judged on criteria pertinent to that program. Needless to say, the ultimate gauge of a teacher education program, whatever its orientation, is the learning achieved by graduates of that teacher education program and their students. However, for reasons that are technical (availability of equipment and facilities, time allocation, etc., which affect students' learning and measurements of learning) and economic (access to funds for expensive longitudinal research is almost nonexistent), such stringent criteria are difficult if not impossible to apply in researching the effectiveness of teacher education programs.

THE KNOWLEDGE BASE

Keep in mind throughout this chapter that though recent research on teacher education will be cited, we have much more knowledge about how to educate teachers than we have the will or ability to translate those findings into teacher education programs. Locke's (1984) concern about the lack of a knowledge base on how to help teachers learn—as compared to what they need to learn —is no longer valid, as current research on sport pedagogy is now more focused on teachers and learning to teach than on research on teaching (Bain, 1990). Locke's (1984) premise about research and the key to PETE reform is worth repeating here:

> "It is naive to believe that research is both necessary and sufficient to effect comprehensive reform in teacher education. A great many of the problems that bedevil teacher educators cannot be solved by research at all. The point at which experts do agree is that major policy issues in our field will be decided in the political arena on the basis of economic and social considerations (Howey & Gardner, 1983) rather than on the basis of research. Caution and a lot of modesty become anyone who wants to work at improving the education of teachers." (p. 5)

THE CENTRAL QUESTION OF TEACHER EDUCATION

Answering the question about the most appropriate content and pedagogy for PETE poses another: What does one see as the central issue of teacher education? According to Tinning (1993), for some the central issues are "How can we train student teachers to become effective teachers?" and "How can we best develop the teaching skills of student teachers?" An example here is warranted. Rickard and Boswell (1991) recently laid out a framework for the design of a teacher education physical education program to influence the teaching abilities of preservice teachers "so that they experience satisfying levels of success in their student teaching and later, in their first teaching position" (p. 31). In describing the knowledge base for these trainees, Rickard and Boswell included

- the knowledge of content rooted in games, gymnastics, and dance (a specific view of content as described earlier),
- subject matter of allied fields (motor development and motor learning are mentioned),
- knowledge of generic pedagogical skills shared by effective teachers in general (reference to teaching effectiveness literature, yet recognizing the importance of linking pedagogy to a specific content domain as in pedagogical content knowledge), and
- conceptualizing year-long school curricula.

Such a model promotes a view of teaching as the development of technical expertise.

For others, the critical issue of teacher education centers around how to educate teachers who reflect on their work from a critical social perspective (Tinning, 1993). Such a model focuses more attention on teaching as a moral and ethical enterprise, forcing teachers to address the consequences of their teaching and their choice of curricular content on pupils' *attitudes* toward physical education. McKay, Gore, and Kirk (1990) laid out general guidelines for a critical teacher education. They suggested:

"[First,] Prospective teachers must understand physical education within the historical and contemporary relations of power between genders, classes, and ethnic groups. Second, neophytes must learn to question how and why physical education takes on its current form and content and be sensitive to the social construction of physical education knowledge." (O'Sullivan, Siedentop & Locke, 1992, p. 275)

These examples are not meant to convey an "either/or" perspective to the design of teacher education programs but to suggest that most programs tend to emphasize one perspective more that the other. Graham (1991) suggested that both perspectives are necessary in the design of PETE programs. Whitson and McIntosh (1990), McKay et al. (1990), and Kirk (1989), would suggest that the more technical orientation to teaching (as I have characterized the Rickard and Boswell framework) is more prevalent in teacher education, and they would rather see a more reflective approach to teacher education as represented by the writings of Bain (1990), Kirk (1989), and Tinning (1992).

STUDENTS OF TEACHING

Regardless of one's perspective of teaching, Tinning (1993) reminds us that in our deliberations about quality programs we cannot ignore the voices of prospective teachers. Locke's (1984) monograph on "Research on Teaching Teachers: Where Are We Now?" was all but silent on preservice teachers' perspectives. We have made significant inroads on this topic in the last decade. Thus I start with a discussion of what we know about recruits to physical education teaching and the potential impact of that literature on the content and design of quality teacher education programs.

IMPORTANCE OF THE ISSUE

What we know about the students of teaching can affect directly the quality of a teacher education program. The growing knowledge base about incoming teacher recruits is critical if we are to design programs built on the assumption that their beliefs and values must be understood and addressed if those programs are to have a substantive impact on their views of teaching and learning in physical education (Dewar & Lawson, 1984; Doolittle, Dodds, Placek, 1993; Hutchinson, 1993; Hutchinson & Johnson, 1993–4; Lortie, 1975). Lortie (1975) took what might be viewed as an extreme position when deciding on the relative merits of one's previous professional experiences and teacher education program when he suggested that biography and pre-career experiences are more important than teacher education. Feiman-Nemser (1983) argued that recruits' beliefs about teaching filter what they are exposed to during their professional education and most adopt ideas from these programs that fit already existing beliefs derived from past experiences. Doolittle et al. (1993) found that incomplete teaching perspectives often "constitute a weak base for the professional identities that formal training tries to shape" (p. 355). As Lawson (1983) suggested, "The concept of successful induction is one in which a recruit's inaccurate subjective warrant is replaced by a new self-image forged out of new ideological commitments and newly acquired knowledge and skill" (p. 13). Lawson (1983) defined the subjective warrant as "each person's perceptions of the requirements for teacher education and for actual teaching in schools" (p. 6). Doolittle et al. (1993) summarized the knowledge base to date on PETE recruits, noting that: "We know that teaching recruits enter professional training programs already having formed images of themselves as teachers (Hutchinson, 1993), exuding high confidence in their own abilities to teach, and being unrealistically optimistic that they will be better able to solve daily problems of teaching than their fellow recruits" (p. 356).

IMPLICATIONS FOR TEACHER EDUCATION

The dominant view of new recruits is that they perceive physical education as being primarily skill oriented, prefer coaching to teaching, and are more conservative than other teachers. Implications for teacher education are obvious and have been frequently cited in that literature. They include:

1. Grounding teacher education programs in the past experiences of new recruits and allowing them to develop an awareness and an appreciation for the legitimacy of their professional history. (Graber, 1991; Schempp, 1989).
2. Ensuring that preservice teachers are prepared to design programs for pupils that serve all students, not only the interests of the skilled and competitive students. Teacher educators must examine carefully what skills and beliefs prospective teachers actually take away from the program, as distinct from the beliefs and skills that were intended by the program (Dewar, 1989).
3. Convincing recruits that learning to teach is a career-long process which involves much more than a love for children (Graber, 1989), as important as that may be.
4. Providing opportunities in the teacher education program for recruits to examine and challenge the structure and function of physical education and sport in a male-dominated society (Bain, 1990; Griffin, 1989).
5. Insuring that supervisors (cooperating teachers and university personnel) recognize that the primary focus of novices is their survival as students, not as teachers. Addressing these concerns and how they might influence their engagement with teacher education assignments is a priority if teacher educators are to acquire positive leverage in shaping preservice students' views (Graber, 1989).

Several studies in physical education have used the Teacher Concern Questionnaire (TCQ) devised by Fuller and Borich (1974) to access teachers' concerns from a developmental perspective. The constructs measure a teacher's concern with self, teaching, tasks, and impact of teaching on students. Results suggest that novice teachers and preservice teachers are more concerned with issues of self, while experienced teachers are more concerned with the impact of their teaching on their students. The results of studies in physical education have been varied, with mixed support for the developmental premise (Wendt, Bain, & Jackson, 1981). Several researchers suggest its contribution to improving teacher education preparation lies in providing supervisory personnel with information on the nature of preservice teachers' concerns that will help focus their assistance to novice teachers (Behets, 1990; Boggess, McBride, & Griffey, 1985; Fung, 1993).

PROGRAM CONTENT FOR PETE: A FRAMEWORK FOR ESSENTIAL TEACHER EDUCATION?

What are the essential elements of content knowledge in physical education? To address this issue, I have drawn on Shulman's (1987) framework of a knowledge base for teacher education.

SHULMAN'S ANALYSIS OF THE
ESSENTIAL KNOWLEDGE BASE

Shulman describes the knowledge base of teaching and different ways of knowing that are important for teachers and necessary for successful practice. Three of Shulman's categories include content knowledge, pedagogical knowledge, and pedagogical content knowledge.

Content Knowledge

What is the appropriate content knowledge for physical education trainees? Recent Academy papers (Corbin & Eckert, 1990) highlighted the struggle over the nature of essential subject matter in our profession. There are some who feel that the essential content for preservice teachers should be closely aligned to physical education in current K–12 schools (sport, games, and fitness activities). Others argue that undergraduate curriculum content should focus on the subdisciplines of physical education (sport psychology, exercise physiology, biomechanics, etc.), with pedagogists then helping prospective teachers apply this "foundational knowledge base" to helping children learn sport, games, and so on.

Those who advocate a teacher education content curriculum aligned with what is taught in K–12 schools disagree considerably about the nature of that content. Some support a sport and games content. Siedentop has been an advocate of this approach, with his Sport Education model (see his chapter in this book). Others advocate the need for what might be described as a more "balanced" presentation of physical activities, recognizing the interests and abilities of all students, not just those girls and boys who benefit from a competitive, "male model of sport" (Wright, 1995).

Those who support curriculum content that reflects more direct links with K–12 physical education content, however defined, face consistent erosion of program time in the physical education undergraduate curriculum for activity performance courses. Siedentop (1989) suggested that "we have arrived at a point in our history where we can now prepare teachers who are pedagogically more skillful than ever, but who in many cases are so unprepared in the content area they would be described as 'ignorant' if the content were a purely cognitive knowledge field (p. 3)." Siedentop noted that no matter how well educated prospective teachers were in the pedagogical domain, they will fail unless they have more time to develop direct expertise in sport forms. The consequence of this deficiency in PETE programs has been, according to Siedentop, teachers who are "ill-equipped to teach anything beyond a beginning unit of activity" (p. 9).

In describing the decline of activity coursework in undergraduate physical education, Siedentop (1989) suggested that the root problem is that the study of

> "sport skill and strategy through experiential learning is not considered of sufficient academic quality to form the core of an undergraduate degree program. Learning basketball, volleyball, and gymnastics—and all the associated issues of training, technique, performance, and strategy—are not worthy of formal academic credit as the central foci of a preprofessional program. If we cannot confront that core problem, and somehow resolve it, physical education in schools is doomed." (p. 8)

Pedagogical Knowledge

Yet Siedentop himself has been ambivalent about the relative importance of content knowledge as compared to pedagogical knowledge in a teacher education program. He has devoted much of his academic career to building the pedagogical knowledge base in physical education in a teacher education curriculum. In another presentation at the 1989 AAHPERD convention, Siedentop (1990) advocated a greater emphasis on pedagogical knowledge, stating that "all failures in teaching derive from a lack of pedagogical skill rather than an inadequate subject matter knowledge" (p. 33). This ambivalence may be representative of the confusion among pedagogy researchers on the relative importance of these two curricular areas in improving PETE programs.

Combining Content and Pedagogical Knowledge

In making a case for the importance of both subject matter knowledge and pedagogical content knowledge in teaching physical education, Tinning (1992) drew on Arnold's (1988) distinction between weak and strong practical knowledge in physical education. Practical knowledge in the weak sense is demonstrated by an individual who can perform an activity (is physically able to do something) but cannot articulate how it is done. Practical knowledge in the strong sense is demonstrated by an individual who can both physically perform an activity or skill and articulate how it is done (Tinning, 1992, p. 3).

Tinning noted that practical knowledge in the weak sense is of little use to teachers, but practical knowledge in the strong sense is to their advantage. Because possessing knowledge about a movement or sport without being able to perform it is a typical occurrence in the coaching world (for example, gymnastic coaches who teach stunts they cannot perform), Tinning (1992) argued that the "essential knowledge for a physical education teacher is knowledge about (i.e., prepositional knowledge) how to perform a practical activity and the corresponding ways of organizing the graded progressive practice necessary to acquire the skill. Being able to also perform the skill might be a bonus but it is not a necessity" (p. 11).

Tinning suggested that while prospective teachers must have practical experiences in sport forms which make up school curricula, performance competence was not absolutely necessary. While teachers may have better insights and understandings of an activity if they can perform it themselves, Tinning believed time devoted to developing such competence is a luxury rather than a necessity. Thomas (1990) has strong commitments to physical activity as a core of any physical education undergraduate program, though he does not address what mastery or expertise might mean. Without such a focus, he asks, "What will happen to a field of study in which the scholars have not mastered and do not understand through experience the essential nature of the field—movement? . . . Simply stated, one who has no expertise in a sport cannot study the skilled nature of the behavior satisfactorily" (pp. 10–11).

PEDAGOGICAL AND PEDAGOGICAL CONTENT KNOWLEDGE: IMPLICATIONS FOR TEACHER EDUCATION

Most teacher educators would recognize the significant contribution of research on pedagogical knowledge (Doyle, 1986; Doyle, 1990; Silverman, 1994; Waxman & Walberg, 1991), and more recently on pedagogical content knowledge (Griffey & Housner, 1991; Rovegno, 1991; Shulman, 1987), to our understanding of learning to teach. A large database exists that describes the skills and knowledge necessary for the management and design of quality instruction in physical education. However, there remain some outliers in the field (Wade, 1991) who insist that "after 20 years there is no published research base that details a systematic investigation of the teaching of physical education, which our current group of students might reflect upon and utilize in developing their own skills as practicing teachers" (p. 209).

In reality, most teacher educators recognize the importance of that knowledge base in developing effective teachers, though most agree that it alone is not sufficient for excellent teacher education (see Rink's and other relevant chapters in this book).

ANALYSIS OF MOVEMENT AND STEP SEQUENCING

Learning to teach also includes the ability of trainees to analyze human movement. It ties together one's knowledge of content with knowledge of pedagogy and one's ability to detect errors with one's knowledge of the appropriate sequence of steps to help students improve their performance. Dodds (1994) noted that "expert teachers of motor skills are qualitatively different from novices in their abilities to detect errors and appropriate aspects of performance" (p. 157). Novices have difficulty extracting the relevant clues from the environment to help their students, and much work has been done to provide teacher educators with a solid understanding of how to do this (Gangstead & Beveridge, 1984; Pinheiro & Simon, 1992). Barrett and her colleagues (Barrett, Allison, & Bell, 1987) have demonstrated that undergraduate physical education majors can learn to detect errors and respond effectively to motor patterns exhibited by their students when they are directly taught observational skills over several field experiences.

The work of my colleagues and several doctoral students at Ohio State has convinced me that a teacher education program must devote substantial time to teaching trainees how to observe and critique athletic performance of novice and intermediate athletes, either using a performance principles approach (Matanin, 1993) or a critical incident approach (Rush, 1990; Wilkinson, 1991). Although there is not currently significant evidence to empirically support my position, I believe time devoted to skill analysis competency, to observe and critique athletic performance, "may provide a better payoff than time spent developing the skill competencies of preservice teachers beyond an introductory level in physical activity content areas" (O'Sullivan & Doutis, 1994).

TEACHER THINKING

In time, research on teacher thinking will also affect teacher education programs. Researchers have used methods such as think aloud, stimulated recall, and process tracing to capture teachers' thought processes. At this stage there is considerable disagreement about the practical value of these findings for the content and practice of teacher education (Clark & Lampert, 1986; Floden & Klinzing, 1990; Shulman, 1986). The case of teacher planning is instructive. The results from research on teacher planning in general education (Clark, 1988; Clark & Dunn, 1992; Clark & Lampert, 1986) and physical education (Stroot & Morton, 1989) show that planning does affect instruction but that teachers do not follow the rational planning model which has been the major strategy used in the professional preparation of teachers. According to Floden and Klinzing (1990): "Current research has yet to provide concrete suggestions for these routines. Perhaps the best teacher educators can do now is to help teachers revise the rational [curriculum] model so that it can be suited to [actual] practice without completely losing its desirable emphasis on the relationship between teaching aims and instructional choices" (p. 18).

RELATING PEDAGOGY TO SUBJECT MATTER

A growing body of literature on teachers' practical knowledge has highlighted the significance of helping undergraduates tie their knowledge of pedagogy to their knowledge of the subject matter—what Shulman (1986)

has termed pedagogical content knowledge (PCK). Shulman defined pedagogical content knowledge as:

> "the most useful forms of representation of those ideas, the most
> powerful analogies, illustrations, examples, explanations, and demon-
> strations—-in a word, the ways of transforming the subject that make
> it comprehensible to others. Pedagogical content knowledge also in-
> cludes an understanding of what makes the learning of specific topics
> easy or difficult: the conceptions and preconceptions that students of
> different ages and backgrounds bring with them to the learning of
> those most frequently taught topics and lessons." (pp. 9–10)

Grossman (1991), in a review of the literature on pedagogical content
knowledge, laid out several implications for teacher education. First,
teacher educators need to take "teachers' prior knowledge of a subject more
seriously" (p. 212). Second, the mismatch between college coursework in
a subject and the K–12 curriculum requires that courses on "subject
specific methods [can] help bridge these gaps by incorporating substantive
discussions about central topics in the field" (p. 212). According to Grossman, "Teachers need pedagogical maps of content, the understanding of
a subject from an explicitly pedagogical perspective that enables teachers
to track students' misunderstandings and guide them toward new conceptions" (p. 213). Given the importance of content knowledge and pedagogical content knowledge, Grossman (1991) advocated a rethinking of the
generalist view of an elementary and middle school teacher and exploring
the potential for building subject matter expertise within collaborative
teaching teams.

In a recent issue of *Quest,* Housner and French (1994) reviewed the
growing knowledge base on teacher expertise and pedagogical content
knowledge in physical education. Dodds (1994) concluded that expert
physical educators have richer, more substantive cognitive representa-
tions of their subject matter, instructional strategies, and the nature
of their students than do novice teachers. Griffey and Housner (1991)
demonstrated marked differences in the planning, interaction, and student engagement for experienced and inexperienced teachers. Novices
reacted to surface issues in the classroom and were more prone to shift
activities during lessons for no obvious curricular reasons. Novices seem to
be caught up in the present moment and, while the routines of experienced
teachers are few, novices do not yet possess them.

A number of modifications to teacher education programs to develop
more sophisticated knowledge about preservice teachers have been suggested in the literature. Berliner (1986) suggested the development and
use of scripted lessons in early field work so that student teachers can
concentrate on ways of presenting the content to students that are both
meaningful and challenging. Livingston and Borko (1989) suggested that
students do less field work and be assigned to teach in areas for which they
have strong content preparation and know the content well in advance.

PROGRAM DESIGN

What do we know about the scope and sequence of content for a teacher education program? Where should subject matter content be introduced and emphasized? When is the most effective time to provide coursework on pedagogy and pedagogical content knowledge? What type of field experiences should be structured for prospective teachers? When and how often? These are some of the questions for which the current literature provides few solid clues. Given the limitations of chapter length, I am going to confine this discussion to what we know about the scope and sequence of field work and student teaching and the implications of that knowledge for how we organize this component of PETE programs.

Much has been written about the role of field work in learning to teach. Study after study confirms the critical role of this experience and the significant contribution of cooperating teachers to the preparation of neophyte teachers (Dodds, 1985, 1989; O'Sullivan, 1990; Schempp, 1989). Other studies recognize that, at times, the influence of poorly organized and unstructured field work on prospective teachers can be weak, contradictory, and ambiguous (O'Sullivan & Tsangaridou, 1992).

EFFECT OF FIELD WORK ON PRESERVICE TEACHERS

In a recent study, Jones (1992) sought to determine how field experiences influenced students to confirm or question their career choices. Positive student reactions and positive feedback from their cooperating teachers were two key factors that confirmed physical education teaching as their career choice. Three factors—off-task student behavior, off-task class behavior, and nonmotivated students during lessons—caused preservice teachers to question their career choices. Jones' study reaffirmed the importance of careful attention to site selection for field experiences, appropriate training of cooperating teachers for their role as teacher educators, and carefully designed opportunities for student teachers to be debriefed on their teaching experiences.

Several studies on field experiences have demonstrated that student teachers become more custodial during student teaching (Schempp, 1989; Templin, 1979) and that sometimes field experiences, if not properly structured and supervised, can be misinterpreted, teaching trainees false ideas, such as that pupil learning is not a high priority. Studies show that preservice teachers attend more to classroom management than to other topics and focus their attention on ensuring that children are busy, happy, and good. Recognizing this is one thing, but knowing how to intervene effectively is another matter. The university supervisor's limited observations and lack of time in the schools reduces the credibility of his or her feedback in the eyes of the cooperating teacher and student teacher. Teaching styles and attitudes of preservice teachers are primarily influenced through the direct tutelage of the cooperating teacher (Randall, 1992). We do know that the cooperating teachers play a key role in this process; their opportunities and willingness to buy into a collaborative educational mission with university personnel are critical. However, assuring that these opportunities are provided is not easy.

DEALING WITH OBSTACLES TO EFFECTIVE FIELD EXPERIENCE SUPERVISION

Randall (1992) highlighted several key obstacles to the effective supervision of field experiences:

1. Students are not prepared for their teaching assignments in schools and do not exhibit the curiosity about the process of becoming a teacher.
2. Lack of communication between university and school supervisors.
3. Lack of a shared understanding of the respective role of each triad member (student, cooperating teacher, university supervisor) in the supervision process.
4. Student teachers lack the kinds of managerial and organizational skills considered necessary by the cooperating teacher.
5. Development of inconsistent goals for student teaching, related to issue 4 above.

In a review of the student teaching literature, Dodds (1989, p. 83) noted that research on field experience is scarce when it comes to providing professors clues about "how they might be more deliberate and effective in using field experiences to intensify their programmatic message to trainees." Dodds presented several guidelines for teacher educators to consider in the development of more effective field experiences:

1. All people associated with field experience don't necessarily share the same teaching perspectives, and thus no training program will strongly affect its students until the perspectives of all participants become broadly similar.
2. Teacher educators must design deliberately progressive, sequential, and well timed field experiences. These experiences must support the programmatic teaching perspective and provide opportunities for trainees to compare and contrast their views of teaching with their education program and the cooperating teachers or clinical educators with whom they are working.
3. Teacher educators must explore implications of sport within field experiences by encouraging open discussion about the effects of sport when its messages are elitist, sexist, and/or homophobic.

4. Teacher educators must attempt to ensure that the processes of reflection and choice become interwoven and apparent in field experiences. A haphazard series of field experiences does little to ensure that a programmatic perspective is transmitted to trainees.

O'Sullivan and Tsangaridou (1992) found that PETE programs producing prospective teachers who show concern for student learning and their teaching effectiveness in learning settings advocate a shared vision (of faculty and school personnel), reflective inquiry, and sequenced, programmatic efforts to studying teaching and use their findings to develop a research-based teacher education program. They also concluded that well constructed, early field experiences can provide opportunities for preservice teachers to explore their understandings of teaching, schooling, and the role of the teacher in educating youth. In short, effective programs provide prospective teachers with knowledge about good teaching and with supervision which enables them to practice and reflect on this knowledge.

In a follow-up study, Tsangaridou and O'Sullivan (1994) showed that carefully designed, reflective assignments help prospective teachers to focus on social and ethical aspects of the teaching and learning setting as well as on the technical aspects of teaching, where much of their initial concern lies (Graber, 1991). These assignments also improved the quality of their reflection, from mere descriptive accounts of teaching events to justifications and critiques of the consequences of their actions for students' behaviors and students' feelings toward each other and their subject matter. Such efforts are small but promising steps in equipping students with the "conceptual apparatus, understandings, and strategies to recognize and engage the hidden learnings present in all teaching" (Tinning, 1992, p. 17).

It is critical, it seems to me, that whatever view of good teaching we hold, we spend more time and energy studying how best to realize our specific visions of PETE programs and produce teachers who embody that view. While we each pursue our vision of what it means to be a good teacher and what it means to have a program that produces such educators, let us support each other in our work and ensure that all of us consciously and otherwise (Bain, 1990) are preparing professionals who will help students enjoy our subject matter in ways that are exciting, accessible, and attentive to their diverse needs.

REFERENCES

Arnold, P. (1988). *Education, movement and the curriculum*. London: The Falmer Press.

Bain, L.L. (1990). Physical education teacher education. In W.R. Houston (Ed.), *Handbook of research on teacher education* (pp. 758–781). New York: Macmillan.

Barrett, K., Allison, P., & Bell, R. (1987). What preservice physical education teachers see in an unguided field experience: A follow up study. *Journal of Teaching in Physical Education, 7,* 12–21.

Behets, D. (1990). Concerns of pre-service physical education teachers. *Journal of Teaching in Physical Education, 10,* 66–75.

Berliner, D. (1986). In pursuit of the expert pedagogue. *Educational Researcher, 15,* 5–13.

Boggess, T., McBride, R., & Griffey, D. (1985). The concerns of physical education student teachers: A developmental view. *Journal of Teaching in Physical Education, 4,* 202–211.

Brophy, J., & Good, T. (1986). Teacher behavior and student achievement. In M. Wittrock (Ed.), *Handbook of research on teaching* (3rd ed., pp. 328–375). New York: Macmillan.

Carnegie Forum on Education and the Economy, Task Force on Teaching as a Profession. (1986). *A nation prepared: Teachers for the 21st century.* New York: Author.

Clark, C.M. (1988). Asking the right questions about teacher preparation: Contributions of research on teacher thinking. *Educational Researcher, 17*(2), 5–12.

Clark, C., & Dunn, S. (1992). Second-generation research on teachers' planning, intentions, and routines. In H. Waxman & H. Walberg (Eds.), *Effective teaching: Current research* (pp. 183–202). Berkeley, CA: McCutchan.

Clark, C.M., & Lampert, M. (1986). The study of teacher thinking: Implications for teacher education. *Journal of Teacher Education, 37*(5), 27–31.

Corbin, C., & Eckert, H. (1990). *The evolving undergraduate major. American Academy of Physical Education Papers, No. 23.* Champaign, IL: Human Kinetics.

Dewar, A. (1989). Recruitment in physical education teaching: Toward a critical approach. In T. Templin & P. Schempp (Eds.), *Socialization into physical education: Learning to teach* (pp. 39–58). Indianapolis: Benchmark Press.

Dewar, A., & Lawson, H. (1984). The subjective warrant and recruitment into physical education. *Quest, 36,* 15–25.

Dodds, P. (1985). Delusions of "worth-it-ness": Field experiences in elementary physical education teacher education. In H. Hoffman & J. Rink (Eds.), *Proceedings on the Second Conference on Preparing the Physical Education Specialist for Children* (pp. 90–109). Reston, VA: American Alliance for Health, Physical Education, Recreation and Dance.

Dodds, P. (1989). Trainees, field experience, and socialization into teaching. In T.J. Templin & P.G. Schempp (Eds.), *Socialization into physical education: Learning to teach* (pp. 81–104). Indianapolis: Benchmark Press.

Dodds, P. (1994). Cognitive and behavioral components of expertise in teaching physical education. *Quest, 46,* 153–163.

Doolittle, S., Dodds, P., & Placek, J. (1993). Persistence of beliefs about teaching during formal training of preservice teachers. *Journal of Teaching in Physical Education, 12,* 355–365.

Doyle, W. (1986). Classroom organization and management. In M. Wittrock (Ed.), *Handbook of research on teaching* (pp. 392–431). New York: Macmillan.

Doyle, W. (1990). Themes in teacher education. In R. Houston (Ed.), *Handbook of research on teacher education* (pp. 3–24). New York: Macmillan.

Feiman-Nemser, S. (1983). Learning to teach. In L. Shulman & G. Sykes (Eds.), *Handbook of teaching and policy* (pp. 150–170). New York: Longman.

Feiman-Nemser, S. (1990). Teacher preparation: Structural and conceptual alternatives. In R. Houston (Ed.), *Handbook of research on teacher education* (pp. 212–233). New York: Macmillan.

Floden, R.E., & Klinzing, H.G. (1990). What can research on teacher thinking contribute to teacher preparation? A second opinion. *Educational Researcher, 19*(5), 15–20.

Fuller, F., & Borich, G. (1974). *Teacher concern checklist: An instrument for measuring concerns of self, task, and impact.* Austin, TX: Research Center for Teacher Education. University of Texas at Austin.

Fung, L. (1993). Concerns among physical educators with varying years of teaching experience. *The Physical Educators, 50*(1), 8–12.

Gangstead, S., & Beveridge, S. (1984). The implementation and evaluation of a methodological approach to qualitative sport skill analysis instruction. *Journal of Teaching in Physical Education, 3,* 60–70.

Graber, K.C. (1989). Teaching tomorrow's teachers: Professional socialization as an agent of socialization. In T. Templin & P. Schempp (Eds.), *Socialization into physical education: Learning to teach* (pp. 59–80). Indianapolis: Benchmark Press.

Graber, K.C. (1991). Studentship in preservice teacher education: A qualitative study of undergraduates in physical education. *Research Quarterly for Exercise and Sport, 62,* 41–51.

Graham, K. (1991). The influence of teacher education on preservice development: Beyond a custodial orientation. *Quest, 43*(1), 1–19.

Griffey, D., & Housner, L. (1991). Differences between experienced and inexperienced teachers' planning decisions, interactions, student engagement, and instructional climate. *Research Quarterly for Exercise and Sport, 62,* 196–204.

Griffin, P. (1989). Gender as a socializing agent in physical education. In T. Templin & P. Schempp (Eds.), *Socialization into physical education: Learning to teach* (pp. 219–234). Indianapolis: Benchmark Press.

Grossman, P. (1991). Mapping the terrain: Knowledge growth in teaching. In H.C. Waxman & H.J. Walberg (Eds.), *Effective teaching: Current research* (pp. 203–215). Berkeley, CA: McCutchan.

Gudmundsdottir, S. (1990). Values in pedagogical content knowledge. *Journal of Teacher Education, 41*(3), 44–52.

Holmes Group. (1986). *Tomorrow's teachers.* East Lansing, MI: Author.

Housner, L., & French, K. (1994). Expertise in learning, performance, and instruction in sport and physical activity, *Quest, 46,* 149–152.

Howey, K., & Gardner, W. (Eds.). (1983). *The education of teachers.* New York: Longman.

Howey, K., & Zimpher, N. (1989). *Profiles of preservice teacher education: Inquiry into the nature of programs.* Albany, NY: SUNY Press.

Hutchinson, G. (1993). Prospective teachers' perspectives on teaching physical education: An interview study on the recruitment phase of teacher socialization. *Journal of Teaching in Physical Education, 12,* 344–354.

Hutchinson, G., & Johnson, B. (1993-1994). Teaching as a career: Examining high school students' perspectives. *Action in Teacher Education, 15*(4), 61–65.

Jones, R. (1992). Student teachers: Incidents that lead them to confirm or question their career choice. *Physical Educator, 49,* 205–212.

Kirk, D. (1989). The orthodoxy in RT-PE and the research/practice gap: A critique and an alternative view. *Journal of Teaching in Physical Education, 8,* 123–130.

Lawson, H. (1983). Toward a model of teacher socialization in physical education: The subjective warrant, recruitment, and teacher education. *Journal of Teaching in Physical Education, 2,* 3–16.

Livingston, C., & Borko, H. (1989). Expert-novice: Differences in teaching: A cognitive analysis and implications for teacher education. *Journal of Teacher Education, 40*(4), 36–42.

Locke, L. (1984). Research on teaching teachers: Where are we now? *Journal of Teaching in Physical Education Monograph, 2.*

Lortie, D. (1975). *Schoolteacher: A sociological study.* Chicago: University of Chicago Press.

Matanin, M. (1993). Effects of performance principle training on correct analysis and diagnosis of motor skills. *Dissertation Abstracts International, 54,* 1724A. (University Microfilms No. 9325550)

McKay, J., Gore, J., & Kirk, D. (1990). Beyond the limits of technocratic physical education. *Quest, 42,* 52–76.

O'Sullivan, M. (1990). Physical education teacher education in the United States. *Journal of Physical Education, Recreation and Dance, 61*(2), 41–45.

O'Sullivan, M., & Doutis, P. (1994). Research on expertise: Guideposts for expertise and teacher education in physical education. *Quest, 46,* 176–185.

O'Sullivan, M., Siedentop, D., & Locke, L. (1992). Toward collegiality: Competing viewpoints among teacher educators. *Quest, 44,* 266–280.

O'Sullivan, M., & Tsangaridou, N. (1992). What undergraduate physical education majors learn during a field experience. *Research Quarterly for Exercise and Sport, 63,* 381–392.

Pinheiro, V., & Simon, H. (1992). An operational model of motor skill diagnosis. *Journal of Teaching in Physical Education, 11,* 288–302.

Randall, L. (1992). *Systematic supervision for physical education.* Champaign, IL: Human Kinetics.

Rickard, L., & Boswell, B. (1991). A framework for preservice instructional development. *Journal of Physical Education, Recreation and Dance, 61*(5), 31–32, 75–76.

Rink, J. (1993). Teacher education: A focus on action. *Quest, 45,* 308–320.

Rovegno, I. (1991). A participant-observation study of knowledge restructuring in a field-based elementary physical education methods course. *Research Quarterly for Exercise and Sport, 62,* 205–212.

Rush, D. (1990). *Improving skill analysis for diving.* Unpublished doctoral dissertation, The Ohio State University, Columbus, OH.

Schempp, P. (1989). Apprenticeship-of-observation and the development of physical education teachers. In T. Templin & P. Schempp (Eds.), *Socialization into physical education: Learning to teach* (pp. 13–38). Indianapolis: Benchmark Press.

Schon, D. (1987). *The reflective practitioner.* New York: Basic Books.

Sebren, A. (1995). Preservice teachers' reflection and knowledge development in a field-based elementary physical education methods course. *Journal of Teaching in Physical Education, 14,* 262-283.

Shulman, L. (1986). Those who understand: Knowledge growth in teaching. *Educational Researcher, 15,* 4–14.

Shulman, L. (1987). Knowledge and teaching: Foundations of the new reform. *Harvard Educational Review, 57*(1), 1–22.

Siedentop, D. (1989, April). *Content knowledge for physical education.* Paper presented at the Curriculum and Instruction Academy on the Implications of the Knowledge Base for Teaching and Teacher Education, at the Annual AAHPERD convention, Boston.

Siedentop, D. (1990). Undergraduate teacher preparation. In C. Corbin & H. Eckert (Eds.), *The evolving undergraduate major. American Academy of Physical Education Papers, No. 23* (pp. 28–34). Champaign, IL: Human Kinetics.

Silverman, S. (1994). Communication and motor skill learning: What we learn from research in the gymnasium. *Quest, 46,* 345–355.

Sparkes, A. (1989). Paradigmatic confusions and the evasion of critical issues in naturalistic research. *Journal of Teaching in Physical Education, 8,* 131–151.

Sparkes, A. (Ed.) (1992). *Research in physical education and sport: Exploring alternative visions.* London: Falmer Press.

Stroot, S., & Morton, P. (1989). Blueprints for learning. *Journal of Teaching in Physical Education, 8,* 213–222.

Taggart, A. (1988). The systematic development of teaching skills: A sequence of planned pedagogical experiences. *Journal of Teaching in Physical Education, 8,* 76–86.

Templin, T. (1979). Occupational socialization and the physical education student teacher. *Research Quarterly, 50,* 482–493.

Thomas, J.R. (1990). The body of knowledge: A common core. In C. Corbin & H. Eckert (Eds.), *The evolving undergraduate major. American Academy of Physical Education Papers, No. 23* (pp. 5-15). Champaign, IL: Human Kinetics.

Tinning, R. (July, 1992). *Teacher education and the development of content knowledge for physical education teaching.* Keynote address for the conference on "The place of general and subject matter specific teaching methods in teacher education," Santiago de Compestela, Spain.

Tinning, R. (1993, July). *We have many ways of making you think. Or do we? Reflections on 'training' in reflective teaching.* Invited address to the International Seminar on the Training of Teachers in Reflexive Practice of Physical Education, Trois Rivières, Quebec, PQ.

Tom, A. (1987). The Holmes Group Report: Its latent political agenda. *Teachers College Record, 88,* 430–435.

Tsangaridou, N., & O'Sullivan, M. (1994). Using pedagogical reflective strategies to enhance reflection among preservice physical education teachers. *Journal of Teaching in Physical Education, 14*(1), 13–33.

Van Manen, M. (1977). Linking ways of knowing with ways of being practical. *Curriculum Inquiry, 6,* 205–228.

Wade, M. (1991). Unraveling the Larry and Daryl magical mystery tour. *Quest, 43,* 207–213.

Waxman, H., & Walberg, H. (Eds.). (1991). *Effective teaching: Current research.* Berkeley, CA: McCutchan.

Wendt, J., Bain, L., & Jackson, A. (1981). Fuller's concerns theory as tested on prospective physical educators. *Journal of Teaching in Physical Education, Introductory Issue,* 66–70.

Whitson, D., & Macintosh, D. (1990). The scientization of physical education: Discourses of performance. *Quest, 42,* 40–51.

Wilkinson, S. (1991). A training program for improving undergraduates' analytic skill in volleyball. *Journal of Teaching in Physical Education, 11,* 177–194.

Wright, J. (1995). A feminist poststructuralist methodology for the study of gender construction in physical education: Description of a study. *Journal of Teaching in Physical Education, 15,* 1-24.

Zeichner, K., & Liston, D. (1987). Teaching student teachers to reflect. *Harvard Educational Review, 57*(1), 1–22.

ACKNOWLEDGMENT

I would like to thank Gary Kinchin, doctoral student in Physical Education Teacher Education at The Ohio State University, for his assistance in the retrieval of literature for this chapter.

CHAPTER 16

Organizational Socialization:
Factors Impacting Beginning Teachers

Sandra A. Stroot

Learning to teach is a complex endeavor, with many variables affecting prospective teachers' progress toward success. In order to better understand the process of learning to teach, it is important to examine stages that a prospective teacher may be expected to move through and the impact that the workplace can have on teachers' success. One of the most important times in a teacher's career is the induction phase, which is described as "a transitional period in teacher education between teacher preparation and continuing professional development, during which assistance may be provided and/or assessment may be applied to beginning teachers" (Huling-Austin, Odell, Ishler, Kay, & Edelfelt, 1989, p. 3). Developmental stages, workplace conditions, and their impact on teachers during the first years of teaching will be discussed in this chapter. In addition, strategies for addressing concerns of beginning teachers as they enter the school setting will be suggested.

CAREER DEVELOPMENT OF TEACHERS

Several models have been presented in an attempt to identify and describe developmental stages of preservice (Caruso, 1977; Fuller & Bown, 1975; Sacks & Harrington, 1982; Yarger & Mertens, 1980) and inservice teachers (Burden, 1980; Gregorc, 1973; Katz, 1972; McDonald, 1982; Peterson,

1979; Unruh & Turner, 1970; Yarger & Mertens, 1980). Most teachers are familiar with discussing the developmental stages of children and adapting tasks and activities to meet each child's needs according to these developmental stages. The same concept applies to teacher development. All of the teacher development models represent a continuum, in which teachers move from feelings of anxiety and concerns for survival to mastery of teaching, at which stage they are fully functioning professionals who are able to address the individual cognitive, social, and emotional needs of their students.

A MODEL OF TEACHER DEVELOPMENT

Katz's (1972) model of developmental stages has been chosen to provide a more in-depth description of teacher development. Katz's model illustrates a developmental progression of stages experienced by teachers already in the school context rather than preservice teachers in teacher preparation programs. A brief summary of stages and assistance for inservice teachers is shown in Figure 16.1.

The Stages

Katz organized a teacher's development into four stages.

Survival.   In the first stage, Survival, merely coping on a daily basis was the main concern, and teachers began to question their competence and desire to teach. Katz stated that this stage could last throughout the entire first year. On-site assistance is needed at this time to provide encouragement, reassurance, and specific skills to help teachers adapt to life in the schools. Assistance should be available in the school setting to assure support during the crises of the first year of teaching.

Consolidation.   By the second year, most teachers have entered the Consolidation stage and have begun to focus on problems and needs of individual children. Again, on-site assistance by someone thoroughly familiar with the context is most helpful. Opportunities to discuss a child's characteristics, and strategies to address individual needs of children are important for teachers at this stage. Experienced colleagues and other professionals who can suggest strategies that have worked for them in the past can provide teachers with ideas to implement in their own gymnasiums.

Renewal.   Teachers in the third stage, Renewal, arc now in their third or fourth year of teaching, and have become competent in the practice. Activities and patterns previously established have become routine and boring, and teachers look for new ideas that provide variety in the teaching setting. At this stage, teachers have become interested in new developments in the area of their specialization, and it benefits them to attend

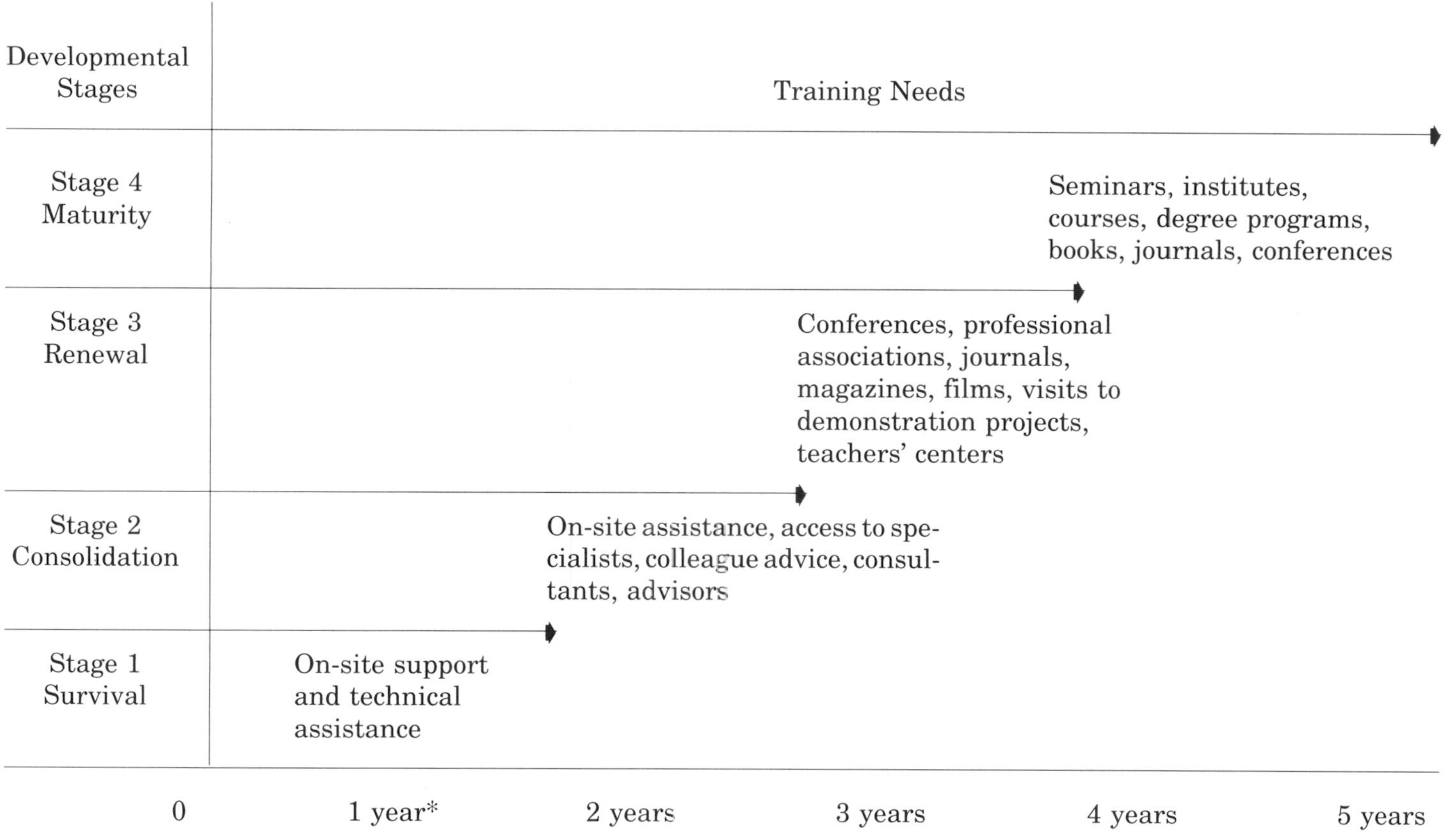

Developmental
Stages

Training Needs

Developmental Stages	0	1 year*	2 years	3 years	4 years	5 years
Stage 4 Maturity					Seminars, institutes, courses, degree programs, books, journals, conferences	
Stage 3 Renewal				Conferences, professional associations, journals, magazines, films, visits to demonstration projects, teachers' centers		
Stage 2 Consolidation			On-site assistance, access to specialists, colleague advice, consultants, advisors			
Stage 1 Survival		On-site support and technical assistance				

*Time periods approximate

Figure 16.1. Stages of development and training needs of preschool teachers

From "Developmental Stages of Preschool Teachers," by L.G. Katz, 1972, *Elementary School Journal*, **73**(1), p. 51. Copyright 1972. Reprinted with permission.

conferences and workshops. Assistance from other teachers at this time comes from exchanging ideas and journals, formal or informal teacher centers, or groups which encourage continued networking are also helpful.

Maturity.   In the final stage, Maturity, teachers begin to ask questions of themselves and their teaching that focus on their insights, perspectives, and beliefs regarding teaching and children. Teachers strive to understand the more subtle meanings of the complex teaching setting. For example, questions may arise regarding the dominant societal values and their impact on disadvantaged children, or examining the appropriateness of state mandates in education. In order to assist teachers as they address these issues, a broad range of reading material and/or conference presentations directed toward changing perspectives would be appropriate.

In addition to these suggestions, it is important for teachers to be able to share their concerns with others at their own stage of development. This reassures teachers that they are not alone, and interactions with others at the same level of development can provide ideas and additional insights to help them overcome the struggles of learning to teach.

Other models mentioned previously follow much the same progression as they examine teacher development over time. Needs of teachers in various stages of development differ, and teacher educators and mentors in school settings must understand these stages if they are to provide appropriate assistance based upon teachers' changing developmental needs.

LEARNING THE ROPES

As we begin to try to understand factors that allow teachers to move through these developmental stages and become effective teachers, we must also understand the process teachers follow as they learn about teaching and what it means to be a teacher. The most prevalent model used to study socialization into physical education has been occupational socialization. Occupational socialization was defined by Lawson (1986) as "all of the kinds of socialization that initially influence persons to enter the field of physical education and that later are responsible for their perceptions and actions as teacher educators and teachers" (p. 107). One important aspect of occupational socialization has been organizational socialization, or "the process by which one is taught and learns 'the ropes' of a particular organizational role" (Van Maanen & Schein, 1979, p. 211). These authors also identified three work orientations that can be adopted by new teachers.

- First, custodial orientation perpetuates the existing system and maintains the status quo.

- Second, content-innovation orientation promotes change in how teachers define and implement the teaching of their own content.
- Third, role innovation redefines the teacher's role as an educator in the school and community context.

These three descriptions reflect different philosophies which influence the amount of control a teacher has over the workplace environment and the process of socialization. Custodial orientation and role innovation, in fact, represent opposite perspectives and outcomes. In the former, the teacher is passive and willing to accept the existing system, and no significant changes occur. In the latter, the teacher is proactive and empowered to make changes and redefine the role of a physical educator in a particular context, and perhaps beyond.

Van Maanen and Schein also described socialization tactics that influence how teachers "learn the ropes" and the outcome of the socialization process. Scenarios representing these tactics were provided by Lawson (1983), as he discussed custodial and innovative orientations. Socialization tactics representing the custodial approach are provided in the first example, and will perpetuate the existing structure. Conversely, the tactics in the second example represent the innovative approach, and will encourage empowerment of the teacher and promote change in the current structure. Examples:

1. Schools with socialization tactics that are collective, sequential, variable, serial, and involve divestiture will breed custodial orientations in new teachers.
2. Schools with socialization tactics that are individual, informal, random, disjunctive, and involve investiture will nurture innovative orientations in new teachers. (p. 7)

Implications for beginning teachers as they are socialized into a new school setting are great. In one sense, the existing system will shape the outcome for the beginning teacher by the socialization tactics in that particular context. Another interpretation is that beginning teachers can become empowered to change the system by choosing socialization strategies that would more likely make these changes possible. The feasibility of beginning teachers making these choices is greatly influenced by the context in which they are working, particularly those conditions that enhance or inhibit their effectiveness.

WORKPLACE CONDITIONS: CREATING A QUALITY ENVIRONMENT

As just mentioned, conditions in which teachers are expected to work are very important to their ability to be effective.

QUALITY OF WORK LIFE INDICATORS

It may be useful to examine Louis and Smith's (1990) Quality of Work Life (QWL) indicators as a framework for understanding workplace conditions as significant variables affecting teaching performance. The intent of these indicators was to "promote working conditions that tangibly contribute to the establishment of a more professional work life and career for teachers" (Louis & Smith, 1990, p. 35). Based on the relationship of organizational contexts to teachers' QWL, seven criteria were identified as indicators of QWL:

- respect from relevant adults;
- participation in decision making;
- frequent and stimulating professional interaction;
- a high sense of efficacy;
- use of skills and knowledge;
- resources to carry out the job; and
- goal congruence.

As Tyson indicated in chapter 4, many factors inherent in the school setting affect teachers' ability to achieve these criteria—and thus their ability to attain the ideal QWL that will enhance teaching performance.

FACTORS AFFECTING QWL

Louis and Smith (1990) also provided specific factors that may serve as reference points toward achieving the seven criteria of QWL. These factors are categorized in three groups and are provided in Figure 16.2.

As teachers enter a school setting, it is important that they begin to examine their workplace conditions relative to the seven QWL indicators and any other relevant environmental influences that may affect their ability to teach. The category of Social/Cultural Changes includes variables which may be the easiest for teachers to control. A teacher can immediately plan a strategy for professional growth, request observations from a trusted peer, and gather information relative to retreats, conferences, and workshops available through the school and professional organizations. Administrative/Political Changes and Technical/Instructional Changes require a different type of intervention, as the extent that these variables can be changed is determined by the institutional flexibility within a system. Although we all know that change cannot be instantly implemented, with persistence, support, and an understanding of criteria that lead toward a quality of work life and enhance the teaching process, change—even systemic change—can (and does) occur.

Social/Cultural Changes	Administrative/ Political Changes	Technical/ Instructional Resources
– Professional growth plans – Expanded teacher roles – Teacher-initiated programs – Peer observations – Retreats or other mechanisms to increase social cohesiveness	– Structures promoting formal participation in making school policy – Strong decentralization to departments	– Restructuring the conditions for teaching and learning: – Alternate schedule – Student empowerment – Parent involvement

In addition, all of the above factors must be examined in light of the local conditions of school-based leadership, students, and the school culture.

Figure 16.2.   Factors that may affect teachers' quality of work life
From "Teacher Working Conditions," by K.S. Louis and B. Smith. In *Teachers and Their Workplace* by P. Reyes (Ed.), 1990, Newbury Park, CA: Sage Publications, Inc. Copyright 1990. Reprinted with permission.

CAREER DEVELOPMENT OF PHYSICAL EDUCATION TEACHERS

What do we know about the people who choose to become physical education teachers? Unfortunately, the information that research has uncovered does not speak favorably about people who enter the physical education profession. Studies have indicated the average grade-point average for students choosing physical education as a profession was lower than university recruits in general (Dewar & Lawson, 1984). Many people who choose physical education for a career, including Judi Sloan, the 1993 Teacher of the Year in the state of Illinois, were average students who received joy and success through physical rather than academic achievements (Williams & Williamson, 1995). As in Judi's case, however, this does not necessarily affect their ability to be effective teachers.

We also know that experiences prior to formal teacher preparation programs have made significant impacts on prospective teachers' decisions to choose physical education as their major area of study (Hutchinson, 1993). Lawson (1983) discussed the experiences throughout life that helped form impressions about sport and the desire to teach, and other research studies have shown that students who choose physical education as a major have had positive experiences in sport (Dewar & Lawson, 1984; Dodds, Placek, Doolittle, Pinkham, Ratliffe, & Portman, 1992). Coaches and physical education teachers were important, positive role models to prospective physical education majors, with coaches being the primary role model for males, and physical education teachers the most influential for females (Dewar, 1989). In addition, the concept called "apprenticeship of observation," which refers to observation and interactions with teachers during pre-college schooling, has influenced prospective teachers' understanding of what it means to be a teacher and of effective teaching (Schempp, 1989). These important people and experiences have helped to guide career choices of physical educators and have influenced the understandings and beliefs of those who have chosen the physical education profession.

Preservice teacher preparation programs play an important role in determining the extent to which beginning teachers are prepared to teach as they enter the school setting. The preservice component of career development is discussed by O'Sullivan in chapter 15 of this book. She indicates that the philosophical base of the teacher preparation program and the strategies used to impart the knowledge of teaching affects the skills and abilities of preservice teachers. Experiences of preservice teachers are important to understand, as they can greatly influence beginning teachers' feelings of success during their initial years of teaching.

INDUCTION INTO THE FIRST YEAR OF TEACHING

In this section, I will identify concerns of beginning teachers in physical education, illustrating these concerns with statements and quotes from various research studies. Also included are stories from beginning teachers who were proactive in their induction year and emerged with feelings of success and accomplishment after their first year of teaching. Suggestions and strategies for assisting teachers as they address concerns much like those mentioned previously are provided, to help make the transition from the university to the school setting a more positive and successful experience for new teachers.

REALITY SHOCK

Reality shock seems to be a major concern of beginning teachers, including physical educators. Reality shock is described as "the collapse of the missionary ideals found during teacher training by the harsh and rude reality of classroom life" (Veenman, 1984, p. 143). When previous experiences do not prepare new teachers for their work environment, overwhelming feelings of inadequacy result in reality shock. The more similar the teaching setting to previous experiences of new teachers, the less reality shock will be an inhibiting factor. Similarly, in a teacher preparation program where teachers are provided with multiple field experiences and opportunities to practice their teaching strategies in diverse settings, less reality shock will occur.

Williams and Williamson (1995) edited a book in which beginning physical education specialists shared some of the important aspects of their first year of teaching in the school setting. Several of these teachers worked in the inner-city schools of Chicago, where the reality of their own lives was very different from the context in which they worked. Statements from several of the teachers reflect the type of reality shock they experienced working with inner-city youth. For example, Tamara's concerns revolved around the students' acceptance of her physical education program. She stated, "I was surprised at the beginning of the year because I thought the kids were going to automatically love everything we were doing. I thought they'd be thrilled to finally have a good PE teacher, but they weren't" (pp. 32–33). Torres stated, "One week there were two shootings outside the school. Thirteen-year-old children were carrying guns and chasing other children" (p. 66). Vince told about his reaction when he realized that a Latin-American boy did not understand English: "I was thrown for a loop at that moment . . . How many times have I stood there talking while the students just looked at me and didn't know what was going on" (p. 39)? Katie commented on her surprise at the issues that she had to address in schools, when she stated, "I never imagined having to deal with substance abuse in my school. I thought that occurred 'somewhere else'" (p. 67). When discussing her expectations about her school setting, Jackie reflected on her critical observations of other teachers, and then stated that she was not realistic about working with students in the cities. She said, "To think I went into this situation thinking it would be great and I didn't have to follow anyone else's structure or rules, it was all up to me . . . It just wasn't like that" (p. 28).

In these examples, the urban setting in which these children lived was reflected in the problems teachers faced in the school setting, and the problems were not familiar to the beginning teachers. They felt helpless and had to learn new strategies for themselves and for their students. In each of these situations, the setting in which these teachers found themselves during their first teaching experience was very different from that which they felt prepared to undertake. Although all of these teachers had early field experiences in urban settings, their new school setting was so different that they experienced a debilitating reality shock as they entered their new position.

Kelley and Mike found teaching positions in school settings which were familiar to them, given their personal and professional backgrounds and experiences. They graduated from a teacher preparation program with several field experiences similar to their first teaching position (O'Sullivan, 1989, p. 240) and found no surprises relative to their responsibilities and expectations. Kelley stated, "The first month I was so uptight and I was not real sure what was expected of me by my principal and what I expected of myself . . . It has been so even keel after that. I have not had ups and downs." Mike felt "that everything he thought would happen has happened." In these situations, the teachers' prior experiences were similar to the situations they faced in their new teaching positions; therefore, reality shock was absent.

WASH-OUT EFFECT

Zeichner and Tabachnick (1981) described the wash-out effect as the period of time when the impact of the teacher education program diminishes. Sometimes the differences in the reality of the school context do not support the goals and philosophies adopted by beginning teachers during the teacher preparation program. It is this situation to which Lawson (1989) referred when he said, "School practices progressively erode the effects of teacher education" (p. 148). The extent that strategies are provided to new teachers to effectively implement learning objectives for students, as well as the support within the school context, will enhance or inhibit a new teacher's ability to actively provide a learning-centered program.

Lisa's description of how her teaching changed over the year provides a clear picture of the wash-out effect:

> At the beginning of the year, I did physical fitness, then basketball . . . By the end of the year, it came down to those kids who wanted to play basketball on one side of the gym and those kids who wanted to play volleyball on the other side of the gym. Some studied for finals while I did work I had to get done before the end of the year — and no one cared . . . I could just see myself falling into a rut and being a roll-out-the-ball-type. (Stroot, Faucette, & Schwager, 1993, p. 381)

Kelbe also recognized changes in her behaviors, as she stated, "I just feel like I'm not teaching, and it really drives me nuts. I have such a phobia about PE teachers that don't teach, and I see myself slipping into that category" (p. 381).

Smyth (1992) described the wash-out effect in the experience of another first-year teacher, Mr. Miller: "Because of lack of support for his efforts to promote skill acquisition, he sought and implemented teaching practices that modified or replaced many of the teaching methods that he had learned in his teacher education program" (p. 19). "Despite initial training, it appears that Mr. Miller's context served to reward a 'busy, happy, and good' curriculum" (p. 17).

In contrast to these teachers, Mike and Kelley did not experience wash-out of the strategies taught to them in their teacher preparation program. They found them to be quite effective in meeting their managerial and instructional goals, and were able to continue to improve on these teaching strategies as the year progressed. Both Kelley and Mike felt their teacher preparation program provided necessary skills for them to be successful, and both felt highly supported by their schools' principals. Mary (Solmon, Worthy, & Carter, 1993) also felt she was well prepared to teach. Despite several hurdles that she had to address during the first year, Mary felt that due to her ability to discipline and control the class, and the administrative support of one of her principals, she was able to meet her goals for the year.

ISOLATION

Physical isolation from other professional adults is a common problem faced by beginning teachers, as so much time is spent interacting with children or young adults (Kurtz, 1983; Ryan, 1979). The fact that physical education teachers are often the only physical education specialists in the school building, especially at the elementary level, exacerbates this problem.

Torres commented on his need to share his frustrations and receive feedback on his teaching when no one was available for him (Williams & Williamson, 1995).

> One day a class didn't go right. I was depressed and the kids were going bonkers. I asked myself, "Am I teaching them anything?" I felt so down and continued to question what I was doing. It made me feel very insecure. I never felt that way before, even when I was student teaching . . . I felt so isolated and didn't have anyone to give me feedback on what was happening in my classes. . . That would have helped a lot. (p. 12)

Jessie and Kelbe both experienced social isolation as they attempted to develop casual interactions with the teachers in their schools (Stroot, et al., 1993). Jessie stated, "I would sit in the faculty room and no one would speak to me. I mean literally no one would speak to me. A casual 'hello,' but I was never included in conversations." (p. 380). Kelbe stated that her lunchtime interactions were very negative, as the conversations became "half-hour bitch sessions" for the teachers as they continued to criticize students and the school. This type of isolation was experienced by Mike, too, who wrote:

> You walk in to get a cup of coffee in the teachers' lounge, or you sit down to eat lunch and there is no real point of interest to get to know you. They have all been together years and years . . . They look at the gym teacher, as they put it, "differently than they would a real teacher." I have heard that. So there is isolation. (O'Sullivan, 1989, p. 235)

Mary was attempting to build a program in two inner-city elementary schools where the previous programs were taught in the throw-out-the-ball style (Solmon, et al., 1993). She encountered resistance, and began to look to others for reassurance and encouragement. Mary's perception is reflected in the following statement: "As the only physical educator in either school, she felt isolated without anyone to turn to for support and advice" (p. 318).

There were a few teachers who did not seem to be isolated in their school context and were able to develop positive relationships with other employees and/or a mentor. Smyth (1995) discussed a beginning teacher, Andy, who was able to establish a close personal and professional relationship with another school employee, Jack. Smyth stated, "Although Andy taught independently of his physical education colleague, he was not alone. He shared an office with the head of maintenance, Jack . . . Andy learned more about working at Brightland from Jack than from anyone else" (p. 206).

Napper-Owen and Phillips (1995) reported an instance in which the researcher acted as a mentor for two beginning teachers. Cathy, one beginning teacher, was able to work well with a physical education co-worker, John, and although she was able to share ideas and camaraderie, she felt there was not enough time to talk with John. Peter, however, felt the other physical education specialists in his district utilized the "throw out the ball" style of teaching, and did not have colleagues with the same philosophical perspective with whom to share professional concerns. The researcher/mentor in this study acted as a professional colleague for both Cathy and Peter to discuss the struggles of teaching physical education. It was through their weekly meetings that the feelings of isolation were diminished for these beginning teachers.

MARGINALIZATION OF PHYSICAL EDUCATION

The legitimacy of physical education as a subject area is a serious issue, not only for beginning physical educators but for many members of the physical education profession.

O'Sullivan (1989) highlighted this issue for beginning teachers as she described a major paradox in the settings in which Mike and Kelley worked. "The struggle for legitimacy of their subject matter was overshadowed by the collegial respect (legitimacy) both teachers received for their managerial rather than instructional abilities" (p. 240). Mike and Kelley were respected for their ability to manage students, but not for their ability to teach. Solmon, et al. (1993) also described Courtney's experiences and stated that ". . . she encountered some difficulty in being taken seriously as a teacher. She believed other teachers perceived her as a supervisor of play rather than a specialist in physical education" (p. 324). Lisa, too, stated that " . . . elementary classroom teachers seemed to value physical education only for the 'prep period' it provided them" (Stroot, et al., 1993, p. 379). Lisa felt that she had no parental support for physical education either. She stated, "The parents supported athletics, and they supported after-school programs . . . but they didn't care what went on in the classroom" (p. 383).

Perceptions of marginalization of physical education as a legitimate subject area were also evident in the statements made by several beginning teachers from Williams and Williamson's (1995) text. Jackie stated, "One thing I had to struggle with was getting rid of the negative stigma of physical education. It was perceived as recess, and that I was there to give the teachers their prep time" (p. 25). Other times, this lack of respect was indicated when parents and administrators complained about the children receiving less than perfect grades on their report cards, as they claimed, "PE is supposed to be students' break time" (p. 32).

Physical education rarely is perceived as a legitimate subject area by education specialists or by the general public. Cartoons and television regularly depict physical education class as playtime for students and physical education teachers as stereotypic, dumb jocks who bumble their way through life. This issue must be confronted by every individual in the physical education profession.

One teacher who seemed to make a positive impact on his school setting was Andy. As reported by Smyth (1995):

Andy was able to become an integral part of the school community in arenas other than the gymnasium. He worked with teachers on special projects, assisted in various academic activities, and obtained appointments to the superintendent's council. As a result of his involvement in various aspects of the school, Andy developed positive relationships with the teachers—relationships that allowed him to be an advocate for physical education, as well as to portray a positive image of himself as a teacher. (pp. 206–207)

WORKLOAD AND ROLE-CONFLICT

Most teachers have six to nine classes per day, as well as additional duties. A number of elementary teachers travel, as their assignments are split between two schools. In some cases, a supplementary contract is provided for other responsibilities, especially coaching at the secondary level. Although Kurtz (1983) reported that, in general education, the most difficult courses were left to beginners, with experienced teachers choosing the best class assignments, there is no real evidence that this is a problem for beginning physical education teachers. Workload, however, has been mentioned by several beginning teachers as an area of concern. Reed (Solmon, et al., 1993) reflected a concern for the number of classes he would teach as well as other variables that would impact his ability to organize time. Reed knew that he would have large classes, increased in size by mainstreamed special education students. He was also concerned about the pace he would have to maintain in order to allow 30 minutes of instructional time for each of his many classes (p. 321).

Most teachers were not concerned about the number of classes that they would teach, but the scheduling and time available for organization and instruction. As stated by Mr. Miller, "The number of classes that I have aren't [sic] really a big problem, but they're really congested" (Smyth, 1992, p. 10). His complaint was that he was unable to have time between classes to organize for the upcoming grade level and activity.

Many concerns focused on the extra duties assigned to the beginning teachers. Kelbe assumed the position of department chair during her first year, and the administrative duties were overwhelming. In addition to ordering equipment, writing the physical education curriculum, collecting plans, and observing and evaluating the teaching of her peers, she was faced with daily interruptions that inhibited her ability to teach.

I feel so scattered in so many directions . . . It's so outrageous. Thirty to 40% of my time . . . is spent trying to find stolen clothes, misplaced things, shoving kids out of the locker room. . . It's a never-ending, constant battle . . . I'm expected to be full-time PE teacher, full-time locker-room attendant, retail clerk, lost and found clerk. I can't teach effectively under these circumstances. (Stroot, et al., 1993, pp. 379-380)

Mike was assigned the extra duty of supervising safety patrol in his elementary school setting, and, as he stated,

This has been a lot of work. I had to have routines established, chain of command, competency tests, established posts, rules of conduct . . . and a demerit system. . . . Being in charge of safety patrol has put me in the added role of disciplinarian. . . . When there are rule violations, they warn, and if it doesn't stop they inform me or send the student to me. (O'Sullivan, 1989, p. 233)

Some teachers who had supplemental coaching contracts felt the pressures of role-conflict and found coaching responsibilities to be very time-consuming. Kelbe and Lisa (Stroot et al., 1993) struggled as they realized the time involved and that the rewards for being a good coach were sometimes greater than for being a good teacher. They also struggled as they realized it was their teaching that suffered. Kelbe stated,

I usually spend 5 hours a day on volleyball. Last night, I didn't get home until 10:30. . . . Right after volleyball practice, we had a coaches' meeting . . . until 10:00. I'm not doing my best as a teacher, and it makes me feel incompetent. (p. 379)

Lisa reinforced this with her comments regarding her struggles.

I didn't have any support for my teaching. They supported me as a coach, but as a teacher, I could do anything or nothing at all. [To] sit on the bleachers and roll out the ball would have been fine. . . . Without anyone caring about what you teach and with so many other responsibilities, it would have been easy for me to do that. (p. 279)

Cathy was one of the few teachers who found limited benefits related to teaching from her supplemental coaching contract (Napper-Owen & Phillips, 1995). Cathy felt that what she learned relative to giving feedback during her coaching experience transferred to her teaching experience. Although she was able to recognize some benefit from coaching, most of the time Cathy found that she did not have the time or energy to implement changes in her teaching that were suggested by her mentor. When changes were suggested, she said, "I'd like to think of maybe doing something like that, but it's hard to do all that with coaching" (p. 322).

MANAGEMENT AND INSTRUCTION CONCERNS

Concerns about management of students, time, and facilities differed according to perceptions of preparation for the context and factors within the school setting. Again, if the prior experiences of teachers provided strategies and skills necessary to work in the setting similar to the one in which they found their first teaching position, the transition was much smoother.

Management Concerns

It seemed the most difficult scenarios were those where teachers familiar with the concerns of students from middle-class backgrounds such as their own were working in inner-city schools where student problems were more severe than anything they had experienced or anticipated. This was reflected in the examples of reality shock reported previously. Along with these examples, students did not seem to care about disciplinary options available to teachers, such as time-outs or detentions.

These teachers found that they were not always able to cope with students' lack of respect, as they challenged teachers' expectations on a regular basis. Katie stated, "The students did not seem responsible for their behavior. They'd just say, 'I have a detention, oh well,' and then probably skip it. The school had no attendance policy." It was frustrating, and without assistance some of the teachers struggled throughout the entire year (Williams & Williamson, 1995, p. 52). The fact that the school administration did not establish or uphold such policies left few options for the beginning teachers—it was virtually impossible for them to find success.

Almost the opposite situation occurred for Kelley and Mike, who both felt that the strategies taught in the teacher preparation program were useful in the school setting and that school administrators supported their efforts as disciplinarians. Their management concerns revolved around getting everything accomplished within limited time constraints rather than the discipline of students.

Instructional Concerns

The most common instructional concern reported by teachers was relative to grading. With several hundred students to grade each quarter, teachers struggled with providing fair evaluations. Several new teachers entered settings where all students received A's, and when attempting to implement a differential grading procedure, they encountered resistance by students, administrators, and parents. Often, this also indicated the lack of recognition for physical education as a legitimate content area. "Parents provide pressure relative to the grading procedure, as indicated by parent comments in Jackie's school, 'How could my kid fail gym. Look, A's and B's all across this stinking report card, and then an F in gym.' That was the most frustrating thing throughout the whole year" (Williams & Williamson, 1995, p. 25). Mike's expectations for student learning also resulted in parent complaints. Mike wrote, "There has been a lot of flack from parents of students who earned a U—unsatisfactory—for the third 6 weeks of the year. 'Failing gym is like failing lunch or recess,' one parent told me." (O'Sullivan, 1989, p. 235). Mary, too, struggled with parent reactions to upholding standards within her program:

> I don't believe in throwing out the ball and letting kids play, and from my understanding, that's the way it has been here. I flunked over half the kids in a class because they did not meet my standards, and when you do that you catch a lot of static. It really hurt me when the parents went directly to the principal instead of coming to me first. I didn't have a chance to handle the problem. (Solmon, et al., 1993, p. 318)

Another instructional problem that was identified by Mike was individualizing activities to meet the varied needs of students in classes. He stated that his major concern was "greater individualization of instruction by matching class activities more closely to student competencies" (O'Sullivan, 1989, p. 233). Goals such as these can only be addressed after management of students is no longer an issue. As Mike has already overcome this hurdle, he was better able to focus on individual student concerns. This ability to focus on individual students reflected a more advanced stage of development for Mike, who continued to grow as a teacher.

INTERACTIONS WITH COLLEAGUES

Recently, collegial interaction has been shown to be one of the most powerful contextual variables which enhances or inhibits beginning teachers' ability to be successful in elementary or secondary settings.

Four of the teachers in Williams and Williamson's (1995) text struggled with their coworkers. Vince stated, "The hardest thing for me this year was getting along with the other physical educator [Connie] and keeping up with the paperwork. Working with Connie has been her way or no way. That made team teaching extremely difficult, since she would not accept any of my ideas" (p. 38). Similarly, Heather commented, ". . . the most difficult thing was working with a teacher I couldn't get along with . . . It was hard working with her. She only graduated four years ago, and already was 'rolling out the ball' . . . She never had anything planned. I still don't know how she got away with it" (p. 3). Torres also had to work with a teacher who held a very different philosophy and was not accepting of any of the suggestions or ideas provided by him, and Joe stated, "My coworker and I did not share ideas" (p. 44). Kelbe (Stroot, et al., 1993) also had differing perceptions and ". . . saw herself and her primary colleague at opposite ends of a continuum regarding expectations for student learning" (p. 378), and Jessie stated that "her teacher education preparation did not prepare her for how to deal with uncooperative colleagues" (p. 382). Smyth (1995) reported Sue's reaction to her colleague whose "teaching styles were fundamentally different." She [Sue] liked to have someone to talk to, particularly about physical education, but increasingly found Bill's presence on the other side of the gymnasium to be more annoying than reassuring and helpful" (p. 204). Sue found it difficult to defend her task-oriented style of teaching when students wanted to play the games that they saw in Bill's class.

As mentioned previously, Andy benefited from the support of Jack the custodian (Smyth, 1995), and Cathy believed that her interaction with John encouraged her professional growth (Napper-Owen & Phillips, 1995). Katie was another of the fortunate teachers. She worked with committed and supportive coworkers who had a positive impact on her first year as a physical education teacher. Katie described her coworkers:

Jane developed a new worksheet for weight training and she shared it with the staff. If I asked her any questions she would tell me whatever I needed to know . . . We also had a really dynamic male teacher . . . We worked together for about a month and I benefited from observing and teaching with him . . . It was inspirational to work with a person who was innovative and truly cared about the outcome of his efforts. (Williams & Williamson, 1995, p. 50)

POLITICS IN THE WORKPLACE

Schempp, Sparkes, and Templin (1993) described the experiences of three teachers during their first years of teaching, and focused on the biographical influences, the role demands, and the impact of the school culture on the lives of these teachers. This article provides insights on the power relationships in schools, and describes the teachers' reactions to the challenges they faced as they negotiated the school system. Schempp, et al. found that school administrators, teachers, and students marginalized physical education as legitimate subject matter. Teacher preparation programs were not perceived as credible, so new ideas that beginning teachers brought into school settings were devalued. As teachers realized concerns in their new setting, they were hesitant to vocalize or take action to resolve the issues. These teachers did not want to feel alienated or put themselves at risk. Compliance and silence allowed the teachers to be accepted by others in the system. With feelings such as these, no change could occur. As noted by several beginning teachers, without consistent support and encouragement, it is extremely difficult for new teachers to implement the knowledge and strategies that would result in a quality physical education program.

Macdonald (1995) examined beginning physical education teachers in Australia, and suggested that tensions between professionalization and proletarianization offer a useful lens through which attrition rates may be understood. She noted the routine and fragmented nature of the professional work; limited authority, responsibility, and autonomy of teachers; and different motivations for men and women to remain in the profession. Again, the question emerges, how can the existing system be modified to enhance the induction process of teachers, increasing the number of high quality professionals who remain in the field?

SUPPORT FOR BEGINNING TEACHERS

Several of the beginning teachers found support through their interactions with their coworkers and other school employees. However, it is also important to examine the extent of support provided by the administrators and by mentoring programs that are designed to assist teachers' entry into the school setting.

Kurtz (1983) stated that beginning teacher supervision usually consists of "one to three formal visits, a few incidental contacts, and a number of group contacts" (p. 44). When beginning teachers need support, reassurance, and assistance during their first year, these few visits are not adequate to meet their needs. There was limited administrative support for the beginning teachers in Williams and Williamson's text (1995). The number of evaluations ranged from zero to two for the entire year. Tamara's quote is typical of many principals, who seem to be supportive but can offer little substantive assistance to these teachers.

> The principal would come over and talk to me when the children were involved in activity. She never gave me any feedback on my teaching . . . She formally observed me once and left without saying a word. Even when I saw her later she didn't mention the evaluation . . . (p. 34)

Kelbe's situation was exactly the same: Her administrator did not provide
feedback or encouragement.

> He [the principal] comes around every once in a while, but he hasn't
> said anything positive. One day, I really had a good lesson in the
> weight room . . . and he stood there about 10 minutes and, then,
> never said a thing . . . (Stroot, et al., 1993, p. 380)

Mentoring for most of these teachers was virtually nonexistent. Courtney, in fact, was left entirely on her own. "Prior to the start of the school
year, the principal informed Courtney that she knew nothing about physical education and would leave everything in her hands" (Solmon, et al.,
1993, p. 323). Courtney expressed her feelings about the lack of support.

> . . . inservice provided for new teachers by the administration was
> somewhat lacking and a source of some concern. She [Courtney]
> regretted that she was not apprised of the details needed for complete
> success at the beginning of the year. "They have a good assertive
> discipline program, but nobody bothered to go over the procedures.
> I have a homeroom and nobody told me what to do during homeroom.
> I just had to feel my way through it. (p. 324)

In Williams and Williamson's text (1995), Heather reported that she
was supposed to work with a mentor in her building; however, the reality
was quite the opposite. Heather stated, "The administration told us at
the beginning of the year to find somebody to be a mentor teacher . . . So
I went to the building and thought, 'There are no PE teachers around
this building. Who is going to be my mentor?'" (p. 2). Heather was put
into an impossible situation—she was told to "find a mentor," yet who
was there to provide encouragement and expertise to the only physical
education specialist in the school?

Several teachers were positively influenced by a mentor. As Jessie
(Stroot, et al., 1993) moved into her first year of teaching, she called upon
her university student teaching supervisor for assistance, and an informal
mentoring relationship was developed. The mentoring relationship continued as Jessie moved into another teaching position during her second
year, and proved to be valuable as she continued to learn to teach. Lisa
also found support as she moved to a new school system during her second
year. In the new setting, she was involved in a formal mentoring program
instituted by the school district, and she also found support through
the district's Coordinator of Health and Physical Education. Lisa was
observed approximately once per week, and feedback and suggestions
were offered. Lisa felt encouragement and support in her efforts to be
effective and was able to move toward that goal as the year progressed.
Katie (Williams & Williamson, 1995) not only had a mentor who "was
always available to answer questions and help with difficult situations"
(p. 50), but, as mentioned previously, had coworkers who were willing to

assist in any way possible to help her through her first year. Peter and Cathy (Napper-Owen & Phillips, 1995) both felt as though they were positively influenced through the induction program.

> Peter believed the feedback he received throughout his first year enabled him to teach more effectively and to apply his undergraduate training. He believed the supervision and assistance encouraged him to explore new methods of instruction and to vary instructional activities. The induction assistance encouraged Cathy to think about her teaching and determine ways to make her teaching more effective. (p. 323)

The scenarios of these beginning teachers reflected several deep concerns that influenced their successful transition from the university to the schools. Workplace factors greatly influenced their perceptions of their success and their role as a physical education professional. It is important that we begin to take an assertive role to modify these conditions, and to help all, not just the lucky ones, to have a positive experience during their first year of teaching. As Sparkes, Templin, and Schempp (1993) note, "At best [the workplace] should promote a positive socialization process whereby all teachers are made to feel welcome, secure, enriched, empowered, and valued in terms of their actual and potential contributions to school life" (p. 386).

CONTINUED CAREER DEVELOPMENT

The scenarios previously cited have all related to the lives of beginning teachers as they learn to work within their school setting. What happens as teachers gain experience? Again, we have different stories.

It seems that some teachers reach a professional crossroads and are able to move through the stages of development and become professionals who positively influence the lives of students. Others just slow down until they are content with "busy, happy, and good" (Placek, 1983).

One study focused on seven effective elementary physical education specialists (including two beginning teachers, Mike and Kelley), whose major goals were student activity and student achievement. These teachers ranged from first-year teachers (Mike and Kelley) to veterans who had 20 or more years of teaching experience. Veterans faced many of the hurdles mentioned by the beginning teachers, but thanks to support and encouragement and their own clear understanding of where they were going, they were able to overcome many of the inhibitors and effectively implement their curriculum. Veteran teachers were able to develop and maintain a learning atmosphere in their classrooms and gain the respect of their colleagues and administrators. These teachers were also very much involved in activities outside of the regular class schedule which had a positive impact on students and the school.

Examples of experienced teachers who continued to struggle are also available in the literature. Templin (1989) described Sarah, a 14-year veteran teacher, who had yet to overcome some of the workplace factors faced by beginning teachers. She stated she felt as though she was "running on ice" as she could not meet her goals for a quality program. Another study examined 11 high school physical education specialists (O'Sullivan, 1994), and again some of the contextual hoops and hurdles disappeared over time, yet some remained. Siedentop, Doutis, Tsangaridou, Ward, and Rauschenbach (1994) stated:

> . . . none of these teachers "threw out the ball" and abdicated their responsibilities as educators. These were serious professionals dealing in their own ways with the contexts in which they performed their professional services. . . . It is our conclusion that gym was "no sweat" for students, and it was "no sweat" for teachers. . . . Other evidence presented in this monograph suggests strongly that physical education was typically marginalized in these schools. Our teachers had little support or pressure to produce a more intense learning ecology; indeed, one might argue that had they done so it might have put them at risk in their school ecologies. Instructional leadership for physical education from school administrators was noticeably absent. (p. 393)

These teachers have negotiated an environment that is acceptable to all who enter the gymnasium. It is questionable, when this negotiation occurs, whether the compromise made by these teachers to adapt to their work environment encourages any additional demands on students or on teachers, even if they result in more effective teaching.

Griffin (1985) described the contextual factors in an urban, multiracial, junior high school which made it virtually impossible for teachers to meet their professional goals. Again, compromises were made in order to survive. Given the extent of the systemic constraints at work in this environment, Griffin recommended, "If there is to be real hope for change, it lies not in finding the right pedagogical stuff but in acting on the right political stuff" (p. 165).

In these examples, the contexts in the elementary and secondary settings seem to be very different. It is difficult, given the limited information at this time, to speculate on the scope of difference and the extent of impact on teachers in each respective setting. Moreover, the urban and suburban settings seem to bring about different challenges. Many of our teachers have not been adequately prepared for urban contexts. One has to wonder if teacher education programs, no matter how good they are, can adequately prepare teachers who are unfamiliar with urban settings to make a smooth transition into a context where major societal problems are reflected in the problems children bring into the schools.

SUGGESTED STRATEGIES FOR BEGINNING TEACHERS

It is obvious from these scenarios that the beginning teachers found mentors to be beneficial in helping them through the transition from the university to the school setting. Teachers with mentors spoke of the positive impact of the emotional and instructional support that they received during their first year of teaching. In these settings, both the formal and informal mentoring models seemed to enhance entry into the schools. It was also apparent that the beginning teachers who had a clear perspective on what they wanted to do and how they wanted to do it eventually found support within their setting and success in accomplishing their goals. These teachers were empowered to be proactive. Workplace conditions, however, vary drastically, and often the beginning teacher must be assertive in order to create a positive work environment.

SEEK OUT MENTORS

The first thing teachers can do to empower themselves is to ask about the availability of mentors. Sclan and Darling-Hammond (1992) provided an overview of state policies regarding beginning teacher performance evaluation. As of 1992, 45 states and the District of Columbia had developed programs and/or requirements for beginning teacher evaluation. As many of these programs also offer support for the beginning teacher, it is important to be aware of the state policy. In addition, beginners could ask about the availability of a mentoring program within the school. For example: What type of mentoring is available? Does this include evaluation? Who chooses my mentor? How often will I see my mentor? What is expected of me? What is expected of my mentor?

In addition to gathering information about the mentoring program, new teachers could ask about opportunities to meet other specialists in a similar content area, both beginners who will be facing the same struggles and veterans who have moved positively and productively through their career path. These people can provide a supportive network to share struggles and ideas to enhance the first years of teaching. Observing peers and having peers observe other teachers will assist and benefit all involved, as ideas and strategies are shared. These relationships will continue throughout a teacher's career and will provide valuable, professional interactions to help each individual continue to grow.

TAKE ADVANTAGE OF PUBLISHED RESOURCES

Current journals and books can be very helpful in providing ideas and suggestions to beginning teachers. Journals which provided ideas specific to the classroom include the *Journal of Health, Physical Education and Recreation* and *Strategies* (both published through the American Alliance for Health, Physical Education, Recreation & Dance, Reston, VA) and *Teaching Elementary Physical Education* (published by Human Kinetics, Champaign, IL). Articles such as Ratliffe's (1987) paper, "Overcoming Obstacles Beginning Teachers Encounter," or "Helping Novice Teachers Handle Discipline Problems," by Fernandez-Balboa (1990) provide very practical suggestions for beginning teachers.

As teachers become members of their state and national professional organizations, many of these journals become available as a part of the membership. In addition, programs to improve teaching for physical educators, like the American Master Teacher Program sponsored by Human Kinetics, offer other valuable resources, where teachers can take workshops and gather resources that are designed for practical implementation. Bain and Wendt's (1983) *Transition to Teaching: A Guide for the Beginning Teacher* provides practical suggestions for management and instruction. One other suggestion is for beginning teachers to read about experiences of teachers in situations much like the ones they are likely to experience. References for all of these suggestions are included in the reference section of this chapter.

BE REFLECTIVE

It is also helpful to create a method to reflect and act upon the struggles and successes encountered throughout a teaching career. One suggestion is to ask a teacher who is observing to begin to gather information relative to established goals for teaching. Systematic observation instruments to code the feedback provided to students or the amount of time children are spending in appropriate activity are examples of what and how information can be gathered. Journal writing is another helpful way to take time to think about strategies that worked and those that did not. Identify concerns, and begin to think of how teachers can modify their teaching to reduce problems and enhance the learning environment. Using these suggestions, begin to create a plan such as the one indicated below to address some of the struggles:

1. What is the first issue/concern that you would like to address in your learning environment?
2. How would you like to address this issue/concern?
3. How would you measure whether your effort was successful?
4. Implement the project.
5. What were the results of your project?
6. Modify the project or identify a new project.

NETWORK

Some concerns identified by beginning teachers were systemic concerns that are difficult to overcome alone. When addressing systemic concerns, the teacher must again ask questions to find out what networking has already occurred and how to become more socially and politically active in these networks. Responsibilities for these issues should be with the veterans, who have already become established in the existing setting. In many cases, however, these veterans have already compromised, so again, responsibility to be proactive falls on the beginner. One of the more recent movements that is an outcome of educational reform is the increased collaboration between universities and public school settings. Such a collaborative project would include university faculty to help teachers as they continue to learn to teach. A collaborative action-research project "brings together teachers, staff developers, and university faculty with the goals of improving practice, contributing to educational theory, and providing staff development" (Oja & Smulyan, 1989, p. 24). Closer interaction between school and university personnel would further ease the transition to the school setting for beginning teachers. Perhaps collaborative groups such as these would also assist in addressing the more difficult systemic concerns that have an overwhelming impact on beginning and veteran teachers alike.

For a beginning teacher who is willing to be proactive in requesting assistance, there are multiple options available. There is no longer a good reason for teachers entering a new school setting to "learn the ropes" in isolation. It does, however, usually take the initiative of the new teacher, because in many cases the system encourages perpetuation of the workplace conditions that have become concerns for the beginning teachers, as discussed in this chapter.

SUMMARY

Implications of the socialization process for teacher education programs and school districts are great. It is important during professional preparation that novice teachers be provided with the knowledge, opportunity, assistance, and support to practice their teaching skills in a variety of settings, including some of the tough urban settings in which beginners are likely to find their first teaching position. In addition, as teachers work in the school setting, the assistance and support suggested by Katz (1972) should be provided to them throughout their career. Collaborative efforts between university and school faculties would help make the transition from the university to the school setting a smooth, successful one for each teacher.

REFERENCES

Bain, L.L., & Wendt, J.C. (1983). *Transition to teaching: A guide for the beginning teacher*. Reston, VA: The American Alliance for Health, Physical Education, Recreation and Dance.

Burden, P.R. (1980). Teachers' perceptions of the characteristics and influences on their personal and professional development. (ERIC Document Reproduction Service No. ED 198 087)

Caruso, J.J. (1977). Phases in student teaching. *Young Children, 33*(1), 57–63.

Dewar, A.M. (1989). Recruitment in physical education teaching: Toward a critical approach. In T. Templin & P. Schempp (Eds.), *Socialization into physical education: Learning to teach* (pp. 39–58). Indianapolis: Benchmark Press.

Dewar, A., & Lawson, H. (1984). The subjective warrant and recruitment into physical education. *Quest, 36,* 15–25.

Dodds, P., Placek, J., Doolittle, S., Pinkham, K.M., Ratliffe, T., & Portman, P. (1992). Teacher/coach recruits: Background profiles, occupational decision factors, and comparisons with recruits into other physical education occupations. *Journal of Teaching in Physical Education, 11,* 161–176.

Fernandez-Balboa, J.M. (1990). Helping novice teachers handle discipline problems. *Journal of Physical Education, Recreation and Dance, 66*(7), 50–54.

Fuller, F.F., & Bown, O.H. (1975). Becoming a teacher. In K. Ryan (Ed.), *Teacher education: 74th yearbook of the National Society for the Study of Education, Part II* (pp. 25–52). Chicago: University of Chicago Press.

Gregorc, A.F. (1973). Developing plans for professional growth. *NASSP Bulletin, 57,* 1–8.

Griffin, P. (1985). Teaching in an urban multiracial junior high school physical education program: The power of context. *Quest, 37,* 154–165.

Huling-Austin, L., Odell, S.J., Ishler, P., Kay, R.S., & Edelfelt, R.A. (Eds.). (1989). *Assisting the beginning teacher.* Reston, VA: Association of Teacher Educators.

Hutchinson, G.E. (1993). Prospective teachers' perspectives on teaching physical education: An interview study on the recruitment phase of teacher socialization. In S. Stroot (Ed.), Socialization into physical education [Monograph]. *Journal of Teaching in Physical Education, 12*(4), 344–354.

Katz, L.G. (1972). Developmental stages of preschool teachers. *Elementary School Journal, 73* (1), 50–54.

Kurtz, W.H. (1983). Identifying their needs: How the principal can help beginning teachers. *NASSP Bulletin, 67,* 42–45.

Lawson, H.A. (1983). Toward a model of teacher socialization in physical education: Entry into schools, teachers' role orientations, and longevity in teaching. *Journal of Teaching in Physical Education, 3*(1), 3–15.

Lawson, H.A. (1986). Occupational socialization and the design of teacher education programs. *Journal of Teaching in Physical Education, 5,* 107–116.

Lawson, H.A. (1989). From rookie to veteran: Workplace conditions in physical education and induction into the profession. In T. Templin & P. Schempp (Eds.), *Socialization into physical education: Learning to teach* (pp. 145–164). Indianapolis: Benchmark Press.

Louis, K.S., & Smith, B. (1990). Teacher working conditions. In P. Reyes (Ed.), *Teachers and their workplace* (pp. 23–47). Newbury Park, CA: Sage.

Macdonald, D. (1995). The role of proletarianization in physical education teacher attrition. *Research Quarterly for Exercise and Sport, 66*(2), 129-141.

McDonald, F.J. (1982, March). *A theory of the professional development of teachers.* Paper presented at the meeting of the American Educational Research Association, New York.

Napper-Owen, G.E., & Phillips, D.A. (1995). A qualitative analysis of the impact of induction assistance on first-year physical educators. *Journal of Teaching in Physical Education, 14*(3), 305–327.

Oja, S.N., & Smulyan, L. (1989). *Collaborative action research: A developmental approach.* London: The Falmer Press.

O'Sullivan, M. (1989). Failing gym is like failing lunch or recess: Two beginning teachers' struggle for legitimacy. *Journal of Teaching in Physical Education, 8*(3), 227–242.

O'Sullivan, M. (Ed.). (1994). High school physical education teachers: Their world of work [Monograph]. *Journal of Teaching in Physical Education, 13*(4), 323–441.

Peterson, A.R. (1979). Career patterns of secondary school teachers: An exploratory interview study of retired teachers (Doctoral dissertation, The Ohio State University, 1978). *Dissertation Abstracts International, 39,* 4888A.

Placek, J. (1983). Concepts of success in teaching: Busy, happy, and good? In T. Templin & J. Olson (Eds.), *Teaching in physical education* (pp. 46–56). Champaign, IL: Human Kinetics.

Ratliffe, T. (1987). Overcoming obstacles beginning teachers encounter. *Journal of Physical Education, Recreation and Dance, 58*(4), 18–23.

Ryan, K. (1979). Toward understanding the problem: At the threshold of the profession. In K.R. Howey & R.H. Bents (Eds.), *Toward meeting the needs of the beginning teacher* (pp. 35–52). Minneapolis, MN: Midwest Teacher Corps Network; and St. Paul, MN: Minnesota University Press.

Sacks, S.R., & Harrington, G.N. (1982, March). *Student to teacher: The process of role transition.* Paper presented at the meeting of the American Educational Research Association, New York.

Schempp, P.G. (1989). Apprenticeship-of-observation and the development of physical education teachers. In T. Templin & P. Schempp (Eds.), *Socialization into physical education: Learning to teach* (pp. 13–38). Indianapolis: Benchmark Press.

Schempp, P.G., Sparkes, A.C., & Templin, T.J. (1993). The micropolitics of teacher education. *American Educational Research Journal, 30*(3), 447–472.

Sclan, E., & Darling-Hammond, L. (1992). *Beginning teacher performance evaluations: An overview of state policies.* Washington, DC: American Association of Colleges for Teacher Education. (ERIC Document Reproduction Service No. ED 341 689)

Siedentop, D., Doutis, P., Tsangaridou, N., Ward, P., & Rauschenbach, J. (1994). Don't sweat gym! An analysis of curriculum and instruction. In M. O'Sullivan (Ed.), High school physical education teachers: Their world of work [Monograph]. *Journal of Teaching in Physical Education, 13*(4), 375–395.

Smyth, D. (1992, April). *"The kids just love him": A first year teacher's perceptions of how the workplace has affected his teaching.* Paper presented at the annual meeting of the AERA, San Francisco.

Smyth, D. (1995). First-year physical education teachers' perceptions of their workplace. *Journal of Teaching in Physical Education, 14*(2), 198–214.

Solmon, M.A., Worthy, T., & Carter, J.A. (1993). The interaction of school context and role identity of first-year teachers. *Journal of Teaching in Physical Education, 12*(3), 313–328.

Sparkes, A.C., Templin, T.J., & Schempp, P.G. (1993). Exploring dimensions of marginality: Reflecting on the life histories of physical education teachers. In S. Stroot (Ed.), Socialization into physical education [Monograph]. *Journal of Teaching in Physical Education, 12*(4), 386–398.

Stroot, S.A., Faucette, N., & Schwager, S. (1993). In the beginning: The induction of physical educators. In S. Stroot (Ed.), Socialization into physical education [Monograph]. *Journal of Teaching in Physical Education, 12*(4), 375–385.

Templin, T. (1989). Running on ice: A case study of the influence of workplace conditions on a secondary school physical educator. In T. Templin & P. Schempp (Eds.), *Socialization into physical education: Learning to teach* (pp. 165–189). Indianapolis: Benchmark Press.

Unruh, A., & Turner, H.E. (1970). *Supervision for change and innovation.* Boston: Houghton Mifflin.

Van Maanen, J., & Schein, E. (1979). Toward a theory of organizational socialization. In B. Staw (Ed.), *Research in organizational behavior* (Vol. 1, pp. 209–261). Greenwich, CT: JAI Press.

Veenman, S. (1984). Perceived problems of beginning teachers. *Review of Educational Research, 54*(2), 143–178.

Williams, J., & Williamson, K.M. (1995). *Beginning to teach physical education: The inside stories.* Dubuque, IA: Kendall/Hunt.

Yarger, S.J., & Mertens, S.K. (1980). Testing the waters of school-based teacher education. In D.C. Corrigan & K.R. Howey (Eds.), *Concepts to guide the education of experienced teachers.* Reston, VA: Council for Exceptional Children.

Zeichner, K., & Tabachnick, R. (1981). Are the effects of university teacher education "washed-out" by school experience? *Journal of Teacher Education, 32*(3), 7–11.

CHAPTER 17

Innovation and Change in Physical Education

Lynn Dale Housner

I can recall vividly the thoughts that went through my mind the night before my first day of student teaching. I was excited to finally put to use the teaching strategies I had learned in my undergraduate teacher education program. Sure, I had been in contact with kids during early field experiences, but these experiences consisted of observing teachers or serving as an aide. The experiences were short, disconnected, and involved only small groups of students.

Tomorrow would be the real thing. I would probably have to wait for a while before the cooperating teacher would allow me to solo, but I felt ready. I was comfortable with planning units and lessons and had already met with the cooperating teacher to get some ideas about the activities that might be taught. I knew about various styles of teaching and had prepared lessons in advance using learning modules, IPIs, reciprocal task sheets, guided discovery, and others. I knew about exercise physiology and how to improve flexibility, cardiovascular endurance, muscular strength, and percent body fat. I had a firm grasp on measurement and evaluation and knew how to design or select tests that measured affective, psychomotor, and cognitive growth. I had taken required courses in a wide variety of team and individual sports as well as classes in ballet, folk dance, ballroom dancing, women's and men's gymnastics, aquatics (lifeguard and water safety instructor certification), and others. So, I had good knowledge and skill in the content of physical education.

I had no idea that student teaching would become a disaster of such proportions that I would actually consider leaving teaching by midsemester. On my first day of student teaching, I showed up well before the cooperating teacher arrived. Just before the first class of students arrived, so did the cooperating teacher. He casually unlocked the equipment room door and waited for the students to arrive. He met the students at the entrance to the gym and when they were lined up he simply said, "Go ahead." The students ran to the equipment room, selected whatever piece of equipment they wanted, and began to play on their own. Students played four-square, dodgeball, kickball, jump rope, and so on; some simply congregated to sit and talk. All of this took place in a single gymnasium of modest size. To this day it amazes me that the children carried out all of this activity without serious injury occurring.

At the end of class, the students tossed their equipment in the equipment room and lined up at the door. The next class was already lined up at the door waiting to enter the gym. At this point, the cooperating teacher gave me keys to the physical education office and equipment room and with a smile that seemed at once sympathetic and sardonic he told me that I was on my own. This was the last time I would see him for any appreciable amount of time for the remainder of the semester. Reluctantly, but with no other options in mind, I told the students to "go ahead," and like the first class they rushed the equipment room, frantically grabbed equipment, and began to play. For each of the classes that followed, I helplessly used the "go ahead" command. I had learned my first routine in the real world.

I survived student teaching by conducting physical education in much the same way. Certainly, I tried to change things; particularly early in student teaching. Nevertheless, the children—who had spent years in physical education at this school—resisted and ultimately the inertia of the program made it too heavy to budge. My university supervisor recognized that my situation was bad and suggested that I just "get through it" and look forward to my first job where I could develop my own program. After all, this was the cooperating teacher's program and I had little authority to make change. Unfortunately, this did not diminish the day-to-day frustrations of conducting bad physical education.

THE SCOPE OF THE PROBLEM

Although I did not know it at the time, my student teaching experience was not unusual. The phenomena I experienced are common in teaching physical education (Stroot, Collier, O'Sullivan, & England, 1994; Templin & Schempp, 1989; Templin, 1988). Specifically, I was deprofessionalized, marginalized, and isolated. I was alone, rarely having contact with other teachers. The cooperating teacher and principal did not observe my classes. The only time I met the principal was early in the semester and he made it clear that as long as I took care of the discipline problems and nobody got hurt I would be doing fine. Also, I did not eat lunch with the other teachers. Rather, I was in charge of playground supervision during lunchtime and ate standing up. Finally, my students, always inquisitive, wondered aloud why someone would need a college education to teach physical education.

This is not to say that all physical education is done poorly. There is considerable literature describing solid programs (McKenzie, Sallis, Faucette, Roby, & Kolody, 1993; Siedentop, Mand, & Taggart, 1986; Wescott, 1992; Wuest & Lombardo, 1994) and skilled teachers in physical education (Griffey & Housner, 1991; Housner & Griffey, 1985; Siedentop, 1989; Templin, 1983). However, although isolated pockets of excellence in school-based physical education exist, too many physical education programs are characterized not only by large classes, poor facilities, and very little administrative support, but also by punishment with exercise, students picking teams, evaluation based on "dressing-out" rather than affective, cognitive, and psychomotor growth, students waiting in lines, sex role stereotyping, and virtually no use of alternative teaching methods to increase levels of student engagement, learning, interactions, problem solving, and so on (Locke, 1992; Norton, 1987).

Articles in recent theme issues of *Journal of Physical Education, Recreation and Dance (JOPERD)* on problems and possibilities (Norton, 1987) and critical crossroads in physical education (Graham & Stueck, 1992) and on secondary physical education in *Quest* (Siedentop & O'Sullivan, 1992) point to the deplorable condition of the vast majority of physical education programs and the need for immediate and dramatic change. Given the epidemic nature of the problems confronting physical education, researchers have argued that positive and substantive change can only be achieved through the use of radical, system-wide strategies (O'Sullivan, Siedentop, & Tannehill, 1994). Locke (1992) goes so far to argue that ". . . it is better to chuck the dominant model (and thereby most school programs) and start over from scratch" (p. 362).

These researchers argue convincingly that systemic change is needed, and I agree. Unfortunately, unlike the massive amount of research documenting the monumental problems related to teaching physical education, there is little available research to guide the process of change in physical education (Locke, 1992; O'Sullivan, et al., 1994); it is not clear what to change, how much to change, and who should initiate change.

We do know that change will be difficult to achieve (Armstrong & Sparkes, 1991). Research indicates that prospective physical education teachers possess well developed understandings about the nature of physical education, acquired over years of participation in school-based physical education programs (Schempp, 1989). One can imagine the perceptions of students regarding physical education at my student teaching site. These beliefs are resistant to change (Ennis, 1994) and often remain largely unaltered by teacher education programs (Doolittle, Dodds, & Placek, 1993). Though prospective teachers acquire new knowledge in preservice and inservice teacher education, when they discover that this knowledge is inconsistent with the actual practices of physical education they tend to disavow what they have learned, and the beliefs accumulated over a lifetime of experience begin to reemerge and dominate (Faucette, 1987; Lawson, 1983). During the course of a career, continual knowledge disavowal can result in a teacher's forgetting much of what he or she learned in preservice education (Kelley & Lindsay, 1977, 1980; Lawson, 1993).

There are factors associated with the context of teaching physical education that contribute to knowledge disavowal. Teacher-coach role conflict, large class sizes, equipment limitations, and so on make it easier for physical education teachers to reject new knowledge and embrace the status quo (Locke, 1990). Add to these factors the isolation, marginalization, and deprofessionalization that accompany teaching physical education, and it is easy to understand how knowledgeable, well intentioned physical educators resign themselves to simply maintaining orderly classes characterized by a "casual" attitude toward instruction (Siedentop, Doutis, Tsangaridou, Ward, & Rauschenbach, 1994).

CHAPTER PREVIEW

The purpose of the present chapter is to provide physical education teachers and teacher educators with strategies that can be used to achieve quality programming in physical education while at the same time contending with deprofessionalization, isolation, and marginalization. The strategies are intended to assist physical educators to continue to develop professionally, develop high-quality physical education programs, and bring their important work to the attention of colleagues, administrators, parents, and politicians. While considering the strategies, the reader should keep in mind that research confirming their efficacy is unavailable; we simply do not yet know whether application of the strategies will have the desired effect.

This chapter is organized in four major sections. In the first section, strategies for reversing deprofessionalization are presented; in the second, strategies to minimize isolation; and in the third, strategies for overcoming marginality. In the fourth section the role of teacher education in changing physical education is discussed. Many of the strategies presented do not fall neatly into one section or another. Rather, they may address several or all of the problem areas simultaneously. An attempt was made to classify the strategies, however, according to the problem area that they address most directly.

REVERSING DEPROFESSIONALIZATION

In physical education there has been and will continue to be an explosion of new knowledge. In a field of study characterized by the rapid expansion of knowledge, obsolescence of knowledge begins to occur shortly after graduation and will continue unless strategies are employed by teachers to keep abreast of new ideas (Kelley & Lindsay, 1977, 1980). Of course, knowledge obsolescence contributes to deprofessionalization. When physical educators are viewed as lacking in the requisite knowledge to provide effective instruction, deprofessionalization occurs and with it the inevitable erosion of perceptions about the importance of physical education. Described below are strategies designed to assist the physical education teacher in staying abreast of new developments in the field and reversing deprofessionalization.

PROFESSIONAL DEVELOPMENT PLANS

In many states, career advancement in teaching is linked directly to demonstrated evidence of professional development (Association of Teacher Educators, 1985). Career ladders or lattices (Chandler, Lane, Bibik, & Oliver, 1988) designate levels associated with improved teaching or performance of new roles and responsibilities. As higher levels are achieved or more diverse roles are taken on, rewards—such as salary increases, opportunities to obtain student teachers, leading staff development workshops, serving as a mentor to less experienced teachers, and so on—are provided.

Although acceptable professional development activities vary from state to state and between school districts within states, historically, three types of activities have been designated as appropriate:

- attending professional conferences where continuing education credits are awarded,
- participating in staff development workshops sponsored by the school district, and
- pursuing an advanced educational degree or graduate coursework beyond the baccalaureate.

Career advancement is also contingent on the teachers' performance in the classroom. The teacher is often required to build a professional portfolio that includes instructional plans, sample tests, instructional materials, and other relevant materials. Observations of teaching performance, interviews, and teaching evaluations collected from peers and students and tests of content knowledge have been suggested as legitimate sources of information regarding professional development (McGreal, 1983).

Career advancement opportunities are available in virtually every school district. These opportunities permit physical educators to advance their careers while at the same time reversing deprofessionalization. It is imperative that the physical educator adopt an assertive, high-profile approach to career advancement. Physical educators' professional development plans should include a variety of activities, such as involvement in professional organizations, attending workshops and conferences, subscribing to professional journals, attending graduate school, and building comprehensive teaching portfolios.

INVOLVEMENT IN PROFESSIONAL ORGANIZATIONS

While it seems obvious that involvement in professional organizations would contribute significantly to the reduction of knowledge obsolescence, surprisingly few physical educators are involved in state, district, or national organizations.

AAHPERD

The American Alliance of Health, Physical Education, Recreation and Dance (AAHPERD) estimates that nationally only 5% of physical education teachers are members, whereas nearly 50% of math teachers belong to the National Council of Mathematics Teachers (Paula Kun, AAHPERD public relations manager, personal communication, August, 1994).

This level of professional involvement is disappointing, particularly when one considers the services available through AAHPERD. For example, each year state, district, and national AAHPERD organizations sponsor conferences designed to bring to the membership the most current thinking regarding quality programming. Unfortunately, these conventions are almost always held during the school year when teachers are unable to attend. In order for teachers to attend conventions, they often must take leave without pay and finance the cost of travel themselves.

Some states have begun to put on summer workshops designed specifically for teachers. A summer program of particular note is the National Conference on Teaching Elementary Physical Education, sponsored by the Council on Physical Education for Children (COPEC), a unit of the National Association of Sport and Physical Education (NASPE), and *Teaching Elementary Physical Education*, a publication of Human Kinetics. During the summer of 1994, the conference was held at the University of Wisconsin at La Crosse and focused on portfolio and performance assessment, inclusion, teaching responsibility, accountability, and early childhood physical education.

AAHPERD publishes a number of journals including the *Journal of Physical Education, Recreation and Dance,* the *Research Quarterly for Exercise & Sport Science, Strategies,* and the *Journal of Health Education.*

In addition, AAHPERD often brings together professionals from higher education, the public schools, and the private sector to develop publications directly related to educational practice. NASPE has recently published two documents that could have a dramatic impact on the way physical education is delivered (Ennis, 1992; Rink, 1992). The first, the NASPE Benchmarks (NASPE, 1992a), provides guidelines pertaining to the outcomes that should be achieved in a quality, daily K–12 physical education program taught by a certified specialist. The second publication, *Developmentally Appropriate Physical Education* (NASPE, 1992b), outlines the educational practices that should be used when teaching physical education.

AAHPERD has also developed brochures, videotapes, slide presentations, and other materials designed to assist the teacher to promote physical education in their school and community. Ironically, while health and physical activity are valued by the public, physical education is often targeted for elimination during times of fiscal austerity. Given the profound, positive effects of moderate exercise on morbidity due to cardiovascular disease—even when other risk factors such as hypertension, high percent body fat, smoking, and high cholesterol are present (Blair, 1993)—it is imperative that physical educators become vocal proponents of the contributions that daily, quality physical education can make to a healthy and active lifestyle.

The above description represents only a summary of a few of the contributions that AAHPERD can make to continuing professional development. Ultimately, however, AAHPERD can make an impact only when the individual physical educator becomes involved. More information about AAHPERD can be obtained by writing to AAHPERD, 1900 Association Drive, Reston, VA 22091-1599 or calling 703-476-3400.

USPE Foundation

The United States Physical Education (USPE) Foundation is a not-for-profit organization whose primary purpose is to provide grants to community and state physical education groups, colleges, and other agencies to conduct advocacy programs in support of quality physical education programs for preschool through 12th grade. Information about the USPE Foundation is available from Human Kinetics, P.O. Box 5076, Champaign, IL 61825-5076 (800-747-4457).

AMTP

Human Kinetics sponsors two special programs for educators, the American Master Teacher Program (AMTP) and Continuing Education Workshops, in addition to producing resources for preschool to 12th-grade physical education. AMTP provides elementary physical educators with practical strategies to help them teach more effectively and offers support, encouragement, and recognition for their accomplishments. Successful completion of all courses and requirements leads to certification as a Master Teacher. The Continuing Education Workshops supply preschool through high school physical educators with information to stay abreast of the latest issues in physical education. Each one-day workshop features a topic developed by such leading physical educators as Daryl Siedentop, Don Hellison, Tom Ratliffe, Don Glover, and Dan Midura. Human Kinetics also publishes *Teaching Elementary Physical Education (TEPE)* and *Teaching Secondary Physical Education (TSPE)* for physical education specialists, teachers, and administrators. The two journals provide insights into issues affecting teachers on a daily basis, illustrate applications of research, promote physical education in the schools, and advocate a high professional standard. Information about AMTP, Continuing Education Workshops, and the journals are available from Human Kinetics, P.O. Box 5076, Champaign, IL 61825-5076 (800-747-4457).

TEACHERS AS ADJUNCT FACULTY

An ideal way for a physical educator to keep abreast of new ideas is to become active in a teacher education program at a local university or college. For instance, a critical role assumed by the physical educator is that of cooperating teacher. In most teacher education programs, cooperating teachers are provided with training via inservice workshops or graduate coursework regarding effective supervision. The focus of these learning experiences is to provide cooperating teachers with up-to-date knowledge and skill regarding curriculum models, instructional planning, teaching styles, classroom management, systematic observation, providing feedback, conducting student teacher conferences, and so on.

Another professional development opportunity available to physical educators is to transform their schools into clinical teaching sites. As a clinical site, the school would serve as a setting for a variety of real-world, educational experiences. Early field experiences and teacher education classes in pedagogy, motor development, skill analysis, and so on could be conducted at the site. Children at the school would provide undergraduate and graduate students with opportunities to obtain hands-on teaching experience.

As physical education teachers develop professionally, opportunities for expanding their role in the teacher education program arise. For example, teacher-faculty exchanges could be arranged where university faculty teach in the schools on a part-time basis while the physical education teacher teaches university classes. Also, the physical educator might be able to teach in the university part-time during evenings or in the summer. Because most institutions of higher education require an advanced degree to teach, physical educators interested in becoming involved in teacher education should make graduate study part of their professional development plan.

TEACHER AS RESEARCHER

In the recent theme issue of *JOPERD* entitled, "Research for and by Practitioners" (Templin, 1992), examples of research are presented in which practitioners generate research questions that derive from their own teaching experience and attempt to answer these questions in collaboration with university researchers (Twine & Martinek, 1992; Williamson, 1992). Bringing teacher educators and practitioners together through school-university partnerships can take many forms, including

- school-centered models of program development,
- professional development schools,
- teacher centers,
- staff development programs, or
- models for action research (Anderson, 1988; Martinek & Schempp, 1988; Sharpe, 1992).

Collaboration between practitioners and teacher educators can be mutually beneficial. Continued professional development, improved research consumption, reduced isolation, and more authentic, school-based educational experiences for preservice and inservice teachers can result from collaboration (Graham, 1988; Templin, 1988).

SELF-MENTORING

A cornerstone of continual professional growth is ongoing reflection about one's knowledge, beliefs, instructional practices, and teaching effectiveness. According to several educational researchers (Ferguson, 1989; Ross, 1989; Roth, 1989), reflective teachers view knowledge as socially constructed, contextually based, indefinite, ephemeral, and adaptable to particular situations. They constantly raise questions regarding the what, why, and how of teaching and test new knowledge in instructional settings. The notion of reflective teaching has recently caught the attention of teacher educators in physical education (Hellison & Templin, 1991; Wuest & Lombardo, 1994). They provide the following suggestions for physical educators reflecting on their own educational practices.

1. Maintain a record of thoughts and reflections through the use of written journals or audiotaped logs. Spend 10 to 15 minutes each day or week reflecting on the nature of the instructional events that took place.
2. Employ systematic observation instruments to obtain data regarding your teaching. Instruments are available to obtain information regarding a wide variety of teaching variables, including feedback, student time on task, use of direct instruction behaviors, teacher-student interactions, and so on. (Darst, Zakrajsek, & Mancini, 1989).

3. Visit and observe fellow teachers using systematic observation systems.
4. Construct a videotape library of teaching cases collected from lessons conducted throughout the school district by experienced teachers.

ESTABLISHING TEACHER CENTERS

Teacher centers can play an important role in the professional development of teachers. A teacher center is typically designed by and organized for teachers to meet their political, social, and educational needs. The teacher center can be located at schools within the district or, if available, at a nearby college or university. Teachers meet once or twice each month to share professional ideas. The advantage of a teacher center is that its functions are flexible and can vary from month to month. Some of the functions of successful teacher centers that I have witnessed are described below.

1. **Staff development center**. It is not unusual to hear physical educators complain about the inservice staff development workshops offered by their school districts. Their primary complaint is that the information provided is either irrelevant or only indirectly related to their jobs as physical education teachers. Teacher centers have obtained approval from school districts to conduct workshops designed specifically for physical educators. For example, some district-wide evaluations of the effectiveness of the curriculum in promoting growth in the affective, cognitive, psychomotor, or fitness domains have been conducted through teacher centers. Also, needs assessments conducted through teacher centers have been used to determine if the curriculum being offered meets the perceived needs of parents and students. Finally, some teacher centers have published newsletters designed to update physical educators about new ideas regarding educational practice.

2. **Educational clearinghouse**. Some teacher centers have operated as clearinghouses for current materials, documents, videotapes, journals, or books. For example, some teacher centers keep libraries of current documents, such as those produced by AAHPERD, and current textbooks on physical education. Also, because leave time and financial support for professional travel to attend conferences is typically unavailable, teacher centers have sometimes sponsored a teacher's attendance at state, regional, or national conventions. They videotape as many presentations as possible, and house these videotapes in the teacher center library for members to view.

3. **Political action center**. Physical education has suffered from the misperceptions of the public. Despite the public relations efforts of AAHPERD, the public remains uninformed about the benefits of physical

education. If physical education is to survive in tomorrow's schools, it is imperative that physical educators convince the public of the contributions made by physical education to the development of children and young adults. For instance, AAHPERD has created brochures, videotapes, slide programs, and, most recently, the Sport and Physical Education Advocacy Kit (SPEAK), all of which explain the benefits of daily, quality physical education programs taught by certified specialists. These materials can be assembled and stored at teacher centers and used to promote physical education at PTA meetings, open houses, school board meetings, city council meetings, and community events. To obtain the promotional materials created by AAHPERD, including SPEAK, write to AAHPERD Publications, Box 385, Oxon Hill, MD 20750-0385 or call 1-800-321-0789.

ELIMINATING ISOLATION

Many of the strategies presented for reversing deprofessionalization also help eliminate isolation. For example, joining a state, regional, or national AAHPERD can bring you in contact with many colleagues on a regular basis. Also, establishing a teacher center can provide meaningful interaction with fellow professionals every few weeks. However, this does not address the problem of isolation that confronts the physical educator on a daily basis, particularly at the elementary level. Often, elementary physical educators are by themselves each day, with little opportunity to interact with other physical education or classroom teachers. The strategies presented below can be implemented in the schools and operate to provide professional interaction on a daily basis.

MENTORING PROGRAMS

A variety of mentoring programs have been established to assist the beginning teacher to acclimate professionally (Huling-Austin, 1992; Stewart, 1992). Typically, a mentoring program links an experienced teacher with a newly inducted teacher. The primary purpose is to help beginning teachers resolve problems they encounter during the early years of teaching. The experienced teacher is provided with time to counsel the beginning teacher about classroom discipline, school policies and procedures, instructional effectiveness, student motivation, and so on. District and regional coordinators of physical education need to explore establishing mentoring programs. Perhaps mentors could be selected from among the active members of a teacher center or on the basis of involvement in professional activities. Ideally, a reward system that might include release time, financial support for professional travel, and so on would be used to encourage the best teachers to become mentors.

JOINING THE TEAM

Placek (1992) has argued that if ". . . we wish to overcome our present marginal status to apply for full membership in the curriculum, we must become proactive to ensure our success" (p. 340). Physical education teachers need to come out of the gymnasium and demand to become an integral part of the school. School faculties often participate in interdisciplinary planning teams that work together to provide students with learning experiences which are at once active, meaningful, developmentally sensitive, and integrated.

There are several reasons why physical education is ideally suited to enliven and bring relevance to academic content through integration. First, students like physical education (Goodlad, 1984); and research indicates that when students like subject matter they attend better and learn more (Hidi, 1990). Second, physical education is active. Physical education, unlike many academic subjects, is noted for less passivity and more active learning (Goodlad, 1984). The child's own body becomes the vehicle through which authentic and relevant learning takes place. Finally, as Lawson (1987), has pointed out, physical education includes a rich, sophisticated body of knowledge that embraces virtually all of the content offered elsewhere in school curricula as "academic."

Integrated/conceptually based curricular models (Placek, 1992) should be explored not only as a way of reinforcing academic content in physical education but, also, reinforcing physical education through academic content. By joining the team and integrating physical education into the curriculum, physical educators inform parents, classroom teachers, and educational administrators about the wide variety of outcomes associated with the body of knowledge in physical education.

OVERCOMING MARGINALITY

Marginality in education occurs when a particular content area is considered less important than others. In physical education, Sparkes, Templin, & Schempp (1993) have argued that, "In the pecking order of subjects, there is powerful evidence that PE gets located at the bottom in British and North American schools . . . Therefore, physical educators teach a subject that tends to be defined as peripheral to the central functions of the school; that is, PE is a marginal subject" (p.387). Paradoxically, at the same time that the importance of school-based physical education has dwindled in the public mind, there has been unprecedented growth in recreation, sport, and physical education programs conducted outside the schools (Brock, 1994; Siedentop, 1992). Parents willingly pay registration fees to enroll their children in a wide variety of physical activity programs, such as tennis schools, gymnastics clinics, summer camps, after-school programs, parent-child classes, and so on, yet pay little attention to physical education classes in the school. Given the obvious interest of parents in providing quality physical activity programs to their children, it seems reasonable to speculate that perhaps it is not the subject matter of physical education, but rather how physical education is provided, that renders school-based programs marginal.

BUILDING EXEMPLARY SCHOOL-BASED PROGRAMS

Building exemplary programs is at the heart of demarginalizing physical education. There is a critical shortage of high-quality physical education programs that facilitate positive growth in the affective, cognitive, psychomotor, and/or fitness domains. It is critical to the survival of physical education that teachers and teacher educators not only build and document the effectiveness of high-quality programs, but also market these programs so that parents, fellow teachers, school administrators, politicians, and, perhaps most importantly, students become aware of what can be accomplished through them.

Despite a poor history in program development research, this area has begun to emerge as an exciting one in recent years. As has been discussed in other chapters, in just the last 5 years, programs employing diverse curricular models such as sport education (Grant, 1992; Siedentop, 1994), fitness education (Wescott, 1992), adventure education (Dyson, 1994), social-development (DeBusk & Hellison, 1989), movement education (Graham, Metzler, & Webster, 1991), and health-related physical education (McKenzie, et al., 1993) have been implemented and evaluated in school physical education programs. Practitioners and teacher educators need to continue to expand on this initial effort. Regardless of the curricular model selected, the key curriculum development principles presented below should be included as part of any attempt to build a quality program.

1. Constraints and opportunities unique to the context need to be determined. The facilities and equipment available in the school and community, the interests and abilities of the students, and the expertise of the teacher all need to be carefully assessed (Ennis, 1992).

2. Community involvement and support should be garnered. Parents, teachers, and students should be involved in the process of program building. Encouraging community involvement will enable the teacher to bring physical education into congruence with the community's perceived needs and interests. It also is an excellent way for the physical educator to educate the public regarding the many positive outcomes associated with a quality physical education program.

3. Realistic learning goals should be established (Ennis, 1992). Because physical education is a rich subject matter domain comprised of myriad

affective, cognitive, psychomotor, and fitness objectives, curricula are frequently comprised of too many learning goals. When building a program, it is important to keep in mind that trying to do too much is usually counterproductive (Graham et al., 1991).

4. Ongoing assessment should be a part of the program. Formative and authentic assessment (Veal, 1992) characterized by connecting assessment to real-life indicators of learning, regular and direct examination of student performance, immediate adjustments to instruction based on students' levels of success, and programmatic modifications based on the learning achieved by students should be integral components in the curricula.

BUILDING EXEMPLARY ALTERNATIVE PROGRAMS

Traditionally, physical education in the United States has been delivered in schools from approximately 8:30 a.m. to 3:30 p.m., Monday through Friday, for nine months each year. Recently, however, educational researchers, administrators, and policy specialists pressed by an array of the burgeoning social problems Tyson noted in chapter 4 (e.g., violence, drugs, unemployment, health, illiteracy) have begun to rethink education as a multidimensional, holistic, and integrated process that can take place both in and outside of traditional school settings. For example, Lawson (1994) has argued that education is more than what goes on in schools: "Pedagogy . . . should include schools, but also teaching-learning acts in homes, neighborhoods, and communities" (p. 66). In support of this notion, Heath and McLaughlin (1993) provide evidence indicating that programs judged most effective by young people are those that take place outside of school.

The movement toward expanding and redefining the nature of schools and educational opportunities points to the need for physical education teachers and teacher educators to "think differently" in order to create alternatives to current school structures, instructional settings, and time distributions characteristic of the multi-activity program format that dominates physical education in the United States (Siedentop, 1992, 1994). Such thinking might include the development of school-based community fitness centers or programs where the "lines between curricular and cocurricular activities are blurred and even eliminated . . . with clubs rather than classes as the main organizing structure" (Siedentop, 1992, p. 70).

Alternate programming would also include at-risk programs conducted after school, on weekends, and during the summer. For example, Jones, Winn, and Dooley (1995) have developed Project Y.E.S., Youth Enrichment Services, which provides inner-city children ages 5 to 13 with a community-based educational program designed to teach academic skills, fitness, and health. Another example of an alternative program comes from Debra Sievert, the New Mexico AAHPERD 1993 Middle School

Teacher of the Year. She has developed a program called Friday Night Live (FNL) that is held every Friday night during the school year from 7:00 p.m. to 9:00 p.m. The purpose of FNL is to provide students the opportunity to get off the streets on the weekend and have fun in a safe, supervised environment. The students are primarily from middle- to low-income homes; many have experimented with drugs and joined gangs. FNL offers them an alternative to such activities.

THE ROLE OF TEACHER EDUCATION IN CHANGE

The strategies provided in this chapter thus far focus primarily on the physical educator. However, teacher educators can and should contribute to change. If newly inducted teachers are to value ongoing professional development, it is important that this process begin during teacher education. Described below are some of the strategies that teacher educators could use to assist prospective teachers to combat marginalization, deprofessionalization, and isolation.

TRANSMISSION OF KNOWLEDGE

The structure of teacher education programs may exacerbate the problem of knowledge disavowal. Teacher education programs often promote knowledge that is isolated and disconnected. Prospective teachers may acquire knowledge but, without an overarching, well connected schemata representing physical education, knowledge becomes inert (Newell & Rovegno, 1990)—theoretically important, but irrelevant to professional practice. If the point of teacher education programs is to help students construct a personally meaningful, well connected, practical body of knowledge, we must also be careful not to hypocritically promote the importance of educational principles such as active learning, curricular relevance, and authentic assessment and then place students in large lecture classes where knowledge is transmitted passively and assessed only through the use of objective tests.

Teacher educators need to begin to explore ways to structure teacher education programs that will overcome student disavowal of and resistance to new knowledge and beliefs. One strategy that warrants attention is the development of programs that illustrate how theoretical knowledge can be translated into practice. If students observe and experience such programs, they might be less likely to complain, "This stuff doesn't work." The emerging research on program development described above should be included as a part of the coursework offered in teacher education programs. Also, the basic instruction program (BIP) in physical education should be viewed as an opportunity to provide a concrete example of the translation of theory into practice (Housner, 1993). The BIP could be a thread that weaves through and interconnects the body of knowledge in physical education.

Shulman (1986) has suggested that using case studies similar to those used in medicine or law could provide the prospective teacher with a vehicle for acquiring knowledge of teaching. Exemplars of expert teaching performance, either written or videotaped, could be used to build a library of cases, each focusing on a different element of pedagogical expertise. In this way, teacher educators would be able to avoid the unpredictable nature of many early observational assignments and systematically direct students' attention to the pedagogical skill under investigation.

Researchers (Copeland, 1989; O'Sullivan, Stroot, Tannehill, & Chou, 1989) have called for the development of teaching simulations as a method to provide preservice teachers with opportunities to practice pedagogical skills and decision making. These types of simulations are based on computer-mediated, interactive, video laser disk technology. Such simulations would enable the teacher to practice clinical reasoning in a realistic setting without the risk associated with actual clinical teaching experiences.

APPLICATION OF KNOWLEDGE

Case studies and simulations appear to have potential for training prospective teachers effectively. Regardless of the types of learning experiences provided through university coursework, however, eventually the student will have to venture into schools to gain a full understanding of how to teach well.

Early field experiences that require prospective teachers to observe and teach in actual classroom settings should be an integral part of teacher education programs. Of course, it is important that these early experiences be brief, controlled, and focused on relatively specific pedagogical skills. Through the course of the professional preparation program, as knowledge about teaching becomes more sophisticated, beginning teachers would be provided with more challenging experiences focusing on increasingly complex combinations of teaching skills.

The settings for field experiences must be carefully selected. Observations and teaching should be conducted in classrooms of experts who not only possess sophisticated knowledge of teaching, but also are able to model, explain, and provide feedback regarding the knowledge and cognitive strategies they use to plan, implement, and evaluate lessons. Teachers selected as clinical instructors should be familiar with the language of teaching effectiveness research. Perhaps formal graduate study or inservice programs could be used to empower teachers to reflectively analyze their own teaching and the teaching of others. In this way, university coursework and experiences in the field would provide beginning teachers with convergent educational experiences that share a common language based upon research on teaching.

Educational coursework and field experiences should facilitate the growth of pedagogical knowledge in undergraduate teachers in training. At this point, the student should be ready to enter student teaching. Regardless of the preparedness of the student teacher, however, research indicates that student teachers and first-year teachers still have knowledge and information-processing deficiencies that should be taken into consideration when designing the student teaching experience.

Livingston and Borko (1989) provide several recommendations for the student teaching experience based on the findings of an expert-novice study of teaching. They suggest that

1. Student teaching assignments should be in an area in which the student is academically well prepared. Student teachers assigned to teach in subject areas with which they are not thoroughly familiar spend planning time learning the content rather than concentrating on learning organizational strategies, instructional techniques, and activity routines that can be used to transmit content to students.

2. The number of courses that student teachers must plan for should be reduced. Student teachers are often overwhelmed when planning for a variety of courses. Unlike experienced teachers, beginners do not have a rich, pedagogical content knowledge to rely on when planning lessons. As a result, planning becomes a lengthy process of constructing instructional activities and teaching strategies. This process invariably reduces the time that student teachers have available for reflecting on their teaching and for mentally organizing their pedagogical content knowledge.

3. Student teachers should have multiple opportunities to teach the same content. Allowing novices to evaluate a lesson and restructure it for a second instructional episode, "contributes to the development of content knowledge and pedagogical reasoning skills" (p. 40).

TEACHER INDUCTION PROGRAMS

As Stroot noted in the previous chapter, teacher education needs to be viewed as a process that spans a teacher's career. Unfortunately, formal teacher education is often considered finished when the preservice teacher graduates and begins his or her first teaching job—and this is probably when the beginning teacher needs assistance the most. During the first years of teaching, the exigencies of teaching, the socialization processes in the workplace, and the implicit beliefs and understandings about the nature of physical education that beginning teachers bring with them often combine to exert considerable pressure to disavow knowledge and accept the status quo. Teacher education programs reinforce this view by cutting beginning teachers loose following graduation. Teacher educators need to explore strategies that provide support for beginners in their first jobs. For example, teacher education programs could establish telephone hotlines that permit beginning teachers who are facing problems to call the institutions that graduated them, where teacher educators would be available to provide advice or even visit the teachers to observe their teaching. A network of advisors could be established by teacher educators in regions throughout the country for teachers working out of state or far from their alma mater. In this way, beginning teachers who need advice could contact teacher educators close to their teaching sites.

Another way for teacher educators to maintain professional contact with newly inducted teachers is to create a newsletter designed to update them about new ideas on teaching physical education. For instance, New Mexico State University published a newsletter, *Sports Tips*, which was sent to all physical education teachers in New Mexico. Each monthly issue provided information about developmentally appropriate practices, safe and unsafe stretching exercises, NASPE benchmarks, and so on. Including newly inducted physical education teachers as contributors to newsletters provides them with a valuable, professional development activity while at the same time encouraging interaction between the practitioner and teacher educator.

CONCLUSIONS

The strategies presented in the preceding pages represent only a small portion of the possible strategies that could be used to promote positive change in physical education. Not discussed were a number of ideas that I have personally seen successfully implemented, such as honors programs in physical education, parents as teachers, majors clubs in teacher education programs, summer sport camps, faculty fitness/wellness programs in the schools, and so on. There is no limit to the ways that physical educators and teacher educators can work to reverse deprofessionalization, eliminate isolation, and overcome marginalization.

This is not to suggest that change will be an easy process. Rather, contextual constraints such as fiscal austerity, large classes, inadequate equipment, and poor facilities combine with isolation, deprofessionalization, and marginalization to make change profoundly difficult in physical education. Despite the difficulty of achieving change, there are several reasons to be optimistic about the possibilities for the future. First, teachers and teacher educators have begun to acknowledge the need for dramatic change in physical education. Second, strategies for promoting change have crept into the physical education research literature. Most of the strategies included in this chapter have been gleaned from articles published in just the last 5 years. Third, examples of commendable traditional and nontraditional programs in physical education exist, even in less than ideal contexts. Although just a beginning, these examples suggest that substantive change can take place.

Even at my student teaching site, change was possible. Following student teaching, the cooperating teacher resigned and I had the opportunity to assume his position for several years. With the help of classroom teachers, I established a group contingency management system that was reinforced every day. The reward for diligently participating in an "instructional program" of physical education was what students valued most: choice. One day each week, I set up three or four learning centers and the students could select the center at which they would participate. Of course, noncompliance meant no choice. Choice was also part of the instructional program. Using task sheets to guide the daily activities in several units of instruction simultaneously, I was able to let students choose the units that they wanted. After a single semester, the management system was no longer needed. The students had begun to realize that learning can be fun.

Change can happen, but only when committed practitioners and teacher educators work in concert. With considerable effort we may someday convince parents, teachers, school administrators, and politicians of the myriad benefits of quality programming in physical education, so they will no longer permit their children to do without it.

REFERENCES

Anderson, W.G. (1988). A school-centered collaborative model for program development. *Journal of Teaching in Physical Education, 7,* 176–183.

Armstrong, N., & Sparkes, A. (Eds.). (1991). *Issues in physical education*. London: Cassell Publications.

Association of Teacher Educators. (1985). *Developing career ladders in teaching.* Reston, VA: Author.

Blair, S.N. (1993). Physical activity, physical fitness, and health. *Research Quarterly for Exercise and Sport, 64,* 365–376.

Brock, B.J. (1994). Recreation programming for the '90s family: Demographics and discoveries. *Journal of Physical Education, Recreation and Dance, 65,* 64–67.

Chandler, T.J.L., Lane, S., Bibik, J., & Oliver, B. (1988). The career ladder and lattice: A new look at the teaching career. *Journal of Teaching in Physical Education, 7,* 132–141.

Copeland, W.D. (1989). Clinical reasoning in novice teachers. *Journal of Teacher Education, 40,* 10–18.

Darst, P., Zakrajsek, D., & Mancini, V. (Eds.). (1989). *Analyzing physical education and sport instruction* (2nd ed.). Champaign, IL: Human Kinetics.

DeBusk, M., & Hellison, D. (1989). Implementing a physical education self-responsibility model for delinquency-prone youth. *Journal of Teaching in Physical Education, 8,* 104–112.

Doolittle, S.A., Dodds, P., & Placek, J.H. (1993). Persistence of beliefs about teaching during formal training of preservice teachers. *Journal of Teaching in Physical Education, 12,* 355–365.

Dyson, B.P. (1994). *A case study of two alternative elementary physical education programs.* Unpublished doctoral dissertation. The Ohio State University, Columbus, OH.

Ennis, C.D. (1992). Developing a physical education curriculum based on learning goals. *Journal of Physical Education, Recreation and Dance, 63,* 74–77.

Ennis, C.D. (1994). Knowledge and beliefs underlying curricular expertise. *Quest, 46,* 164–175.

Faucette, N. (1987). Teachers' concerns and participation styles during in-service education. *Journal of Teaching in Physical Education, 6,* 425–440.

Ferguson, P. (1989). A reflective approach to the methods practicum. *Journal of Teacher Education, 40,* 36–41.

Goodlad, J. (1984). *A place called school.* New York: McGraw-Hill.

Graham, G. (1988). Collaboration in physical education: A lot like marriage? *Journal of Teaching in Physical Education, 7,* 165–175.

Graham, G., Metzler, M., & Webster, G. (1991). Specialist and classroom teacher effectiveness in children's physical education: A 3-year study. *Journal of Teaching in Physical Education, Monograph, 10*(4).

Graham, K., & Stueck, P. (Eds.). (1992). Critical crossroads: Decisions for middle & high school physical education. *Journal of Physical Education, Recreation and Dance, 63*(2).

Grant, B.C. (1992). Integrating sport into the physical education curriculum in New Zealand secondary schools. *Quest, 44,* 304–316.

Griffey, D.C., & Housner, L.D. (1991). Planning, behavior, and organizational climate differences of experienced and inexperienced teachers. *Research Quarterly for Exercise and Sport, 62,* 196–204.

Heath, S.B., & McLaughlin, M.W. (1993). Building identities for inner-city youth, In S.B. Heath & M.W. McLaughlin (Eds.), *Identity and inner-city youth: Beyond ethnicity and gender* (pp. 1–12). New York: Teachers College Press.

Hellison, D.R., & Templin, T.J. (1991). *A reflective approach to teaching physical education.* Champaign, IL: Human Kinetics.

Hidi, S. (1990). Interest and its contribution as a mental resource for learning. *Review of Educational Research, 60,* 549–571.

Housner, L.D. (1993). Research in the basic instruction program. *Journal of Physical Education, Recreation and Dance, 64,* 53–58.

Housner, L.D., & Griffey, D.C. (1985). Teacher cognition: Differences in planning and interactive decision making between experienced and inexperienced teachers. *Research Quarterly for Exercise and Sport, 56,* 44–53.

Huling-Austin, L. (1992). Research on learning to teach: Implications for teacher induction and mentoring programs. *Journal of Teacher Education, 43,* 173–180.

Jones, D.F., Winn, G.L., & Dooley, E.A. (1995). Project Y.E.S.: A break from tradition. *Journal of Physical Education, Recreation and Dance, 66*(2), 41–47.

Kelley, E., & Lindsay, C. (1977). Knowledge obsolescence in physical education. *Research Quarterly, 48*, 463–474.

Kelley, E., & Lindsay, C. (1980). A comparison of knowledge obsolescence of graduating seniors and practitioners in the field of physical education. *Research Quarterly for Exercise and Sport, 51*, 636–644.

Lawson, H. (1987). Teaching the body of knowledge. The neglected part of physical education. *Journal of Physical Education, Recreation and Dance, 58*, 70–72.

Lawson, H.A. (1983). Toward a model of teacher socialization in physical education: The subjective warrant, recruitment, and teacher education. *Journal of Teaching in Physical Education, 3*, 3–15.

Lawson, H.A. (1993). Teachers' uses of research in practice: A literature review. *Journal of Teaching in Physical Education, 12*, 366–374.

Lawson, H.A. (1994). Toward healthy learners, schools and communities. *Journal of Teacher Education, 45*, 66–70.

Livingston, H., & Borko, H. (1989). Expert-novice differences in teaching: A cognitive analysis and implications for teaching. *Journal of Teacher Education, 40*, 36–42.

Locke, L. (1990). Why is motor learning ignored?: A case of ducks, naughty theories, and science. *Quest, 42*, 134–142.

Locke, L. (1992). Changing secondary school physical education. *Quest, 44*, 361–372.

Martinek, T.J., & Schempp, P.G. (Eds.). (1988). Collaboration for instructional improvement: Models for school-university partnerships. *Journal of Teaching in Physical Education, 7*, 157–259.

McGreal, T.L. (1983). *Successful teacher evaluation*. Alexandria, VA: Association for Supervision and Curriculum Development.

McKenzie, T.L., Sallis, J.F., Faucette, N., Roby, J.J., & Kolody, B. (1993). Effects of a curriculum and inservice program on the quality and quantity of elementary physical education classes. *Research Quarterly for Exercise and Sport, 64*, 178–187.

National Association of Sport and Physical Education. (1992a). *Outcomes of quality physical education*. Reston, VA: American Alliance for Health, Physical Education, Recreation and Dance.

National Association of Sport and Physical Education. (1992b). *Developmentally appropriate physical education practices for children*. Reston, VA: American Alliance for Health, Physical Education, Recreation and Dance.

Newell, K., & Rovegno, I. (1990). Commentary—motor learning: Theory and practice. *Quest, 42*, 184–192.

Norton, C.J. (Ed.). (1987). High school physical education: Problems and possibilities. *Journal of Physical Education, Recreation and Dance, 58*(2).

O'Sullivan, M., Siedentop, D., & Tannehill, D. (1994). Breaking out: Codependency of high school physical education. *Journal of Teaching in Physical Education, 13*, 421–428.

O'Sullivan, M., Stroot, S., Tannehill, D., & Chou, C. (1989). Interactive video technology in teacher education. *Journal of Teacher Education, 40*, 20–26.

Placek, J.H. (1992). Rethinking middle school physical education curriculum: An integrated thematic approach. *Quest, 44,* 330–341.

Rink, J. (1992). The plan and the reality. *Journal of Physical Education, Recreation and Dance, 63*(2), 74–77.

Ross, D.D. (1989). First steps in developing a reflective approach. *Journal of Teacher Education, 40,* 22–30.

Roth, R.A. (1989). Preparing the reflective practitioner: Transforming the apprentice through the dialectic. *Journal of Teacher Education, 40,* 31–35.

Schempp, P.G. (1989). Apprenticeship-of-observation and the development of physical education teachers. In T. Templin & P. Schempp (Eds.), *Socialization into physical education: Learning to teach* (pp. 13–38). Indianapolis: Benchmark Press.

Sharpe, T. (1992). Teacher preparation: A professional development school approach. *Journal of Physical Education, Recreation and Dance, 63,* 82–87.

Shulman, L.S. (1986). Paradigms and research programs in the study of teaching: A contemporary perspective. In M.C. Wittrock (Ed.), *Handbook of research on teaching* (3rd ed., pp. 3–36). New York: Macmillan.

Siedentop, D. (Ed.). (1989). The effective elementary specialist study [Monograph]. *Journal of Teaching In Physical Education, 8*(3).

Siedentop, D. (1992). Thinking differently about secondary physical education. *Journal of Teaching In Physical Education, 63,* 61–72, 77.

Siedentop, D. (1994). *Sport education: Quality PE through positive sport experiences.* Champaign, IL: Human Kinetics.

Siedentop, D., Doutis, P., Tsangaridou, N., Ward, P., Rauschenbach, J. (1994). Don't sweat gym! An analysis of curriculum and instruction. *Journal of Teaching In Physical Education, 13,* 375–394.

Siedentop, D., Mand, C., & Taggart, A. (1986). *Physical education: Teaching and curriculum strategies for grades 5-12.* Palo Alto, CA: Mayfield.

Siedentop, D., & O'Sullivan, M. (Eds.). (1992). Secondary school physical education. *Quest, 44*(3).

Sparkes, A.C., Templin, T.J., & Schempp, P.G. (1993). Exploring dimensions of marginality: Reflecting on the life histories of physical education teachers. *Journal of Teaching In Physical Education, 12,* 386–398.

Stewart, D.K. (1992). Mentoring in beginning teacher induction: Studies in the ERIC data base. *Journal of Teacher Education, 43,* 222–226.

Stroot, S.A., Collier, C., O'Sullivan, M., & England, K. (1994). Contextual hoops and hurdles: Workplace conditions in secondary physical education. *Journal of Teaching in Physical Education, 13,* 333–360.

Templin, T. (Ed.). (1983). Profiles of excellence: Fourteen outstanding secondary school physical educators. *Journal of Physical Education, Recreation and Dance, 54,* 15–36.

Templin, T. (1988). Teacher isolation: A concern for the collegial development of physical educators. *Journal of Teaching in Physical Education, 7,* 197–205.

Templin, T. (Ed.). (1992). Research for and by practitioners. *Journal of Teaching in Physical Education, 63,* 11–25.

Templin, T., & Schempp, P. (Eds.). (1989). *Socialization into physical education: Learning to teach.* Indianapolis: Benchmark Press.

Twine, J., & Martinek, T.J. (1992). Teachers as researchers: An application of a collaborative action research model. *Journal of Physical Education, Recreation and Dance, 63,* 22–25.

Veal, M.L. (1992). The role of assessment in secondary physical education: A pedagogical view. *Journal of Physical Education, Recreation and Dance, 63*(2), 88–92.

Wescott, W.L. (1992). High school physical education: A fitness professional's perspective. *Quest, 44,* 342–351.

Wiggins, G. (1989). Teaching to the (authentic) test. *Educational Leadership, 46,* 41–47.

Williamson, K.M. (1992). Relevance or rigor: A case for teacher as researcher. *Journal of Physical Education, Recreation and Dance, 63,* 17–21, 25.

Wuest, D., & Lombardo, B. (1994). *Curriculum and instruction: The secondary school physical education experience.* St. Louis: Mosby.

CHAPTER 18

Enhancing Learning:
An Epilogue

Catherine D. Ennis
Stephen J. Silverman

This project began one evening while we were having dinner in Washington, DC. What started as a social occasion turned into business and an in-depth discussion about physical education. We believed that a collection of the accumulated research in our field was needed. We, as physical education researchers, knew there was a vast reservoir of published work, but that it was not summarized and collected for easy access. As we indicated in the first chapter, we also realized that the field had become specialized. Many of the chapters we envisioned would be valuable not only for teachers, teacher educators, and beginning graduate students, but also for researchers in sport pedagogy who wanted to keep up with other subareas.

As we discussed the need for this volume, we were mindful that some scholars in other areas (most notably Wade, 1991) did not believe there was an accumulated body of literature in physical education. We hope you'll agree, after reading this text, that the body of literature has grown considerably in the last decade and that it is of increasing importance in physical education teaching, teacher education, and curriculum! And, as you surely will have noted, it has the potential to influence physical education.

It should be obvious from reading the preceding chapters that schools and physical education classes are complex places and that no one research result will immediately provide the silver bullet for improvement.

Each of us must use the research on physical education to inform our professional judgment, considering our workplace and the many contextual factors that interact with any changes we would make. The way informed professionals use the knowledge base in teaching physical education, in curriculum development, and for preparing future teachers will affect the growth of the field. As many of the contributors noted, the perceived problems with school physical education are remediable. We should be optimistic because research results may suggest alternatives to some of the problems of current practice. As Berliner (1987) has noted, the knowledge base of teaching can help transform the teaching profession.

Many issues—for example, measurement and assessment, curriculum development, and instructional effectiveness—were discussed in chapters specifically focusing on them and also in other chapters. This demonstrates the complex nature of physical education teaching and the need for professionals to be widely informed. Although, as we discussed previously, research often is conducted on discrete subareas, teaching physical education is the intersection of these subareas. We have tried to make connections among the chapters in this book, but many more are desirable and possible.

We hope the diversity of our field, evidenced both in the topics addressed by researchers and the methods they employ, will continue to grow. Without ongoing, focused work by researchers in a variety of areas and with a variety of methods, we will not continue the progress that is evidenced throughout this volume. We hope that those contemplating a research career will see opportunities in sport pedagogy and that teachers and teacher educators will look for opportunities to apply what they've read here. The vitality of physical education necessitates that we continue to grow by using what we've learned and attempting to learn more. As a field, we have grown greatly, but we still have much to learn. Important research questions will continually evolve. If physical education and sport pedagogy are to grow, we must expand our knowledge—and use it to inform practice.

REFERENCES

Berliner, D.C. (1987). Knowledge is power: A talk to teachers about a revolution in the teaching profession. In D.C. Berliner & B.V. Rosenshine (Eds.), *Talks to teachers* (pp. 3–33). New York: Random House.

Wade, M.G. (1991). Unravelling the Larry and Daryl magical mystery tour. *Quest, 43*, 207–213.

INDEX